The fading miracle

Four decades of market economy in Germany

Herbert Giersch
Karl-Heinz Paqué
Holger Schmieding

CAMBRIDGE
UNIVERSITY PRESS

Published by the Press Syndicate of the University of Cambridge
The Pitt Building, Trumpington Street, Cambridge CB2 1RP
40 West 20th Street, New York, NY 10011–4211, USA
10 Stamford Road, Oakleigh, Melbourne 3166, Australia

© Cambridge University Press 1992

First published 1992
Reprinted 1993
First paperback edition 1994

Printed in Great Britain by The Bath Press, Bath

A catalogue record for this book is available from the British Library

Library of Congress cataloguing in publication data

Giersch, Herbert.
The fading miracle: four decades of market economy in Germany / Herbert Giersch,
Karl-Heinz Paqué, Holger Schmieding.
    p.   cm. – (Cambridge surveys in economic policies and institutions)
ISBN 0 521 35351 3
1. Germany (West) – Economic policy. I. Paqué, Karl-Heinz. II. Schmieding, Holger.
III. Title. IV. Series.
HC 286.G54 1992
338.943'009'045-dc20   91–22347 CIP

ISBN 0 521 35351 3 hardback
ISBN 0 521 35869 8 paperback

The fading miracle provides a lucid account of economic policy in West Germany from the late 1940s up to the present, and has been carefully updated to include a survey of the way Germany has reacted to the new challenges presented by the unification of the two German states in 1990. Five distinct eras are covered: the early post-war misery ending with the celebrated liberal reforms of June 1948 which laid the ground for the so-called social market economy; the miraculous growth spurt in the 1950s; the golden years of full employment and demand management from the early 1960s up to the worldwide caesura of the first oil crisis in 1973; the fifteen years of slack growth thereafter; and, most recently, the dramatic political and economic unification which set up a challenging new agenda for policymakers.

For all these five periods, the authors describe and evaluate the major policy controversies and decisions as well as the actual path of economic history. Particular emphasis is placed on the characteristically German institutions of policy counselling and their role in policy formation. Although the book mainly addresses students of economics, it is most valuable reading for anybody with a keen interest in economic policy matters and the economic history of Europe.

Cambridge surveys in economic policies and institutions

The fading miracle
Four decades of market economy in Germany

Cambridge surveys in economic policies and institutions

Editor
Mark Perlman, Professor of Economics, University of Pittsburgh

Economic ideas are most obviously revealed through economic policies, which in turn create and are implemented by economic institutions. It is vital, therefore, that students of economics understand the nature of policy formation, policy aims, and policy results. By examining policies and institutions in a detailed yet accessible manner, this series aims to provide students and interested lay-people with the tools to interpret recent economic events and the nature of institutional development, and thus to grasp the influence of economic ideas on the real economy.

Other books in the series

Shigeto Tsuru *Japan's capitalism: creative defeat and beyond*

Contents

Figures

Tables

Preface

This book is an essay in applied economics, not in economic history. To be sure, history is its subject matter, but the main interest of the authors – all of them economists – was to describe and evaluate a long chain of events in the light of their own economic understanding. Hence, the book is addressed above all to students of economics and interested laymen, not necessarily professional historians who would like to learn new facts about West German post-war economic history. The reader we have in mind should be familiar with the basic tools of economic reasoning and should have a keen interest in history; no more is required.

Reality can hardly be understood unless it is deliberately simplified by abstraction. We had to abstract from numerous facts and relationships that others might have wished to stress. Admittedly, the choice is subjective: idiosyncrasies may have come in, though we tried to avoid them. No doubt, Marxists would have seen things through different conceptual glasses. But we believe that our 'individualistic approach', which regards markets rather than classes as the decisive force of economic history, yields a quite consistent interpretation of actual events, at least in the case of West Germany since the Second World War.

In our view, the main lesson comes down to one fundamental proposition: miracles emerge when spontaneity prevails over regulation, and they fade when corporatist rigidities impair the flexibility for smooth adjustment. At the time of writing, dramatic developments in Central and Eastern Europe gave rise to a renewal of beliefs in market spontaneity, thus tentatively confirming our own views and hopes. The 1990s will provide further tests of our proposition in Western as well as in Central and Eastern Europe. But one can speak of miracles only when favourable developments come as a surprise. Where they are desperately longed for, as they are now in the eastern part of the (re-)united Germany and elsewhere in Central and Eastern Europe, they will be seen as the fulfilment of justified hopes. And they may not emerge as easily, since hungry people are tempted to eat the fruits before they are ripe.

Not only the miracle, but also the fading of the miracle provides important lessons. Corporatism and bureaucracy are strong forces, leading potentially everywhere to a politicization of economic life. For a while, they may be held back or brought into service of rapid market growth when people or the public can be made to believe that distributional quarrels will close growth opportunities to the detriment of all, eventually leading to a zero-sum society. But politicians, bureaucrats and leaders of corporatist organizations have too short and too partial a view to meet the concerns of market-orientated economists. No doubt, the narrow interests of the practitioners of the corporatist system will often gain the upper hand, so that the economy is bound to slow down under the impact of mounting regulations and higher taxes, rising costs and shrinking profit margins.

External economic relations may serve as an accelerator. As we observed, this holds true in a slowdown as much as under conditions of fast growth. Trade liberalization in an upswing helps to enhance the supply responsiveness of a domestic economy under demand pressure; and allowing more imports to come in facilitates import liberalization in other countries. Such market integration amounts to a widening of the scope for gainful specialization – from an inter-industry to an intra-industry division of labour. Much mutual learning and much technology transfer go along with this process. In reverse, we observe induced protectionism emerging under conditions of relative stagnation; it makes matters worse.

In interpreting West German post-war economic history and policy along these lines, we found no basic contradictions between the course of events and the teaching of the great Ordoliberal Walter Eucken, who, half a century ago, stressed the link between theoretical reasoning and institutional description in the form of what he called thinking in 'economic orders', in types of institutional settings or frameworks.

Naturally, there is a basic methodological shortcoming. Economics correctly advises us to think in terms of opportunity costs, i.e. to compare alternatives. Interpreting historical events, imputing consequences to 'causes', any kind of valuation and any assessment would thus require counterfactual analyses. To be honest, if we made them, we mostly kept them at the back of our minds. The reason is simple: there are always far too many alternatives, including some possibilities one can think of only with the benefit of hindsight and some which have never been discussed anywhere.

As far as the period of the West German economic miracle – i.e. the late 1940s and the 1950s – is concerned, we believe that events took a course for which there was hardly any better realistic alternative. But for the slowdown we cannot be so sure. The senior author's record of (mostly unheeded) advice and policy criticism reminds him of some alternatives that appeared to be better ex-ante. Would they have also turned out better ex-post? The answer is that we just cannot know with any degree of certainty. Alternative paths of history are as hypothetical as ex-ante descriptions of alternative policy proposals sometimes demanded by policy-makers in the interests of keeping their freedom of choice. And just as an ex-ante discussion of policy alternatives can raise the intellectual level of the economic policy debate, we feel that counterfactual historical analysis may be worth more intellectual effort than could be invested in writing this book. Nevertheless, readers interested in such counterfactual reflections will find fertile ground in numerous passages referring to the actual policy debate.

In recent years, the progress of history even outpaced the work on this book. When the authors started to write the initial drafts, the unification of divided Germany was still a distant dream; by the time we put the finishing touches to the manuscript, East Germany had already merged with the West. For this fortunate and originally unforeseen reason, this book covers the entire time span in which West Germany existed as a separate economic entity with its own particular economic policies (mid 1948 to mid 1990) and the brief time span of the post-war chaos (1945 to mid 1948) which preceded the formation of West Germany.

By its very nature, an essay in applied economics should not be structured like a piece of historiography: the thread of economic reasoning all too often requires a deviation from historical chronology. Therefore we subdivided West German post-war history into four periods – 1945–8, 1948–60, 1960–73 and 1973–89 – each of which can sensibly be treated as a period with its own characteristic problem setting. For reasons of analytical convenience, we dealt separately with the domestic and the international aspects of economic policy in each of these periods (except the very short first one). Needless to say, such a separation of issues must remain to some extent arbitrary, because, in actual practice, domestic and international matters are often closely intertwined. Nevertheless, we think that the opportunities, challenges and pressures emanating from international trade and finance have been important enough for West Germany's economic development to deserve a somewhat extensive and thus separate treatment. The dramatic events of German unification in 1990 are covered in a separate chapter, the only one that has been updated and revised for the paperback edition. All major sections of the book are self-contained: the reader who is short of time may turn to any of them without prior digestion of the preceding paragraphs. This is why we deliberately allowed for some minor overlapping of issues between the sections.

Writing this book would have been impossible without a basic consensus among its authors. This consensus led to a virtually unlimited mutual confidence during the drafting period and helped to avoid counterproductive disputes when the drafts were subjected to scrutiny. The book may be considered a by-product of learning from each other during a period of more than five years. Only if the book's gestation period is taken to be so long as to include several workshops under his auspices could the senior member of the team accept a fair share in whatever credit may be associated with its authorship.

As any economist knows, a division of labour can be highly productive: it saves costs and raises output per unit of time. Applied to interpersonal cooperation, the division of labour can also help to improve product quality. Should this apply to this book, the authors would feel reassured. Naturally, the division of labour had a wider scope. It included the participants of various workshops devoted to the subject, notably Christoph Buchheim, Gerhard Fels, Stephan Heimbach, Renate Merklein, Karl Schiller and a large number of associates of the Kiel Institute of World Economics, in particular Alfred Boss, Joachim Fels, Erich Gundlach, Henning Klodt, Enno Langfeldt, Joachim Scheide, Stefan Sinn and Frank D. Weiss. Some of them prepared papers illuminating certain aspects, developments or episodes; others made specific points to correct our judgements. Of course, the usual disclaimer applies: any remaining shortcomings are the sole responsibility of the authors.

Finally, we are indebted to Andreas Freytag and Thomas Ilka for research assistance, to Simone Schmieding for taking care of the manuscript, and to Thomas Tack for supporting our editorial efforts. We also thank Patrick McCartan and Pauline Marsh of Cambridge University Press for their excellent cooperation in the final stages before publication. The whole enterprise has greatly profited from the intellectual atmosphere and the facilities of the Kiel Institute of World Economics.

1   Stylized facts 1948–1990

On 18 October 1952, a British weekly published a survey on the performance of the West German economy since the Second World War. Its general message was plain: unconditional acknowledgement of a wholly unexpected economic recovery, the so-called German miracle, and warm praise for the sound economic policies that had brought it about. On 15 October 1966, the same paper carried another survey of this type called 'The German Lesson', in which the acknowledgement and praise of fourteen years earlier had become a quite enthusiastic – although not uncritical – celebration of the virtues of an export-orientated economy German style, with its excellent industrial relations and its reasonable macroeconomic policies. For all occasional caveats, West Germany appeared as a shining counter-model to the Britain of the day, with its economy inflicted by sclerotic diseases and maltreated by macroeconomic stop-and-go shocks. On 7 May 1988, about six weeks before the fortieth anniversary of the West German currency reform, the same paper published a leading article on the state of the West German economy. Under the highly suggestive headline 'Wunderkind at 40' and below a front cover showing a fat middle-aged man, unmistakably German in appearance, the article conveyed the picture of a rich, saturated and stodgy economy with not much zeal for growth and not enough flexibility for structural change left over from the days of its youth; the prospects for the future were painted in somewhat gloomy colours, and there was no talk any more of an enviable German model.[1]

These three judgements by outside observers give an impressionistic outline of what may be called the fading German miracle. In this first chapter, we shall evaluate whether, by and large, the statistical facts on the economic performance of West Germany bear out this picture. In doing so, we shall focus on three aspects of this performance, namely economic growth, structural change, and macroeconomic stability. The

---

[1] For the three articles, see *The Economist*, 'The German Economy – Divided it Stands' (18 October 1952); 'The German Lesson' (15 October 1966); 'Wunderkind at 40' (7 May 1988).

chapter will be essentially descriptive, with no attempt to establish an economic explanation of historical developments. Of course, all facts are theory-laden, and the selection and presentation of statistics is never independent of some prior theoretical prejudice. Hence it should not be surprising if some later economic interpretation is foreshadowed in the sketch of facts we present below.

1   Economic growth

Figure 1 shows the average annual growth rate of real gross domestic product (GDP) in West Germany from the currency reform in mid 1948[2] until 1990. If one abstracts from the pronounced cyclical movements which the graph reveals, the time span of forty-two years may be conveniently divided into five distinct periods (1948–50, 1950–60, 1960–73, 1973–80 and 1980–90), with each period having a lower average annual growth rate than the preceding one.

Clearly, the most exceptional of these periods was 1948–50, with growth rates above 15 per cent p.a. This was the time of a drastic reorganization of the domestic structure of production in the aftermath of the currency reform and the comprehensive freeing of prices in June 1948. At a virtually constant level of employment until spring 1950, most of the observed output growth was due to an increase in working hours and to the productivity gains of repairing the war-damaged capital stock and reshuffling resources from less to more efficient uses. This speedy recovery from the early post-war misery was the first stage of the German miracle, but it hardly delivers a sensible performance standard for intertemporal or international comparisons. It should and will be treated as exceptional.

The 1950s were the second – and arguably the main – stage of the German miracle: from 1950 to 1960, real GDP grew by an average of 8.2 per cent p.a., a higher rate even than at business-cycle peaks in later years. Only once in this period, during the downturn of 1958, did the growth rate drop below 6 per cent p.a. At some time in the late 1950s and early 1960s, the trend growth of real GDP seems to have slowed down significantly.

---

[2] The immediate post-war period from May 1945 to June 1948 is excluded for two reasons. First, it was a time of almost complete price and production controls by the Allied authorities of occupied Germany, with the economy moving from a virtual standstill of production to a modest utilization of the – badly damaged – capital stock. To call this process 'growth' would be misleading; it was more like an initial restarting (and repairing) of the economy's machinery. Second, there are no national accounts statistics available for this period, and the commonly used index of industrial production gives a partial and fairly distorted picture of total economic activity. For details on this period, see Chapter 2 below.

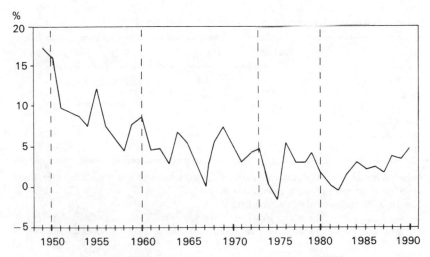

Figure 1. Growth of GDP in West Germany 1949–90.
Notes: Average annual growth rate of GDP at constant prices. For 1949 annualized growth rate relative to GDP in second half of 1948; for 1948/9–1959/60 excluding the Saar and Berlin.
Source: Statistisches Bundesamt; own calculations.

If the boom year 1960 is taken as a plausible endpoint of the miraculous post-war growth dynamics, it is easy to recognize the following thirteen years up to 1973 as a period of a still very satisfactory growth performance (around 4.4 per cent average annual increase of real GDP), but also of quite violent business fluctuations. This period covers the first genuine recession with (slightly) negative growth (1966/7) and the very powerful recovery thereafter.

As in many other industrialized countries, the oil price shock in the boom year 1973 marks an economic watershed between the still golden 1960s and early 1970s and the much more troubled later years. From 1973 to 1980, average growth stood at a meagre 2.2 per cent p.a., with the deepest post-war recession in 1974/5 leading to significantly negative growth and the later recovery being on the whole much more moderate than in earlier times. Whether the second oil price shock around 1980 and the ensuing recession of 1981/2 really indicate the beginning of a new period with still lower trend growth than before may be open to doubt, since the unusually long and slow recovery after 1983 gained momentum towards the end of the decade. From 1980 to 1990, GDP grew at an annual average of 2.1 per cent, only marginally less than in the period 1973–80. In any case, it is indisputable that trend growth slowed down after 1973 and did not recover to prior levels until the late 1980s. Hence, viewed as a whole,

Table 1. *Growth performance of selected countries 1950–89*[a]

	1950–60	1960–73	1973–80	1980–9
West Germany[b]	8.2	4.4	2.2	1.9
France	4.6	5.6	2.8	2.1
Italy	5.6	5.3	2.8	2.3
United Kingdom	2.8	3.1	0.9	2.7
United States	3.3	4.0	2.1	3.0
Japan	8.8	9.6	3.7	4.2

Notes: [a] Average annual growth rate of gross domestic product (for the United States and Japan: gross national product) at constant prices.
[b] For 1950–60 excluding the Saar and Berlin.
Sources: Statistisches Bundesamt (for West Germany), OECD (for all other countries 1960–89), and *The Economist* (1985) (for all other countries 1950–60); own calculations.

the historical pattern of West German economic growth from 1948 to the late 1980s appears to be quite compatible with the picture of a gradually fading miracle.

This conclusion receives support from an international comparison of growth performances. Table 1 presents the average annual GDP growth rates of the six largest industrialized countries for the periods 1950–60, 1960–73, 1973–80 and 1980–9. For the 1950s, the general message is unambiguous: economic growth in West Germany was outstanding, much faster than in the United Kingdom, the United States and France, but also significantly faster than in Italy, which is usually regarded as another country with an economic miracle at that time. Only Japan slightly outperformed West Germany, but Japan in the 1950s was just on the verge of becoming a modern industrial society and still had a vast catch-up potential to tap, presumably much more so than West Germany. The change from the 1950s to the 1960s is most remarkable: while Japan, France, the United States, and to some extent even the United Kingdom entered a golden age with higher growth than in the previous decade, West Germany faced a quite dramatic growth deceleration which pulled it down to a poor fourth rank of the countries in the table. Only Italy experienced a slowdown as well, but it was clearly minimal compared to West Germany's. Thus, by the 1960s, the long-term growth dynamics had already become weaker in West Germany than in its continental EEC partner countries, and it has remained so up to the second half of the 1980s.

In the period 1973–80, growth rates dropped sharply in all countries relative to earlier years, but the prior growth ranking in Table 1 is mostly preserved, with the growth rate in West Germany being again slightly

Table 2. *The growth of output, inputs and productivity 1950–89*

	1950–60[a]	1960–73	1973–80	1980–9
(i) Real GDP	8.2	4.4	2.2	1.9
(ii) Active labour force	3.3	0.3	0.0	0.3
(iii) Labour volume	0.9	−0.8	−1.0	−0.3
(iv) Labour productivity	7.3	5.2	3.2	2.2
(v) Capital stock	4.8	6.1	3.8	2.8
(vi) Capital productivity	3.4	−1.6	−1.6	−0.9
(vii) Joint factor productivity	6.9	3.0	1.6	1.2

Notes: (i) gross domestic product at constant prices; (ii) number of employed persons (incl. self-employed); (iii) number of hours worked by active labour force; (iv) gross domestic product at constant prices divided by number of hours worked; (v) gross fixed capital (excl. non-commercially used housing) at constant prices; (vi) gross domestic product at constant prices divided by capital stock as defined in note to (v); (vii) weighted productivity of labour and capital as defined in notes to (iv) and (vi), with weights being 0.7 for labour and 0.3 for capital.
[a] Excluding the Saar and Berlin.
Sources: Statistisches Bundesamt and Bundesanstalt für Arbeit; own calculations.

higher than in the United States. In the 1980s, however, the picture changed again and the relative decline of West Germany reached its nadir: while the United Kingdom, the United States and, to a lesser extent, Japan, managed to accelerate the growth of their economies, all continental European countries fared even worse than before, with growth rates now between 1.9 and 2.3 per cent p.a.; among the EEC countries West Germany found itself at the lower end, lagging behind France, Italy, and the United Kingdom. Hence, after all, the fading German growth miracle seems to be a case not only of absolute slowdown in historical terms, but also of relative decline by international standards. Only recently, in 1989/90, does the West German economy seem to have regained a higher rank in the growth league. Whether this indicates a trend reversal or merely a transitory deviation remains to be seen.

By definition, an economy's output growth is due to an increase either of factor inputs or of factor productivity. Table 2 shows average annual growth rates of labour input, the capital stock, and various measures of productivity for the West German economy in the four relevant periods. As to labour input, the table indicates that the active labour force (including the self-employed) increased quite fast in the 1950s (by 3.3 per cent p.a.) and much slower thereafter. In terms of labour volume (i.e. the total number of hours worked), the 1950s are the only one of the four periods with an increase, since the sharp rise of the number of persons employed was sufficient to overcompensate the reduction of working hours per employee (largely because of longer holidays and a shortening of the working week). From the early 1960s onwards, the labour volume decreased quite steadily. With these trends in mind, it does not come as a surprise that the overall slowdown of output growth has been somewhat more dramatic than the slowdown of labour productivity growth, which actually declined from 7.3 per cent p.a. (1950–60) and 5.2 per cent p.a. (1960–73) down to 3.2 per cent p.a. (1973–80) and 2.2 per cent p.a. (1980–9).

As to capital, the picture is quite different: after having reached 4.8 per cent p.a. in the 1950s, the long-term growth rate of the capital stock peaked at 6.1 per cent p.a. in the period 1960–73, a time of very high saving and investment shares in gross national product. From this peak level, capital formation slowed down to 3.8 per cent p.a. (1973–80) and 2.8 per cent p.a. (1980–9), broadly in line with the deceleration of labour productivity growth. As a consequence, capital productivity – measured as GDP per unit of capital at constant prices – followed a most characteristic path: while it grew sharply in the 1950s by an average of 3.4 per cent p.a., it declined in the remaining three periods by an average of 1.6 per cent p.a. from 1960 to 1980 and 0.9 per cent p.a. from 1980 to 1989. Apparently, a process of capital deepening, which had set in with the investment boom in the 1960s, pulled down capital productivity in the face of a gradually shrinking labour volume.

To isolate those factor productivity gains (or losses) that are due to technical progress and structural change, not just to some sort of capital (or labour) deepening, a measure of joint factor productivity must be used. Needless to say, any such measure is very crude, as it involves a weighted average of capital and labour productivity growth, with the appropriate weights depending on the parameters of the production technology in the economy. Making some standard assumptions of the growth accounting literature,[3] we arrive at the numbers in Table 2 for the four relevant periods. As it turns out, the growth of joint factor productivity slowed down quite dramatically from 6.9 per cent p.a. in the 1950s to 3 per cent p.a. in 1960–73, 1.6 per cent p.a. in 1973–80, and 1.2 per cent p.a. in 1980–9. If the respective growth rates of labour productivity are recalled, it becomes clear that – on the statistical grounds of growth accounting – almost half of the labour productivity growth since 1960

---

[3] Following Maddison (1987), pp. 658ff., we assume a Cobb-Douglas technology with constant returns to scale and constant factor shares in value added. Numerically, we assume the labour share to be 70 per cent and the capital share to be 30 per cent. Note that the results in the table are quite robust with respect to changes of the numerical assumptions in the empirically relevant range.

Share of total
employment (%)

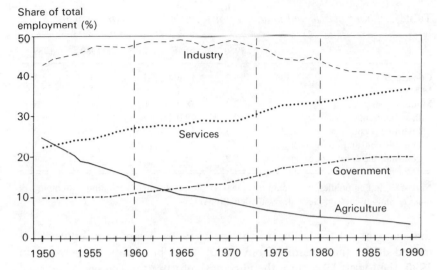

Figure 2. Structural change of the West German economy 1950–90.
Notes: Agriculture including forestry; industry including construction;
services including trade and transport; government including social
security administration and private non-profit organizations; for the
years 1950–9 excluding the Saar and Berlin.
Source: Statistisches Bundesamt; own calculations.

should be attributed to capital deepening, not to structural change or
technical progress.

2   Structural change

West German economic growth was accompanied by distinctive structural
changes. Figure 2 shows the development since 1950 of the shares in total
employment of four sectors:[4] agriculture, industry, services and the public
sector. Some features of Figure 2 are worth noting: (i) agriculture suffered
a sustained decline from about a quarter of total employment in 1950
down to well below 5 per cent in 1990. While this shrinkage went on
throughout the sample period, its speed diminished markedly over time,
with the bulk of the decline occurring prior to 1980, most of all in the
1950s and 1960s. (ii) Broadly speaking, industry passed through three
stages. From 1950 until the early 1960s, its employment share grew from
about 43 to 49 per cent. After some years of merely cyclical variation,

---

[4] To keep the presentation simple, we do not show sector shares in value added. By and
large, they confirm the picture conveyed by the employment shares and the qualitative
interpretation in the text.

Table 3. *Share of selected industries in total industrial employment^a (%)*

	1950	1960	1973	1980	1989
Construction	16.2	15.6	15.2	14.3	12.3
Mining	9.9	6.4	2.6	2.6	2.3
Manufacturing	73.4	78.0	82.2	83.1	85.5
Basic materials	19.0	18.0	17.4	17.3	16.5
Investment goods	25.3	33.8	40.3	42.6	47.2
Durable consumption goods	23.2	21.0	18.8	17.7	16.3
Non-durable consumption goods	5.9	5.3	5.6	5.5	5.4

Note: ^{a} Excluding utilities, but including construction; employment excluding self-employed.
Source: Statistisches Bundesamt; own calculations.

the share began to decline in the early 1970s. From then onwards, it moved down quite steadily from about 49 to just below 40 per cent in 1990, the lowest level since the currency reform. (iii) The net winners of structural change have been private services and the public sector. The former expanded their share in total employment throughout the four decades, starting at 22.3 per cent in 1950 and arriving at well above 35 per cent in 1990. As in industry, the greatest upward leap occurred in the 1950s, but unlike in industry, the expansion continued in later years, albeit at a somewhat slower pace. In turn, the employment share of the public sector stagnated in the 1950s at around 10–11 per cent, but moved up most of the time thereafter from 11 per cent in 1960 to about 20 per cent in 1990.

The fact that industry's share in total employment did not decline until the early 1970s is quite unusual by international standards. In other advanced industrialized countries, the process of deindustrialization started earlier, usually in the late 1950s and early 1960s. To locate the centre of the peculiar dynamics of West German industry, we shall look at the structural change within industry itself. Table 3 presents the shares in total industrial employment of construction, mining and manufacturing as well as four branches of manufacturing in the five years 1950, 1960, 1973, 1980 and 1989 which make up the boundaries of our four relevant growth periods. The table shows quite clearly that, at all times, manufacturing was the engine of industrial growth, or at least a brake on its decline: the employment share of construction fell from close to 16 per cent in 1950 to about 14 per cent in 1980 and 12 per cent in 1989; mining shrank dramatically from a share of about 10 per cent in 1950 to 2.6 per cent in 1973 and stagnated thereafter; only the share of manufacturing climbed up continually, from about 73 per cent in 1950 to more than 85 per cent in 1989. Within manufacturing, the trend was also unambiguous: while the relative importance of basic materials and consumer goods industries declined, investment goods industries increased their share in total industrial employment from about one-quarter in 1950 to almost one-half in 1989.

3   Macroeconomic stability

In the so-called stability law of June 1967, the West German legislator declared four major macroeconomic targets to be achieved at any time. Roughly speaking, these targets are a steady path of growth,[5] full employment, price stability and external balance. How did the West German economy fare by these widely accepted standards?

(i) Steady growth. Cyclical fluctuations of output growth are a common feature of the last forty years of West German economic history, with the most violent movements taking place in the 1960s and 1970s (see Figure 1). However, the fluctuations of output growth rates are themselves no reliable indicator of cyclical business conditions since they reflect both long-run supply and short-run demand variations. Instead, Figure 3 presents a widely used measure of capital stock utilization of the West German economy.[6] If the level of the boom year 1970 is taken as the reference standard (1970 – 100), the figure shows that capital stock utilization varied from about 93 to 102. The extremely high levels of the early 1950s must be interpreted as altogether exceptional, another indicator of a sort of miracle: they should not be given too much importance in the overall picture.

The cyclical pattern in the figure is easily discernible: recession troughs at the beginning of the sample period in 1949/50, and again in 1954, 1958, 1963, 1967, 1971, 1975, and 1982; boom peaks in 1953, 1955, 1960, 1965, 1970, 1973, 1979, and 1989/90. Particularly severe recession troughs fell in the years 1958 (at least relative to the unusually high prior peak level), 1967, 1975 and 1982, and the most marked booms in the mid 1950s,

[5] The law itself speaks of 'steady and adequate growth'. Whatever 'adequate growth' means, it is certainly not a genuine target of short-term macroeconomic stability. Having dealt with long-term growth above, we shall just leave it out at this point.

[6] If one defines the business cycle as a sequence of changes in the utilization of an economy's productive potential, and if one further assumes that, in the short run, this potential is constrained by the capital stock – and not the labour supply – it makes good sense to take the utilization of the economy's capital stock as a proxy for the state of the business cycle. Note that in periods of chronically full or overemployment, the labour supply – and not the capital stock – may become the relevant constraint. In fact, West Germany was in a state of full or overemployment most of the time in the period 1960–73; however, it still had a foreign worker supply in southern Europe to tap, so that the domestic labour supply constraint was not binding after all.

1970 = 100

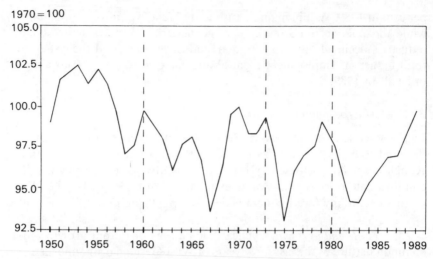

Figure 3. Index of capital stock utilization in the West German
economy 1950–89.
Note: for 1950–9 excluding the Saar and Berlin.
Sources: for 1950–9: Deutsches Institut für Wirtschaftsforschung,
Berlin (adjusted to the levels of later years); for 1960–89: Institut für
Weltwirtschaft, Kiel.

in 1960, 1970, 1979, and 1989/90. With the possible exceptions of the
long and forceful upswing in the early 1950s until about 1956 and the
equally long, but much slower recovery after 1982, the cyclical fluctuations
reveal quite sizeable amplitudes which did in fact translate into the fairly
unsteady output growth pattern of Figure 1. Hence, as far as mere
stabilization of the business cycle is concerned, the performance does not
look very impressive.

(ii) Full employment. The West German unemployment record
since the currency reform in mid 1948 may be divided into five major
periods (see Figure 4): from mid 1948 to 1950, a sharp increase of the
unemployment rate from below 5 to more than 10 per cent; from 1950
to 1960, a gradual and sustained decline from above 10 down to about
1 per cent, only briefly interrupted by the business downturn of 1957/8; from
1960 to 1973, a fairly constant minimal unemployment rate at about 1 per cent,
with only one sharp temporary rise to 2.1 per cent in the recession around
1967; in 1974–80, a sharp rise from 1 up to 5 per cent in 1975, followed
by stagnation and a meagre one percentage point decline towards the end
of the 1970s; in 1980–90, another rise, this time from about 4 to over 9
per cent in 1983, followed by stagnation and – at the end of the sample

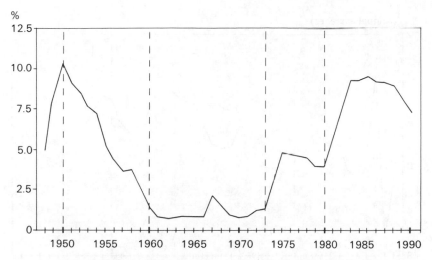

Figure 4. The unemployment rate in West Germany 1948–90.
Notes: for 1948 only second half of the year; for 1948–59 excluding the Saar and Berlin.
Sources: until 1952, Bundesminister für Arbeit; from 1953, Bundesanstalt für Arbeit.

period – some improvement in the range of two percentage points. What appears to be striking about this record is the fact that cyclical forces do not play the dominant part: from 1950 to the early 1970s, business upswings and downturns coincided with variations in the unemployment rate, but the movements were obviously minor compared to the overall downward trend in the 1950s and the stagnation at a very low level in the 1960s. In later years, recessions coincided with sharp rises of unemployment to new dimensions, but the following booms did not reverse the prior rises; thus, since 1973/4, a kind of asymmetric pattern has emerged which also defies any straight account of unemployment in terms of cyclical forces.

If we look over the last forty years, it is clear that a state of full (or even over-) employment had been reached in the early 1960s, after a decade of spectacular rises of employment (see Table 2). However, since the mid 1970s and even more so since the early 1980s, unemployment has re-emerged as a persistent feature of the West German economy. Hence, one of its major macroeconomic targets – full employment – has not been realized. In this respect, the recent macroeconomic performance in West Germany is quite unsatisfactory, although still somewhat better than in most other industrialized European countries.

% (Annual averages)

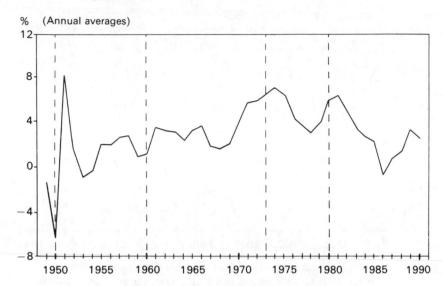

Figure 5. Price inflation in West Germany 1949–90.
Notes: for 1949 annualized growth rate relative to second half of
1948; for 1948/9–1959/60 excluding the Saar; up to 1950 consumer
price index for representative household (four persons); from 1951
onwards deflator of private consumption expenditure.
Source: Statistisches Bundesamt; own calculations.

(iii) Price stability. By international standards, the rate of
inflation has been comparatively low in West Germany throughout the
last forty years. From a historical perspective, however, the performance
is mixed (see Figure 5): after some violent price movements in the early
1950s – mainly through the stagnation in 1949/50 and the Korea boom
thereafter – West Germany's consumer price inflation was kept in the
range of 1–4 per cent p.a. until the late 1960s, with a slight upward trend
and a visible cyclical pattern. This rather calm picture changed dramatically in the early 1970s, when inflation soared from still below 2 per cent
p.a. in 1968/9 to about 7 per cent p.a. in 1973/4 and, after a temporary
decrease in the second half of the decade, again up to 6.3 per cent p.a.
in 1980/1. Both bursts of inflation followed major oil price shocks and
temporarily rapid expansions of the money supply. From 1980/1 to 1985/6,
price inflation was cut down to virtually zero, but more recently it has
resurfaced again, albeit at moderate rates.

(iv) External balance. As to the external balance, the West
German economy did in fact perform extraordinarily well by all conven-

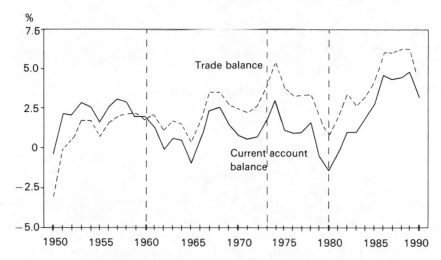

Figure 6. External balance of the West German economy as a share of GNP 1950–90.
Note: for 1950–9 excluding the Saar and Berlin.
Sources: Deutsche Bundesbank, Statistisches Bundesamt; own calculations.

tional standards, although one must keep in mind that these standards have a strong mercantilistic flavour and may not be a helpful guide in many historical circumstances.[7] Figure 6 shows two selected measures of external balance as a percentage of GNP from 1949 to 1990. If we take the current account balance as a rough ex-post measure for the marginal relevance of external constraints to the domestic economy due to internal overspending ('living beyond one's means'), then the West German record is no doubt a very successful one: in only seven out of the 42 years of the sample period has the West German economy ended up with a current account deficit. These years were 1949, 1950, 1962, 1965 and 1979–81. The deficit in 1962 was more or less the ex-ante approved outcome of a deliberate policy measure, the revaluation of the West German currency in 1961. Only in 1949/50, 1965, and again 1979–81 did external deficits play a prominent role in considerations of macroeconomic policies, driving them into an explicitly contractionary stance. Note also the interesting fact that – abstracting from cyclical variations – the current account surplus as a share of GNP was highest in the 1950s and again in the 1980s, but somewhat lower in the two decades in between.

[7] See our later discussion of the persistent West German current account surplus in the 1980s in Chapter 6, Section B.2 below.

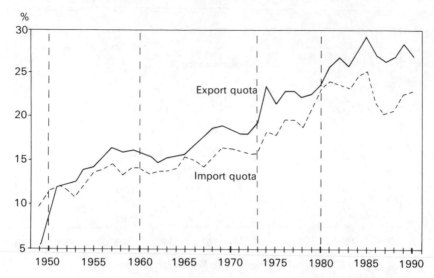

Figure 7. Export quota and import quota in West Germany 1949–90.
Note: for 1949–59 excluding the Saar and Berlin; export (import)
quota defined as value of exported (imported) goods divided by GNP.
Sources: Deutsche Bundesbank, Statistisches Bundesamt; own
calculations.

The main force behind the comfortable external position of the West
German economy was the persistent surplus on trade account (see Figure
6): after the two early years of deficit (1950/1), the trade balance remained
positive throughout, with a clear tendency of the surplus to rise over time
as a percentage of GNP. This rise helped to compensate for the deficits
in the service and transfer balances which gradually emerged as a
consequence of West Germany's increasing travel bill abroad, the remittances made by foreign workers to their home countries, and transfers to
developing countries and the EEC budget.

It is important to note that the almost persistent state of trade surplus
coincided with a rapid integration of the West German economy into
world markets. As Figure 7 shows, the trend growth of export and import
values outpaced the long-term increase of GNP so that both the export
and the import quota rose continually, with a particularly pronounced
upswing in the 1950s. Hence the data do in fact point to an important
role of exports as a driving force of West German economic growth; at
least in the early years, there was something like a German export miracle.

In summary, the stylized facts of the West German economic performance since the currency reform in 1948 indicate that it may deserve two

cheers rather than three after all. As to the speed of growth (and also structural change), the story is one of sharp rise and gradual fall: exceptional dynamics in the 1950s, no more than average speed in the 1960s and 1970s, and slow pace in the 1980s, though possibly with a slight acceleration in the very recent past. As to standard criteria of macroeconomic stability, it is a story of external success, but also of at least partial internal failure, with the most unfortunate monument of failure being the persistently high unemployment rate in the last decade.

2 1945–1948: establishing a liberal order

For Germany and all other countries liberated from the Nazi dictatorship, the end of the Second World War created the opportunity for a better beginning. In the following three years, the newly gained freedom of the German people already manifested itself in an intense political debate and a vigorous cultural life, at least in those parts of the former Reich now occupied by the Western Allies. At the same time, however, the standard of living fell to a dismally low level, far worse even than the economic hardship endured at the height of the hostilities. In the memory of Germans who lived through these days, it is not the war itself but the three years after which have become deeply engrained as the time of hunger and misery when even the Catholic Archbishop of Cologne publicly encouraged his flock to go on stealing the food and the coal they needed to survive the winter. In early May 1947, the food rations issued in major industrial centres of Western Germany were down to 740–800 calories per day,[1] i.e. roughly one-quarter of the pre-war consumption of 3,000 calories. And while industrial production in the rest of Western Europe already exceeded its 1938 level by 7 per cent in 1947, West German factories still churned out no more than 34 per cent of their pre-war output.[2] There was hardly any hint of an economic miracle to come.

In this chapter, we shall first examine what had gone wrong in the occupied country during the first three years after the war (Section 1). Next, we shall turn to the rise of the peculiar German brand of economic liberalism which laid the intellectual foundations for the regime switch from a centrally administered to a basically free-market economy in mid 1948 and which remained the quasi-official credo of West Germany's economic policy thereafter (Section 2). Finally, we shall discuss the main elements and the immediate impact of the reforms of June 1948 (Section 3), while the subsequent sustained recovery that lasted throughout the 1950s will be dealt with in Chapter 3.

[1] See Balabkins (1964), p. 115.
[2] See Economic Cooperation Administration (1951), p. 98.

1   Post-war misery

(a) Economic collapse. Three months after the end of hostilities
in Europe, the leading statesmen of the United States, the United Kingdom
and the Soviet Union met at Potsdam in the vicinity of Berlin to discuss
the future shape of Germany. The three victors approved the de facto
cessation of the former German territories east of the rivers Oder and
Neisse to Poland and the Soviet Union, and confirmed their earlier
decisions to divide the remainder of the country into occupation zones –
with France being allotted a zone of its own in the South-West – and to
administer these four zones as one economic unit. However, this projected
joint administration never materialized because of inter-Allied quarrels.
The military commanders of each zone thus assumed complete control
over the economies of their respective parts of the country.

The three Western Allies were facing a huge task. Taken together, their
zones that eventually were to become West Germany covered 52 per cent
of the Reich territory. Before the war, 57 per cent of the German
population had lived there, producing some 61 per cent of Germany's
industrial output – but only about 43 per cent of the basic foodstuffs,
above all grain and potatoes.[3] Organized economic activity had virtually
ground to a halt. Although the overall destruction which bombing raids
had dealt to the capital stock was fairly limited,[4] the damage was
distributed very unevenly. Even many basically intact factories were
paralysed because suppliers of essential inputs had been bombed out.
More importantly, the transport system had collapsed, as most bridges
had been knocked down and the bulk of the railway equipment was no
longer serviceable. In addition, 20 per cent of all residential buildings –
and 50 per cent of those in the cities subjected to major attacks – had
been destroyed or heavily damaged.[5] To make matters worse, the
population in the western part of the country was increasing sharply from
some 39 million in 1939 to 46 million in mid 1948; about 8 million people
were expellees from the formerly German-inhabited parts of eastern Europe
or refugees from the Soviet zone of occupation.[6]

To prevent the temporary economic collapse from turning into a chronic
crisis, the economy would have needed three features: (i) an incentive
system for channelling manpower and physical resources into the most
productive repair activities and for converting armaments production to

[3] Statistisches Bundesamt, *Statistisches Jahrbuch* (1953), pp. 13ff., excluding Berlin and the
Saar.   [4] See The United States Strategic Bombing Survey (1945).
[5] *Ibid.*, pp. 12ff., 51, 127; unlike all other figures, these numbers refer to the entire Reich
territory.   [6] Statistisches Bundesamt, *Statistisches Jahrbuch* (1953), p. 50.

the best civilian uses; (ii) an opportunity to expand industrial production and to export manufactures in exchange for food in line with the comparative advantages of Western Germany (which includes the Ruhr valley, i.e. the industrial powerhouse of the late Reich); and (iii) a chance to import capital, which – unlike the complementary factors of manpower and skill – had become relatively scarce.

In fact, Allied policy ran counter to these needs, at least for the time being. Initially, the victors' attitude towards the future of Germany was guided by the harsh vision of Henry Morgenthau, the US Secretary of the Treasury in the latter years of the war, and Harry D. White, then chief of the Treasury's monetary research department, who had worked out a blueprint for turning the industrial heartland of the European continent into a country of peaceful farmers and craftsmen. Although the actual White–Morgenthau Plan was quietly shelved soon after Roosevelt and Churchill had accepted the idea at their second Quebec summit in September 1944, its spirit remained evident in the first Allied decisions on economic policy. For the US zone, this spirit was manifest in the Joint Chiefs of Staff directive JCS 1067 of April 1945, which required that the US military authorities 'impose controls to the full extent necessary to achieve the industrial disarmament of Germany' and forbade them to take major 'steps (a) looking toward the economic rehabilitation of Germany or (b) designed to maintain or strengthen the German economy'.[7] For Germany as a whole, the Morgenthau spirit shaped the economic provisions of the Potsdam Protocol of August 1945. This agreement called inter alia for the drastic contraction of German industry in general and heavy industry in particular, along with a sweeping decentralization and decartelization, for the maintenance of 'peaceful' (i.e. light) industries and for the development of a large agricultural sector.[8] To put this accord into practice, the Allies worked out a 'level of industry plan' (March 1946) which restricted overall industrial output to 55 per cent of the 1938 level and earmarked the equipment to be shipped abroad as reparations.[9]

As a whole, the policies of industrial disarmament, of artificially emphasizing agriculture, of restricting or virtually prohibiting foreign trade (including the import of raw materials needed to attain even the permitted level of industrial output) and, most unpopular, of extracting reparations in kind by dismantling and forcibly exporting capital goods were likely to delay and impede the country's economic recovery. Worst

---

[7] US Department of State (1947), pp. 155–6.   [8] *Ibid.*, pp. 159–60.
[9] In the case of the machine tools industry, for instance, one of the traditional strengths of the German economy, only 11.4 per cent of the pre-war capacity was to be retained in the country: US Office of Military Government for Germany OMGUS (1946), pp. 207–15.

of all, however, the Allies decided to keep almost the entire Nazi system of directing the economy intact.

   (b) The centrally administered economy. From 1936 onwards, the Nazis had converted the still predominantly capitalist German economy into a centrally administered system geared towards the needs of the totalitarian state, most of all the ambitious rearmament drive. Unlike the situation in command economies of the Soviet type, however, the means of production remained – at least nominally – in private hands. Within the rigid frame set by the Nazi economic legislation, the quest for private profitability and for keeping one's own firm intact could play a role besides the overriding imperative of meeting the prescribed targets. In sociological terms, this meant that entrepreneurs as a social group (or class) did not vanish.

   The main pillars of the Nazi economic legislation had been the fixing of prices, wages and rents at their levels of autumn 1936, the rationing of consumer goods and foodstuffs, the central allocation of labour, raw materials and major commodities, a system of compulsory delivery quotas for farmers, and a tight regulation of housing. During the war, the economic system resting on these pillars had served its purpose of extracting savings for the rapid build-up of the armaments industry reasonably well. After the war, a competent central administration might have engineered a substantial recovery, at least for some time, provided it could have gathered adequate information about the resources available, the damages to be repaired and the structural changes required. Yet after the breakdown of the previous administration, the collapse of communications and transportation and the severe post-war disruptions of the pattern of production, this was clearly not feasible. Furthermore, the fragmentation of the Reich as well as the gradual build-up of new German authorities, reaching from the local level upwards to the states (*Länder*) and the zones, implied that a totally different system of planning had to be erected, which could not rely on the previous institutions. The focus on small administrative units, which was most evident in the American zone, meant that basic services within a region could be restored without unnecessary delays, while inter-regional and interzonal ventures like the reconstruction of transport links typically took much longer. More importantly, as authority in day-to-day affairs rested mostly with German regional bodies under the supervision of the respective occupying power, there was an inherent bias against an economically rational division of labour between firms in different administrative units.

   Given these gross inefficiencies in the administrative allocation of inputs and the distribution of output, which went far beyond the usual deficiencies of command economies, the fixing of wages, prices and rents at their 1936 level had particularly bad consequences. They were discernible both on the microeconomic and the macroeconomic level. As to the micro-level, the rigid structure of relative prices did not reflect the post-war scarcities, which differed markedly from pre-war conditions. Therefore, price signals could not steer resources into the most productive uses, not even in those cases where the administrative system had left sufficient room for individual initiative. As administrative allocations were inadequate and unreliable, firms increasingly took to self-production of inputs, thus reducing the overall allocative efficiency even further. Leaving aside some minor adjustments in the price structure, it was only the prices for 'new' goods which were flexible, in the sense that, when these goods were introduced, their prices could be determined on the basis of what the authorities accepted as current costs. The result of these microeconomic distortions was rather curious. On the one hand, there were no adequate economic incentives to spur on the production of bottleneck commodities like fertilizers and coal-mine equipment. On the other hand, firms could fare comparatively well by securing attractive prices for luxurious or semi-luxurious commodities which had not been available before the war and for which prices had therefore not been fixed previously. Naturally, a flood of such 'new' goods as fancy and innovative ash trays, lamps, dolls and chandeliers poured forth. Thus, in the midst of post-war misery, West Germany turned into a 'hair-oil ash-tray herb-tea economy'.[10] Between mid 1946 and mid 1948, the glass and ceramics industry and the musical instruments and toys industry were by far the most rapidly growing sectors of the West German economy, with employment increasing by 113.5 and 108.4 per cent respectively, about five times as fast as overall employment.[11]

In the macroeconomic domain, the frozen price level did not stand in any realistic relation to the current money supply. After 1932, a ruthlessly expansionary monetary policy had created an inflationary pressure which could only be held in check by the price freeze of 1936 in the first place. On top of this, the financing of the war through the printing press pushed up the money supply roughly tenfold,[12] whereas at the end of the war, industrial production dropped to about a quarter of what it had been before. With more money chasing fewer goods at fixed prices, Germany found itself in a state of 'repressed inflation'.[13] The official money lost its

[10] Röpke (1951), p. 271; see also Balabkins (1964), p. 161.
[11] Ehret (1959), p. 65; the numbers refer to the Bizonal (US–British) area only.
[12] For exact figures on circulation, see Buchheim (1988), p. 199.
[13] Röpke (1947), p. 57.

value not via rising prices (open inflation) but via a spreading reluctance to accept this money as a medium of exchange.

Because of the almost complete repudiation of the official currency, the classical form of black marketeering, i.e. the exchange of goods against the official money at unofficially high prices, played only a minor role.[14] Instead, cigarettes replaced the Reichsmark as the standard means of payment and short-term store of value in day-to-day transactions. On the unofficial markets, the exchange rate between Reichsmark and cigarettes, i.e. the Reichsmark price of cigarettes, was flexible. Therefore, counter to Gresham's Law, which holds for money of different inherent qualities at fixed exchange rates, the 'good money' (cigarettes) drove out the 'bad' (the Reichsmark).

Even more importantly, firms and individuals resorted to illegal bilateral barter and to complicated compensation deals, often involving arduously worked out chains of bilateral trade to finally get hold of scarce inputs. Both the need to have a sufficient supply of commodities at hand for eventual bartering and the general flight into physical assets as the only reliable stores of value (*Flucht in die Sachwerte*) resulted in a large-scale hoarding of raw materials and semi-finished products.[15]

As money and money wages had virtually lost their meaning, firms with goods that were directly usable or readily saleable on the illegal markets used wage payments in kind to reduce widespread absenteeism and to improve work discipline. Firms lacking this resort tried to restructure their output mix so as to have something barterable themselves. Between city and countryside, a specific type of barter economy came into being which Henry C. Wallich has aptly described as follows: 'Each day, and particularly on weekends, vast hordes of people trekked out to the country to barter food from the farmers. In dilapidated railway carriages from which everything pilferable had long disappeared, on the roofs and on the running boards, hungry people travelled sometimes hundreds of miles at snail's pace to where they hoped to find something to eat.'[16]

To sum up, the peculiar combination of an ineffective administrative allocation of resources, of illegal markets and of excess liquidity in face of rigidly fixed prices gave rise to widespread inefficient self-production, to very high transaction costs and to a very unfavourable ratio of stocks to output in an economy desperately short of raw materials. Neither sound money nor flexible relative prices were available as the means for coordinating the complex division of labour which is the hallmark of a modern economy. Eventually, as the administrations increasingly lost their

---

[14] See Mendershausen (1949), pp. 652–4.   [15] See Buchheim (1988), p. 195.
[16] Wallich (1955), p. 65.

grip on the economy, only about half of the output was available through legal channels according to some reports. The rest was hoarded or used for nominally illegal, but widely tolerated, compensation deals and for black-market transactions.[17]

As to the macroeconomic performance, the post-war misery showed up in a rundown of the capital stock and a low level of production. In principle, the partial and unevenly distributed destruction of the capital stock should have made investments highly profitable both in repairing existing and installing new equipment for widening bottlenecks. Instead, investment dropped by an even larger percentage than overall production. Inadequate profit opportunities were the major, but not the only, reason for this. Although actual plant removals and reparations from the British and American zones in the first three years after the war were much smaller than had been announced and expected, the long uncertainty due to protracted and indecisive inter-Allied negotiations meant that businessmen were reluctant to devote resources to the build-up of fixed assets which might eventually be confiscated. Three years after the war, the capital stock was 21 per cent below its peak level of 1944 and still 7.3 per cent below its 1945 level, with the machines being on average older than before.[18]

Although some progress was made in comparison with the collapse at the end of the war, industrial production between 1945 and early 1948 limped at around one-third of its 1938 level. Not even the production ceilings permitted by the Level of Industry Plan of March 1946 were in fact reached. And although the basic philosophy of Allied policy immediately after the war had been to strengthen agriculture, food output fell from 70 per cent in 1946/7 to 58 per cent of its pre-war level in 1947/8,[19] a development attributable above all to a lack of fertilizers and machinery and to an exceptionally cold winter. To prevent widespread starvation, the US and, to a lesser extent, the UK financed huge imports of food, amounting to a total of 1.5 billion dollars in the first three years after the war.[20] Nevertheless, the food rations actually issued frequently fell below the target of 1,550 calories. The economy hit rock bottom in early 1947, when lack of energy caused widespread industrial stoppages. In spite of sufficient stockpiles at the mines, not enough coal was delivered to the factories, to the power plants and to ordinary citizens, simply because rail transport failed and waterways were frozen. In the course of 1947, industrial production picked up again. But until mid 1948, it still did not exceed half of pre-war output levels.

---

[17] See Balabkins (1964), p. 147.   [18] See Krengel (1958), pp. 16, 49–53.
[19] Statistisches Bundesamt, *Statistisches Jahrbuch* (1953), p. 15.   [20] See Niklas (1949), p. 13.

As time went by, the extremely sluggish recovery in production and the miserable levels of consumption did not fail to affect the philosophy of the Allies in general and the Americans in particular. In its rigid form, JCS 1067 had guided the policy of the US military governor in his zone for some six months. Thereafter, the practical task of securing the survival of the population gradually became the major concern, first for the US military authorities in the US zone of occupation and – with a time lag – for their superiors in Washington. As tales of German misery began to make some impression on the general public in the US, Congress became reluctant to foot the bill of the policy of German industrial disarmament by financing food imports.

The gradual change in the philosophy of the US – whose influence on their British and French Allies was growing because of the economic difficulties of the two latter countries at home[21] – manifested itself in a number of steps towards supporting a German recovery. (i) JCS 1067 was increasingly ignored; in July 1947, it was replaced by a new directive (JCS 1779), which stipulated the creation of stable economic and political conditions. On this basis, the Level of Industry Plan was – at least for the American and the British zones – revised in late August to permit Germany to retain sufficient capacity to approximate the 1936 level of output. (ii) The original British plans to nationalize basic industries were scaled down and eventually shelved. (iii) The burden of reparations was eased.[22] (iv) To permit a more rational inter-regional economic adminis-tration, the American and the British zones were fused into what became known as 'Bizonia' at the beginning of 1947. (v) Resources were shifted to apparent bottlenecks, notably the railway system, after the plight of the winter of 1947.[23] (vi) First attempts were made to restore a normal, though rigidly controlled, flow of trade with the outside world.

(c) The sorry state of foreign trade. In the first three years after the war, the development of external trade lagged far behind the reconstruction of West Germany's internal economy, which was sluggish enough. While in 1947 industrial production had reached 39 per cent of

---

[21] The attitude of the British had never been as harsh as the original US intentions. Still, the recovery in the British zone was delayed by the ineffective mechanism of central planning within each zone, on which the British put more emphasis than the US. In the French zone of occupation, the economy was directed from the outset towards the needs of recovery in France. Forced exports to France and the requisition of roughly 10 per cent of production by the occupational authorities did not allow for a continuous and thorough recovery of the economy; see Abelshauser (1979), pp. 229f.

[22] For a detailed assessment of the reparations burden, see Buchheim (1990), pp. 77–99.

[23] As late as June 1948, only 47 per cent of all locomotives were serviceable: Statistisches Bundesamt, *Wirtschaft und Statistik* (1949/50), p. 26.

the 1936 level, there were hardly any commercial exports at all. This was all the more unfortunate since the disruption of almost all economic links between Western Germany and the Eastern half of the former Reich had reduced the opportunities for an internal division of labour. Hence, the need for an exchange of goods and services with foreign countries was far greater than before the war.

The reasons for the sorry state of foreign trade lay in the economic policies pursued in the first three to four years after the war. With Germany's unconditional surrender in early May 1945 the Allies had assumed complete control of all internal and cross-border transactions, including even private business contacts with foreigners. Initially, all foreign trade was virtually prohibited except for the compulsory exports of coal, coke, timber and scrap and the aid-financed imports of food. In the absence of a joint administration of Germany, the trade monopoly of the Military Government meant in fact that every occupying power had almost complete freedom of action in its own zone. Broadly speaking, the French attached priority to rebuilding the coal and chemicals industries as convenient sources for French imports, while the production of goods for local consumption was in general neglected; the British tried to make sure that exports of coal (and other raw materials) reached high levels, while, sometimes for domestic protectionist reasons, they showed less enthusiasm for reviving exports of German manufactures, and the Americans generously supplied food aid while the debate on the desired future of Germany went on between late adherents of a watered-down Morgenthau Plan in Washington and pragmatists like General Clay, the Commander of the US Forces in Germany.[24]

The first significant improvement came about at the beginning of 1947, when the Joint Export and Import Agency (JEIA) of the Anglo-American bizone made some efforts to promote commercial exports and even to reduce red tape, albeit with rather limited success. In 1947, West German imports amounted to 843 million dollars, with goods worth 600 million dollars financed by foreign aid, while exports stood at a meagre 318 million dollars.[25] Furthermore, the commodity structure of trade was grossly distorted. Traditionally, Germany had exported finished manufactured goods in exchange for raw materials, food and some manufactures. In 1947, external sales of finished manufactures were almost negligible, amounting to 11 per cent of all exports compared to 77 per cent in 1936. Instead, raw materials (mainly coal and timber) made up 64 per cent of the exports; semi-finished products (almost exclusively coke and scrap)

[24] See Clay (1950).
[25] Bank deutscher Länder, Geschäftsbericht für das Jahr 1950, p. 46.

came second with 24 per cent. In 1936, the share of these categories had been less than 10 per cent each. On the other hand, 92 per cent of imports were foodstuffs, roughly three times the 1936 share.[26]

On top of the Allied trade restrictions and the bureaucratic red tape, the monetary arrangements made sure that West German producers had little interest in exporting goods and that foreign customers were rather reluctant to buy them. Apart from a minor foreign exchange retention quota introduced in Bizonia in September 1947,[27] German firms were paid in almost useless Reichsmarks for their exports, while local markets offered at least opportunities for profitable barter transactions. Thus, producers had hardly any incentive to go beyond their export obligations.[28] Internally, a chaotic multiplicity of product-specific exchange rates was supposed to equate the fixed internal price of merchandise to the corresponding price on the world market (0.24–0.80 dollars per Reichsmark). Externally, the Allies had originally insisted on conducting Germany's foreign trade in dollars, although – because of a lack of convertible foreign exchange – almost the entire Western European trade was governed by bilateral trade agreements. At given prices and exchange rates, German products were not attractive enough to make other countries want to spend their scarce dollars on them.

(d) Towards new policies. The change for the better was prepared by a political reassessment of the European economic and political situation, most of all in Washington. In 1947, the recovery of Western Europe as a whole was jeopardized by a major transatlantic balance-of-payments crisis. In the US, the exceptionally large European balance-of-payments deficit was correctly interpreted as caused in part by the virtual absence of the continent's traditional industrial heartland, Germany, from European trade circuits. Politically, the unresolved state of affairs and the economic distress in the centre of Europe were seen as playing into the hands of local communist parties and the Soviet Union.

---

[26] 1947 figures: JEIA, March 1949, pp. 18f.; JEIA numbers differ slightly from those of German sources. The official numbers for overall exports may have to be adjusted upwards by up to 20 per cent to account for widespread illegal trade at the borders. Interestingly, the typical pattern of smuggling was the import of money substitutes such as coffee and cigarettes for exports of high-quality and low-weight manufactures such as clocks, cameras and optical instruments: Motz (1954), p. 68. During the post-war misery, sound money was obviously needed more than anything else.

[27] For details on the retention quota, see Motz (1954), pp. 29–32.

[28] In any case, the almost ridiculously painstaking administrative control did nothing to make exporting appear an attractive option. For example, a West German manufacturer of leather goods who had secured seventeen export orders worth 2,000 dollars at the Cologne fair in autumn 1947 had to fill in 1,343 forms, 561 of which were translations into English. See Meyer (1953), pp. 258–85.

With communists pushing their way into power in the East European countries occupied by the Soviet Union and given the increasingly uncooperative attitude of the Soviets with respect to the administration of Germany, the Western Allies finally decided to disregard Soviet reservations and go ahead with rebuilding the economy in their three zones of occupation and – if necessary – to establish a separate West German state.

By 1948, with the abandonment of the original Allied policy, the time had come to put the economy in the three Western zones on a sound footing. In preparation for a currency reform, the Western Allies established a central bank (Bank deutscher Länder) in March 1948.[29] While the need for a new money was obvious, the question of the future economic system of Germany remained still open. At this point, German economists and politicians reappeared on the scene. The outcome of the fierce internal debate on fundamental issues of economic policy and the ensuing power struggle between political parties within Western Germany turned out to be the decisive factors.

2   The rise of Ordoliberalism

The unconditional surrender of Nazi Germany in 1945 and the subsequent occupation by the Allies ended twelve years of intellectual autarchy and opened the country to the ideas discussed and tried elsewhere. Nevertheless, the doctrine which eventually shaped the actual economic system of the emerging West Germany was, among the ideologies competing for influence, the most home-grown one. The concepts of the disparate group of scholars, journalists and politicians that became known under the brandname of 'Ordoliberalism'[30] were based on the daily experience of German post-war misery, i.e. the gradual breakdown of the system of central planning which the victors had inherited from the Nazis, and the lunacies of a monetary regime in which cigarettes had replaced the debased Reichsmark as the common store of value and medium of exchange. More fundamentally, 'Ordoliberalism' was deeply rooted in a particular perception of Germany's economic and political history that

---

[29] See Möller (1976), pp. 453–6.

[30] The term 'Ordo' was chosen by Walter Eucken, a leading neoliberal scholar from Freiburg University, to establish a link between the German neoliberal concept of an economic order and the medieval idea of 'Ordo', that is the natural and harmonious state of affairs to be detected by scholarly discussion and to be approached in reality by appropriate policies. For simplicity's sake, we include under the heading of 'Ordoliberalism' all those proponents of liberal ideas who subscribed to the basic tenets of this doctrine, whether they used this name themselves or not.

offered an answer to the question of how Nazi totalitarianism could have risen in the country of Kant, Goethe and Beethoven.

   (a) The Ordoliberal interpretation of Germany's economic history. With the Industrial Revolution in full steam from the 1830s onwards, economic liberalism had gained ground in the patchwork of Germany's princely states. The German customs union (Zollverein) of 1834 laid the economic foundations for the subsequent political unification. In its first decade, the German Reich of 1871 was almost a haven of laissez-faire liberalism. However, according to the Ordoliberal interpretation, economic freedom was endogenously eroded by the rise of private economic power. Unchecked by measures to safeguard competition, monopolies as well as cartels and organized interest groups had blossomed and eventually acquired sufficient influence to become important powers in the political arena. The laissez-faire economy was gradually transformed into a corporatist system. Important steps in this direction were Chancellor Bismarck's turn towards a protectionist tariff policy (*Schutzzollpolitik*) after a cyclical slump in the late 1870s and a decision of the Supreme Court in 1897 which explicitly legitimized the formation of cartels.

   After the defeat in the First World War, the weak governments of the Weimar Republic (1918–33) tried to broaden their popular appeal by bending down to sectional interests. However, the resulting interventions into the free play of market forces created new, often unforeseen, distortions in the economic system – necessitating further interventions or even leading into self-perpetuating intervention spirals (*Interventionsspiralen*) that caused additional damage.[31] Thus, the state fell prey increasingly to the thriving private-interest groups lobbying for restraints on competition in order to secure rents for themselves (*Der Staat als Beute*). The inherent corporatist inefficiencies and inflexibilities delayed Germany's recovery from the Great Depression (1929–32). And this intermeshing of economic and political power (*Vermachtung der Wirtschaft*), of the private and the public domain, prepared the ground for the final and ultimately fatal concentration of all economic and political power in the hands of the totalitarian Nazis.[32] Initially, the full employment policy of public works and monetary expansion to which the Weimar Republic resorted towards the end of the Great Depression in 1932 and which the Nazis adopted from 1933 onwards was quite successful in

---

[31] Mises (1926).
[32] See Hayek (1944), who, although himself not an Ordoliberal in the strict sense, has expounded this essential Ordoliberal interpretation most forcefully in his famous warning against 'The Road to Serfdom'.

bringing down unemployment. However, as this policy continued even after the Depression had been overcome, a general price and wage freeze had to be ordered in late 1936 to prevent a surge of inflation. Even before the war, this rigid regimentation of economic life developed into an almost full-blown system of central administration, although firms remained nominally private and independent. By its very nature, a central administration has the tendency to legitimize its existence and power by imposing national goals, in the most extreme case by starting a war.[33] In the eyes of the Ordoliberals it was both the lack of adequate safeguards against the rise of private power and the weakness of the state which ultimately caused the replacement of economic and political freedom by an unrestrained dictatorship.

  (b) Individual freedom and a strong state. Being liberals in the European sense of the word,[34] the Ordoliberals emphasized individual freedom as the overriding normative principle. For some of them, this choice of first priority was based on a philosophy of 'natural law'; for others, it was the logical implication of their Christian belief in the equality of all human beings as autonomous subjects created in the image of God. True to classical liberal tradition, the Ordoliberals interpreted the notion of individual freedom in a negative sense – as the scope for free and self-determined individual action to be shielded from intrusions and arbitrariness. While the classical liberals had maintained that the law was mainly to protect the individual against government coercion, the Ordoliberals went one step further. In accordance with their perception of Germany's economic history, they attached equal importance to safeguarding individual freedom against intrusions by private agents, especially monopolies, cartels and organizations of vested interests. The key to the preservation of liberty was to prevent any concentration of power. In the political sphere, the classical separation of powers (legislature, executive, judiciary) was to serve this purpose; in the economic sphere, intense competition on free markets was to ensure the dilution of private power. Thus, apart from protecting individual freedom under the law in the political domain, the government was assigned the task to ensure that, in the economic domain, competition was not eroded endogenously. Hence, the German Ordoliberals demanded more than the minimal state

---

[33] See Müller-Armack (1946); Eucken (1948).
[34] Throughout this book, we use the term 'liberal' in the classical European meaning of a political philosophy which puts much confidence in the decentralized coordination of economic and social activity. In our terminology, the American meaning of the term 'liberal' would have to be broadly classified as 'social democratic'.

(*Nachtwächterstaat*) of laissez-faire liberalism. They explicitly advocated a strong state.[35] Broadly speaking, government was to gain this strength vis-à-vis sectional interests and to preserve its status as the impartial and incorruptible arbiter of the economic process against short-term interventionist temptations by limiting its own scope to a few essential tasks.[36]

The Ordoliberals argued that, in a given framework and with adequate safeguards, the economic process would spontaneously lead to optimal results, i.e. a dilution of power and an efficient allocation of resources. The state was held to be capable of establishing and maintaining a liberal economic order, but not of intervening into the economic process on a large scale. In the same vein, the human mind was held to be capable of consciously designing a desirable economic constitution, but not of centrally administering the complexity of a modern economy. In this sense, the Ordoliberals were predecessors of the modern school of 'Constitutional Constructivism', although their respective intellectual edifices rest on different normative premises.[37] Modern constitutionalists stress that agreement among the parties concerned is the relevant normative criterion. Behind a veil of uncertainty over the precise distributional setting, a unanimous agreement on general and durable rules is conceivable; in a given situation in which the major distributional consequences of a decision are known, it is not. Therefore the state should devise a constitution but refrain from meddling with day-to-day processes. On the other hand, the Ordoliberal case for general rules and against interventionism was instead based on the insight and experience that, by creating new distortions, interventions tend to undermine the entire economic order and, hence, individual liberty. Furthermore, the erosion of liberty in one sphere would spread to all spheres of life. If economic choice was lost, political freedom was endangered as well because of the inherent interdependence of both domains ('Interdependenz der Ordnungen'[38]). This thinking in terms of institutional settings or frameworks ('Denken in Ordnungen'[39]), this emphasis on the question of how any measure affects the entire order was one of the characteristic hallmarks of Ordoliberalism. It reflects as much the insight into the repercussions of interventions as the typically German tendency to discuss issues in broad fundamental rather than narrow pragmatic terms.

[35] Rüstow (1932), p. 68.
[36] This concept of the strong but limited state seems to be inspired by the German (or rather Prussian) ideal of the civil servant (*Beamter*). If he were guaranteed a permanent employment at an acceptable salary and equipped with clear-cut and practical rules, this impartial civil servant would not succumb to any influence-peddling from interested parties. See Willgerodt (1989), pp. 31–60.   [37] Vanberg (1988), p. 28.
[38] Eucken (1952), p. 180.   [39] *Ibid.*, p. 19.

Having studied or even personally witnessed the rise of external protectionism and internal interventionism and finally the switch towards central planning and political totalitarianism, the Ordoliberals were profoundly sceptical of unrestrained evolutionary processes of any kind. Therefore, they called for an active anti-cartel and anti-trust policy. According to them, a powerful public agency has to supervise the behaviour of market participants sufficiently to prevent any severe form of collusion, cartels and abuse of monopoly power. In cases of natural monopolies, the government has to force participants to refrain from using their market power so that the outcome is actually the same 'as if' unrestrained competition had in fact prevailed.[40] As German scholars, some prominent Ordoliberals tended to take their insights to logical extremes. Thus, competition had not only to be safeguarded but actually to be organized by the state ('Der Wettbewerb – eine staatliche Veranstaltung'[41]) – in quite the same way in which a sports race needs an organizer to invite participants and a referee to ensure that rules of fair play are observed.[42]

(c) The Ordoliberal economic order. The principles of the Ordoliberal economic constitution, that is the competitive order, were formulated most cogently by Eucken (1952). The basic task was to maintain a well-functioning price mechanism based on the highest possible degree of competition. All other constitutive principles of the competitive order are no more than an outflow of this general requirement: (i) monetary stability is to ensure that price signals are not affected by inflationary distortions; (ii) free market entry for new firms and for products from abroad is to increase competitive pressure and to thwart attempts at rent-seeking by closing markets; (iii) the institution of private property is to stimulate an efficient use of resources and to prevent any concentration of the means of production in the most unwarranted hands, those of the state; (iv) freedom of contract is to give the agents the opportunity to make their own choices; (v) liability for economic decisions, in modern terms the internalization of external effects, is to link individual self-interest to the common weal; and (vi) the constancy of economic policy is to make

---

[40] Miksch (1947), p. 101; Eucken (1952), p. 295. In their theoretical writings, prominent Ordoliberals like Miksch and Eucken emphasized the notion of 'perfect' competition. It remains unclear how much practical importance they attached to this theoretical concept. Some of their publications convey the impression that they actually wanted the state to ensure that, within the competitive order, competition ought to verge on the textbook ideal of 'perfect' competition. Here, the number of participants is so high that none of them has any influence whatsoever on the result.   [41] Miksch (1947), p. 11.
[42] For this analogy, see Giersch (1988b), p. 5.

government behaviour predictable and thus reduce the margin of error in the decisions of private agents.

Eucken and the other Ordoliberals assigned priority to the policy of maintaining this economic order. But in addition to *Ordnungspolitik*, the Ordoliberals advocated interventions to correct unwarranted developments endogenous to the market system. Eucken explicitly stated 'regulative principles' which were needed even if perfect competition were in fact realized.[43] Besides strict regulation of monopolies that cannot be broken up, Eucken pleaded for progressive income taxation as an acceptable and to some extent desirable means of social policy and for minimum wages set by the government in times of recession if the labour supply reacted perversely, i.e. if more rather than less labour were supplied after a decline in the wage rate. But he firmly believed that a general rise in the standard of living would bring about a normal labour-supply reaction. According to Eucken, the state should in some instances go beyond a rule-orientated policy and interfere with the market process ('Prozeßpolitik') to affect outcomes. Nevertheless, his regulative principles do not amount to any licence for unrestrained interventionism. For instance, if a full employment policy by credit expansion was likely to distort relative prices and create inflationary pressure, it had to be ruled out from the start.[44]

The approach of thinking in terms of the general order (*Denken in Ordnungen*) comes out most clearly in the so-called conformability principle. Of all possible courses of action, the one which was most compatible with a free society and a market economy, and which was least likely to create new distortions that might require further interventions, was to be chosen.[45] As specified by Röpke, interventions should correct the outcome of the market process, for example, through direct transfers and subsidies.[46] But the government should not interfere with the market mechanism itself by, say, fixing prices or quantities. Furthermore, interventions should promote and not impede the working of the market forces: whereas so-called preservation subsidies were to be inadmissible, adjustment assistance might be acceptable.

While 'Ordoliberalism' is the commonly used expression for the underlying set of ideas, the term 'social market economy' became the brandname both for the blueprint of a desirable economic order which the Ordoliberals advocated and for the actual economic system of West Germany since June 1948. The term 'social market economy' had been

[43] Eucken (1952), p. 291.   [44] *Ibid.*, pp. 225, 254–5.
[45] See Watrin (1979), p. 421.   [46] Röpke (1942), pp. 252–8; (1944), pp. 78ff.

coined by Müller-Armack.[47] However, the meaning behind the attribute 'social' remained somewhat obscure. It was one of the issues on which the Ordoliberals differed most.

All maintained that the replacement of central planning by free markets would be a social act per se by giving rise to an efficient use of resources and to productivity increases. Those who had suffered most from the debased currency, from corruption-prone rationing and illegal black markets were the poor and the weak, i.e. those most in need of protection against distress. Furthermore, abolishing central planning and authoritarianism would in itself help to redress the growing subordination of individuals to the state, a march into dependence which Eucken (1948) had diagnosed as the 'new social problem'. Consequently, Eucken and the other members of the 'Freiburg Group' of neoliberals saw little need for a social policy that went beyond establishing a competitive order with a limited redistribution of income by progressive taxation and some basic welfare provisions. On the other hand, Müller-Armack and other scholars inspired by the social teachings of the Catholic Church called for a much more comprehensive and outcome-orientated approach to the 'social question', excluding neither the fixing of prices and wages in exceptional circumstances nor far-reaching interventions into the housing market.[48] Quite astonishingly, even Röpke (1944), who – on most counts – was one of the most stringent and consistent of the German neoliberals, advocated some explicit social engineering in order to prevent excessive urbanization and to preserve the rural and small-town lifestyle of farmers and craftsmen. At least to Röpke and Müller-Armack the attribute 'social' was supposed to mean more than basic welfare provisions.

(d) The political and academic debate. Immediately after the war, the differences of opinion on the proper role of social policy in a market economy did not yet matter much. The real issue was whether there should be a market economy at all. Neither of the two largest political parties was genuinely convinced of the merits of free markets: while the Social Democratic Party (SPD) favoured extensive central planning and a nationalization of major industries in line with the example set by the British Labour Party in the UK, the major conservative party, the Christian Democratic Union (CDU/CSU[49]), advocated – albeit in vague terms – the nationalization of basic industries and a 'considerable' degree of economic planning 'for a long time to come' in its Ahlen programme

---

[47] Müller-Armack (1946), pp. 80ff., 109.   [48] *Ibid.*, pp. 110ff.
[49] To be precise: the CDU/CSU comprises both the Christian Democratic Union (CDU) and its slightly more right-wing Bavarian counterpart, the Christian Social Union (CSU).

of February 1947.[50] Until early 1948, the debate between (i) outright socialists (often encouraged and supported by the British), (ii) Keynesians who vaguely stressed the need for government interventions and expansionary demand policies (often backed by the numerous New Dealers among the American administrators and advisors) and (iii) the Ordoliberals was not won conclusively by any side. In the aftermath of the acute supply crisis of 1947 the liberals at least managed to gain attention, though not widespread support, in the public debate. It was only through a number of fortuitous circumstances that an Ordoliberal programme could finally be implemented.

Until early 1948, West Germany seemed to be set to replace the post-war chaos eventually by some mild form of (democratic) socialism, at least in economic matters. When the Bizonal Economic Administration was established in January 1947, the SPD managed to have Viktor Agartz elected as director. Agartz, a trade unionist with strong Marxist leanings, was a staunch supporter of economic planning and political centralization. Under his auspices, the administration expanded considerably relative to the size of its precursors in the American and the British zones. The SPD, viewing the Economic Administration as the nucleus of a future German central government, was confident that its socialist – albeit never clearly defined – economic programme would be implemented in due course. However, the proponents of free or at least freeish markets were thrice lucky:

(i) Agartz resigned on 1 July 1947 after a row with British experts on his plan to place the coalfields of the Ruhr valley under German control. This provided the conservatives and liberals with an unexpected opportunity. One week earlier, a Bizonal parliament (the Wirtschaftsrat) had been constituted. In this provisional legislative body, into which the democratically elected parliaments of the states (*Länder*) sent their representatives, the CDU/CSU and the liberals could – together with some assorted right-wing parties – muster a small majority over the SPD (and the communists). Alarmed that the SPD had successfully monopolized the posts of ministers of economics in all West German state governments, the Wirtschaftsrat twice rejected a proposal to keep the Bizonal Economic Administration in the hands of the SPD. On 24 July 1947, the SPD threw up its hands in despair and retreated into opposition, confident that once the first general parliamentary election had taken place, it would gain control of the entire administration anyway. Thus the CDU/CSU could nominate the directors

[50] See Müller (1982), p. 30.

of all five branches of the Bizonal administration.[51] In combination with the diminishing Allied interest both in tight control over the economy for the purpose of industrial disarmament and in a nationalization of basic industries, this change meant that the more extreme versions of socialism had lost out politically, at least for the time being.

(ii) In late January 1948, the Allies forced Johannes Semler, the new – and vaguely liberal-conservative – director of the Economic Administration, to resign. Semler had pointed out in a well-publicized speech that corn which was part of the US shipments of food aid was traditionally considered as *Hühnerfutter* in Germany, i.e. fodder for chicken and not food for people. Unfortunately for him, the term was translated into English as 'chicken feed', which the Allies took as an insult. In early March, the Wirtschaftsrat elected the staunchly liberal Ludwig Erhard as Semler's successor.[52]

(iii) Even before Erhard took office, an Independent Advisory Council of Academic Economists to the Bizonal Economic Administration had been instituted in late January 1948. Because of the initiative of the liberal-minded deputy director of this Administration, the Ordoliberals were prominently represented on the new Council (inter alia Böhm, Eucken, Miksch, Müller-Armack). As it turned out, their ideas for decontrolling the economy were accepted by a majority of Council members. Thus, Erhard could count on strong intellectual support from a prestigious body.

The major issues in the academic debate came out clearly in the Advisory Council's first report of 1 April 1948, which contained a majority and a minority opinion.[53] There was a general consensus that the introduction of a new and stable currency could put an end to repressed inflation and would thus make the macroeconomic reason for a comprehensive control of prices and production obsolete. Hence, the return to sound money should be coupled with a reform of the economic system in general. But what sort of reform? The majority pleaded for a genuine market economy, albeit with fixed prices for some 'socially sensitive' goods during a period of transition. The minority made a case for a mixed economy, i.e. for the parallel existence of markets and central planning, with the latter being drastically overhauled to make it more effective. Broadly speaking, the minority view was a watered-down version of Kromphardt's original vision of 'market splitting and core planning' ('Marktspaltung und Kernplanung'[54]). Kromphardt, himself a member

---

[51] For a detailed account, see Eschenburg (1983), pp. 376–96.
[52] For a brief biography of Erhard, see Willgerodt and Peacock (1989), pp. 2–3.
[53] Wissenschaftlicher Beirat (1973), report of 1 April 1948, pp. 1–6.
[54] Kromphardt (1947).

of the Council, had proposed an ingenious way to make planning more rational: the rationing cards given to consumers should be passed on by the shops to the producers, to whom raw materials would then be allocated according to the number of cards (or points) received, i.e. according to the quantities actually sold through the official channels. Black markets should be legalized to give firms an accepted outlet for any surplus they managed to produce out of their allocated inputs. The switch from illegal to legal fringe markets would reduce transaction costs and widen bottlenecks in the administered core of the economy.

Such a system would undoubtedly have made the contemporaneous mix of official planning and illegal markets more effective by improving the administrative allocation of resources within sectors producing goods for final consumption. However, it would still have presupposed the comprehensive use of rationing cards, which consumers had learned to despise. More fundamentally, it would not have made the central planners' task of determining the allocation of resources much easier: in a complex pattern of a division of labour with several intermediate stages of production, issuing rationing cards which final consumers pass on to producers would not have made much of a difference. In all but the final stage of production, the planners would have had to rely on their accustomed – and ineffective – methods of guessing demand and supply without a direct feedback from the economic agents affected.

In the Advisory Council's first report, the differences of opinion between the Ordoliberal-inspired majority and those academics who by and large supported Kromphardt's reasoning manifested themselves on several counts. While Ordoliberals generally advocated the liberalization of markets as the major means to raise production and, as a consequence, investment, the minority saw the need for an administrative channelling of resources into investment as the only way of attaining the necessary high rate of capital accumulation. Thus, the minority did not want to rely on voluntary savings as the main source of investable funds and on market prices as signals to steer these funds into the most productive uses. And while the majority pleaded for a radical turn towards markets to make the currency reform and hence the transition from a barter to a money economy an instant success, the minority warned against insurmountable difficulties of adjustment in the short run and called for a much more gradual approach – without making it altogether clear whether the administrative system should be retained or eventually abolished. In line with this pessimistic assessment of the supply elasticity of free markets the minority maintained that, beyond the basic necessities which even the majority wanted to remain centrally administered for a limited period of time to cushion the social disruptions of the change of regime, a large number of manufactures and many essential raw materials should be subject to price and production controls. Whereas the Ordoliberals stressed the unleashing of market forces, which they expected to lead to an increase in production as the most social of all policies, the minority wanted to rely on fixed prices and a rationing system to protect the needy against deprivation.

The academic debate found its close counterpart in the political arena. Just before the currency reform, the Bizonal parliament discussed a proposal to endow the directors of the economic and the agricultural administration with the right to lift price controls and the rationing systems for most goods without further prior approval by parliament. While liberal and conservative politicians put forth more or less the Ordoliberal arguments, the Social Democrats emphatically warned against a sweeping liberalization. Unlike the minority of the Advisory Council however, the SPD mainly stressed the danger of inflation[55] once prices were set free rather than the need for retaining the discredited rationing cards for consumer goods. On 18 June 1948, the majority of the Wirtschaftsrat voted to grant Erhard the authority to liberalize markets that he had asked for. The stage was finally set for radical change.

3   The liberal reforms of June 1948

(a) The reform package. Having won the decisive vote in the Bizonal parliament, Erhard felt free to go ahead with his liberal blueprint. He complemented the currency reform and the so-called little tax reform, both of which had been basically worked out by the Western Allies, with the reinstitution of a market economy in the Bizone in late June 1948.

The actual currency reform was enacted by the three Military Governments on 20 June 1948.[56] It consisted of three major steps, namely (i) a drastic contraction of the money supply by the introduction of the Deutsche Mark to replace the Reichsmark, (ii) a restructuring and consolidation of existing private and public debt, and (iii) the establishment of strong institutional safeguards against future inflationary policies.

(i) A strictly limited amount of cash could be exchanged into DMarks at a conversion rate of 1:1. As an initial endowment, every individual thus received 40 DMarks immediately and a further 20 DMarks two months later. Firms were granted an allowance of 60 DMarks per employee, while public authorities received the equivalent of one month's revenue. All

---

[55] See Müller (1982), pp. 119–25.
[56] For a detailed description of the prehistory of the currency reform and of the measures enacted, see Möller (1976), pp. 433–83.

private cash balances and bank deposits, including savings accounts and time deposits, exceeding these allowances were to be scaled down by a factor of ten.[57] Half of this amount was immediately available, i.e. after the income tax office had checked the registered sums for prior tax evasion. The fate of the blocked half was decided in late September, with 35 per cent (of the original total) being cancelled, 10 per cent being released and 5 per cent being credited to a special account for investment purposes. Thus, the effective conversion rate turned out to be 10:0.65 instead of 10:1 for balances exceeding 600 Reichsmarks.

(ii) While the official prices and all recurrent payments such as wages, rents and social security payments remained unchanged (1 RMark = 1 DMark), almost all debts were devalued by a factor of ten. The Reichsmark balances and the Reich bonds held by the commercial banks were wiped out. Instead, the banks received low-interest 'equalization claims' amounting to roughly 4 per cent of the Reich debt at the end of the war.[58] To restore their liquidity, the banks were granted deposits with the central banking system equal to 15 per cent of their demand deposits plus 7.5 per cent of their time and savings deposits. As these reserves exceeded the new minimum requirements by 50 per cent, the banks were thus given considerable leeway for credit expansion.

(iii) To protect the new currency, the Allies established two institutional safeguards against future financing of public debt by money creation. First, with the currency reform, the Bank deutscher Länder became the sole provider of legal tender; contrary to the wishes of many German experts, the new central bank was to be independent from the government and all other political bodies.[59] And second, the Military Governments explicitly forbade excessive budget deficits. Article 28 of the Conversion Law stated that expenditures of public authorities must be covered by current income. The procurement of funds by means of credit should be lawful only in anticipation of future revenues.[60]

A few days after the currency reform, the system of central planning was abolished in the Bizone. Although the guidelines on the decontrol of the economy (Leitsätze) which the Bizonal parliament had passed on 18 June 1948 had not yet been approved by the Allied Bizonal Control Office,[61] Erhard lifted the price controls for almost all manufactured goods and some foodstuffs in the following week. And as Erhard did not renew the directives on the rationing of goods and the central allocation of

---

[57] The respective deposits of public authorities were cancelled altogether.
[58] See Gundlach (1987), p. 21.   [59] Möller (1976), p. 455; Müller (1982), p. 137.
[60] Law No. 63, US Zone, June 1948; WiGBl., 48. Beilage, No. 5, p. 19; cited in Mendershausen (1949), p. 660.   [61] They were approved on 30 June 1948.

resources which expired at the end of June,[62] the Bizonal economy started into the second half of 1948 with genuinely free markets in almost all goods for which the price controls had been removed. The most notable exceptions from the sweeping decontrol were basic foodstuffs, most raw materials (such as coal, iron, steel and oil),[63] wages, rents and rates for basic public services such as electricity, gas and water. Broadly speaking, those commodities in which the Allies had a particular political interest (i.e. coal and steel) and those goods and services which were considered to be especially important for the poor remained under administrative control.

Simultaneously with the currency reform, the Military Governments enacted changes in the tax system geared towards promoting the formation of capital. Because of French objections, this tax reform was by no means as radical a departure from the prohibitively high taxes on income – which the Allies had levied in 1946 – as the German administration had demanded. None the less, this 'little tax reform'[64] cut the personal income taxes by roughly one-third (the top marginal rates had stood as high as 95 per cent in 1946),[65] reduced the corporate income tax from 65 to 50 per cent and offered important tax exemptions for income saved and invested. On the other hand, a high excise tax on coffee was introduced, while many local taxes were substantially raised.[66] As a whole, the tax changes were designed to improve the incentive to save and invest.

Contrary to the drafts of German experts, the currency reform was not immediately complemented by a redistribution of wealth to achieve an equalization of war and post-war burdens (*Lastenausgleich*). By its very nature the sweeping cancellation of existing monetary debt, i.e. the core of the currency reform, was bound to reveal that savers in general – and the bombed out and the expellees in particular – had lost their wealth while the owners of undestroyed real assets had not. Therefore American and German experts working on blueprints for a monetary reform had originally insisted on a link with the *Lastenausgleich*. However, the German politicians did not object very loudly when the Allies separated the two issues and assigned the technically difficult task of devising the *Lastenausgleich* by the end of 1948 to the German authorities.[67]

---

[62] Buchheim (1988), p. 221.
[63] However, the administered prices for many of these goods were raised.
[64] Mendershausen (1949), p. 659.   [65] Boss (1987), p. 4.
[66] Mendershausen (1949), p. 660.
[67] The first preliminary law on relief for the victims of the war, of expulsion, the Nazi tyranny, and the currency reform was, however, not enacted prior to August 1949. The law on the *Lastenausgleich* proper was passed three years later. It provided for a special tax of 50 per cent on all wealth holdings at the time of the currency reform, payable in yearly instalments over the next decades. As the valuation clauses were very generous, far less than 50 per cent of mid 1948 wealth was eventually redistributed: Schillinger (1985), pp. 283–90; for further details, see Chapter 3, Section A.3.

(b) The impact of the reforms. The radical currency reform was an immediate and tremendous success. Virtually overnight, the Bizone took the great leap from the stage of primitive bilateral barter to that of genuinely multilateral exchange with money as the means of deferred payments. On the morning after the introduction of the Deutsche Mark, people accepted money in exchange for goods and labour services, the shop windows were full of products which had previously been unavailable – at least legally – and black and grey markets were reduced to an almost negligible role. Most of all, 'the gray, hungry, dead-looking figures wandering about the streets in their everlasting search for food came to life as, pocketing their 40 DMarks, they went on a first spending spree'.[68] The sudden reappearance of goods in the shops thus had a tremendous psychological effect: it finally instilled people with the sense of a new beginning.

Soon after the reforms it became clear that the transformation of the country was not just due to shops putting goods on sale which they had previously hoarded or peddled illegally. In fact, production soared: in the second half of 1948, industrial output grew at an annualized rate of 137 per cent, with the 1936-based index of production leaping from 50 in June to 57 in July and 77 in December.[69] Roughly one-third of this increase was attributable to a higher productivity per hour, and the remainder to a rise in the number of hours worked. Under the new regime, the incentive to work in factories rather than spending time in searching and bartering for food and other basic necessities was restored. While the industrial workforce grew by 13.1 per cent, workers stayed at work for 42.4 hours per week in December 1948, 4.2 hours longer than they had in June.[70] The most notable increases in production occurred in some of those sectors of manufacturing for which the price controls had been lifted (vehicles, electrical equipment, textiles and shoes), while comparatively little progress was made in industries which remained under tight control, i.e. coal mining and iron ore production.[71]

Concurrent with the rise in the utilization of existing capacity, the post-war rundown of the physical capital stock was finally stopped and the formation of new capital picked up again. Because of the post-war slack of investment and, less importantly, the dismantling of machinery, the capital stock in industry had gone down by 7.3 per cent between the

[68] Wallich (1955), p. 71.
[69] Adjusted for number of working days: Ritschl (1985), p. 164.
[70] Statistisches Bundesamt, *Wirtschaft und Statistik* (1949/50), pp. 12–13, 157. In the following years, the working week lengthened even further to an average 46.5 hours in 1949 and 48.2 hours in 1950, Statistisches Bundesamt, *Statistisches Jahrbuch* (1953), p. 506.
[71] Statistisches Bundesamt, *Wirtschaft und Statistik* (1949/50), p. 15.

end of the war and the reforms of June 1948.[72] In the second half of 1948 the capital stock started to grow again at an annualized rate of 5.6 per cent. Thus, parallel to the boom in production, the basis for future growth was laid. Surprisingly, the investment surge could be funded, although private households – given the opportunity to convert cash balances and bank accounts into goods – turned into net dissavers;[73] aggregate investment was financed mainly from high business profits, but also from foreign aid and the fiscal surplus of the public sector, which amounted to about 1.5 per cent of GNP between the currency reform and the end of March 1949.[74]

This thoroughly positive empirical assessment of the liberal reforms is based mostly on the official index of Bizonal industrial production in 1948. Considerable doubt has been cast on the reliability of these numbers and with them the decisive importance of the reforms by Abelshauser (1975). Pointing out that the immediate pre-reform figures may have significantly understated true activity as firms did not report part of the output which they hoarded in anticipation of the reform, Abelshauser employs the statistics on the electricity consumption of industrial firms to re-estimate actual output. According to his revised figures, industrial production in the last quarter of 1948 was just 33 per cent instead of 51 per cent above the level of six months earlier. Although this would still constitute a substantial gain, he concludes that what happened after the currency reform was mainly a continuation of the general recovery which had set in after the sharp crisis of early 1947.

Abelshauser's arguments have received considerable attention. At first glance, they look quite convincing. The official production indices for May and June 1948 give in fact implausibly low figures for some specific consumption goods (for example, shoes: 47 per cent of 1936 production in April 1948, down to 28 per cent in June and up to 61 per cent in July).[75] Although Abelshauser may thus have a point in some instances, his case is still unconvincing for a variety of reasons: (1) the incentive to under-report actual output was in general weak before the reforms.[76] (2) The basic assumption of Abelshauser's re-estimate, namely a constant ratio of the input of electricity to output, does not hold. As Ritschl (1985, pp. 140ff.) has shown, the productivity of electricity rose in line with the volume of industrial production. This makes the official figures which imply that firms put electricity to better use after the reform than before

[72] Krengel (1958), p. 16; Statistisches Bundesamt, *Statistisches Jahrbuch* (1952), p. 454; these numbers include the French zone.   [73] Buchheim (1988), p. 229.
[74] Gundlach (1987), p. 29.
[75] Statistisches Bundesamt, *Wirtschaft und Statistik* (1949/50), p. 88.
[76] See Buchheim (1988), p. 225; Wünsche (1979), p. 38.

look more plausible than the re-estimated ones. (3) Even if we accept the notion that the official figures for May and June 1948 are biased downwards because firms secretly hoarded part of their output in anticipation of the reforms, this is, strictly speaking, no argument against the significance of the regime switch. It is an open question whether firms would – amid the general shortage of inputs – have produced these extra goods at all if they had not expected to be able to sell them for real money in the near future. (4) The crucial months of 1948–9 in West Germany came as close to a controlled experiment as one may ever get in economic policy: the new currency was introduced in both the Bizone and the French zone, but in the latter area the first important decontrol measures were not enacted prior to early 1949. Until the reforms of late June 1948, industrial production had been roughly on a par in both parts of Western Germany. Thereafter, a sizeable gap appeared between the rapid progress made in the Bizone and the much slower pace of recovery in the French zone, a gap which began to narrow once markets were liberalized in the French zone as well (see Figure 8). (5) In a broader perspective, the comparison between East and West Germany illustrates the fundamental importance of the regime switch. Until 1948, the economic situation was roughly similar on both sides of the Elbe. Ever since the regime switch towards a market economy in the West, East Germany – which was gradually transformed into a Soviet-type economy by its communist rulers – lagged behind dramatically.

Despite the spectacular advance of aggregate supply in real terms, the entire reform venture was actually put in jeopardy in autumn 1948 by an unexpected surge of monetary demand. Prior to the currency reform, Erhard and the Advisory Council to the Federal Minister of Economics[77] had predicted a deflation. However, both the money supply and the velocity of money increased by more than had been anticipated. The gradual conversion of old Reichsmark balances into DMarks, the paying out of the second instalment of the initial personal allowance and the considerable credit expansion in the banking system based on the generous initial endowments with central bank deposits made the quantity of money (M3) grow from 6.5 billion DMarks at the end of July to 10.4 billion DMarks three months later and 13.1 billion DMarks at the end of the year.[78] Furthermore, the velocity of money rose dramatically as firms managed to get along with surprisingly small cash balances while consumers looking at shop windows stocked with readily available goods

[77] See Müller (1982), p. 108; Wissenschaftlicher Beirat (1973), report of 12 June 1948, p. 7.
[78] Bank deutscher Länder, *Monatsberichte* (January 1949), p. 38; (February 1949), pp. 17, 38; own calculations.

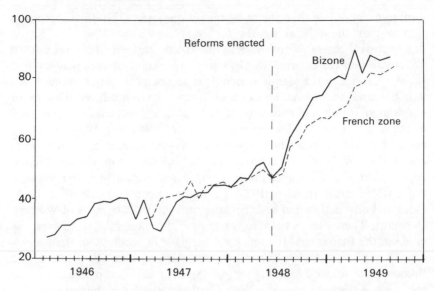

Figure 8. Industrial production before and after the liberal reforms of
June 1948.
Notes: Official index of industrial production, 1936 = 100; Bizone:
British and US zones of occupation.
Source: Ritschl (1985), p. 164.

for the first time for more than five years saw little point in holding cash
or saving money.

The unleashing of pent-up demand became almost instantaneously
visible in prices. In the first four months after the reform, consumer prices
(as measured by the cost of living index) rose at an annualized rate of
33.1 per cent. Producer prices increased even more rapidly, at an
annualized rate of 45 per cent.[79] The fate of the new currency as well as
the liberalization of markets was endangered. Both the inflation and the
first administrative reaction, namely to reduce the conversion rate for
Reichsmark accounts into DMarks from 10:1 to 10:0.65 on 1 October
1948 undermined public confidence in the new money. In autumn 1948,
the first signs of an imminent repudiation of the paper money appeared,
namely a re-emergence of bartering arrangements and a renewed hoarding
of inventories.[80] On 12 November 1948, the trade unions called for a
one-day general strike to protest against the inflationary consequences of
Erhard's economic policies. Somewhat surprisingly, the major concern of

[79] The difference was largely due to the fact that the former index includes housing rents,
transport and other services for which the still-administered prices remained constant,
while the prices for most of those producer goods which remained under administrative
control were raised.   [80] Wallich (1955), p. 74.

the unions was inflation itself, not a genuine deterioration of the standard of living in real terms. Because of a roughly parallel increase in prices and nominal wages, real purchasing power had not diminished substantially in the post-reform inflation.[81] As the unions demanded the declaration of a 'state of economic emergency', the installation of a price commissioner with far-reaching powers, a reversion to an administrative allocation of most manufactures and the nationalization of basic industries and banks, the general strike was widely considered to strengthen the case for a return to an administered economy.[82] Except for one token concession on which the Military Government insisted, namely the establishment of a toothless independent price council, the West German authorities kept their nerve. In November, monetary policy tightened. The central bank raised the reserve requirements from 10 to 15 per cent and froze – with some minor exceptions – the aggregate amount of credit outstanding.[83] As a consequence, the pace of monetary expansion slowed, with M3 rising from 11.5 billion DMarks at the end of October to 13.1 billion DMarks two months later.[84]

In late 1948, the economy began to cool off. After the inflationary burst in summer and early autumn, the price level was approaching the limit set by the monetary frame and the fiscal surplus; in addition the anticipation of the first Marshall Plan imports may have eased inflationary pressures somewhat.[85] Between October and December the annualized increase of consumer prices dropped to 8.8 and that of producer prices to 2.9 per cent. The final victory of the new currency became evident in the exchange rate against its commodity substitutes, i.e. in the prices of tobacco and coffee. On 15 December 1948, these goods were traded for half of their pre-reform prices.[86]

It has sometimes been asserted that a turnaround in economic policy as tough and sweeping as the German liberal reforms of late June 1948 would have been next to unthinkable in a genuine democracy. However, the most contentious part of the reforms, namely the sudden decontrol of most parts of the economy, had been endorsed by two German parliamentary bodies, the Wirtschaftsrat (the representatives of the freely elected state parliaments of the Bizone) and the Länderrat (the representatives of the Bizonal state governments). Although a majority of West Germans did favour the reintroduction of price controls at the height of

---

[81] Although wages remained under administrative control until early November, the Military Government had authorized wage increases of up to 15 per cent in late April 1948: Müller (1982), p. 152. This leeway was almost completely exploited during the summer so that wages did not lag far behind prices.   [82] See Müller (1982), p. 168.
[83] See Möller (1976), p. 468.
[84] Bank deutscher Länder, *Monatsberichte* (February 1949), pp. 17, 38; own calculations.
[85] See Borchardt and Buchheim (1987), pp. 327f.
[86] Statistisches Bundesamt, *Wirtschaft und Statistik* (1949/50), pp. 932ff.; own calculations.

the post-reform inflation, public opinion changed once the initial upheaval was over. In late 1948, the liberal and conservative parties, which had backed Erhard, increased their share of the popular vote in local elections in the British zone. More importantly, the theme of free markets versus a return to administrative control became the dominant issue in the campaign for the elections to the first West German Bundestag in mid 1949. Contrary to the expectations of many observers, a conservative–liberal coalition gained the upper hand against the Social Democrats. With a liberal reform radical enough to attract widespread attention and to confer noticeable benefits to a great number of people, the conservative and liberal parties had paved the way to becoming the dominant combination of forces in West German politics for almost two decades.

3   1948–1960: spontaneous growth

For most of the time in the twelve years after the currency reform, the development of the West German economy turned out to be a virtually unqualified success, with fast growth, tolerably low price inflation, a rapidly declining level of unemployment and an increasingly secure external balance. In the following two sections, we shall ask why this was so and, in particular, what contributions economic policy made to this apparently miraculous performance. For expository convenience, we shall deal separately with matters of the domestic and the international realm (Sections A and B respectively).

A   Overcoming capital shortage and unemployment

By late 1948, most independent observers agreed that the liberal reform of June 1948 had initiated a quite dramatic revival of the West German economy, with production soaring well above even the most optimistic expectations and inflation soon running out of steam.[1] With the reform having basically succeeded, the policy debate took a slight turn away from the abstract philosophical issue of the vice or virtue of a social market economy to the more pragmatic question of whether the early expansionary momentum could be transformed into a sustainable non-inflationary process of cumulative supply-side growth at a full utilization of the economy's productive potential, above all the rapidly growing labour force. With the benefit of hindsight, it is clear that the following period of 15 to 18 months – a time of consolidation, if not of slight recession – was to become decisive in this respect. Therefore, this period deserves careful examination, both as to its actual economic development and as to the most exciting and paradigmatic policy debate which it brought about.

---

[1] See the *Financial Times* of 26 August 1948, 'Recovery in Western Germany – Currency Reform Succeeds in its Two Main Objects', and *The Economist* of 2 October 1948, 'Western Germany on its Feet'.

1   The critical period 1949/50

The beginning of the consolidation can be marked by the turn of the years 1948/9, when price inflation gave way to a significant deflationary tendency, with an average monthly decrease of the price level of about 0.5 per cent in 1949 and even 1.0 per cent in the first half of 1950. In part, this was just a quite natural reaction to the prior upsurge of prices after the restrictive measures of the Bank deutscher Länder, which had tightened the economy's liquidity belt. In part, however, it was a genuine cooling of the business climate. Despite a noticeable slowdown of economic growth relative to the spectacular rise right after the currency reform, industrial production still grew by 24 per cent in 1949 and by about 12 per cent in the first half of 1950; as far as it is measurable at all, the growth of real GDP was well above 15 per cent p.a. throughout the period.[2] However, the labour market began to look somewhat gloomy. To many experts' surprise, the unemployment rate had not substantially surpassed the 5 per cent mark in the second half of 1948, despite mounting structural adjustment pressures in the aftermath of the currency reform and despite a still rapidly growing labour force; this changed in the period 1949/50, when the rate moved up continually to a peak of 12.2 per cent in March 1950. The balance of aggregate employment growth changed accordingly: while, from June to December 1948, 230,000 new jobs were created, 1949 brought a net employment loss of about 150,000 jobs. Not before the second quarter of 1950 did a marked increase of employment signal a turning of the cyclical tide.

Given this macroeconomic picture, it is clear that the bulk of aggregate output growth in the period 1949/50 was due to gains in labour productivity (output per worker). These gains came about through essentially two distinct supply-side forces which had been freed by the liberal reform in June 1948 and which continued to work all through the temporary cyclical slowdown of demand growth: a rapid reconstruction of the capital stock and a powerful structural adjustment of employment.

As to reconstruction, it soon became obvious that a good part of the capital stock which had been damaged but not destroyed in the war could be fairly quickly repaired and put to use again. These repair investments raised output per worker for two reasons. In a quantitative sense, they allowed working hours to return to normal levels, from about 42 in 1948

---

[2] On an annualized basis, real GDP (in prices of 1936) grew by 17.3 per cent p.a. from the second half of 1948 to 1949, and by 16.3 per cent p.a. from 1949 to 1950. See *The Economist* (1985), p. 36 and Statistisches Bundesamt, *Statistisches Jahrbuch* (1955), pp. 510–11.

to 48 hours per week in 1950.[3] In a qualitative sense, they pushed up output per working hour, since they provided industrial workers with a first post-war endowment of properly functioning capital equipment. Thus, the economy's machinery was literally switched on again in the two years following the liberal reform, so that it was probably not before mid 1950 that anything like a normal utilization of productive capacities could be reached, independent of cyclical forces. With full analytical justification, this process may be called 'reconstruction'.

Below the surface of a more or less stagnating overall employment, a vigorous and fast process of structural adjustment took place, again a mere continuation of developments which had set in straight after the currency reform. In the second half of 1948, the net increase of employment by 230,000 had come about as the balance of 600,000 new jobs in expanding and 370,000 lost jobs in contracting sectors. In the year 1949, employment increased by 260,000 in the expanding sectors and shrank by 410,000 in the contracting ones, leading to a net loss of 150,000 jobs.[4] With an overall level of employment in the range of 13 to 14 million people, this turns out to be the fastest structural adjustment in the history of the West German economy. Apparently, the liberal reform led to a thorough reorganization of the economy's production structure, mostly independently of short-term cyclical factors. This conjecture is strongly confirmed by the fact that the intersectoral pattern of structural change did not change from the second half of 1948 to early 1950. In the two years before the currency reform, employment had grown in all major sectors except agriculture, with the most rapidly expanding sectors being textiles, clothing, timber products, musical instruments, toys, glass and ceramics. With the currency reform, this grossly distorted growth[5] came to an end, and industries like iron and steel, metal manufacturing and vehicles took the lead in the growth race together with 'productive' services such as banking, transport and insurance, mostly at the expense of agriculture and some 'overgrown' consumer goods industries. In agriculture and forestry alone, 350,000 jobs were lost in the eighteen months after the currency reform.[6] Clearly, this rapid reshuffling of labour was bound to leave deep traces in any aggregate productivity statistics.

As overall business conditions normalized, the forces of structural change led to a pronounced regional imbalance of the (growing) unemployment. For the simple reason of geographical and cultural proximity

---

[3] See Statistisches Bundesamt, *Statistisches Jahrbuch* (1955), p. 469.
[4] See Ehret (1959), pp. 78–9, and Barnikel (1959), pp. 25–33.
[5] As to the distortions, see Ehret (1959), pp. 63–6, and Chapter 2 above.
[6] See Ehret (1959), pp. 78–9.

to their former homes, the bulk of the almost 9 million German refugees (or, in official language, expellees and immigrants)[7] were crammed into the rural areas of the North (Schleswig-Holstein, Lower Saxony) and the South-East (mostly northern Bavaria), where a large number of them found temporary work and shelter on farms.[8] The unexpected rapid upswing after the currency reform helped to ease the structural adjustment, but in 1949 and early 1950, the expansionary forces were simply not strong enough to allow for an immediate integration of the emerging rural surplus labour. As a consequence, an extremely skewed regional pattern of unemployment emerged: by the turn of the year 1949/50, the unemployment rate in the two northern states Schleswig-Holstein and Lower Saxony stood at 26.3 and 17.3 per cent respectively, compared to a rate of 4.5 per cent in urban and industrialized North Rhine-Westphalia and 4.6 per cent in the area of the later state of Baden-Württemberg; at the same time, the share of expellees in unemployment varied across states from 58.5 per cent in Schleswig-Holstein and 43.4 per cent in Lower Saxony down to 13 per cent in North Rhine-Westphalia and well below 5 per cent in Rhineland-Palatinate (as compared to a national average of 35.1 per cent). No doubt, the regional imbalance of unemployment in West Germany reached a historical peak at the beginning of 1950.[9]

So much for the state and development of economic affairs during the consolidation period 1949/50. With a stable and even declining price level but a rapidly rising unemployment rate, the attention of the general public, of economists and politicians gradually moved from monetary stability to unemployment. As to the diagnostic part of the economic policy debate, there was no real disagreement that the main cause of unemployment had to be found in one major fact, namely the severe shortage of capital. In modern terminology, the standard capital shortage story of a contemporaneous professional economist may be told as follows.

Immediately after the war, Germany found itself with a part of its capital destroyed or at least damaged through bombing raids and its population dramatically increased through the influx of refugees. Until

---

[7] In West Germany, two types of German refugees were distinguished: those who came from the formerly German-inhabited regions east of the rivers Oder and Neisse; and those who fled from the Soviet-occupied zone, the later German Democratic Republic. The former were called 'expellees' (*Vertriebene*), the latter 'immigrants' (*Zugewanderte*). In mid 1948, there were about 7 million, and by 1950 almost 8 million expellees in West Germany; the number of immigrants stood at 1.3 million in 1949 and increased rapidly in the early 1950s to reach almost 2 million as early as 1952. For further statistical details, see Bundesminister für Vertriebene (1953), especially p. 8.

[8] This is true above all for the 6 million or so expellees who arrived until 1946 and who temporarily swelled 'employment' in agriculture.

[9] See Paqué (1987, 1989a), who presents various (modern) measures of regional mismatch for West Germany in 1949/50 and at later times.

the currency reform, this abrupt shift of factor endowments did not push up the unemployment rate, simply because industrial and agricultural employers could well afford to pay wages in an almost worthless currency. In the overcrowded rural areas of the North and the South-East, many refugees began to work on farms, so as to secure a bare minimum of subsistence; most probably, their marginal product was extremely low – if not negative – so that employing them came close to being a charitable act on the part of the farmers. As earning money had a low survival value compared to black-market activities, work discipline was bad and absenteeism very common in the official (i.e., money-wage) part of the economy. Hence, there was a hardly quantifiable, but certainly substantial amount of hidden unemployment. All this changed with the currency reform, which swept away the monetary distortion from the employers' profit-maximizing calculus and thus revealed the real extent of the capital gap: with fixed proportions of capital and labour prevailing in the short run and capital being the constraint, industrial firms had to lay off part of their labour force; similarly in agriculture, where the short-run potential of substituting labour for capital had already been stretched to its limits. As agriculture had temporarily absorbed most of the refugees in the first place, the readjustment to normal economic conditions quite naturally led to a marked regional disparity of unemployment between the rural and the industrial regions. Hence, with profits at a high and wages at a miserably low level, the only feasible medium-run solution to the unemployment problem was seen to be a rapid and sustained growth of the capital stock – including housing – combined with a movement of abundant labour away from the rural areas to the industrial centres, where the marginal efficiency of capital was highest because of the enormous physical productivity of repair and modernization investments in existing plants.[10]

This story gives a very plausible explanation for the unemployment in the consolidation period 1949/50, even from today's perspective. It also finds considerable support in later empirical studies which unanimously estimate so-called structural unemployment at that time to be well above 50 per cent.[11] Note that, in this respect, the term 'structural' did not

[10] This kind of reasoning can be found in many academic publications on the matter, be they written by Keynesians or Ordoliberals. See, for instance, Arbeitsgemeinschaft deutscher wirtschaftswissenschaftlicher Forschungsinstitute (1950), pp. 4–7; Quante (1950), p. 385; Wissenschaftlicher Beirat (1973), report of 26 February 1950, paras. 7–12, and, with some provisos concerning the widespread exclusive preoccupation with capital shortage, Röpke (1950), pp. 36–50.

[11] See, for example, Ehret (1959), p. 103 with an estimate for December 1949 and Wagenführ (1950), p. 80 with an estimate for February 1950. The methodology of these estimates was still very poor from an econometric standpoint; however, their results find some support in a modernized estimate by Paqué (1989a).

literally mean a mismatch between actual labour supply and actual labour demand with the effective constraint on employment being the mobility of the labour force between regions, sectors or occupations; rather it meant a – mostly regional – mismatch between actual labour supply and a potential labour demand, which would be forthcoming if sufficient capital were available, with the effective constraint being not mobility but the supply of capital. Thus interpreted, structural unemployment is identical to capital shortage unemployment as defined above.

Note that factor prices – notably the wage rate – played no significant role in the contemporaneous diagnosis of unemployment.[12] Most observers considered wage levels to be extremely low, although, by international standards, labour did not fare as badly as one might expect in a war-damaged economy: expressed in dollars at the official exchange rate, the average hourly wage of an industrial worker in 1949 (1950) was $0.34 ($0.30) in West Germany, compared to $1.38 ($1.44) in the United States, $0.58 ($0.44) in the United Kingdom, $0.26 ($0.23) in France and $0.24 ($0.23) in Italy.[13] Of course, such calculations must be taken with more than a grain of salt, since currency misalignments and hefty exchange-rate adjustments in the late 1940s may distort the picture; however, the numbers do at least broadly indicate that, in terms of wage levels, West Germany was lagging only behind the Anglo-American world, but not behind the other major continental countries.

In any case, profits were quite high and growing in the whole period 1949/50. This can be inferred from the figures in Table 4, which show changes of labour productivity, nominal and real wages, producer prices in industry and consumer prices in general for the two years after the currency reform. In the first six months – the time of the boom – industrial wages rose by 15 per cent, just enough to compensate for the sharp increase of consumer prices by 14.3 per cent and thus to keep real wages more or less constant. With labour productivity rising by 17.7 per cent and producer prices by about 3.5 per cent, the 15 per cent nominal wage increase left industry with a wide margin of additional profits. This apparent moderation of wage demands before and after the official lifting of the wage stop in late September 1948[14] has been widely acclaimed as

[12] The remarkable exception is Röpke (1950), who mentions the wage level's being out of line with full employment marginal productivity of labour as a possible explanation for at least some unemployment (pp. 45–6). However, he does not elaborate on the point, and the main thrust of his argument falls within the domain of capital shortage (pp. 44–7).

[13] Own calculations on the basis of data from *The Economist* (1985), Part III. The currency conversion rates used are yearly averages based on Bank für Internationalen Zahlungsausgleich (1951), p. 139.

[14] Note that the official wage stop was not enforced strictly. Even before November 1948, nominal wage increases were granted with the permission of the Allied authorities. See Chapter 2, Section 3 above.

Table 4. *Productivity, wages and prices after the currency reform[a]*

	30 June 1948– 31 December 1948	31 December 1948– 31 December 1949	31 December 1949– 30 June 1950
(i) Labour productivity	17.7	26.0	8.8
(ii) Nominal wages	15.0	8.4	2.1
(iii) Consumer prices	14.3	−6.3'	−5.7
(iv) Producer prices	3.5	−5.7	−2.0
(v) Real wages	0.6	15.6	8.3

Notes: [a] Rates of change (in per cent).
(i) Index of output per manhour in industry (1936 = 100); (ii) index of gross hourly earnings per worker in industry; (iii) consumer price index for representative household (four persons; 1950 = 100); (iv) index of producer prices in industry (1950 = 100); only available from 31 July 1948 on; figure in table is estimated, based on backward extrapolation to 30 June 1948; (v) nominal wage index as defined in note to (ii) divided by consumer price index as defined in note to (iii).
Source: Statistisches Bundesamt; own calculations.

a major contribution of the unions to West German reconstruction. The following year of consolidation brought a remarkable further improvement in profit margins in industry, despite the temporarily worsening business climate: only about half of the 26 per cent gain in labour productivity over the year was passed on in wage increases and price reductions. Hence, in spite of a sizeable rise of real wages by 15.6 per cent, industry could keep a large chunk of the productivity gains in the form of retained earnings for investment. This trend continued in the first six months of 1950, although at a somewhat slower pace. Hence, after all, labour-market observers in late 1949 and early 1950 were quite justified in leaving wages and labour costs out of their diagnosis of unemployment: given the state of wages and profits in 1949/50 and the presumably very low elasticity of short-term substitution in production between labour and the existing capital stock, the cause of unemployment was to be located in capital shortage proper, not in the level of labour costs.

The broad consensus on the cause of unemployment did not entail an agreement on cures to be applied. The most important and controversial statements of prominent economists and politicians about full employment policy were made at about the time of peak unemployment from, say, spring 1949 to late 1950. We shall pick out three paradigmatic positions which played a major part in the policy debate as well-argued cases based on different conceptions of the role of government, namely

(i) the Keynesian position as presented by Erich Preiser and the working group of the German Economic Research Institutes, with Fritz Baade of the Kiel Institute of World Economics as its intellectual pacemaker;
(ii) the dogmatic liberal position as presented by Wilhelm Röpke;
(iii) the pragmatic liberal position as presented by the Advisory Council to the Federal Minister of Economics, with members including prominent Keynesians: Wilhelm Kromphardt, Hans Peter, Erich Preiser, Karl Schiller and Gerhard Weisser, as well as outspoken liberals: Franz Böhm, Walter Eucken, Leonhard Miksch, Alfred Müller-Armack, and Theodor Wessels.

These three positions will be briefly summarized, juxtaposed and evaluated below in so far as they had implications for the central policy question whether and how the capital shortage could and should be overcome by government action.

(i) The Keynesian position. German Keynesians usually pleaded for a combination of three measures: expansionary monetary policy, special tax incentives for saving, and investment planning (*Investitionslenkung*). The macroeconomic part of their argument – for instance, as elaborated by Preiser (1950)[15] – ran as follows.

Additional investment is needed to overcome the capital shortage. There are two ways of financing this investment at a given level of production and income: through an increase in current saving at the cost of current consumption – the classical way – or through money creation – the Keynesian way. The classical variant has the drawback that, be it through an increase of taxation or a rise of the interest rate, it entails a mere shift of aggregate demand away from consumption to investment, but no change of its level. As, in a state of unemployment equilibrium, production and income are determined by aggregate demand, there will be no change in income and hence no secondary effects on consumption and saving – in short, no self-perpetuating multiplier process which may move the economy closer to full employment. The capital shortage will only be reduced to the extent of the initial cut in consumption, no matter how this cut has come about. Not so in the Keynesian variant: as the initial investment is financed through money creation, there will be no reduction of consumption either through higher taxation or through a rise in the interest rate. In unemployment equilibrium, income will rise by the amount of additional investment; thus an expansionary multiplier process is set in motion which leads to income-induced increases in both saving and consumption. As the induced consumption demand meets a supply which

---

[15] Similar arguments were made by Schiller (1951) and by Quante (1950).

is price inelastic in the short run, prices and – at given nominal wages – profits in the consumption goods industries will rise. If the process is now left to itself (without further monetary alimentation), the original investment will eventually be financed through an income-induced rise in (voluntary) saving by private households and through a consumption-induced rise of profits and thus retained earnings in the consumer goods industries. Hence the multiplier process ends up financing itself, albeit at the cost of rising prices of consumer goods. However, this cost can be avoided if the expansionary monetary policy is combined with the introduction of a system of tax incentives for saving which is precisely targeted at skimming off the consumer demand push resulting from the investment-induced income expansion. Of course, such a policy cuts off all secondary effects of the multiplier process by preventing consumption from rising with income so that the overall expansion just equals the original increase in investment, i.e. the investment multiplier equals one, a result which parallels the celebrated Haavelmo Theorem of a balanced budget multiplier. Only by starting another round of money-financed investment can – and should – the expansionary effect be perpetuated.

The analytical difference between a Keynesian policy *without* and a Keynesian policy *with* tax privileges for saving is obvious: without the privileges – the 'British-Keynesian' way – investment is at least partly post-financed through an (involuntary) inflation tax on consumers; with tax privileges – the 'German-Keynesian' way – it is exclusively post-financed through voluntary (but note: subsidized) saving. To Preiser and most other prominent German Keynesians, it was precisely this quality of raising voluntary saving ex-post and thus avoiding inflation which made this peculiar policy mix so attractive for West Germany at a time when the classical variant of saving through consumption restraint was held to be unfeasible since the propensity to consume appeared to be extremely high, and the conventional Keynesian variant of forced saving carried with it the danger of initiating an inflationary spiral, with all its negative consequences for external stability.

Apart from their macroeconomic argument for monetary expansion and tax reform, Keynesians made a strong welfare economic case for planning[16]: major growth bottlenecks, above all in housing and transportation, could easily be recognized, but not easily broken without government interference, since the private rate of return in these important

---

[16] See, for instance, Arbeitsgemeinschaft deutscher wirtschaftswissenschaftlicher Forschungsinstitute (1950), Ch. 11, most contributions to the conference on full employment held by the Economic Institute of the Unions in Oberhausen, March 1950 (see Wirtschaftswissenschaftliches Institut der Gewerkschaften (1950)) and, less dogmatically, Wissenschaftlicher Beirat beim Bundesministerium der Finanzen, report of 25 June 1950, para. 6.

fields was apparently too low to attract a socially desirable amount of capital. In addition, the German capital market was extremely narrow, so that the process of channelling business savings (profits) into socially desirable uses was seriously constrained anyway. Hence, extensive government intervention was required both in the shape of direct public investment to break bottlenecks, and in the shape of a tax reform aimed at promoting private investment in social bottleneck fields and improving the efficiency of capital markets by removing overdrawn tax privileges for self-financing.

(ii) *The dogmatic liberal position.* Even among liberal economists, Wilhelm Röpke was practically alone in making a clear-cut case for higher interest rates as a necessary step towards overcoming the capital shortage. His argument – presented most cogently in a controversial evaluation of German economic policy in summer 1950[17] – ran along the following neoclassical lines. By definition, a capital shortage can only be overcome through saving, be it forced or voluntary. Variants of forced saving are outright taxation, open inflation, which raises business profits (retained earnings) at the cost of real wages, or suppressed inflation (through price controls), which leads to a quantitative rationing of consumption demand. While taxation might be justified within very narrow limits to finance public investments in carefully selected fields, the other two variants were simply unacceptable in a country like Germany, with its record of disastrous inflation and its more recent experience of central planning (*Bewirtschaftung*). Variants of voluntary saving include genuine household as well as business saving out of current income. Extensive business saving through retained earnings had the drawback of distorting the allocation of capital at least in a country like West Germany, where the capital market was still in its infancy; hence, one should rely mainly on household savings and also capital imports.

As to households, Röpke recognized a genuine conflict between their high time preference due to the long period of war and post-war misery and the economy's urgent need for capital to secure full employment in the future. As, at least in the longer run, the interest rate is the price of time – and not the price of liquidity – this conflict of the (perfectly legitimate) demands of the present and the future must be reconciled by a rise in the interest rate, even if the price to be paid is a less than maximum, but nevertheless intertemporally optimal capital accumulation. Of course, a rise of the interest rate to its equilibrium, or in Wicksellian terms, to its natural level would necessarily reduce investment demand. Yet it was

[17] See Röpke (1950), Ch. 8.

by no means clear whether this would also reduce the volume of realized investment: at a less than equilibrium rate, investment was supply-constrained by savings, so that the level of realized investment might well increase along with the (positively) interest-elastic supply of savings. Furthermore, the rise in the interest rate would lead to a readjustment of the investment structure towards the formation of capital with a particularly high marginal efficiency, i.e. – in Röpke's empirical judgement about West Germany in 1950 – those projects which satisfy demands in the near future at the cost of those aimed at the more distant future.

To summarize, it was the interest rate which Röpke regarded as the main regulator of the intertemporal allocation of resources, and not some supposedly objective criteria of urgency which direct the decisions of central planners. Röpke was ready to grant that, at the given level of still heavy regulation and price controls in certain asset markets (for instance, the housing market), a certain degree of corrective government intervention – including the provision of tax privileges – was probably warranted so as to secure enough capital formation despite an artificially low market rate of return. Nevertheless, he emphasized that government intervention was only justified as a temporary emergency measure, to be called off as soon as free-market pricing was re-established everywhere, which, at any rate, should happen as soon as possible. In this sense, Röpke was highly critical of (Keynesian) attempts at government planning to break apparent bottlenecks; instead, he strongly advocated the re-establishment of free and, as he assumed, efficient capital markets in all fields, no matter how 'visible' and 'urgent' the investment needs appeared to be.

In the same vein, Röpke argued in favour of substituting private foreign savings for official foreign aid, which was expected to be cut back anyway. In his view, only a steadfast policy of economic liberalization was appropriate to regain the confidence of foreign investors in the West German economy and thus allow the private capital inflow to increase and supplement domestic savings.

(iii) The pragmatic liberal position. If we interpret the Keynesian and the dogmatic liberal standpoints as opposite ends in a spectrum of opinions about the scope of deliberate expansionary measures and government intervention in the face of the capital shortage in 1949/50, we shall have to place the position of the politically influential Advisory Council to the Federal Minister of Economics somewhere in the middle. In its main reports on unemployment, capital shortage and monetary policy (reports of 8 May 1949, 26 February 1950 and 10 June 1950),[18]

---

[18] See Wissenschaftlicher Beirat (1973), pp. 37–40, 65–71, 81–5.

the Council struck a delicate balance between Keynesian macro and neoclassical price theory.

In its statements on monetary and credit policy, the Council by and large followed Keynesian-type reasoning, albeit with a particularly pronounced anti-inflationary undercurrent. In the report of 8 May 1949, the Council emphasized the need for moderately expansionary open-market operations, which should be accompanied by an active market policy (*Marktpolitik*) to cut down on monopolistic profit margins; these were considered to be at least partly responsible for excessive price levels. Increasing competition between industrial producers would drive up productivity, thus allowing wages and incomes to rise; with appropriate tax incentives for household saving, this rise could then be transformed into an increase in saving (not in consumption).

Thirteen months later, in its report of 10 June 1950, the Council fully endorsed Preiser's Keynesian concept of pre-financing investment through money creation. As a complement to the investment push, the Council recommended creating the conditions for a more efficient capital market. Unlike Röpke, however, the Council did not go as far as to make a case for free and thus presumably high interest rates; instead, it pleaded for tax incentives for saving and a systematic reduction of bond price risk through open-market operations by the central bank (*Kurspflege*), which comes down to a policy of pegging the interest rate, again a strongly Keynesian element.

In its main report on unemployment and capital shortage (26 February 1950), the Council advocated credit expansion provided that – after pre-financing investment – the required growth of aggregate supply would be forthcoming so as to avoid any inflationary pressure. The Council also recommended introducing tax privileges for special forms of saving (*Zwecksparen*), especially in the field of housing investment. Besides, it argued in favour of a general cut in individual and corporate income taxation, with tax savings being transformed into a compulsory loan (*Zwangsanleihe*) to be held in the form of bonds or stocks; thereby, firms should not be allowed to use their tax savings for additional self-financing except in very narrowly defined circumstances. With respect to direct labour-market interventions, the report flatly rejected any kind of rationing of the labour supply, be it through compulsory short-time work, new public work programmes (*Notstandsarbeit*) or the prohibition against holding more than one job at a time. However, government support for refugees and other labour-market fringe groups was explicitly endorsed provided the support was linked to an active job search by the recipients and not just granted as an unconditional cash allowance.

To summarize, the major thrust of the report was a combination of moderate credit expansion to pre-finance investment with no Phillips-curve-type concession to inflation, of active tax policy to encourage capital formation and to channel savings into bottleneck fields, and of a social policy to facilitate labour-market adjustment with no direct public work programmes involved. The ideological picture of government which this conveys is that of a public authority which is in principle liberal-minded, but which has at the same time the right and the paternalistic duty to impose distortions on the price system so as to secure an adequate growth for the economy to the long-term benefit of all. It is a highly pragmatic version of economic liberalism, far from a socialist-minded intervention-ism, but also far from any ideal of laissez-faire.

From a modern welfare theoretic point of view, it is certainly Röpke's dogmatic liberalism which, of the three positions sketched above, provides the most convincing answer to the question of how to overcome a serious capital shortage, namely through a rise in the price of time: the interest rate. All other variants of increasing saving entail at least some elements of coercion and distortion: in the case of tax privileges for saving, taxpayers are forced to carry the burden of subsidizing (voluntary) saving; if the tax privilege depends on the type of saving (for example, housing loans), an element of distortion is added, although it may just be a compensation for other market interventions, such as rent control. Of course, Keynesians and the Advisory Council were well aware of this simple point. It remains all the more striking that they did not feel obliged to consider seriously the alternative of letting the interest rate adjust to the observed scarcities. Clearly, the welfare economic basis of their argument was poorly developed; instead, somewhat cruder notions of maximizing growth and capital accumulation prevailed.[19]

Politically, the pragmatic liberal and, to some extent, the Keynesian ideas had distinctive advantages over Röpke's more radical line: they conveyed the picture of an active government which not only recognized

[19] As to the macroeconomic part of the argument, the essentially Keynesian line of reasoning as presented by Preiser and the Advisory Council had some serious analytical flaws: at no point did it clearly distinguish between the stock demand for money (hoarding) and the flow demand for savings, with, at a given money supply, the former having a deflationary effect on aggregate demand and the latter having no effect at all as long as the velocity of money and hence money demand remains constant. Instead, it was simply assumed that an increase in consumption demand raises prices while an increase in investment demand does not. However, it is the stock demand for money and the price elasticity of the aggregate goods supply, not a trade-off between saving and consumption, which eventually determine whether a monetary expansion leads to more real economic activity or more inflation. True, by expanding the aggregate production capacity of the economy, investment does – and consumption does not – increase future goods supply, but this is a medium- or long-run effect which may not prevent immediate inflationary pressures from emerging. Apparently, Preiser and many other economists simply assumed that the capacity effect of investment would be large and come about fast.

the capital shortage, but also did something about it. To let market forces run their merciless course without any substantial policy commitments by the public authorities might have overstretched the readiness of the population to adjust to economic conditions which were harsh enough anyway. Given this kind of political constraint on any conception of economic policy, the pragmatic position of the Advisory Council deserves much credit as a remarkably liberal stance which made its most far-reaching compromises with interventionism precisely in that field where they were likely to hurt least: in the field of promoting capital formation for future growth.

What was the answer of economic policy to the cyclical downturn and the rise of unemployment in 1949/50? In the domain of demand management, nothing dramatic happened, at least during the year 1949: after the inflationary pressure had finally abated in the first quarter of 1949, the Bank deutscher Länder began to release the monetary brakes. The discount rate was reduced from 5 to 4.5 per cent in May and to 4 per cent in July, where it stayed until, in the autumn of 1950, the balance-of-payments crisis during the Korea boom led to a rise to 6 per cent.[20] In March 1949, prior credit ceilings were lifted and, in the second half of the year, reserve requirements were successively scaled down.[21] All these measures were kept deliberately cautious so as not to rekindle inflation and thus endanger the still very shaky external balance; they were about in line with the recommendations of the Advisory Council to the Federal Minister of Economics, who, in its report of 8 May 1949, pleaded for a moderate credit expansion.[22] As to fiscal policy, a tiny programme of no more than 300 million DMarks to finance selected investment and export projects was initiated in August 1949. Calls for more daring expansionary steps – especially from Social Democrats and union leaders – could be heard frequently throughout 1949; yet they did not have the sense of urgency necessary to provoke any major public debate. Remarkably enough, the cyclical downturn played no significant part in the political prelude to the first federal parliamentary elections in August 1949; on the contrary, the Christian Democrats could base their campaign right on the apparent success of the social market economy, a strategy which paid off handsomely at the polls.

By early 1950, however, the economic policy debate heated up considerably. With the number of unemployed surpassing the magic 2 million threshold in February 1950, there was some objective economic back-

---

[20] On the balance-of-payments crisis, see Section B.2 of this chapter.
[21] For details, see Wallich (1955), pp. 79–87.
[22] See Wissenschaftlicher Beirat (1973), pp. 81–5.

ground for a change of mood. To be sure, a number of curious political accidents added fuel to the flames: in December 1949, the newly established West German government had presented a confidential memorandum to the Organization of European Economic Co-operation (OEEC) in which the prospects of the West German economy for the next two years (until 1952) of the Marshall Plan aid were outlined.[23] This memorandum was no master piece of economic diplomacy: in its main political sections, it concluded with the gloomy prediction that, even with fairly optimistic assumptions, there were few chances for the West German economy to overcome its most urgent bottlenecks in the supply of capital and housing and thus to reduce unemployment in the next two years. Given the economic facts of the day, this was by no means an unrealistic assessment. Politically, it was certainly meant to underline the further urgent need of foreign support. Unfortunately, this plausible strategy backfired completely: to the apparent surprise of the West German government, the Economic Co-operation Administration (ECA) – the American body supervising the implementation of the Marshall Plan – was appalled by the picture of gloom which, in American eyes, looked more like a cry for help than a sensible programme for viability. Therefore, in February 1950, the ECA issued a memorandum of its own in which the West German government was openly blamed for its all too passive attitude towards the problem of mass unemployment. As to economic policy, the ECA called for a more aggressive monetary and credit policy to give a boost to investment demand, and a more prominent role for public works programmes.[24] This critique was all the more trenchant because, up to this point, the American administration had given steadfast support to the liberal economic policy stance as personified by Ludwig Erhard, who was the Minister of Economics in the centre–right coalition government in West Germany since 1949. Naturally, the unions and the Social Democratic opposition widely acclaimed this kind of unexpected support for their cause. In early March, the West German government replied by issuing a counter-memorandum which basically restated its diagnosis of capital-shortage unemployment and listed all the relevant policy measures that had already been taken or were planned for the near future. Meanwhile, the government had received backing from the Advisory Council, which, in its report of 26 February 1950, more or less endorsed the government's position.

The reaction of the government turned out to be well balanced and to the point: it was uncompromising as to the general policy maxim that price stability and external balance deserved priority over short-term

[23] For the Marshall Plan, see Section B.2 of this chapter.
[24] For the text of the memorandum, see *Die Neue Zeitung* of 20 February 1950, 'Wortlaut des alliierten Memorandums'.

employment gains, thus signalling to the ECA that a change of philosophy was and remained out of the question. At the same time, it was politically pragmatic enough to calm its critics by announcing two additional public projects: a work-creation programme (volume: 0.9 billion DMarks) and a housing programme (volume: 2.6 billion DMarks). Both of these programmes (just like the earlier one of August 1949) were expected to have a short-run expansionary effect through a pre-financing commitment by the central bank.[25] In the event, the extent of pre-financing of all three programmes together remained well below 1 billion DMarks all through 1950, with the bulk of the more important work-creation and housing programmes carried out in the autumn of 1950 when the Korea boom and the subsequent balance-of-payments crisis had set in; in any case, the programmes amounted to no more than 3 per cent of aggregate gross investment in 1950.[26] No doubt, this was a very modest political yield of the ECA warnings, so that, on balance, the West German government came out as the net winner of what the press christened the 'Memorandum War'.[27]

As to the supply side, the government showed even less inclination to develop anything like a counter-cyclical policy activism. The reason for this relaxed attitude was simple: the core of what most economists persistently recommended for speeding up capital formation, namely massive tax incentives for saving and investment, had already been introduced in the Tax Law Adjustment Acts of June 1948 and April 1949 so as to prevent the very high income tax rates fixed by the Allied authorities from stifling the motivation of the population to work and save. The privileges included accelerated depreciation allowances for capital expenditures incurred in repairing war-damaged equipment (para. 7 (a) of the Income Tax Law), for new residential property (para. 7 (b)) and for new industrial, commercial and agricultural plants (para. 7 (e)), tax deductions for housing loans (para. 7 (c)), shipbuilding loans (para. 7 (d)) and special forms of saving such as life insurance premiums and contributions to building societies (para. 10).[28] In 1950, the total amount deducted from individual and corporate income tax according to para. 7 (a)–(e) of the Income Tax Law was about 0.9 billion DMarks, i.e. 4.2 per cent of the aggregate gross income of all individual and corporate tax returns; 48 per cent of this amount was expenditure on repairing

---

[25] For the text of the German 'counter-memorandum', see *Die Neue Zeitung* of 6 March 1950, 'Bundesregierung beantwortet alliiertes Memorandum'.

[26] Own calculations from the data in Bank deutscher Länder (1951), p. 27, Table 6.

[27] For a contemporaneous summary of the 'Memorandum War', see *The Economist* of 11 March 1950, 'Economic Dogmatism in Germany'.

[28] For a detailed description of these income tax provisions, see Boss (1987), pp. 31–4.

war-damaged equipment, and about 30 per cent was housing loans.[29] These numbers suggest that the tax privileges had great importance for capital formation; however, as they were designed and implemented before unemployment reached its most threatening dimension (i.e. before mid 1949), they can hardly be regarded as a conscious political answer to the unemployment problem. Parallel to the cuts of marginal tax rates in later years, the privileges were removed or restricted in applicability. Neither was there any speeded-up effort in 1950 to raise the efficiency of capital markets; in fact, a law with this explicit aim was passed no earlier than December 1952, when the unemployment problem had already lost a good deal of its urgency. Nor was there any deliberate effort to raise public investment: in the early 1950s, the government's share in capital formation came close to one-quarter of total investment expenditure, with the bulk of public engagement falling into the fields of housing, transportation, schooling and the subsidization of private industry. No doubt, these investments helped to overcome serious bottlenecks in the economy's capital stock (especially in transportation).[30] However, they were simply part of a long-term strategy to stimulate economic growth, with no regard to the particular cyclical conditions and the temporary rise of the unemployment rate.

All this conveys the impression that the government did not really see the need for taking any exceptional steps to reduce unemployment. Of course, there were quite a few laws passed in 1949/50 which had immediate relevance for the labour market, for instance, the resettlement orders of November 1949 demanding an organized movement of 300,000 refugees away from Schleswig-Holstein, Lower Saxony and Bavaria to other states, the first housing law of April 1950 providing a legal framework for government intervention in the housing market, and the many laws on welfare matters which gave particular support to labour mobility, above all of refugees.[31] Again, this legislation was based much more on medium- and long-term visions of economic growth and social equity than on short-term considerations of full employment. After the main economic course had been set in 1948 and 1949 towards capital formation, the government was apparently ready to sit back and watch the capital stock growing.

[29] Own calculations on the basis of data from Statistisches Bundesamt (1956), pp. 22, 35, 59, 66.
[30] For more details on public investment, see Wallich (1955), pp. 169–71.
[31] For details, see Wallich (1955), pp. 273–9. Most importantly, the so-called Emergency Aid Law (*Soforthilfegesetz*) of 1949 and the Law for the Equalization of War Burdens (*Lastenausgleichsgesetz*) gave generous support to refugees willing to make a new economic start.

This attitude was greatly rewarded by the fortuitous business upswing which set in with the worldwide Korea boom in early summer 1950. From March to December 1950, the index of industrial production rose by a sensational 32.3 per cent, i.e. on an annualized basis by 45.3 per cent, a rate never reached again thereafter. Within a few months, a surge of exports and domestic absorption led to more than full capacity utilization of the capital stock and to plenty of new orders, especially in the investment goods industries, a traditional strength of the German economy. As other countries – above all the United Kingdom and the United States – absorbed their (non-inflationary) economic potential much earlier than West Germany, the prior cautiousness of the Bonn government proved to be a blessing, whereas the execution of the special employment and housing programmes decided upon in early spring looked increasingly ill-timed. In a way, the Korea boom provided the West German economy with a Keynesian stimulus just at a time when it was most needed and popular; as the boost did not come from government spending, all those negative crowding-out effects of an increase in public expenditure on domestic investment could be avoided. The only (modest) price to be paid for the boom was a sharp but temporary hike of imported price inflation and a short-lived – though politically critical – balance-of-payments crisis.[32]

It was not only the business climate, but also the general outlook of economists as to the major deficiencies of the West German economy which changed considerably with the Korea boom, as two important academic conferences in West Germany on full employment during the year 1950 clearly show. When, in March 1950, British and German economists – admittedly all of them Keynesians or Marxists – came together at a conference of the Economic Research Institute of the Unions, there was a broad consensus among them that, on top of capital shortage, a cyclical trough was responsible for the high unemployment.[33] By October 1950, at the meeting of the German Economic Association, there was an equally broad consensus among participants – Keynesians and liberal economists – that the focus of attention should increasingly shift from macroeconomic to structural issues, i.e. to the newly emerging acute bottlenecks in the productive potential of the economy.[34] Also, for years to come, the Advisory Council did not place the issue of unemployment at the centre of any of its reports: matters of international finance and trade integration moved into the foreground instead.

[32] See Section B.2 of this chapter.
[33] See the contributions in Wirtschaftswissenschaftliches Institut der Gewerkschaften (1950).
[34] See the contributions in Albrecht (1951).

Table 5. *The growth of aggregate expenditure items^a at constant prices (annual averages, % p.a.)*

	1950–5	1955–60	1950–60
Private consumption	8.6	6.9	7.8
Government expenditure	7.0	9.1	8.0
Private investment^b	12.4	6.4	9.4
Exports	17.5	9.6	13.5
Total expenditures on domestic output^c	10.3	7.6	8.9

Notes: ^{a} All four expenditure items defined according to standard national accounts conventions at constant 1976 prices.
^{b} Gross investment in plant and equipment (i.e. excluding change of inventories).
^{c} Excluding change of inventories.
Source: Statistisches Bundesamt; own calculations.

2   1950–1960: the demand side

The Korea boom marks the beginning of the second stage of the German miracle: in the following decade, real GDP more than doubled and output per worker increased by almost 75 per cent. As to the macroeconomic performance, the decade may sensibly be divided into two sub-periods: the five years from the Korea boom to the sharp cyclical upswing in 1955, a time of altogether spectacular output growth (on average about 9.5 per cent p.a.), a persistently high utilization of the capital stock and – after the short inflationary hike of the Korea boom – of virtual price stability; and the five years from 1955 to 1960, a time of a pronounced cyclical pattern with one significant business downturn (1957/8) and something like a rebirth of price inflation. We shall look successively at the macroeconomics of these two periods.

Viewed from the expenditure side of national accounting (see Table 5), the main pillars of the economic expansion in the period 1950–5 were exports and private investment, which, in real terms, grew by 17.5 per cent and 12.4 per cent p.a. respectively, much faster than private consumption (8.6 per cent p.a.) and government expenditure (7.0 per cent p.a.). Apparently, a buoyant demand for West German goods on world markets drove firms into a very high rate of capital stock utilization (see Figure 3); this spurred the demand for new capital equipment, which further supported the expansion and thus led into a kind of virtuous circle.

In this process, expansionary macroeconomic demand policies played almost no active role. As to monetary policy, the Bank deutscher Länder counteracted the price inflation and the increasing current account deficit of the Korea boom with sharply restrictive measures, above all with an upward shift of the discount rate from 4 to 6 per cent in October 1950. This was a major counter-cyclical effort to curb the dramatic increase of domestic absorption which helped to overcome the balance-of-payments crisis.[35] From mid 1952 onwards, inflation gave way to a slight deflationary trend, and the current account moved into a healthy surplus which was to remain a persistent feature of the West German economy until 1962. Given these positive signals, the monetary authorities loosened the credit brakes: until June 1954, the discount rate was successively reduced from 6 to 3 per cent, where it stayed until August 1955. Similarly, the lending rate for ordinary bank credits declined from a high of 10.5 per cent in 1951 to a low of 7.9 per cent in 1955.[36] Note, however, that these changes did not mean anything like a deliberate shift towards an explicitly expansionary monetary policy; rather they figure as a passive accommodation to the diminishing pressures of price inflation and external imbalances. To some extent, the gradual decline in nominal interest rates may also reflect an underlying change on the real side of the economy: with a fast-growing capital stock, the economy's need for new capital equipment became somewhat less pressing, so that a decline in the profitability of investment and thus in the real rate of interest was quite likely anyway.[37] Hence, both in monetary and in real terms, the development of interest rates looks more like a natural outcome of fast export-led supply-side growth than of any active liquidity policy of the central bank.

As to fiscal policy, it was a time of rapid surplus accumulation: throughout 1951–6, the West German government[38] ran a considerable budget surplus which, from 1952 on, amounted to about 3 per cent of GNP.[39] The reasons for this surplus were both political and economic. Politically, the West German government was accumulating funds to finance at some future date an expensive programme of rearmament which

---

[35] See Section B.2 of this chapter.

[36] Annual averages; data taken from Deutsche Bundesbank (1988), p. 3.

[37] Note that any such change of the 'natural rate of interest' could not show up in actual bond markets simply because there was a tight control of emissions and an upper ceiling for nominal long-term interest rates on bonds of 6.5 per cent. See Wallich (1955), pp. 184–6.

[38] In what follows, the term 'government' means all public bodies on the federal, state and local level.

[39] The budget balance is defined as the consolidated balance of the whole public sector at all levels (federal, state and local) excluding the social security administration; the surplus is even higher when one includes the social security system, since it ran a surplus of its own in the range of 1 per cent of GNP. All numbers on budget balances in the text are taken from national accounts statistics and thus follow standard national accounts conventions. In 1953, the budget surplus even reached about 10 per cent of GNP. This altogether exceptional level was basically due to a non-anticipated repayment of funds to cover occupation costs by the Allied forces.

was more or less on the agenda from 1951 onwards. Because of political difficulties – above all the refusal of the French parliament to ratify the treaty of the European Defense Community in 1954 – the project was delayed for a few years until West Germany joined NATO in 1955 and thereafter began to set up its armed forces. Economically, it is safe to say that the government and its public finance experts persistently under-estimated the growth of the economy and thus of tax revenues, so that – ex-post – the budget balance turned out more favourable than expected. In any case, there was not much political talk about using the accumulated surpluses for the purpose of countercyclical spending projects, simply because, in those years, the autonomous growth of the economy looked more than satisfactory: if anything, fiscal policy had a slightly pro-cyclical bias.[40]

In summary, the period 1950–5 really deserves to be called a time of spontaneous growth: for four years after the Korea boom, the macro-economic sky was so bright that business cycles played no part in politics. After all, the campaign leading up to the federal elections in 1953 was again fought with almost no reference to macroeconomic difficulties. Without taking pains to justify its economic policy stance, as had still been necessary in the 1949 campaign, the Christian Democrats – Chan-cellor Adenauer's party – could gain an easy victory. Also, cyclical issues played a very minor part in the analysis of the Advisory Council to the Federal Minister of Economics: from June 1951 to September 1955, only three short reports[41] were concerned with the state of the business cycle, two of which asked how the rapid expansion could be secured. None of them contained any explicit call for cyclical activism.

From the expenditure side of national accounting (see Table 5), the second half of the 1950s appears to be much more normal than the first. With 7.6 per cent p.a. in real terms, the growth of total expenditure on domestic goods was still exceptionally rapid, but the composition of expansion now looked more balanced than before: exports still ran ahead, now followed by government spending, and – at a distance – private consumption and investment, yet differences in growth rates were clearly much less pronounced than in the earlier five-year period. Apparently, growth was still export-led, but not to the extent of prior years; a kind of normalization had set in.

Also, macroeconomic stability returned to the economic policy agenda, albeit – by the standards of later decades – in a still quite undramatic

---

[40] See Sachverständigenrat (1964), p. 101.
[41] See reports of 9 October 1951, 17/18 January 1953 and 10 January 1954, reprinted in Wissenschaftlicher Beirat (1973), pp. 135–7, 169–71, 213–16.

form. The starting-point was the extraordinary boom in 1955, with a real GDP growth of 11.9 per cent p.a., an extremely high degree of capital stock utilization, a virtual depletion of domestic labour reserves – the unemployment rate fell below 3 per cent in the summer months – a noticeable, though still moderate, acceleration of price inflation to above 2 per cent p.a., and a significant drop of the current account surplus due to the high level of internal absorption. Given these facts, the central bank switched its monetary stance from passive accommodation to active restraint: in three steps from August 1955 to May 1956, the discount rate was raised from 3 to 5.5 per cent, the highest level since 1952, and a number of complementary measures of tight credit were taken.[42] This policy had the full backing of the Advisory Council, which, in its report of 11 October 1955, recommended a sharp restriction on credit expansion. However, in the political realm, the final step of these measures in May 1956 provoked the first serious clash between the stability-orientated Bank deutscher Länder and Chancellor Adenauer: with an eye to the federal parliamentary elections scheduled for the autumn of 1957, Adenauer was afraid of a policy-induced cyclical backlash. In a public speech in Cologne, he openly criticized the central bank for having incurred the risk of a recession; in the same vein he blamed 'his' Ministers of Economics and Finance, Ludwig Erhard and Fritz Schäffer, for having publicly praised the restrictive policy measures without prior consultation in the cabinet. This political skirmish did not have serious consequences, since academic economists, the liberal press and to a large extent the general public (including the unions!) firmly supported the course of the Bank deutscher Länder, so that Adenauer finally gave up his tactically motivated opposition. However, the incident itself was widely acclaimed as a paradigmatic case for a central bank which is independent of any government interference into monetary affairs.[43]

As to the cyclical effects of the new monetary stance, Adenauer's intuition was not bad at all: from 1955 to 1958, the expansion slowed down substantially and finally ended in a moderate recession, with the growth of real GDP dropping to a low of 4.4 per cent p.a. in 1958. In fact, the year 1958 became the first one since 1950 with a slight increase in the annual average unemployment rate, from 3.7 to 3.8 per cent. The recession coincided with a general downturn in world markets, so that it is difficult to judge by how much it was home-made or imported. The

[42] For details, see Scheide (1987a), p. 15; Emminger (1976), pp. 492–3, and Schlesinger (1976), pp. 589–91, who emphasizes that – given the cyclical state of the economy – the tightening of monetary policy came somewhat late.

[43] On the political details of the controversy, see Schwarz (1981), pp. 323–4, and Schlesinger (1976), p. 590.

truth may lie in the middle: with a tight credit market, private investment stagnated in 1957, but recovered in the following year; in turn, exports still grew fast in 1957, but virtually stagnated in 1958.[44] Hence, most probably, domestic forces initiated and international forces prolonged the slowdown. In any case, the slight recession helped to stabilize price inflation at 1–2 per cent p.a. and to push up the current account surplus to its prior level of about 3 per cent of GNP. Given the apparent determination of the monetary authorities to reduce inflationary pressures even at the cost of some cyclical downturn, the outcome looks very much like a 'wanted recession', i.e. a slowdown of growth which was deliberately taken into account to stem an overbrimming boom.[45]

With currency reserves piling up and the economy cooling off, the central bank – since 1957 called the Deutsche Bundesbank[46] – released the monetary brakes again; thus, inter alia, the discount rate was successively reduced from its peak of 5.5 per cent in mid 1956 to a low of 2.75 per cent in the first ten months of 1959.[47] Again, these moves look more like a passive reaction to weakening cyclical pressures than an aggressive expansionary stance. Nevertheless, they laid the monetary ground for another sharp recovery in 1959–60; with this recovery, the economy finally moved into a state of overemployment which was to become the long-term benchmark for the 1960s.

As to fiscal policy, the period 1955–60 brought a significant change: the end of strict fiscal discipline. The budget surplus of the public sector shrank markedly, from 4–5 per cent of GNP in 1954/6 to 1.5–1.8 per cent in 1958/9; in the boom year 1960, it rose again to 3 per cent, but sharply declined thereafter. This change had essentially three causes. First, the rearmament programme finally got underway, so that part of the prior surplus simply lost its rationale. Second, the federal government loosened its pursestrings a little, as many critical observers recognized with disdain. This became most evident in 1956, the fiscal year before the federal elections, when the government went ahead with distributing a whole bunch of 'social gifts' in the form of expenditures or tax concessions granted to special interest groups.[48] With fast-growing tax revenues, the

---

[44] The numbers from the national accounts statistics are the following ones: private investment in real terms (excluding inventories) rose by 0.3 per cent in 1957 and 4.4 per cent in 1958, and the export volume by 11.4 per cent in 1957 and 1.8 per cent in 1958.

[45] The strongly anti-inflationary rhetoric of the Bank deutscher Länder in its monthly reports of early 1956 supports this interpretation.

[46] On 1 August 1957, the Bank deutscher Länder was legally replaced by the Deutsche Bundesbank as the West German central bank. This legal change had no economic consequences; institutionally, the new central bank was virtually identical to the old one.

[47] See Scheide (1987a), p. 14, and Schlesinger (1976), pp. 590–1.

[48] For details, see Schwarz (1981), pp. 324–7.

budget still looked basically sound, so that this opportunistic strategy did not backfire immediately; however, as many of these fiscal gifts had a built-in permanency, they certainly shifted the long-term base-line for the budget in normal times away from surplus to equilibrium or even deficit. Third, in the only significant cyclical downturn of the 1950s in 1957/8, the public budget took over the role of an automatic stabilizer to some extent: while nominal public spending grew at a fairly constant rate of 10–11 per cent p.a. from 1956 to 1960, tax revenues followed a strongly pro-cyclical path, and so did the budget surplus, which reached a low of 1.5 per cent of GNP in the main recession year 1958.[49] Many economists regularly demanded that the counter-cyclical automatism of tax revenues should be supplemented by deliberate changes on the expenditure side of the budget (such as shifting public investments from boom to recession times). The most urgent and politically weighty arguments of this kind came from the Advisory Council in its report of 11 October 1955 and from the Board of Governors of the Bundesbank, who, in November 1959, published a resolution calling for a contractionary government budget to support the monetary authority's efforts to curb the inflationary expansion.[50] All in all, these calls were in vain as public decision-making on all levels was too inert to allow for the required flexibility, not to speak of the lack of honest will on the side of politicians who found themselves under permanent lobbying pressures.

3   *1950–1960: the supply-side miracle*

As we have seen, demand management played an accommodating rather than an active role in the macroeconomics of the 1950s. Hence, the key to the extraordinary growth performance must be found on the supply side: what made the West German economy meet all the powerful waves of export-led demand without serious inflationary strain?

With the benefit of hindsight, it is quite evident that the starting conditions for a sustained supply-side expansion were much better than many contemporaneous observers realized. This was so for two main reasons. First, more than one-third of the large number of unemployed were expellees from the former eastern provinces, a stock of surplus labour which was comparatively mobile, easily assimilated, highly motivated and fairly well educated. In addition, a steady stream of particularly well-qualified immigrants from East Germany (the German Democratic

---

[49] See Sachverständigenrat (1964), p. 101.
[50] See Wissenschaftlicher Beirat (1973), pp. 288–9, and Deutsche Bundesbank, *Monatsberichte* (November 1959), p. 3.

Table 6. *Migration in West Germany 1950–88[a]*

| Period[b] | Migration quota | | | Share of systematic in total interstate migration |
| | Total | Intra-state | Inter-state | |
	(1)	(2)	(3)	(4)
1950–54	6.4	4.6	1.8	32.8
1955–59	6.4	4.6	1.8	12.1
1960–64	6.1	4.3	1.6	5.3
1965–69	6.1	4.3	1.8	6.2
1970–74	5.9	4.2	1.7	6.0
1975–79	4.8	3.5	1.3	6.5
1980–84	4.6	3.4	1.2	8.0
1985–88	4.2	3.1	1.1	9.4

Notes: [a] From 1950 to 1958 excluding, and from 1959 to 1988 including the Saar and Berlin.
[b] All numbers are period averages of respective annual averages.
(1) Number of intra-national (i.e. intra-state plus inter-state) migration cases as a share of the West German population (in per cent).
(2) Number of intra-state migration cases as a share of the West German population (in per cent).
(3) Defined as $\Sigma\ M_i/P$ (in per cent), with M_i being the number of immigration cases in state i and P being the size of the West German population.
(4) Defined as $0.5 \cdot \Sigma\ |M_i - E_i|/\Sigma\ M_i$ (in per cent), with M_i being the number of immigration cases and E_i the number of emigration cases in state i.
Source: Statistisches Bundesamt; own calculations.

Republic) supplemented the labour force throughout the 1950s; as they moved right into the industrial centres of North Rhine-Westphalia and southern Germany, where the need for labour was most urgent, they figured as an almost ideal additional source of supply elasticity. It is worth noting that the 1950s were the period of the largest internal migration in the history of West Germany as a separate economic entity (see Table 6): over the whole decade an average of 6.4 per cent of the population per year moved between communities, 4.6 per cent within and the remaining 1.8 per cent between states. More importantly, the share of systematic interstate in total interstate migration (i.e. loosely speaking the share of one-way long-distance migration mostly from north to west and south-west) was extraordinarily high: 32.8 per cent in the first half and 12.1 per cent in the second half of the 1950s, as compared to 5–10 per cent in later decades. No doubt, the labour force was very flexible; this made it relatively easy to overcome temporary regional or sectoral shortages and thus to avoid early supply-side constraints to growth.[51] Second, profits had been high in the two years after the currency reform, so that firms were able to finance additional investment in plant and equipment as soon as capacity utilization moved up again. Thus, the surge of export demand in the wake of the Korea War did no more than give West German industry a powerful signal when and where to expand capacities in order to grow into a new international division of labour.[52]

Given these favourable initial conditions, it is not altogether surprising that the West German economy could enjoy an accelerator-type virtuous circle: export demand spurred investment, which not only fuelled domestic demand, but also enlarged the capital stock and thus led to a cumulative widening of the economy's productive capacity, and to a sustained absorption of the surplus labour. Because of its traditional export orientation, West German manufacturing – above all the investment goods industries – was bound to take over the role of a growth locomotive (see Table 7): in the first half of the 1950s, the production index of manufacturing increased by an average of 13 per cent p.a., and its employment by 7 per cent p.a.; the investment goods sector alone grew by a breathtaking 16.7 per cent p.a. in production and 9.6 per cent p.a. in employment. The fast growth continued in 1955–60, although the rates of increase were all lower and the intra-sectoral differences somewhat less pronounced. Note that the two non-export-orientated industries outside manufacturing, mining and construction, could still expand in the first half of the decade, mainly through the widespread use of coal as an input in heavy industry and the boom in residential construction to overcome the extreme housing shortage; however, both fell back in later years, since oil was increasingly substituted for coal and the demand for homes approached a first temporary saturation.

Quite naturally, the fast supply-side expansion allowed hefty labour productivity gains to be realized. They were due both to the introduction of new and modernized capital equipment, and to an inter-sector structural change to the advantage of high-productivity manufacturing, which sucked up labour not only from the pool of unemployed, but also from low-productivity agriculture. In turn, the movement of workers and previously self-employed farmers to higher-paid jobs in industry put pressure on agriculture to speed up modernization through rationalization investments, which further improved the overall productivity growth performance.

---

[51] For statistical details on regional and sectoral labour mobility in the 1950s, see Paqué (1987), pp. 6–9.
[52] For West Germany's return to the world market, see Section B of this chapter.

Table 7. *Production and employment in selected industries*[a]

| | 1950–55 | | 1955–60 | |
	Q	E	Q	E
Construction	13.5	7.6	6.7	0.3
Mining	5.0	2.4	0.6	−2.7
Manufacturing	13.0	7.0	7.7	3.5
of which				
Basic materials	11.9	5.4	7.7	2.9
Investment goods	16.7	9.6	8.4	5.5
Durable consumption goods	10.9	6.0	7.0	1.5
Non-durable consumption goods	9.5	4.5	6.8	2.4

Notes: [a] Average annual increase (in per cent).
Q: index of net production.
E: number of employed persons.
Source: Statistisches Bundesamt; own calculations.

All in all, West Germany's return to the world market initiated a long chain of efficiency gains through capital formation and structural change which gave the economy a miraculous appearance of growth dynamics. For a virtuous circle of this kind to carry an economy all the way from a state of extreme capital shortage to a state of extreme labour shortage, two major conditions have to be met. First, there must not be any longer-term profit squeeze (for instance, through aggressive wage increases), so that the profitability of investment remains high and thus persistently invites firms to close the capital gap. Second, there must not be any major counterproductive institutional reform projects which would reduce the elasticity of aggregate goods supply by, for example, discouraging capital formation and/or work effort. As we shall see below, both conditions were met in the West Germany of the 1950s.

(1) Wage policy. As a whole, the 1950s were a time of decreasing labour costs and widening profit margins (see Table 8): the nominal wage level rose fast (7.9 per cent p.a.), but its rise was outpaced by the combined increase of labour productivity (5.7 per cent p.a.) and producer prices as measured by the value-added deflator (3.0 per cent p.a.), so that real unit labour costs (RULC) declined. This holds for both the first and the second halves of the decade, with the decline being somewhat more dramatic in the early than in the later years. Looking over the yearly changes of RULC, we can see that a rough cyclical pattern emerges, with marked

Table 8. *The determinants of labour costs 1950–60[a]*

	(1) W	(2) LP	(3) PC	(4) PV	(5) PV/PC	(6) RULC
1950–51	15.8	7.0	8.2	11.8	3.4	−3.2
1951–52	8.3	6.9	1.4	4.7	3.2	−3.3
1952–53	5.9	6.0	−1.0	−1.3	−0.4	1.2
1953–54	5.0	4.7	0.2	−0.3	−0.5	0.6
1954–55	8.1	7.8	1.4	2.1	0.7	−1.8
1955–56	8.0	4.6	1.9	2.7	0.8	0.6
1956–57	6.6	3.6	2.5	2.8	0.4	0.0
1957–58	6.9	3.5	2.7	2.9	0.2	0.4
1958–59	5.6	6.6	0.8	1.6	0.9	−2.5
1959–60	9.0	6.8	1.1	3.2	2.0	−1.0
1950–55	8.6	6.5	2.0	3.3	1.3	−1.3
1955–60	7.2	5.0	1.8	2.6	0.8	−0.5
1950–60	7.9	5.7	1.9	3.0	1.1	−0.9

Notes: [a] Average annual rates of change of selected variables (in per cent).
(1) W = wage level defined as average gross yearly earnings of employees (including social security contributions of employers); (2) LP = labour productivity defined as gross domestic product at constant prices divided by active labour force; (3) PC = private consumption deflator; (4) PV = deflator of value added (i.e. gross domestic product); (5) PV/PC = ratio of PV to PC as defined in note to (4) and (3) respectively; (6) RULC = real unit labour cost defined as W/(LP·PV) as defined in notes to (1), (2) and (4) respectively.
Source: Statistisches Bundesamt; own calculations.

decreases in the upswings 1950/1, 1954/5 and again 1958–60, and only slight increases in between. Note that the ratio of producer to consumer prices PV/PC (column 5 in Table 8) follows a very similar intertemporal pattern as RULC, albeit in reverse: all major RULC decreases have a counterpart in substantial increases of PV/PC, and both columns reveal a clear-cut cyclical pattern. In economic terms, this means that – de facto – wage policy allowed firms to keep their terms-of-trade gains as profits for investment purposes. By definition, these gains are due to the manifold divergences between the structure of production and that of consumption, i.e. – in the 1950s – to the large terms-of-trade gains of both West German exports relative to imports[53] and investment goods relative to consumption goods. Thus, through this peculiar kind of wage moderation in the form of disregard for the terms-of-trade gains in times of business-cycle upswings, the profitability of investment was kept high.

[53] For details on the terms-of-trade gains, see Section B of this chapter.

Why did labour – represented by unions[54] – allow this to happen? After all, the principle of *Tarifautonomie* (autonomous collective bargaining) was re-established by law in April 1949, and it gave unions and employers' associations the right to negotiate over working conditions and wages without any government interference, even without compulsory arbitration by the government, which had still been the last resort in the legal framework of the Weimar Republic from 1919 to 1933. Hence, in principle, the unions had a free hand to pursue an aggressive wage policy. There are at least four plausible (and non-exclusive) explanations for the unions' apparent restraint which may be summarized under the headings (i) organizational weakness, (ii) political distraction, (iii) economic surprise, and (iv) social responsibility. We shall discuss each of them briefly.

(i) It has been argued, for instance, by Olson (1982), that the caesura of a lost war and foreign occupation destroyed the traditional network of distributional coalitions in West Germany; as a consequence, unions lost part of their power and political strength. Thus, for a decade or so, there was plenty of scope for the economy to grow unburdened by the corporatist sclerosis which is typical of stable democratic societies.[55]

This theory contains an important element of truth for the explanation of union behaviour in the first two years after the currency reform of June 1948. Before that date, unions had been particularly favoured by the Allied authorities in receiving permission and support for the rebuilding of their organizations since union leaders had been quite consistently in opposition to the National Socialist regime. Yet, the currency reform destroyed much of their funds, so that for a while they were simply not able to carry out any major strike. When the economy was flourishing, however, this soon changed and strikes became financially feasible again, probably as early as 1950. Note in this respect that the West Germany of the 1950s may be considered a paradise of peaceful

---

[54] West German unions are organized on an industrial level, which means that all unionized workers of a given branch of industry, irrespective of their occupation, are members of one single union. Collective agreements are concluded on a regional basis, i.e. roughly on the level of states, with employers mostly organized on an industry level as well; a considerable number of large companies negotiate their own arrangements. As all sixteen industrial trade unions are associated in an umbrella organization, the 1949-founded Deutscher Gewerkschaftsbund (DGB), the industrial and regional wage bargaining is de facto heavily synchronized, with some industries like metal-manufacturing playing a leading role as a pacemaker for wage-setting. Another central organization – the Deutsche Angestelltengewerkschaft (DAG) – comprises mainly salaried employees of all branches of industry. Although it is not organized on an industry basis, the DAG and the unions representing individual industries usually adopt the same practice as far as the conclusion of collective agreements is concerned. In addition, there are several small unions of Christian orientation which do not play any significant part in collective bargaining. For details, see OECD (1979), pp. 58–67, and Paqué (1993a), pp. 209–24.

[55] See Olson (1982), pp. 75–6.

labour relations compared to other industrialized countries such as the United Kingdom, the United States, France or Italy and compared to its own past of the Weimar Republic. Yet, by West Germany's later standards, the period was not quite so calm: out of eight years in the period 1950–90 in which more than one million working days per year were lost through strikes, four – 1951, 1953, 1954 and 1957 – fell into the 1950s.[56]

Other indicators also point in the direction of organizational strength rather than weakness. Throughout the first half of the 1950s, the unionization rate was high, both by international standards and by historical standards of later periods: in 1951/2, more than 45 per cent of all employees were union members,[57] more than at any other later time of West German economic history up to the present. Until about 1965, this share declined to about 36 per cent, mostly through the sharp increase of employment of workers who were still non-unionized; however, in the 1950s, the absolute number of union members still grew by an average of about 1.6 per cent p.a. Hence, it would be somewhat misleading to speak of a dramatic weakening of the unions' (numerical) power base. The same holds for the unions' voice in politics and economic policy counselling. As to politics, it is clear that the centre–right federal government as a whole and the Ministry of Economics in particular had, if anything, an anti-union bias. Nevertheless, it would be wrong to regard the unions' umbrella organization – the 1949-founded Deutscher Gewerkschaftsbund (DGB) – as politically powerless: its first president, the prestigious Hans Böckler, was on good terms with Chancellor Adenauer (whom he had known well from the 1920s, when Adenauer was the mayor of Cologne). Most notably, the fierce political debate on the co-determination law in 1950/1 was settled by the deliberate use of the personal ties between the Chancellor and the union leadership.[58] In addition, the Labour Ministry was traditionally open-minded towards labour and union concerns. As to economic policy counselling, the unions' Institute of Economic Research in Düsseldorf – until the mid 1950s headed by the radical Marxist economist Viktor Agartz – played a much more prominent role in the policy debate than it did in later years. At that time, today's impressive battery of independent institutions of economic research and policy advice was not yet fully developed, so that even the unions' academic voice – although clearly biased – could hardly be missed in the public.

On a more general political level, Olson's theory of corporatist weakness

---

[56] See, inter alia, Langfeldt (1987), p. 28.
[57] *Ibid.*, p. 28; Langfeldt includes all employees belonging to a union which is affiliated to one of the three umbrella organizations DGB (Deutscher Gewerkschaftsbund), DAG (Deutsche Angestelltengewerkschaft) and DDB (Deutscher Beamtenbund).
[58] See Schwarz (1981), pp. 128–30.

as applied to post-war Germany is fundamentally at odds with the observations of contemporaneous critics of growing corporatist power. As early as 1955, the renowned liberal historian Theodor Eschenburg published a brilliant booklet on the rule of associations and federations (*Herrschaft der Verbände*)[59] in which he gave many convincing (and apparently altogether typical) examples of the dense network of influence and even infiltration which all major interest groups – be they political, religious or economic – maintained not only in politics, but also in public administration. Hence, to view West German society in the 1950s as temporarily released from the detrimental grip of interest groups through the long-lasting blow of war-time destruction and foreign occupation is to miss a good deal, if not the core, of the spirit of the age.

In summary, the image of organizationally weak unions is hardly borne out by the facts, except in the first two years after the currency reform, when strike funds were still insufficient. If at all, the 'weakness' of the unions must have been of a more indirect sort.

(ii) Wallich (1955) has argued that West German unions were distracted from pursuing an aggressive wage policy by their own syndicalist demands for co-determination, which provoked a heavy political controversy over the passing of two laws, the *Mitbestimmungsgesetz* in 1951 and the *Betriebsverfassungsgesetz* in 1952.[60] As both laws were bound to set the frame for industrial organization in the decades to come, it is not surprising that the unions – just like the employers' associations and the confederation of industry – took them very seriously and invested much effort and political argument in lobbying for their respective cause. Clearly, the protracted controversy over these laws makes Wallich's point look plausible: given the strong syndicalist aspirations of German unions which go back to the 1920s, it would have been a quite rational strategy for them to stand still temporarily at the wage front so as not to endanger the far more daring prospect of a thoroughly syndicalist 'industrial democracy'. Nevertheless, it is only a very partial explanation of union restraint in the 1950s, since the co-determination issue virtually disappeared from the political agenda after 1952. Furthermore, the final outcome of the two laws – especially the later one – was widely regarded as a bad defeat for the unions' cause; hence, one should have observed something like a backlash thereafter, with wage policy becoming more aggressive. However, it took another two years until, in 1954, hefty wage increases were demanded and granted; fortunately, they did not lead to a sharp increase of real unit labour costs, since the boom pushed up labour productivity growth to a quite unexpected degree.

---

[59] See Eschenburg (1955).   [60] Wallich (1955), pp. 307–10.

(iii) This leads to the theory of economic surprise, which states that union wage demands were not particularly cautious and restrained, but persistently outpaced by the actual supply-side expansion and the resulting labour productivity gains; thus, what may have looked ex-ante like an aggressive wage policy turned out to be quite moderate in terms of real unit labour costs. Of course, it is impossible to test this hypothesis rigorously since at that time no serious quantitative forecasts of macroeconomic variables were made which could serve as a basis for identifying the price and productivity expectations of the relevant economic agents; neither does the prior economic history yield a firm basis for modelling something like adaptive expectations, since it would obviously be far-fetched to assume that the extraordinary events of the early years after the currency reform were – in some way or another – extrapolated into the future.

Nevertheless, there are at least two more general observations which lend some support to the theory in question. First, the 1950s must be considered as a time of large and increasing wage drift. Figure 9 shows the intertemporal pattern of wage drift for the investment goods industry:[61] in any single year, the effective wage rose faster than the contractual minimum wage, with the drift widening in the second half of the decade. This is somewhat unusual: in other periods of unemployment such as after 1973, wage drift followed a strongly cyclical pattern, being positive in booms and often turning negative in cyclical downswings, when extra payments were increased at a lower rate than the contractual minimum wage. This indicates that, in the 1950s, union demands quite persistently lagged behind what firms could bear. Without any recourse to strong elements of positively frustrated expectations, i.e. a general underestimation of the trend growth of productivity, it is hard to rationalize this kind of moderate union behaviour.

Second, the rhetoric of the unions and the counter-rhetoric of business and the liberal press were by no means moderate throughout. In particular, Viktor Agartz – until the mid 1950s chairman of the unions' Economic Research Institute – repeatedly called for sharp wage increases either by criticizing productivity guidelines for wage policy or by arguing for a kind of purchasing-power theory of wages which stated, in a quite unqualified fashion, that wage increases spur a non-inflationary economic expansion by fuelling demand and by forcing firms to raise labour productivity through rationalization investments. In 1954, it was widely acclaimed that

---

[61] For expository convenience, only data for the investment goods industry are used; however, about the same intertemporal pattern of wage drift is detectable for other branches of industry. See Statistisches Bundesamt, *Wirtschaft und Statistik* (1961), pp. 680–3.

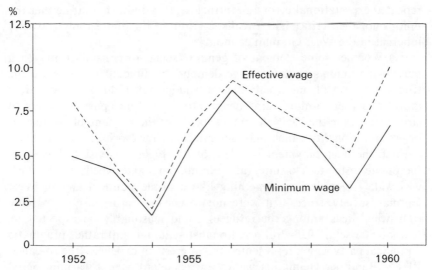

Figure 9. Wage drift in the investment goods industry 1952–60.
Note: Average annual increase of contractual minimum and effective hourly wage in the investment goods industry (index change in per cent).
Source: Statistisches Bundesamt: own calculations.

these calls were a prelude to the first major wave of strikes for higher wages in autumn 1954.[62] On the other hand, the repeated warnings by the liberal press that the wage claims made at the time were likely to lead to an inflationary spiral quite often had a tone of deep concern and urgency, especially in the boom periods 1950/1, 1954/5 and 1959/60.[63] In the same vein, the Minister of Economics Ludwig Erhard, repeatedly issued passionate *Maßhalteappelle* ('calls for moderation') to the public which were intended to ease inflationary pressures through moral persuasion.[64] Apparently, most professional observers consistently underestimated the potential for productivity growth. Of course, by any scientific standards, all these verbal statements are no more than soft evidence of

[62] See, inter alia, *Die Zeit* of 28 January 1954, 'Ein lohnpolitischer Fanfarenstoß – Die neuangelegte "Gruppentheorie" des Herrn Agartz gibt doch etwas zu denken'; *Der Volkswirt* of 30 January 1954, 'Lärm an der Lohnfront'; *Frankfurter Allgemeine Zeitung* of 18 July 1954, 'Expansive Lohnpolitik heute?'; and *The Economist* of 14 August 1954, 'Strike and Boom in Germany'.
[63] See, inter alia, *Der Volkswirt* of 11 August 1950; Theo Eymüller, 'Radikale Lohnforderungen'; *Frankfurter Allgemeine Zeitung* of 28 July 1951, Hans Roeper, 'Die Lohnschraube'; *Handelsblatt* of 23 September 1955, C. O. Heuser, 'Droht uns ein großer Katzenjammer?'; *Handelsblatt* of 17 December 1959, 'Vor Welle neuer Lohnforderungen'; *Frankfurter Allgemeine Zeitung* of 21 December 1959, E. G. Vetter, 'Sturmzeichen in der Lohnpolitik'.   [64] See Schwarz (1981), p. 324.

repeated expectational errors; nevertheless, they indicate that neither the unions nor their critics had a realistic vision of the high supply elasticity inherent in the West German economy.

(iv) Whether some element of genuine social responsibility played a part in the union's cautious wage demands is difficult to say, since the true motivation of union activities is usually well hidden in a cloud of moral and pseudo-moral arguments. However, three particular sets of circumstances in the 1950s do in fact speak for the working of an element of group rationality which may deserve the name 'social responsibility'.

First, the unemployment problem of the 1950s was visibly linked by the public to the task of integrating immigrants and expellees. This task was widely regarded as something like a prime political aim of West German society, since, if it were not reached, a resurgence of extreme right-wing ideas among the refugees could reasonably be expected. A temporary rise in 1950–2 of a nationalist – though still rather pragmatic – political party which represented the interests of expellees (the so-called BHE – Bund der Heimatlosen und Entrechteten) gave a warning signal that a right-wing potential of this kind might in fact become a threat to political stability;[65] as the unions as a whole had left-wing and anti-nationalist leanings, some wage restraint to ease the integration of refugees would certainly have been the rational answer.

Second, the trauma of inflation remained severe, particularly among low- and middle-income workers who had lost most of their savings in the currency reform. Clearly, an aggressive stance in wage policy which would have run the risk of spurring a wage–price spiral was not very popular among the rank-and-file, and union leaders could not simply by-pass this mood. Thus, the repeated warnings of the liberal press not to rekindle inflation might have frightened the average union member more than was officially admitted.

Third, the positive developments of the early 1950s may have contributed to a calming down of the workers: even with some restraint, real wage growth by itself looked more than satisfactory for workers and gave them the confidence that, even without any turn to militancy, many of their material aspirations might be fulfilled within a fairly short time horizon. Only abstract notions like a (properly measured) shrinking wage share in national income might have motivated them to increase their demands; however, with the spirit of hard work prevailing after the misery of the early post-war years, these notions looked fairly academic. Thus, the repeated attempts of union economists to bring the wage share to the

[65] On the BHE, see *ibid.*, pp. 50–1, 119–20, 166–9.

attention of the public did not initiate anything like a persistent mass movement for higher wages.

In summary, all four explanations of union restraint have their part to play: organizational weakness in the years 1948–50, but not later; political distraction in the period 1951/2; economic surprise and rational elements of social responsibility throughout, but probably to a slowly decreasing extent, since people gradually became accustomed to high growth and the most urgent social problems were obviously solved. Hence, it is not surprising that the first significant 'wage revolution' was to happen in 1960, at the beginning of a new decade.

(2) Institutional reform. The 1950s were a time of important new laws in the realm of economic and social policy. We shall consider this legislation only to the extent that it is likely to have exerted a substantial impact on the economy's aggregate supply elasticity, i.e. on the supply and allocation of labour and capital, and on the efficient working of the market order in general.

As to the supply and allocation of labour, three reform packages stand out: (i) the step-by-step income tax reforms from 1948 to 1955, (ii) the laws on the equalization of war burdens in 1949 and 1952, and (iii) the restructuring of the old-age pension scheme in 1957.

(i) To ensure a balanced government budget in the occupied German territory, the Allies imposed a steeply progressive income tax schedule in 1946, with marginal tax rates reaching prohibitive levels at very low nominal incomes.[66] A somewhat more moderate tax schedule was introduced with the currency reform in June 1948; by all conventional standards, however, it was still very progressive, with marginal tax rates reaching about 80 per cent at a yearly gross income of 80,000 DMarks (in 1986 prices).[67] As mentioned above, the potential disincentive effect on work effort and saving were strongly mitigated by the long list of tax exemptions for certain kinds of capital formation. In the subsequent reform steps of 1950, 1953 (the so-called little tax reform) and 1955 (the so-called grand tax reform), the schedule was significantly flattened for all income ranges, with the top marginal tax rate fixed at 55 per cent. At the same time, most of the prior tax concessions for capital formation and the rebuilding of war-damaged equipment were either completely abolished or restricted to selected groups, mostly the refugees.[68] As these concessions had played a tremendous quantitative role, the reforms were

[66] See Wallich (1955), pp. 66–7; Boss (1987), pp. 4–5.   [67] See Boss (1987), p. 22.
[68] For details, see *ibid.*, pp. 31–4.

bound to have only minor incentive effects on work effort, at least in the higher income brackets; taking a long-run perspective, however, they were clearly necessary steps in the direction of a supply-friendly non-distortive tax system.[69]

(ii) There was a general consensus in the late 1940s that the burden of war damage and destruction was very unequally distributed in the population. For example, refugees lost their homes and all their belongings, while many other people were fortunate enough to incur no capital losses. Besides, the currency reform had been carried out without much social cushioning, so that some fundamental correction of wealth distribution was widely considered to be overdue. The task was tackled with the Emergency Aid Law (*Soforthilfegesetz*) in 1949, which fixed preliminary rules for compensation payments, and the Law for the Equalization of War Burdens (*Lastenausgleichsgesetz*) in 1952, which set the definitive legal framework. Taken at face value, this law had quite outstanding egalitarian features: its main point was a wealth tax of 50 per cent levied on all property held (and assessed) on the day of the currency reform; the tax revenue was to be paid into a fund from which legitimate claimants received compensation for war losses of their property. Of course, it was technically impossible to enforce an immediate payment of the huge sum of 84 billion DMarks which the tax was calculated to raise in revenues; therefore, the tax liability was due to be paid in annuities up to the year 1979.

Theoretically, the two laws on the equalization of the war burdens were remarkable achievements of redistribution without any excess burden: a large share of the country's wealth was to be reshuffled, and nobody could escape it by substituting leisure for work, since capital values were calculated ex-post. In practice, the achievement looked much less impressive, at least in quantitative terms: as property values shot up in the 1950s because of fast economic growth and later on a creeping inflation, the effective transfer as a share of current national wealth was sharply reduced. As early as the late 1950s, it did not play any major part in the people's minds. After all, it was the very success of the West German economy which reduced an originally daring venture to a quite marginal affair.[70]

---

[69] Nevertheless, complaints by economists were justified to the effect that many tax concessions which obviously had no convincing economic or social rationale remained untouched in the reform simply because lobbying groups strongly resisted cutbacks to their disadvantage. See Dreißig (1976), p. 713.

[70] On the genesis of the *Lastenausgleichsgesetz*, see Stolper (1964), pp. 317–19, and Schwarz (1981), pp. 166–9. An idea of collective burden-sharing also underlay the so-called Emergency Aid to Berlin (*Notopfer Berlin*), which was introduced in October 1948 to help the city of West Berlin to overcome its economic difficulties caused by geographical isolation and political uncertainty. Broadly speaking, the Emergency Aid to Berlin was

(iii) In the 1880s, Otto von Bismarck had established a social security system which was to encompass a more or less compulsory public insurance for old age, health, accidents and disability.[71] By and large, this system survived the late Kaiserreich, the Weimar Republic and both World Wars; in the 1920s, it was supplemented by a public unemployment insurance which crowded out prior private insurance schemes run and financed by the unions. In essence, the social security system came down to a compulsory public insurance provision for a large section – mostly the less wealthy – of the population, with half of individual insurance contributions paid by the employers and half by the employees. In the case of old-age pensions, the insurance was funded, but from the mid 1920s no longer fully funded. Because of the currency reform in 1948 – or more precisely, because of the suppressed inflation which preceded it – the capital stock of the pension fund had been grossly devalued; to prevent the pensions from falling below subsistence levels, annual parliamentary decisions on pension increases broadly in step with the rise of the wage level had become the rule in the first few years of the Federal Republic of Germany. The bulk of these increases was financed by the current stream of contributions, so that the pension scheme had already de facto moved a good distance away from a funded to a pure pay-as-you-go system. Nevertheless, there was close to a consensus that pensions were in general much too low and that, in due course, an overhauling of the scheme should be on the political agenda.

In his message to the newly elected parliament in 1953, Chancellor Adenauer promised a thoroughgoing reform of the whole social security system. After much political haggling, the reform was finally limited to old-age pensions.[72] By the pension reform law (*Rentenreformgesetz*) of 1957, the pay-as-you-go principle was legally sanctioned. In addition, pensions were 'dynamized', i.e. – roughly speaking – the annual increases were officially linked to the rise of gross wages. To be sure, the actual implementation of the index link between pensions and wages still had to be confirmed by a yearly parliamentary decision; but at least until the mid 1970s, this decision proved to be a mere formality.

The whole reform was very popular, not least because it led to a hefty increase in pensions by 60–75 per cent in one stroke. This once-and-for-all

set as a fixed levy on gross income, at the beginning about 1 per cent, and after 1951 a higher percentage share of gross income. In the mid 1950s, the revenue of the Emergency Aid to Berlin amounted to about 6 per cent of total tax revenue. In 1956, it was abolished for individuals, but not yet for corporate income tax returns. For details, see Boss (1987), pp. 40–1.

[71] On the history of the German social security system from imperial times to the early 1980s, see Hentschel (1983), pp. 11–29.

[72] For the political details of the reform debate, see Schwarz (1981), pp. 327–36.

rise was granted a few months before the federal parliamentary elections in September 1957, so that no pensioner could miss the message of public generosity; the absolute majority which the Christian Democrats reached for the first (and so far the last) time in post-war parliamentary history was at least partly due to this kind of well-timed 'bribery'. However, among liberal economists and even within the cabinet – notably in the Ministries of Economics and Finance – there was no lack of critical voices whose arguments were logically impeccable and far-sighted: a pay-as-you-go system postpones the burden of payment for the pensions of today's working population to future generations; if, in addition, pensions are indexed to gross wages, the burden of payment as a percentage of the gross wage increases whenever the age structure, i.e. the ratio of pensioners to workers, worsens. As the social security contributions in a non-funded system look very much like an ordinary tax – after all, a 'payroll tax' – any increase of contributions may lead to the same disincentive effect on work effort as a straight income tax increase. All this became relevant in later decades and provoked much political lamentation about a crisis in the old-age pension scheme. In the 1950s, however, these problems did not yet show up: to finance current pensions, a moderate increase of the respective payroll tax rate from 5 per cent in 1954 and 5.5 per cent in 1955/6 to 7 per cent of gross income in 1957 was sufficient;[73] as there was an almost parallel cut of the contribution to unemployment insurance from 2 per cent in 1954 to 1 per cent of gross income in 1957, all this looked quite acceptable. For a while, the reform seemed to give everybody a free lunch, but it was bound to raise some major supply-side issues in the future.

As to the supply and allocation of capital, three major reform projects deserve mentioning: (i) the Investment Aid Law (*Investitionshilfegesetz*) of January 1952, (ii) the Law for the Encouragement of the Capital Market (*Kapitalmarktförderungsgesetz*) of December 1952, and (iii) the public support of investment in housing as fixed in a number of housing laws beginning in 1950.

(i) The Investment Aid Law was one of the few excursions of the West German government into deliberate investment planning: the so-called bottleneck sectors – mining, steel and energy – which had for long been subject to price controls were to be given a chance to overcome their narrow constraints of self-financing so as to invest in carefully chosen projects which were particularly important for widening the productive capacity of the economy as a whole. For this purpose, business at large was forced to give a (compulsory) credit of 1 billion DMarks to a special

---

[73] For the numbers, see Bothe (1987), p. 22.

fund; the individual contributions to the credit fund were calculated on the basis of prior profits in 1950 and 1951. A board of fund administrators then had to decide which projects were worthy of being carried out; this was done on the basis of quotas for the different industries which were fixed by the Minister of Economics beforehand, presumably on the basis of some informal calculation of social rates of return.[74] In addition, special accelerated depreciation allowances were granted for firms in the bottle-neck sectors. The law was set to expire after two years, i.e. at the end of 1954.

It is very difficult to evaluate whether and to what extent the law really helped to widen serious bottlenecks. The relatively short duration of the measures and their limited scope make it hard to imagine a counterfactual scenario, with market forces given a chance to do the required work. In any case, the bottlenecks emerging in the Korea boom were finally overcome, but the question whether this was to any significant extent due to the Investment Aid Law or simply the natural consequence of rapid growth throughout the economy remains unanswered.

(ii) Until the mid 1950s, there was no free market for bonds in West Germany. Through a virtually complete control of emissions, the long-term interest rate was limited to 5 per cent p.a. on mortgage and 6.5 per cent p.a. on industrial bonds so as to avoid squeezing credit for residential construction while housing rents were still fixed. Naturally, the effect was to reduce the scope of the capital market for all users. As a consequence, the emission of securities played no more than a marginal role for business finance; instead, investment was mainly financed by tapping retained earnings which were large because of high profits, and by bank loans. In the early 1950s, the narrowness of the capital market had become a recurrent theme of economists' complaints: the Advisory Council alone dedicated three reports exclusively to this topic, in which an increasingly urgent case was made for at least a partial liberalization of the bond market.[75] This finally happened through the Law for the Encouragement of the Capital Market (*Kapitalmarktförderungsgesetz*) of December 1952, which removed the interest-rate ceiling. In addition, tax concessions were granted for the interest on bonds issued by public authorities and by those private or semi-private institutions acknowledged as acting in the public interest (for instance, by investing in low-rent housing);[76] industrial bonds were subjected to a flat 30 per cent coupon

[74] For details on the Investment Aid Law, see Stolper and Roskamp (1979), pp. 395–6, Roskamp (1965), p. 168, and Boss (1987), pp. 38–40.
[75] See Wissenschaftlicher Beirat (1973), pp. 101–8 (report of 10 December 1950), pp. 139–42 (report of 4 February 1952), and pp. 151–3 (report of 6 July 1952).
[76] For details of the law, see Wallich (1955), pp. 185–6, and Boss (1987), pp. 37–8.

tax instead of ordinary income tax. The law was set to expire at the end of 1954, and from then on, the market for long-term bonds was basically free and undistorted by tax reliefs for housing. Clearly, the law had the – merely compensatory – purpose of keeping funds in housing investments, despite an increase of interest rates on industrial bonds which could be expected for the time after the liberalization. As such, it was a mere appendix to the regulation in the (politically sensitive) housing market.

(iii) At least until the mid 1950s, there was an extreme housing shortage in West Germany, and no major political force dared to advocate anything resembling a free-market solution to this problem, since it would have resulted in an extremely unpopular drastic rise in rents. Instead, rent control, which had been common in the Weimar Republic, was simply retained. To increase the supply of residential housing despite artificially low rents, an elaborate system of heavily subsidized and tax-favoured social construction (*Sozialer Wohnungsbau*) was established with the so-called first housing law (*Erstes Wohnungsbaugesetz*) of 1950. Note that this happened on top of the generous tax privileges which already existed for housing investments. More than one-half of all funds channelled into housing in the 1950s were public, either in the form of expenditure on public projects, cash subsidies or foregone tax revenues. Clearly, this was a major effort in investment planning, which, in quantitative terms, turned out to be quite successful: from 1949 to 1959, 5.1 million dwelling units were built, more than half a million a year. Whether a more liberal solution would have been equally successful is a matter of speculation; theoretically at least, a system with free rents, but a 'social cushion' of earmarked transfers to people in need, could have done the same job, maybe with fewer negative by-products in the form of poor housing quality and architectural blunders in urban design which were deplored in later decades. Still more importantly, a liberal solution could have avoided the strangling of the market for long-term industrial bonds so that firms in the early 1950s would have had easier access to household (and foreign) savings. After the housing shortage had been mitigated somewhat, rent control was set to be gradually abolished. However, there was nothing like a free housing market until 1963; even then, a stiff system of regulations to protect tenants' rights remained.[77]

As to the general market order of the economy, two major projects stand out: (i) the so-called Law against Restrictions of Competition (*Gesetz gegen Wettbewerbsbeschränkungen*) and (ii) the legislation concerning co-determination (*Mitbestimmung*).

[77] For a summary evaluation of West German housing policy in the 1950s, see Stolper (1964), pp. 315–17.

(i) In Ordoliberal philosophy, which underlies the design of the West German social market economy, a thoroughgoing anti-trust and anti-cartel legislation has a central place: it is to ensure that free markets do not degenerate through private collusive arrangements or company mergers into cartels or trusts which exercise considerable monopolistic power and control the entry and exit conditions of their markets. Traditionally, German law had been relatively kind to private market restrictions: the cartel law of 1923 did not outlaw cartels, but merely prohibited a vaguely defined abuse of cartel power. After the liberal reforms of 1948, a long and severe controversy arose about how far a prohibition of cartel-like arrangements should be carried: most economists – among them the Advisory Council to the Federal Minister of Economics[78] – favoured tough anti-cartel rules, while the West German confederation of industry and business at large preferred a much softer line. In 1957, after almost ten years of political haggling, a new German cartel law was finally passed. In principle, it outlawed cartels, but it left enough room for many far-reaching exemptions such as cartels for the purposes of regulating the restructuring of an industry, discount conditions and international trade practices. In addition, any cartel could be permitted by the Minister of Economics if there were major public interests at stake.[79] Furthermore, a newly established federal cartel office was to supervise the market behaviour of firms with a so-called market-dominating position. In practice, however, the office had very little factual power, since it turned out to be quite difficult for it to acquire the relevant information on firms' market activities. In general, it is safe to say that the efficiency of the West German market economy as a competitive supply-side machine was the outcome much less of internal market supervision via some public agency than of external pressure from world markets.

(ii) Co-determination had been a long-standing aim of German unions, going back to the time after the First World War when works councils with still very limited responsibilities were established. After the Second World War, the political climate looked quite favourable for a substantial deepening of 'industrial democracy' simply because, in the iron and steel industry of the British zone, which included the important Ruhr area, labour directors had already been installed on the company boards by the Allies so as to prevent the former owners from taking

---

[78] See, above all, its report of 24 July 1949, on fundamental questions of cartel legislation, reprinted in Wissenschaftlicher Beirat (1973), pp. 41–5.

[79] For a summary of the West German anti-cartel and anti-trust legislation, see Stolper (1964), pp. 291–3, and Langfeldt (1987), pp. 17–19.

control again. Broadly speaking, a parity-model was realized, with the eleven members of the supervisory board comprising five representatives from both capital and labour, and one neutral member who was to be nominated by the other directors. On the board of managers, there was one labour representative responsible for matters of personnel. He could be appointed only with the explicit consent of the works council and the relevant industrial unions.

This parity model was set to expire as soon as a freely elected West German parliament had decided on a new form of labour representation. Not surprisingly, the unions recognized the opportunity for lobbying for retaining co-determination in the iron and steel industry and for demanding a more syndicalist structure of the economy as a whole, with industrial councils and chambers above the company level being established and subjected to a fair amount of union control. In effect, these demands came close to abolishing the decentralized market economy in favour of a syndicalist and at least partly planned system. After a heavy political controversy, the steelworkers' union called a one-day strike to underline their legislative demands. This happened in early January 1951, right at the peak of the Korea boom, so that a longer stoppage in the iron and steel industry would have hit the economy very badly indeed. In a kind of last-minute summit meeting, Chancellor Adenauer and the DGB Chairman Hans Böckler struck a deal: the status quo was to be preserved, but more far-reaching syndicalist demands were rejected. The West German parliament finally passed a co-determination law (*Mitbestimmungs-gesetz*) to this end on 23 February 1951, but in opposition to the liberal party, which regarded Adenauer's concessions as an unacceptable break with the principles of a market economy. In fact, the risks were high, since the model of co-determination had only been tested for a very short period in the quite unusual circumstances of the years 1948–50. Whether the elements of syndicalism at the company level, which the law provided, were to hamper economic efficiency in the future was unclear.

A year later, the same type of controversy arose again when the passage of the so-called Company Statute Law (*Betriebsverfassungsgesetz*) moved on to the agenda of parliament. As the status quo in industries other than iron and steel was not a parity model, the unions had a much weaker bargaining position than in the prior debate. Given the strong opposition of the liberals and the business wing of the Christian Democrats in the government coalition, a general extension of the iron and steel model to the rest of the economy was out of reach. The framework which was finally adopted in October 1952 gave just one-third of the seats on the supervisory board to labour representatives; again, the responsibility of the works councils was restricted to personnel matters. The commercial part of business remained completely out of labour's control.[80]

In general, the experience with co-determination in iron and steel and, in the less extended form, in the rest of the economy turned out to be better than many businessmen and economists had expected: at the level of the individual firm, the cooperation between capital and labour worked quite smoothly, at least in the 1950s and early 1960s. It is hard to say whether this was due to the economy's fast overall growth, which made all potential conflicts look less acute, or to the particular character of the works councils, which, as experience showed, were much more down-to-earth in their demands than union leaders, who were not attached to the interests of a single company. For the time being, the economy was spared major social conflicts which might have paralysed its capacity to respond quickly to the requirements of structural change. However, in the longer run, fears of syndicalist dangers remained and would prove justified if, for whatever reason, labour turned more militant.[81]

On the whole, the major institutional reform projects of the 1950s may deserve the attribute 'supply-friendly', at least under the prevailing favourable economic circumstances and social climate of the decade. Most importantly, income taxes were cut and capital formation and housing were subsidized, so that – despite lingering price controls in these fields – the successive widening of the economy's capacities was not hampered; by the mid 1950s, the long-term capital markets were basically liberalized and the main distortions in favour of housing removed. However, it should not be forgotten that some significant liabilities were created which could turn into major problems in due course. This holds above all for the pension reform and the new dimensions of syndicalism. Yet for the time being, the balance was clearly positive.

[80] For the genesis and details of the co-determination and the company statute law, see Stolper (1964), pp. 327–9, Hentschel (1983), pp. 247–54, and Langfeldt (1987), pp. 12–16.
[81] It is interesting to see that independent Anglo-American observers were at first heavily critical of the law as a major defeat to the German market economy, but later took notice of the reasonably good experience. See, inter alia, The Economist of 10 February 1951, 'Trade Union Triumph in Germany'; the Financial Times of 21 July 1952, 'German Labour in Management'; the Wall Street Journal of 16 October 1956, 'German Experience in Labor Management Program is Described'; The Economist of 16 August 1958, 'Germany's Syndicalist Experiment'.

B   Returning to the world market

West Germany's economic performance in the first twelve years after the liberal reforms of 1948 has been widely acclaimed as an outstanding success. The most spectacular feature of the post-war miracle, and perhaps the key to understanding why it could happen at all, was the country's rapid re-emergence as one of the major trading nations of the world. In 1948, the western occupation zones of the former Reich had been an impoverished place dependent upon foreign aid to pay for two-thirds of its desperately needed imports.[1] By the mid 1950s, i.e. within less than a decade, West Germany had managed to boost its exports ahead of imports to such an extent that it came under almost permanent attacks from international organizations for its allegedly excessive trade surpluses. And by 1960, West Germany's share of both world imports and exports exceeded even those which the much larger German Reich had attained before the war. Below, we shall inquire into the causes and consequences of West Germany's spectacular return to the world market. The major internal causes of West Germany's supply elasticity in the face of burgeoning world demand have been dealt with above. After a brief survey of basic facts, we shall thus concentrate on how the initial external constraints were overcome and on the contribution of trade policy to the West German export miracle.

A casual look at some statistics shows how remarkable the development of West Germany's foreign trade really was in the twelve years under consideration. After a jump by 84.4 per cent p.a. in the two years from 1948 to 1950, admittedly from an extremely low level, exports continued to grow at an average annual rate of 16.1 per cent in real terms throughout the 1950s. Imports lagged behind with growth rates of 26.8 and 15.0 per cent respectively (see Table 9). Thus, West Germany reduced its trade deficit to a negligible amount[2] by 1951 and managed to run a sizeable surplus thereafter. Roughly in line with the cumulative trade surplus (7.3 billion dollars from 1951 to 1960), the foreign exchange reserves of the central bank increased from 0.16 billion at the end of 1950 to 7.8 billion dollars a decade later.[3]

The favourable development of West Germany's trade balance is attributable not only to the growth in volumes but also to a change in prices. From 1950 to 1960, the commodity terms of trade (average value of exports divided by average value of imports) improved by 40 per cent. This was not due only to lower prices for imports of important raw materials such as oil. For finished manufactured goods alone, the ratio

[1] Bank deutscher Länder (1951), p. 46.
[2] 35.5 m. dollars: Statistisches Bundesamt, *Statistisches Jahrbuch* (1953), p. 307.
[3] Statistisches Bundesamt (1974), pp. 92, 94, 161.

Table 9. *West Germany's foreign trade 1936–60*[a]

						Rate of growth[c]		
	1936[b]	1948	1950	1955	1960	1948–50	1950–60	1948–60
Imports								
Values	0.68[e]	1.55	2.70	5.82	10.17	31.9	14.2	16.9
Volumes[d]	2.40	1.68	2.70	5.67	10.94	26.8	15.0	16.9
Exports								
Values	0.81[e]	0.64	1.98	6.14	11.42	75.7	19.1	27.1
Volumes[d]	2.29	0.58	1.98	4.89	8.85	84.4	16.1	25.5
Balance of trade	0.13	−0.91	−0.72	0.32	1.25			
Terms of trade[e,f]	125	120	100	121	140			

Notes: [a] In billion dollars.
[b] Western parts of the German Reich.
[c] In per cent p.a.
[d] In 1950 prices; because of the difficulties of computing 1948 dollar prices, the 1948 numbers are indicative only.
[e] Converted at 4.20 RM = 1 dollar.
[f] 1950 = 100.
Sources: Statistisches Bundesamt and OEEC Foreign Trade Statistics; own calculations.

of export to import prices increased by 50 per cent, i.e. by even more than average. Germany's traditional strength in the production of capital goods paid off handsomely in the 1950s, when these goods were in particularly high demand on the world market. In addition, the change in relative prices testifies to the improving quality and sophistication of these export goods.

Together with the growth of trade volumes, the commodity structure of imports and exports changed. While foodstuffs had made up more than half of imports in 1948, manufactures were the most important category by the end of the 1950s (see Table 10). On the export side, raw materials and semi-manufactures (mainly coke and scrap) which had accounted for an extraordinarily high share of exports in 1948 were replaced by manufactures as the dominant category. Broadly speaking, the changes in the commodity structure of imports and exports between 1948 and 1955 are best described as a return to 'normal' conditions, i.e. to the trade pattern of the German Reich before the war, while the subsequent development can be interpreted as a first step towards an intensification of intra-industry trade, i.e. of exchanges of similar commodities between countries with similar factor endowments. A look at the breakdown of trade by regions (see Table 11) confirms that 1948 was still a year in which the pattern of trade was grossly distorted. Because of the aid-financed

Table 10. *Commodity structure of West Germany's foreign trade 1936–89 (respective share in % of total)*

Imports	1936[a]	1948[b]	1950	1955	1960	1965	1970	1973	1979	1985	1989
Foodstuffs	28.6	56.6	40.5	25.9	22.5	20.4	16.5	16.9	11.5	10.4	9.5
Stimulants	6.9	1.1	3.6	5.3	3.8	3.5	2.6	2.4	2.2	2.1	1.6
Raw materials	37.2	23.1	29.6	29.8	21.7	16.2	13.5	12.9	14.6	12.4	6.4
Semi-manufactures	17.8	14.3	13.8	20.1	18.9	15.3	16.1	14.8	17.2	18.7	12.5
Manufactures	9.4	4.9	12.6	19.0	32.2	43.5	50.0	51.8	53.3	54.8	68.5
Semi-finished goods	5.2	2.9	6.3	11.3	13.5	14.8	15.5	15.7	14.5	13.3	15.0
Finished goods	4.2	2.0	6.3	7.7	18.7	28.8	34.5	36.1	38.8	41.5	53.5

Exports	1936[a]	1948[b]	1950	1955	1960	1965	1970	1973	1979	1985	1989
Foodstuffs	1.2	0.4	1.4	2.2	1.9	2.3	3.0	4.0	4.3	4.2	4.2
Stimulants	0.6	2.3	0.9	0.5	0.4	0.5	0.5	0.5	0.7	1.0	0.8
Raw materials	8.8	25.2	14.0	6.1	4.6	3.6	2.5	2.3	2.1	1.6	1.2
Semi-manufactures	9.6	29.8	18.9	12.7	10.4	8.7	7.6	7.4	7.9	7.6	5.7
Manufactures	79.7	42.3	64.8	78.5	82.4	84.5	85.8	85.2	84.4	84.9	87.9
Semi-finished goods	26.9	22.4	22.3	18.5	20.2	18.6	18.4	18.7	18.7	17.3	16.9
Finished goods	52.8	19.9	42.6	60.0	62.2	65.9	67.4	66.6	65.7	67.7	71.0

Notes: [a] German Reich.
[b] Bizonia.
Source: Statistisches Bundesamt.

food imports from the US and the Allied efforts to supply Western Europe with West German coal, coke, timber and scrap, 56.8 per cent of all imports came from North America, while 86.7 per cent of exports went to Western Europe. By 1950, the pattern had returned to a state that could be called normal, with the share of exports to North America subsequently growing and that to Western Europe declining throughout the 1950s. Note, however, the redirection of trade from Eastern to Western Europe after the war: while trade with Eastern Europe had lost its prior importance almost completely, Western Europe had by 1950 assumed a double role as (West) Germany's major supplier and customer, which before the Second World War had quite naturally fallen to the entire continent, East and West.

As to world markets, the rapid rise of West Germany's share in world trade reveals the extent to which it outpaced its competitors. Back in 1948, barely 1.2 per cent of world exports had come from West Germany; until 1960, its exporters expanded their slice of the world markets by a

Table 11. *Regional structure of West Germany's foreign trade 1937–60 (% of total)*

Imports	1937[a]	1948	1950	1955	1960
Western Europe	36.2[b]	28.1[b]	52.4	50.8	54.0
North America	6.3	56.8	15.6	15.0	16.0
Eastern Europe	17.2	1.5	2.6	2.2	4.0
Rest of the world	40.3	13.6	29.4	32.0	26.0

Exports	1937[a]	1948	1950	1955	1960
Western Europe	52.0[b]	86.7[b]	72.0	64.8	63.5
North America	4.1	4.2	5.7	7.2	9.0
Eastern Europe	16.2	2.4	3.7	2.0	3.9
Rest of the world	27.7	6.7	18.6	26.0	25.6

Notes: [a] German Reich.
[b] Excluding Spain.
Sources: Statistisches Bundesamt and OEEC Foreign Trade Statistics; own calculations.

factor of nine. West Germany's corresponding share in world imports trebled from 2.9 per cent in 1948 to 8.9 per cent in 1960. As far as the importance of foreign trade for the domestic economy is concerned, the share of exports in GNP soared from 3.8 per cent in the second half of 1948 to 16.8 per cent in 1960, while the import share rose from 5.9 to 15.0 per cent respectively.

1   The dismal starting-point

The first and most obvious explanation for the spectacular expansion of West Germany's foreign trade in the late 1940s is that it did have to start from an abysmally low basis in the first place. As has been outlined in Chapter 2, Section 3 above, foreign trade on commercial terms had played hardly any role at all in the first three years after the Second World War. The major reasons for this were tight Allied control, the lack of incentives to export and the discrimination of West Germany's soft-currency trading partners against its overpriced dollar exports. Over the course of 1948 and 1949, the situation gradually changed. As of 1 December 1948, the Bizonal Joint Export and Import Agency (JEIA) restricted itself to a mere ex-post control of private trade contracts for most products. Six months after the trade agency of the French zone (OFICOMEX) had been merged with JEIA in mid April 1949, the Allied trade bureaucracy was finally abolished altogether.[4] The unified exchange rate of 0.30 dollars per Reichsmark (and later DMark), which was applied for most products since the spring of 1948, created some link between external and internal prices. Furthermore, the introduction of sound money for internal use in June 1948 ended the anti-export bias of the previous pattern of internal barter arrangements; it thus gave a first significant stimulus to private cross-border exchanges. And to circumvent the dollar clause, which had originally been confirmed by JEIA in its decree No. 1 in early 1947, JEIA soon commenced concluding bilateral agreements with foreign countries, although the first twenty agreements of 1947 and 1948 were, unlike some of the subsequent accords, much too rigid to be of great practical importance.[5]

By late 1949, the institutional setting governing West Germany's foreign trade had thus 'normalized' in a very peculiar sense: it closely resembled that of most other West European countries. Unfortunately, this regime did not make very much economic sense either. All over Europe, in fact everywhere outside the dollar area, cross-border transactions were severely hampered by the lack of international liquidity, i.e. a lack of dollars. Economically, the emergence of this much-deplored post-war 'dollar gap' is easy to explain: any money – for exchanges within and between countries – has to be based on trust in its future acceptance by one's partners in exchange. Trade and payments figures, the fashionable 'dollar shortage' talk and the rates at which major West European currencies were traded on the free market in Switzerland (Figure 10) point to a gross undervaluation of the dollar in the post-war period. At the official rates, no other major currency looked sound enough to be trustworthy or even to be credited with some expected revaluation. Thus, every country had an incentive to refuse to accept any currency but dollars in exchange for its goods. Because of the severe shortage of money that could be used as a store of value and medium of exchange in transactions between currency areas, the world outside the dollar area turned to barter trade, i.e. to a network of bilateral agreements specifying in detail the quantities and values of goods to be exchanged. Such agreements had played a major role in international trade since the Great Depression of the 1920s. They were to make sure that no partner ended up with a deficit that would have had to be settled in scarce dollars, or at least with no bilateral deficit exceeding a fixed limit called 'swing'.

In the very first stage of the rebuilding of previously severed trade links, such bilateral agreements do not necessarily obstruct the growth of trade

---

[4] Its functions were taken over by the authorities of the very recently established Federal Republic, although West Germany's commercial policy remained subject to Allied control until its admission to the General Agreement on Tariffs and Trade (GATT) in October 1951.   [5] Erhard (1954), p. 85.

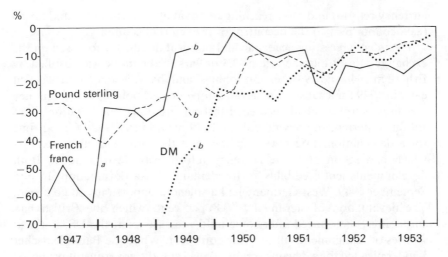

Figure 10. The overvaluation of major West European currencies
1947–53: Deviation of market exchange rate (Zurich rate for
banknotes) from official dollar parity.
Notes: *a*Devaluation. *b*Currency realignment of September 1949.
Source: Bank für Internationalen Zahlungsausgleich; own calculations.

volumes. However, they clearly distort trade flows, hinder a specialization
according to comparative advantages, impede a truly multilateral system
of exchange and prevent a further expansion of trade once the scope for
gainful bilateral exchanges is exhausted. To replace them with some sort
of multilateral trading system was therefore essential for the return to an
economically sensible international division of labour. However, before
we turn to those efforts to redress the sorry state of affairs that were
undertaken on the international level, we first have to answer the question
why West Germany did not resort to unilateral actions to escape the
straitjacket of bilateralism in the first place.

When the Federal Republic of Germany was founded in late 1949, the
conduct of cross-border transactions in Europe was remarkably similar
to the state of West Germany's internal economy before the liberal reform
of June 1948: the repressed inflation and the subsequent lack of sound
money had their counterpart in the overvaluation vis-à-vis the dollar and
the ensuing dollar gap; the administrative control over prices and
production and the internal barter trade was paralleled by the network
of bilateral trade agreements between currency areas. Despite the obvious
success of the internal reforms of the previous year, the West German
authorities did not try to link the attainment of statehood with a sweeping
external liberalization, i.e. with a thorough devaluation (analogous to the

currency reform) and a far-reaching removal of import quotas and tariffs (as a counterpart to the decontrol of the internal economy).

The most interesting academic and political discussion focussed on the exchange rate. While the rate of 0.3 dollars to the mark was justified by Erhard in 1948 and 1949,[6] export lobbies[7] and the Advisory Council called early in 1949 for a substantial devaluation once the policies of tight money and fiscal surpluses had succeeded in bringing down the inflation rate.[8] By this criterion, the second half of 1949 would have been a good time for a devaluation. Prices were falling, and the rapid growth in exports which had set in after the currency reform was slowing down. Both developments lent credibility to the demands for a devaluation. In mid September 1949, West Germany had a splendid opportunity to go ahead. The devaluation of sterling by 30.8 per cent, which the British had surprisingly announced after some mild pressure from the US, initiated a series of realignments all over the continent. While the Bank deutscher Länder pleaded for a devaluation by 20 per cent, the government proposed a rate of 25 per cent to the Allied High Commission, which still had the last say. After a fierce internal debate – with France trying to secure favourable prices for its imports of West German coal – the Allies finally approved a devaluation by 20.7 per cent to 4.20 DMark per dollar. Incidentally, this rate coincided exactly with the pre-war dollar parity of the Reichsmark.[9] As most of West Germany's trading partners had gone further, the trade-weighted exchange rate of the DMark after the realignments was even 1.2 per cent higher than before.[10] By now, the Advisory Council had toned down its demand for a realistic valuation of the DMark. In a report issued in mid December 1949, it still argued for bringing internal prices in line with the external ones by appropriate 'stable exchange rates without foreign exchange controls in the long run'.[11] However, the Council opposed an immediate adjustment which would have raised import prices. As an alternative, it proposed a 50 per cent dollar retention quota for exporters. In other words, the Council pleaded for split exchange rates for the time being, despite the negative allocative consequences which such differentiation would entail.

Although the centre–right government had been elected on a basically free-market platform, four objections against a radical liberalization of external transactions were apparently decisive: (i) the apprehension that a sufficiently large devaluation would make socially sensitive food imports

---

[6] *Ibid.*, pp. 82–3.   [7] On the attitude of exporters see Jerchow (1982), pp. 280ff.
[8] Wissenschaftlicher Beirat (1973), report of 17 January 1949, pp. 23–7.
[9] On these discussions see the *Wall Street Journal* of 13 October 1949; Tüngel (1949), p. 1; Schwarz (1981), p. 61.   [10] Schmieding (1989a), p. 256.
[11] Wissenschaftlicher Beirat (1973), report of 18 December 1949, p. 56.

from the US more expensive; (ii) the fear that this would induce an inflationary wage–price spiral just after the post-currency-reform inflation had run out; (iii) the desire to increase productivity and to keep price inflation in check by exposing firms – via an overvalued exchange rate – to fierce external competition; and (iv) the trade policy argument that one's own import barriers should be used as a means to prise foreign markets open.[12] In effect, having first adopted the rigid European regime of trade and payments controls, West Germany now opted for the Western European way towards removing them, i.e. for a long detour.

Our attention will thus shift from the West German to the Western European level. In particular, we will look at three US initiatives which helped to shape the regime governing Western Europe's – and West Germany's – trade and payments from 1948 onwards: the Marshall Plan, the Organization for European Economic Co-operation (OEEC) and the European Payments Union (EPU).

2   European liberalization and the Marshall Plan

(a) The Marshall Plan. In principle, the economic problem underlying the bilateral trading practices could have been solved easily: the trade and payments restrictions were caused by Europe's lack of international liquidity, i.e. dollars. Hence, a hefty revaluation of the dollar in terms of gold or a corresponding devaluation of European currencies in terms of dollars would have been the obvious remedy. Nevertheless, the governments of both the US and the European countries were rather reluctant to change the parities. First of all, since the traumatic – though misinterpreted – experience with the currency instabilities of the interwar period, a stable external value of one's money in nominal terms was widely regarded as being highly desirable per se. Furthermore, a kind of 'elasticity pessimism' prevailed among academics and politicians, i.e. the belief that trade volumes would react only slowly to price signals: after a devaluation, the desired improvement of Europe's aggregate trade balance vis-à-vis the US would come about only with a long and sustained J-curve-type delay – if it were to happen at all. Quite naturally, European governments favoured narrowing the transatlantic payments imbalance through US aid, even if the continuation of the exchange-rate misalignment implied that the severe restrictions on currency movements involving dollars (currency inconvertibility) and on transactions that gave rise to currency movements (import quotas, discrimination against dollar imports in general) had to be maintained for quite some time.

[12] See Erhard (1954), p. 215.

In the first years after the war, the Americans dealt with the 'dollar gap' by providing aid to prevent 'unrest and diseases' in Europe. In the meantime, they used the leverage which this aid gave them over European countries to pursue their idea of an international economic order. This order was supposed to be characterized by liberal trade practices on a non-discriminatory basis (to be supervised by the envisaged International Trade Organization, which later materialized in the watered-down version of the GATT), by some credit facilities for countries in the process of reconstruction (the World Bank), and by stable exchange rates (the International Monetary Fund). But the organizations which were actually established from 1944 onwards were – at least for the time being – far too weak to cope with the extraordinary problems of European reconstruction after the war.

Shocked by the European balance-of-payments crisis of 1947, and scared that parts of Western Europe might become communist, the US, as the only country capable of shaping the international economic order, changed tack. Amidst lively debates within the American administration about the appropriate course of policy, the US turned towards an increased involvement in economic decision-making in Europe.[13] With the announcement of the European Recovery Program (ERP) – the so-called Marshall Plan – on 3 June 1947, the Americans demonstrated how they intended to help Western Europe. They decided to replace the previous short-run relief efforts by medium-term aid for reconstruction, to provide Europe with some liquidity necessary for the conduct of intra-European trade on a multilateral basis, i.e. without the need to balance trade bilaterally, and to push for the removal of restrictions on intra-European exchanges.

Until April 1948, the details of the Marshall Plan were elaborated in negotiations between the US and Western European countries. On the part of the US, the Paris-based Economic Co-operation Administration (ECA) was to evaluate the aid requests and to supervise the actual disbursements. On the part of Western Europe, the Organization for European Economic Co-operation (OEEC) was founded for the purpose of coordinating aid requests and promoting the liberalization of trade and payments within Europe. Note that the inclusion of West Germany in the OEEC was the first step towards the rehabilitation of the country on the international level, although the three occupation zones were initially represented by the Allied authorities. Whereas the US had invited all European countries besides Spain to participate, Eastern Europe had to abstain because of a veto by Stalin.[14]

---

[13] See Tumlir and La Haye (1981), pp. 375–7.
[14] To compensate his satellite states in Eastern Europe, Stalin founded the Council for Mutual Economic Assistance CMEA in 1949.

Marshall Plan expenditures started in April 1948 and reached their peak in the US fiscal year 1949 (July 1948–June 1949). In mid 1952, when expenditures were less than half of what they had been three years ago, the Marshall Plan was replaced by the much less generous Mutual Security Assistance scheme.[15] Some 88.3 per cent of the entire ERP aid disbursements were outright grants, 11.7 per cent were in the form of long-term credits on favourable terms.[16] The Marshall Plan dollars mainly served to finance European imports of agricultural products (food, feed, fertilizer: 32.1 per cent of all ERP shipments) and raw materials plus semi-finished products (48.3 per cent, mostly fuel and cotton). Only 14.3 per cent of the entire amount was used for machinery and vehicles, i.e. genuine investment goods, and in the case of West Germany, much less (3.3 per cent).[17] In the importing countries, the national currency equivalent of the import values financed by Marshall Plan aid was deposited in special accounts. These so-called counterpart funds were at the disposal of national governments, albeit under the supervision of the ECA. They were usually made available as credits for specific investment purposes on concessional terms. On the one hand, these funds supplemented domestic sources of capital, and on the other, they made it easier for governments to direct resources into politically desired uses and thus strengthened state control over Western Europe's economies. Fortunately, the latter aspect played hardly any role for West Germany, which – unlike most other Western European states – had already liberalized most sectors of the internal economy in mid 1948.

All in all, the European countries received roughly 12 billion dollars of Marshall Plan assistance from the US between April 1948 and June 1952, a sum that was tantamount to roughly 2.1 per cent of the recipients' GNP in this period. Recently, the traditional view that this transfer of resources made a considerable contribution to the economic recovery of Western Europe has come under heavy attack.[18] A comparison of the aid receipts of individual countries (as a percentage of their GNP) and their economic performance as measured by the growth of GNP and exports reveals no clear-cut picture. While, for instance, Austria obtained comparatively large amounts of aid and achieved high rates of growth, it was easily outperformed by West Germany, which had received much less per

[15] The European Recovery Program formally gave way to Mutual Security Assistance on 30 December 1951. Because of the US appropriations practice, the entire US fiscal year (July 1951–June 1952) should be included in the Marshall Plan period, though.

[16] Agency for International Development (AID) (1971), p. 68; own calculations.

[17] Including iron and steel as well as iron and steel products, Milward (1984), pp. 101f. As the actual aid-financed shipments may have released funds for other imports, these figures may not give a correct impression of the structure of the additional European imports made possible by the ERP.

[18] See, inter alia, Cowen (1985); Milward (1984), pp. 90–125.

Table 12. *Marshall Plan aid and economic performance*

	GNP 1950 in bill. $	Aid receipts[a] in:		Real growth rates[b] of:			
		m. $	% of GNP[c]	GNP	Industrial production	Exports	Gross capital formation
Austria	2.430	703.5	7.2	8.66	12.82	22.30	16.87
Belgium–Luxemburg	7.052	324.8	1.2	3.87	2.92	8.71	3.66
Denmark	3.348	271.2	2.0	3.79	3.96	15.46	7.46
France	29.090	2862.6	2.5	4.26	4.47	17.08	−0.56
West Germany	23.310	1317.2	1.4	13.32	20.37	50.09	20.12
Greece	2.185	773.7	8.9	9.01	14.69	17.76	4.55
Italy	15.165	1253.5	2.1	6.05	9.96	8.68	11.79
Netherlands	4.976	980.6	4.9	5.18	7.63	23.89	2.96
Norway	2.720	263.6	2.4	3.34	7.26	7.54	3.61
Portugal	1.398	41.6	0.7	3.71	—	4.87	1.98
Sweden	6.520	82.1	0.3	3.59	2.48	7.54	2.11
Turkey	2.300	213.1	2.3	7.39	8.36	12.81	—
United Kingdom	37.337	2690.7	1.8	2.71	4.03	4.40	2.92
Ireland	1.086	146.5	3.4	3.07	7.78	12.92	6.00
Iceland	0.110	29.3	6.7	1.63	—	0.71	—
All recipients[d]	139.027	11954.0	2.1	5.27	7.71	13.3	—

Notes: [a] Total expenditures, adjusted for the reallocation of aid via bilateral drawing rights 1948/9.

[b] 1948–53 average (gross capital formation: 1948–52 average), in per cent p.a.

[c] Aid receipts divided by four times the GNP of 1950.

[d] Excluding the working capital of the European Payments Union, which amounted to 350 m. dollars. Spearman rank correlation coefficients between aid receipts in per cent of GNP and (i) GNP growth: 0.18; (ii) export growth: 0.36; (iii) growth of industrial production: 0.54, and (iv) growth rate of gross capital formation: 0.28.

Sources: Agency for International Development (1971), Bank für Internationalen Zahlungsausgleich (various issues), Donovan (1987), Milward (1984), OEEC, *Foreign Trade*, Series I, various issues; own calculations.

unit of its GNP (see Table 12). That there was no clear link between a country's Marshall Plan receipts and growth performance is hardly surprising. The funds were allocated among the beneficiaries according to their respective balance-of-payments situation vis-à-vis the countries with a convertible currency ('the dollar area'), not according to an evaluation of investment needs or of how the resources could be employed most productively.[19]

Given the interventionist economic policies of many Western European countries, the Marshall Plan was indeed helpful. Nevertheless, a turn-around in internal economic policies along the lines of the West German reforms of June 1948 would probably have been much more beneficial. In case of such a change, a short-term infusion of public funds for the transition period might still have been a good thing. Longer-term aid, however, would have been unnecessary and perhaps even unwarranted. As far as West Germany is concerned, the Marshall Plan receipts were not a major cause of the growth spurt that set in after the reforms of mid 1948. In fact, the first large shipments did not arrive until early 1949, i.e. at a time when the economy had already started to cool off again. Note, however, that the anticipation of the first Marshall Plan deliveries may have helped at the margin to mitigate the price inflation which developed in the West German economy during the first months after the liberal reforms of June 1948.[20] Sure enough, the Marshall Plan – and the food aid of the previous three years – had significantly alleviated West Germany's balance-of-payments constraint until 1950. And given the dismal state of agriculture in the aftermath of the post-war misery, the food deliveries were indeed a welcome supplement to domestic production. Yet, with less Allied red tape for exporters, a realistic valuation of the DMark and access to short-term credits on commercial terms to cushion the immediate J-curve effect of a DMark devaluation, West Germany should not have needed any aid to pay for its food imports.

Despite its rather minor economic importance, the European Recovery Program had two notable and positive political consequences: (1) the generous American payments to France and the UK made it easier for these countries to accept the politically contentious reintroduction of West Germany into the politics and trade circuits of Western Europe; (2) the shift of the US emphasis from short-term relief to medium-term aid for reconstruction was interpreted as a lasting US commitment to staying in Western Europe and thus enhanced investors' confidence in the political stability of this part of the continent.

---

[19] See Abelshauser (1989), p. 94.
[20] See Borchardt and Buchheim (1987), pp. 317–48; Abelshauser (1975), p. 169.

(b) Towards regional multilateralism: the OEEC and the EPU.
One of the main objectives of the Marshall Plan had been to smooth the
way towards a liberalization of intra-European trade and payments. In
this respect, the programme turned out to be a success. With its offers of
economic assistance, the US coaxed the sometimes reluctant Western
European states into establishing the OEEC. Although this collective body
of Marshall Plan recipients did not become the powerful supra-national
predecessor of a European Economic Union that the US had envisaged,[21]
it turned into a quite effective instrument of liberalization. Immediately
after a well-publicized speech in which the US Marshall Plan administra-
tor, Paul Hoffman, had urged Western Europe towards rapid progress in
early November 1949, the OEEC Council of Ministers decided to abolish
quantitative restrictions on 50 per cent of intra-OEEC trade within six
weeks. This liberalization requirement was raised to 60 per cent in the
autumn of 1950 and to 75 per cent in February 1951. In early 1955 the
quota was finally set at 90 per cent.[22] A few months after the first steps
towards an intra-European liberalization in the narrow sense of the word,
i.e. the removal of quantitative restrictions on the imports of goods, the
first and rather futile steps towards a multilateral settlement of intra-OEEC
payments imbalances were replaced by the much more comprehensive
European Payments Union (EPU) in mid 1950.[23]

The EPU was to a large extent the brainchild of the US Economic
Co-operation Administration (ECA). Despite initial objections by the US
Treasury, which had advocated a strengthening of the IMF,[24] the ECA
had initiated negotiations over a regional multilateral clearing mechanism
in Europe. As a supplement to the OEEC, the EPU was designed to
advance European economic integration in two ways: (i) under the EPU
regime, all intra-EPU payments were to be settled monthly on a strictly
multilateral basis, thus reducing the overall need for transaction balances
in transferable currencies (i.e. the dollar) and removing the rationale for
a bilateral balancing of trade in the area covered by the EPU arrangements;[25] (ii) the EPU was to provide for the automatic extension of limited

---

[21] See Milward (1984), pp. 56–89.   [22] Ehmann (1958), pp. 23–52.
[23] For details of the pre-EPU clearing arrangements see Triffin (1957), p. 149; for a detailed
    analysis of the EPU see Kaplan and Schleiminger (1989).
[24] See Triffin (1957), p. 136.
[25] The EPU was more than an intra-European organization. The clearing mechanism
    encompassed European payments balances with the entire monetary areas of the OEEC
    countries, including overseas territories and all members of the sterling area such as India,
    Pakistan and South Africa. All in all, the EPU area accounted for 57.4 per cent of world
    exports and for 61.7 per cent of world imports in 1950. The actual clearing operations
    were carried out by the Bank for International Settlements in Basle, while the adminis-
    tration of the EPU was placed in the hands of a Paris-based managing board operating
    under the supervision of the OEEC Council, which in turn had the exclusive authority
    to take all major decisions.

balance-of-payments credits from countries with net surpluses in intra-EPU exchanges to net debtors, with the credits being backed up by 350 million dollars of Marshall Plan aid.[26]

To the surprise of European policy-makers and the utter dismay of the Bonn government, the elaborate system almost broke apart within a few months under the strains of a severe West German balance-of-payments crisis. For the first time in the history of the Federal Republic, an external disequilibrium threatened to become a binding constraint on the development of the internal economy. Even more importantly, this was the last time that the essence of the liberal economic system which West Germany had adopted in mid 1948 was actually put in jeopardy. Hence, this crisis deserves to be analysed at some length.

(c) The 'German crisis'. From a West German perspective, the European Payments Union semed destined for a good start. In June 1950, the last month not covered by the EPU, the balance-of-payments problems following the minor realignment of currencies and the removal of quantitative restrictions affecting roughly 50 per cent of private imports from OEEC countries in late 1949[27] had been largely overcome. The overall trade deficit had narrowed to 45 million dollars in June, with exports rising rapidly (63 per cent up on the monthly average of the second quarter of 1949) while imports stagnated.[28] However, the outbreak of war on the Korean peninsula changed the picture dramatically. The run on raw materials and the hoarding of consumer goods propelled West Germany into an unexpected balance-of-payments crisis. By the end of September 1950, i.e. within the first three months of regional multilateral clearing via the EPU and before the EPU directorate had even met for the first time, West Germany had exhausted almost 60 per cent of its EPU quota, while all other member countries (or currency areas respectively) exhibited hardly any deficit at all. The deterioration of the West German EPU position even accelerated in October. After the implementation of the OEEC decision to raise the percentage of 'liberalized' private

---

[26] In the EPU agreement, which was signed on 19 September 1950 and covered intra-EPU payments from 1 July 1950 onwards, the contracting parties specified the details of this credit mechanism: every member country was allotted a quota amounting to roughly 15 per cent of its 1949 trade volume with OEEC members. Within the limits set by these quotas about 60 per cent of net deficits or surpluses with the Union were to be settled by the extension of credit and 40 per cent in gold or dollars. In case the net cumulative deficit of a country surpassed its quota, the difference had to be settled entirely in gold. For details, see EPU (1959), p. 19.

[27] On 30 October 1949 West Germany unilaterally abolished quotas on 37.4 per cent of private imports from OEEC countries. Furthermore, bilateral trade agreements provided for the removal of most quantitative restrictions on German imports from a variety of countries. For details see Schmieding (1987), p. 37.

[28] Schmieding (1987), Tables 5 and 6.

imports from OEEC countries to 60 per cent in early October (with the emphasis on raw material imports), the West German monthly trade deficit with the EPU area went up from 7 million dollars in June 1950 to a record 71 million dollars. To combat this surge in imports, an ad hoc inter-ministerial import committee (*Einfuhrausschuß*) and the central bank moved to dampen internal demand and, hence, imports in the second half of October 1950: outstanding import licences, for which contracts had not been signed, were cancelled; applicants for new licences were obliged to deposit 50 per cent of the value of the desired imports until the goods had actually entered the country (25 per cent as of 23 December); and banks were subjected to a host of restrictions, including outright credit ceilings and an increase in minimum reserve requirements with the central bank by about 50 per cent on average.[29] The exchange rate was not altered, although the Advisory Council to the Federal Minister of Economics now strongly advocated a devaluation.[30]

The discussion of the West German crisis by the EPU directorate and the OEEC Council was based on the report of two independent experts, Per Jacobsson and Alec Cairncross. Having scrutinized the West German economy, they came to the conclusion that the patient was basically healthy.[31] On 14 November, when West Germany's cumulative deficit had already surpassed its quota, the OEEC Council decided to extend a special credit of 120 million dollars designed to cover up to two-thirds of the expected German EPU deficit in the months until April 1951, provided the West German government submitted a credible programme for the restoration of external balance. This condition was formally met by the West German government in early December, although the parliamentary debate on tax increases, the core of the proposed measures, did not start prior to March 1951.[32]

Meanwhile, the October measures were showing some effect. The trade deficit with the EPU area went down to an average of 40 million dollars for November to February. However, even a reduced deficit still implied a deterioration of the West German cumulative balance with the EPU. At the end of January 1951 the Bank deutscher Länder enacted new credit restrictions. When the West German cumulative balance with the EPU surpassed a deficit of 450 million dollars, the import committee suspended the previous relaxation of quantitative controls on 22 February. It temporarily ceased to issue new import licences six days later. In spite of

---

[29] For a detailed account of these measures, see Wallich (1955), p. 236, and Bank für Internationalen Zahlungsausgleich (1951), pp. 50–1.
[30] Wissenschaftlicher Beirat (1973), report of 5 November 1950, pp. 93–6.
[31] Jacobsson and Cairncross (1950).
[32] Bank für Internationalen Zahlungsausgleich (1951), pp. 50ff.

grumblings about a German return to mercantilist trade practices in some West European countries,[33] the EPU directorate accepted the West German measures, thus barring other member states from retaliating against West German exports.

This 'Korea crisis', i.e. the balance-of-payments problems which went along with the inflationary demand-pull initiated by the fighting on the Korean peninsula, provided the last serious political challenge to West Germany's fledgeling liberal economic order. As at the height of the post-currency-reform inflation in autumn 1948, not only the details but the essence of the social market economy were put in jeopardy. By early 1951, even the conservative Chancellor, Konrad Adenauer, the Minister of Finance, Fritz Schäffer, and the Allies urged Erhard to return to a central administration and distribution at least of major raw materials. Even a general price freeze was seriously discussed.[34] Adenauer came very close to sacking his Minister of Economics, i.e. the man whose rotund face furnished with a thick cigar had become the popular symbol of the market economy. A notorious optimist, Erhard stuck to his predictions that the trouble would disappear within a short time or – in other words – that the adjustment flexibility of the market economy was far greater than expected by his opponents.

Once again, Erhard turned out to be right. From March 1951 onwards, the West German overall balance of trade and its EPU position improved dramatically, with West Germany repaying the special assistance credit in May – five months ahead of schedule. It even turned into a net creditor to the EPU by November 1951, a position the country continued to hold until the EPU was abolished in late 1958. In compliance with requests by the EPU directorate and under the supervision of a mediation group of three independent experts appointed by the OEEC Council, the ad hoc import committee gradually resumed issuing new import licences in spring 1951, although the reimposed quantitative restrictions were not lifted prior to January 1952.[35]

The speed of improvement in the West German payments position gives rise to the question how severe the crisis had actually been in the first place. For a thorough evaluation, the following points have to be considered:

(i) Except for January 1950, a month in which imports were extremely high because of the removal of quantitative restrictions on roughly 50 per

[33] Erhard (1954), pp. 108–9.   [34] Schwarz (1981), pp. 126–7.
[35] For 57 per cent of private OEEC imports, a share that increased to 76 per cent in April and to 81 per cent in August 1952: Schmieding (1987), p. 10.

cent of private imports from the OEEC area in mid December 1949, *exports* had been rising at a higher rate than imports in terms of values and volumes throughout 1950 and 1951.[36] As exports increased from a lower level, this discrepancy of growth rates could go along with a temporary balance-of-trade deterioration in late 1950. This imbalance would soon have corrected itself, provided that no major change of trend had occurred.

(ii) Prior to the Korea boom, *capacity utilization* in West Germany had been lower than in other industrial countries. Hence, West Germany had more scope for expansion of output. This necessarily implied a surge in raw material imports in advance of any substantial increase in production for internal and external markets. At least some imported raw materials were likely to find their way into export products eventually.

(iii) The run on imports, especially on raw materials, had led to a substantial worsening of West Germany's *terms of trade* – on top of the already severe deterioration in the wake of the currency realignment in late 1949.[37] With Soviet troops located on its eastern border, the hoarding of raw materials (and consumer goods) was more pronounced in West Germany than elsewhere. However, the accumulation of stocks would not have gone on indefinitely, while higher import prices were bound to dampen import expenditures anyhow, although with a J-curve-type delay.

(iv) The *terms of payments* for West Germany's foreign trade had changed for the worse. West Germany's customers postponed payments for exports, while imports had to be paid for immediately. This change alone accounted for a shortfall of foreign exchange receipts of 65 million dollars vis-à-vis the EPU area in the second half of 1950.[38] However, payments were not likely to be delayed indefinitely unless war actually broke out in Europe. Furthermore, the Bank deutscher Länder had already taken an important step towards halting the hidden flight of capital by raising interest rates in October 1950. In the first half of 1951 the terms of payments for West Germany's foreign trade normalized.

(v) One of the most striking features of West Germany's trade in 1950 was the change in the *regional profile of imports*. On account of the drastic decline of imports financed by US aid,[39] the intra-European liberalization measures of late 1949 and mid 1950, and the opportunity to increase imports of raw materials from the non-metropolitan EPU countries, the share of imports originating in the EPU area went up by 23 percentage

---

[36] Schmieding (1987), Table 6.   [37] *Ibid.*, Table 7.
[38] Bank für Internationalen Zahlungsausgleich (1951), p. 48.
[39] From 80 million dollars per month in 1949 to 40 million dollars per month in 1950.

points to 68 per cent. At the same time, the share of exports to the EPU area declined by 8 percentage points to 77 per cent in 1950. This redirection of trade and the delay in foreign payments for West Germany's exports mentioned above account to a large extent for the rapid exhaustion of the West German EPU quota at the time of an export boom.[40]

All in all, the changes in the West German balance of payments in late 1950 and early 1951 hardly deserve the label 'German crisis'. While the restrictions on the expansion of internal credit may have been justified to check the rise of prices during the Korea boom, the suspension of import liberalization was certainly not warranted by the actual development of trade. However, this criticism can hardly be directed at the West German authorities, whose foreign exchange reserves were running out. Rather, it points to a deficiency of the international financial system, namely to the lack of an adequate source of credit on commercial terms for a country experiencing rapid and healthy growth. The EPU quota, based on 1949 trade figures which had been very small indeed for West Germany, was certainly not sufficient. Acknowledging this fact, the EPU raised the West German quota to 500 million dollars in late 1951. Nevertheless, the lack of an international capital market remained a potential obstacle to growth.[41]

In spite of the West German deliberalization in early 1951, the handling of the German crisis and the rapid improvement in the West German payments position in the same year greatly enhanced the prestige of the EPU and the OEEC. The measures adopted by West Germany and the EPU set a precedent for other crises to come. By extending temporary balance-of-payments credits, the EPU and the OEEC Council enticed those debtor countries which were about to exceed their quotas to adopt more restrictive monetary and fiscal policies and to relax any reimposed import control within a short period of time. As negotiations over the terms of renewal of the EPU were held every year since the initial agreement on each country's financial obligations to the EPU had expired in 1952, creditor countries had some leverage to nudge debtors towards less expansionary demand policies and a more liberal trade and payments regime. On the other hand, countries accumulating claims on the union in excess of their quotas were themselves urged by the OEEC to liberalize their imports further.[42]

---

[40] Schmieding (1987), p. 12.
[41] Until the issue of Germany's external indebtedness was finally resolved by the London Debt Agreement in early 1953, West Germany was de facto excluded from the international capital market. Because of the pervasive systems of exchange controls this market was itself rather underdeveloped.   [42] See Schmieding (1989a), pp. 256–9.

3   *Turning into a pacemaker for liberalization*

(a) The re-emergence of tariff policy. Unlike other restrictions, tariffs as the traditional tool of commercial policy had exerted no influence on the tiny volume and the structure of German imports in the first years after the war. Until the end of 1946, tariffs were hardly collected at all in the three Western zones of occupation. Even the re-enactment of the pre-war tariff in the Anglo-American Bizone in early 1947 and in the French zone a few months later scarcely affected German consumers, as internal prices were fixed by the Allied authorities anyhow. Given the comprehensive system of administrative import controls, tariffs remained largely irrelevant even after the reforms of June 1948. By the time tariffs actually started to play at least a minor role for the volume and structure of imports, i.e. after the removal of quotas on 50 per cent of private imports from the OEEC countries at the end of 1949, the debate about West Germany's tariff policy had already begun in earnest, both between competing local lobbies and between the West German authorities and the Allies.[43]

In the years 1948/9, the Allies had set the stage for the debates to come. At the first round of GATT negotiations in Geneva, the US had brought it about that West Germany, without being a contracting party to the General Agreement on Tariffs and Trade, was granted 'most-favoured nation' (MFN) treatment by thirteen of its most important trading partners on 14 September 1948. This was a remarkable step. After the First World War, the victors had obtained MFN treatment from the German Reich without granting a reciprocal concession.[44] Still, a subsequent Allied decision on 8 August 1949 that West Germany was to extend MFN treatment to all countries regardless of the beneficiaries' policies vis-à-vis West Germany ('statement of Annecy') was considered 'unilateral servitude' by many Germans, including Erhard.[45]

The chance for the West German authorities to reshape the future structure of tariff protection came a few months later. As a preparation for the third round of GATT negotiations in Torquay (England) in 1950 and 1951, the specific 'Bülow tariff' dating back to 1902 had to be replaced by an ad valorem tariff specifying products according to the 1948 'Brussels nomenclatura'. In May 1949, a working group in the Bizonal Economic Administration had still discussed a plan to abolish all tariffs on manufactures vis-à-vis countries applying most-favoured nation treatment

[43] See Jerchow (1979), pp. 254–79; Weiss et al. (1988), pp. 103–13.
[44] Möller (1981), pp. 356–60.   [45] Erhard (1954), p. 210.

to West Germany's exports;[46] on 11 October 1949, however, the federal government appointed a committee including representatives of industrial and agricultural organizations and the trade unions to work out a new tariff schedule. In the hearings before and the discussions within this committee, representatives of industry argued for low tariffs in general (except for fertilizers, some other chemicals, electrical products and a few other commodities) and for a far-reaching reduction of tariffs on agricultural products in particular. This was meant (i) to ensure admission into the GATT to the benefit of West Germany's exports, (ii) to lower the cost of imported raw materials and (iii) to reduce prices for essential goods as a means of moderating wage demands. This point of view was largely supported by the Ministry of Economics and the trade unions, while many conservative politicians lent an ear to the agrarian lobby, who argued for high tariffs on agricultural products (and low tariffs on fertilizers).[47]

The tariff that emerged out of this intense debate was explicitly designed to give the West German negotiators in Torquay considerable bargaining power and scope for reciprocal tariff reductions.[48] The rates proposed by the tariff committee were in general considerably higher than the corresponding rates in the old 'Bülow tariff', although West Germany had been invited to the Torquay conference on the condition that it would not use the introduction of a new tariff schedule as a convenient opportunity to increase import duties. As a consequence, the Allied High Commission did in fact demand substantial reductions of the proposed duties on many agricultural products, on chemicals, fertilizers, electrical goods and some other commodities.[49] However, when the West German parliament turned out to be very reluctant to yield to this pressure, the Allies dropped most of their demands in 1951.

Meanwhile, the West German representatives negotiated in Torquay on the basis of a proposed tariff that had not yet been approved by parliament and the Allies. In the course of these negotiations, West Germany made 'concessions' (i.e. the reduction or at least the binding of tariff rates) on 32 per cent of its tariff positions. Nevertheless, the new import duties finally enacted on 1 October 1951 were, according to some calculations, on average three times as high as the 'Bülow' rates.[50] In line with standard mercantilist practices, the lowest tariffs were levied on imports of raw materials and intermediate products. For the time being West Germany assumed a middle position between high-tariff countries such as the United Kingdom, France and Italy on the one hand and

[46] Verwaltung für Wirtschaft (1949), pp. 265–9.   [47] See Jerchow (1979), pp. 266–8.
[48] Erhard (1954), p. 215.   [49] See Jerchow (1979), pp. 265ff.
[50] Rittershausen (1955), p. 12.

low-tariff countries such as Belgium, the Netherlands, Sweden and Switzerland on the other.

In Torquay, West Germany had achieved its overriding goal: admission into the GATT. However, while the representatives of agriculture were content with the Torquay results, many industrialists and Ludwig Erhard were somewhat disappointed. West Germany had obtained fewer 'concessions' from its partners than the export-orientated branches of industry had hoped for – and had in turn reduced fewer tariffs than its negotiators had in principle been willing to. The fact that West Germany had previously increased tariff rates to obtain bargaining chips helps to explain this partial failure. Assuming that West Germany would cut these tariffs anyhow, its partners at the bargaining table were reluctant to offer 'concessions' in exchange.[51] Indeed, on 10 October 1951, West Germany unilaterally reduced some of its left-over bargaining tariffs.

   (b) Towards unilateral liberalization. The most remarkable features of West Germany's trade policy in the first years after the country had come into being in late 1949 was that it tried to behave almost exactly like everybody else. Its tariff policy was designed to put the new state in a bargaining position similar to that of other countries, and its attitude towards non-tariff barriers to trade was tailor-made to fit into the West European framework, institutionalized in the form of the OEEC and the EPU.

For the period from late 1949 to early 1953, liberalization almost exclusively meant the removal of quantitative restrictions on imports from the EPU area and, with a slight delay, from other non-dollar countries. The motives behind these early measures (including the reliberalization after the 'German crisis') can be summarized as follows: (i) Trying to become a respected member of the Western world, West Germany took great pains to comply with the rules conceived mostly by the ECA and laid down by the OEEC. (ii) The liberalization was meant to ensure reciprocal concessions from fellow OEEC members and – with respect to countries that had entered into bilateral agreements with West Germany – to widen the potential for the growth of exports, a scope given by the sum of West German imports from the country concerned and the respective swing credit. (iii) To enhance the growth of output in general and of exports in particular, the removal of quotas on imports of raw materials and other 'essential' goods not produced locally was given top priority, notably vis-à-vis countries outside the dollar area. (iv) And, at least by Erhard and some economists like Röpke (1950), integration into

[51] See Erhard (1954), p. 219.

the world market was correctly seen as a powerful tool to prevent a recartelization. In the early post-war years, this issue had dominated the thinking of many Americans calling for a new and thoroughly liberal Germany.

After 1952 the determinants of West Germany's trade policy changed: concerns about imported inflation came to the fore. The priority which the central bank – and the general public – attached to price-level stability manifested itself in a comparatively restrictive monetary policy. Between 1950 and 1958 the price level, as measured by the GNP deflator, rose at an annual average of 3.4 per cent in West Germany as opposed to 5.5 per cent elsewhere in the OEEC.[52] At fixed nominal exchange rates, West German suppliers became ever more competitive. When the initial disturbance of the 'Korea crisis' had been overcome, the West German trade and current account swung into surplus. From then on, policy-makers were faced with growing surpluses on both accounts.

The desire to keep the corresponding inflow of exchange reserves and hence the threat to internal monetary stability in check by relaxing import restrictions became the overriding imperative of West Germany's trade and payments policy. As a low-inflation country piling up the largest cumulative surplus relative to its quota within the EPU, West Germany turned into a pioneer of European liberalization; from 1953 onwards, it took unilateral steps ahead in times of cyclical upswings while some debtor countries temporarily reintroduced severe trade restrictions. In mid 1958, 94 per cent of all West German private imports (equal to 82.6 per cent of its overall imports) from the OEEC were free of quantitative restrictions (see Table 13).[53]

Up to this point, the West German liberalization efforts have been presented as if they had hardly been affected by any kind of protectionism. In fact, protectionist pressure groups were quite active and, in some cases, remarkably successful. As to the removal of quotas, the freeing of raw material imports posed no major obstacle, while the liberalization of imports of foodstuffs lagged behind consistently as it encountered fierce resistance from the influential agrarian lobby. Note that Table 13 actually understates the extent of quantitative restrictions on food and feeding-stuff imports: the markets of many agrarian products were so tightly controlled by 'orderly market regimes' (*Marktordnungen*) in West Germany that trade in these products was not counted as 'private trade' by the OEEC and thus not included in the official liberalization statistics.

---

[52] OECD (1970), p. 13; own calculations.
[53] The numbers for West Germany's imports from the whole world except Eastern Europe were almost identical: 93.5 and 82.8 per cent respectively (sources: see Table 13).

Table 13. *Liberalization of West Germany's private OEEC imports*[a,b]

	30 June 1950	15 August 1952	31 December 1954	30 September 1956	30 June 1958
All goods	47 (56)	80.9 (65)	90.1 (83.0)	91.5 (88.8)	94.0 (82.6)
Food and feeding stuffs		71.5	79.4 (79.3)	81.3 (82.7)	85.4 (78.8)
Raw materials		90.7	97.8 (91.6)	98.0 (97.6)	99.3 (88.7)
Manufactures		80.0	93.8 (78.2)	96.2 (84.8)	98.2 (79.3)

Notes: [a] Percentage share of imports without quantitative restrictions at the given date; weighted with 1949 import shares; in brackets: OEEC average, base year 1948.
[b] State imports were exempted from the OEEC liberalization requirements.
Sources: Bank für Internationalen Zahlungsausgleich (1954/5), p. 111; European Payments Union (1955/6), p. 26 (1957/8), p. 26; Presse- und Informationsamt der Bundesregierung (1952), p. 114; (1953), p. 150.

As far as manufactures are concerned, the almost permanent pressure brought upon West Germany by the OEEC and the international bodies helped to overcome internal resistance against the abolition of import quotas. Based on a report by the International Monetary Fund (IMF) according to which West Germany could no longer justify quantitative restrictions with the GATT-conformable argument of a balance-of-payments crisis, the GATT asked the West German authorities in autumn 1957 to lift most of these quotas and to apply for temporary waivers for the remaining ones. The ensuing negotiations took two years. West Germany finally yielded to many of these demands. The most notable exceptions were the quotas on textiles, many of which were to become part of the first Cotton Textile Agreement in 1961, and the majority of restrictions on agricultural imports, which finally became an ingredient of the Common Agricultural Policy of the European Economic Community in the 1960s.[54]

The interplay of macroeconomic considerations, organized interest groups and pressures from abroad was even more visible in the field of tariffs in the mid 1950s. From early 1954 to late 1957, the foreign exchange reserves of the central bank increased by 15 billion DMarks. Amidst this swelling influx of reserves, West Germany tried to use unilateral tariff cuts and the relaxation of administrative controls as a substitute for a revaluation of its currency, at least vis-à-vis other European countries. In this sense, West Germany's almost dogmatic adherence to the principle of fixed parities, which had initially delayed the liberalization of imports

[54] On the evolution of the EEC agricultural policy, see Chapter 4, Section B.1

Table 14. *Tariff protection 1951ᵃ and 1958*

	Nominal tariffsᵇ		Effective tariffsᶜ		Ratio of effective tariffs	Production indexᵈ
	1951	1958	1951	1958	1951/58	1958 (1951 = 1)
Industryᵉ	16.0	9.6	19.6	10.6	1.85	1.54
Production goods	16.1	9.0	25.5	13.6	1.88	1.47
Investment goods	14.5	8.6	8.9	4.5	1.98	1.77
Consumption goods	17.8	12.0	26.9	16.8	1.60	1.38
Agriculture	8.9	8.1	7.4	7.8	0.95	1.28

Notes: ᵃ Tariff schedule of 1 October 1951.
ᵇ Individual tariffs weighted with sales receipts in per cent.
ᶜ Effective tariffs of thirty-three branches of industry weighted with gross value added.
ᵈ Index of net production (agriculture: sales receipts 1951/2, 1958/9), adjusted for change in GNP-deflator.
ᵉ Excluding mining and food industry. Effective tariff protection computed according to the formula in Donges et al. (1988); input–output matrix based with some minor adjustments on the input–output table for 1954 in Stäglin and Wessels (1969).
Source: Schmieding (1989a), p. 260.

and the growth of exports, later on facilitated its integration into the world market. Pointing at rising consumer prices, Erhard secured five major rounds of unilateral tariff reductions between 1955 and 1957.[55] By justifying tariff cuts with the argument of price-level stability, Erhard succeeded in overcoming the resistance from import-competing industries to a considerable extent. All in all, the average nominal tariffs in indu⸱⸱. decreased from 16.0 per cent in October 1951 to 9.6 per cent in early 1958, while the level of effective tariff protection went down from 19.6 to 10.6 per cent (see Table 14).

However, as in the case of quantitative import restrictions, organized interest groups were able to shape the sectoral profile of protection. Contrary to the wishes of Erhard and the Social Democrats,[56] who had advocated linear cuts, i.e. tariff reductions affecting all imports alike, the actual measures passed by parliament were highly differentiated. A simple rule of thumb helps to explain a good deal of the sectoral pattern of these

[55] See Schade (1963), pp. 91–105; Ehmann (1958), pp. 103ff; and Erhard (1957), pp. 210ff.
[56] In the federal parliament, the SPD repeatedly pleaded for far-reaching linear tariff reductions, while members of the conservative–liberal parties (CDU/CSU and FDP) demanded exemptions for agriculture and individual industries; see Deutscher Bundestag (1953–7), pp. 3333–43 (27 January 1955), p. 5829 (19 October 1955), pp. 8176–83 (22 June 1956), pp. 12263–4 (23 May 1957).

cuts: the slower a sector of the economy was growing between 1951 and 1958, the more it could prevent tariff reductions. The effective tariff protection of agriculture, whose sales receipts increased only marginally in real terms, even rose slightly from 7.4 to 7.8 per cent.

In contrast to Olson's celebrated hypothesis,[57] the comparatively successful liberalization of West Germany's external economy in the 1950s cannot be explained by a general weakness of organized interest groups caused by the disruptions of war, occupation and the division of the country.[58] From the very beginning, the major interest groups participated actively in the process of trade policy formation.[59] However, protectionist pressures were dampened by the comparatively strong position of the central umbrella organizations of capital and labour vis-à-vis sectoral lobbies. As a comprehensive organization, the German Federation of Trade Unions (DGB) often acted as an advocate of consumer interests rather than a lobby for workers in particular sectors. In the preparatory committee for the new West German tariff schedule (1949–50) the DGB explicitly participated as the consumers' representative. In mid 1950, the DGB first demanded sweeping reductions of many proposed tariffs. This is all the more remarkable since the unemployment which had become visible after the currency reform of 1948 had reached its peak in early 1950. The expected benefits of liberalization, namely lower prices and high productivity, frequently outweighed the anxieties against import-induced structural change throughout the 1950s.[60]

In order to reconcile the interests of the export-orientated and the import-competing branches of industry, the Federation of German Industry (BDI) pleaded for a general opening of markets, although with numerous exceptions and on the basis of strict reciprocity.[61] However, the BDI's resistance to Erhard's unilateral steps was mitigated by pressure from abroad. From 1953 onwards, the OEEC and the GATT repeatedly asked West Germany for a unilateral liberalization to reduce the growing current account surpluses, sometimes backing their demands with unveiled threats of retaliation. Interestingly, some of the major points made by the BDI against a unilateral liberalization were quite sound. In the last analysis, neither the price level (Erhard's argument) nor the balance on current account (the standard OEEC argument) depends on the level of protection. In the long run, the liberalization of imports is no adequate

---

[57] Olson (1982), pp. 75–6.   [58] See Chapter 3, Section A.3.
[59] See Jerchow (1979), pp. 265ff.; Erhard (1954), pp. 210ff.
[60] On the stance of the unions in the mid 1950s, see the report on the Hamburg Congress in: DGB (1956), pp. 691–2; the regular reports on the progress of liberalization in DGB (1951–8), especially (1957), pp. 115, 287, 310, 493; and Braunthal (1965), p. 331.
[61] See BDI (1949/50), pp. 10ff., (1953/4), pp. 101ff., (1955/6), p. 101, (1957/8), p. 105; Braunthal (1965), pp. 327–31.

substitute for a revaluation. Even under a regime of fixed exchange rates, liberalization tends to promote export growth, directly by reducing the internal price of imported raw materials and intermediate products and indirectly by enhancing productivity growth and putting downward pressure on wages, albeit with a delay. Thus, the cyclical downturn in the US and in Europe in late 1957 and 1958, which reduced foreign demand for West German exports, did more to relieve the pressure on the German Mark than all the measures directed at imports. It remains an odd feature of West Germany's economic history that two ultimately misdirected arguments served to promote the right thing: the liberalization of West Germany's foreign trade.

West Germany's progress towards freer trade was paralleled by moves towards currency convertibility. The removal of import quotas and the multilateral settlement of intra-EPU payments balances from mid 1950 onwards were by themselves important to reinstate money as the medium for conducting cross-border exchanges. After 1951, West Germany moved towards convertibility on current account first within the EPU area, next with all countries besides the hard-currency dollar area and finally with the latter area as well. In 1952, payments for trade in services between West Germany and the EPU area were liberalized; one year later the same step was applied to income transfers.[62] From April 1954 onwards, the DMark became freely convertible for residents of an increasing number of non-dollar countries.[63] At the same time, a gradual hardening of the terms of bilateral trade and payments arrangements with non-EPU countries and a hardening of the EPU agreement[64] itself made the discrimination between the dollar area, i.e. the countries whose currencies were fully convertible, and the rest of the world increasingly obsolete.

Note that from late 1955 onwards the EPU turned into an almost bilateral affair. Low-inflation West Germany accumulated high surpluses in excess of its quota, forfeiting dollar payments it would have been entitled to receive from the union. Via the EPU mechanism, West Germany extended credits to high-inflation France, whose position with the EPU deteriorated rapidly. This increasing imbalance was bound to bring down the EPU eventually. In late 1958, following a cyclical downswing and a drastic change in French policies,[65] France finally agreed to dissolve the

---

[62] Wallich and Wilson (1981), p. 402.   [63] Ehmann (1958), pp. 68ff.

[64] On 30 June 1954 the initial gold-free tranche for debtors within the EPU was abolished, and thirteen months later the share of gold (or dollars) in any future settlement was raised to 75 per cent; for details see the annual reports of the EPU, especially EPU (1959), pp. 17–26.

[65] The French franc was twice devalued in 1957 and 1958. Furthermore, after de Gaulle's rise to power in 1958, France adopted an austerity programme called 'Plan Rueff' that had been approved by the OEEC and the IMF.

EPU as of 27 December 1958; with the exception of Greece (which followed in May 1959), Iceland and Turkey, all OEEC members restored external convertibility of their currency into dollars for current transactions on this day.

West Germany went one important step further and removed most of the remaining restrictions on capital flows in late 1958 and early 1959. Because of the unresolved problem of the country's external indebtedness, a restoration of convertibility for capital transactions had hardly been an issue until 1952. Most capital transactions had been simply prohibited. Two important steps paved the way towards an integration into the international capital market: the negotiated settlement with Israel of 1952, which obliged West Germany to pay 3.5 billion dollars as restitution over the course of the next 12–14 years, and the London Debt Agreement of early 1953, which cut the external indebtedness – pre-war and post-war debt including obligations incurred under the Marshall Plan – by more than 50 per cent from 29.3 to 14.5 billion DMarks.[66] After the latter agreement had come into force as at mid September 1953, West Germany swiftly began to lift the tight restrictions on capital flows. Given the central bank's fear of an uncontrolled capital influx that would boost the money supply at the fixed exchange rate, the liberalization of capital outflows usually preceded that of inflows. In a similar vein, restrictions on transactions with non-dollar countries were lifted earlier than those vis-à-vis the dollar area.

By the end of 1958, i.e. more than ten years after the US had put the issue of European liberalization forcefully on the agenda, the Western part of the continent had finally returned to more or less liberal trade and payments arrangements. Sure enough, this was a remarkable development. Nevertheless, the achievements of this period should not be counted as an unqualified success. All in all, Western Europe, including West Germany, had taken the long road to multilateral trade and currency convertibility. Through a reluctance on both sides of the Atlantic to revalue the dollar or to devalue European currencies, the lack of international liquidity had retarded the removal of barriers to trade and payments for more than a decade. Unfortunately, the short way to currency convertibility, i.e. the option of genuinely flexible or at least readily adjustable exchange rates, was hardly considered at all by policy-makers in the late 1940s and early 1950s.[67] Milton Friedman first presented his – by now famous – 'Case for Flexible Exchange Rates' in

---

[66] Erhard (1954), p. 268.
[67] Even Ludwig Erhard, who sometimes toyed with the idea of flexible exchange rates in the early 1950s (Erhard (1953), p. 133; Erhard (1954), p. 83; *Deutsche Zeitung* (18 October 1952)) did not press this point in the policy debate.

a memorandum written in late 1950.[68] However, he did not yet convince policy-makers and fellow economists that any shortage, be it the lack of a commodity or the lack of international liquidity, would correct itself if the relative prices concerned were allowed to move freely according to relative scarcities. Lower exchange rates vis-à-vis the dollar, be they determined by the market or be they the result of a devaluation in a regime of otherwise fixed parities, would have made Europe attractive for foreign investors. Provided that restrictions on the free flow of capital had been relaxed accordingly, this inflow of capital should have shortened the time needed for reconstruction and the partial catching up with the US. At the same time, a higher dollar would have subjected the American economy to more competitive pressure. Under such a regime, productivity could have increased at an even more rapid rate on both sides of the Atlantic.

Instead of realigning currencies sufficiently, the US and Europe had simply opted to wait for Europe's special post-war import needs to abate before they took decisive steps to liberalize European imports from the technologically most advanced area. The US provided Western Europe with some international liquidity necessary for the transition to regional multilateralism. Apart from its political dimension, American pressure – and payments – to further the economic integration of Europe can be seen as an attempt to hasten the change in the regional structure of European import demand by removing intra-European barriers to trade and payments and by integrating West Germany into the European economy. Interestingly, the major beneficiaries of Marshall Plan aid in absolute terms, namely the United Kingdom and France, were exactly the two countries which went through recurrent balance-of-payments crises in the 1950s. On the other hand, West Germany – which had suffered a net outflow of resources in the post-war period if war reparations and the costs of military occupation are deducted from the Marshall Plan payments and the other receipts of foreign assistance[69] – experienced an unprecedented export boom, outstandingly high rates of economic growth and a rapid accumulation of foreign reserves. Although it had started from a much lower base, the West German standard of living eventually surpassed those in the United Kingdom and France.

As far as West Germany's trade policy is concerned, the Allies have to be credited with initiating the first West German steps away from war-time autarchy after 1947. However, it was for endogenous reasons that West Germany gradually turned into a pacemaker for liberalization. With less

[68] Friedman (1953), p. 157.
[69] For a detailed comparison of outflows and receipts, see Buchheim (1990), pp. 69–99.

inflation than almost everywhere else in Europe and benefiting from its traditional strength in high-quality goods, which were in high demand in Europe and beyond, West Germany started to accumulate huge balance-of-trade surpluses. With a relatively far-reaching and rapid liberalization of imports and a faster growth of productivity than in most other EPU countries, West Germany outpaced its OEEC partners in terms of export and import growth and gained market shares overseas while other European countries became slightly more dependent on intra-European exchanges. Most importantly, West Germany increased its share of the North American market more rapidly than the rest of the OEEC.

Having started as an impoverished country with an overvalued currency and tight controls on cross-border transactions, West Germany was transformed by a combination of luck (high demand for German capital goods) and policy (less inflation than abroad) into a country enjoying all the benefits of export-led growth. With its attempt to fend off an imported inflation via unilateral liberalization at fixed exchange rates, this process even tended to feed on itself. As the removal of barriers to imports raised the degree of internal competition and hence the elasticity of domestic supply, West Germany's increasingly liberal trade policy contributed significantly not only to the growth in exports but also to the economic miracle itself.

4   *The emergence of 'little Europe'*

With the end of the EPU in late 1958, it may have seemed as if European regionalism had finally given way to a healthy multilateralism. However, a serious relapse into a new kind of regionalism had already set in some time ago. At the beginning of 1958, West Germany and five other countries in Western Europe formed a European Economic Community. As the EEC was to become ever more important for West Germany in later decades, the emergence of this narrow 'little European' club merits a good deal of attention.

While the OEEC used part of the Marshall Plan aid to promote the abolition of quantitative restrictions above all on intra-European trade, early attempts to establish a Western European customs union had but two meagre results, namely the customs union between Belgium–Luxemburg and the Netherlands and the standardized Brussels tariff nomenclatura of 1950. For the time being, the issue of mutual tariff cuts was left to the General Agreement on Tariffs and Trade (GATT) with its two basic principles of non-discrimination between members in the form of unconditional most-favoured nation treatment (MFN) and of reciprocal liberalization. To solve the free-rider problem inherent in any unconditional MFN treatment, the first four GATT rounds were structured according to the 'principal-supplier rule': each country negotiates over a certain tariff with its major supplier(s) only. Thus, the four rounds of multilateral negotiations between 1947 and 1956 were little but a multiplicity of simultaneous bilateral talks.[70] Over the course of the 1950s, the drawbacks of this approach became clearly visible: (i) Participants can gain bargaining chips by increasing tariffs beforehand. (ii) High-tariff countries have few incentives to reduce import duties on products which are mainly supplied by a low-tariff country. (iii) The overall success depends critically on the attitude of the major participants. If an important trading nation is not willing to lower its tariff barriers substantially, this has the awkward consequence that the opportunities for reciprocal liberalization between other members are diminished as well, since these countries would have to extend any deal to a quantitatively important free-rider without getting anything in return. Consequently, the first GATT round (Geneva, 1947), with tariff cuts of 19 per cent on average, was a success, mainly because the US had pushed for substantial progress. The results of the three following rounds were rather disappointing,[71] because the US administration had been granted little leeway for reciprocal liberalization by the US Congress. As it turned out, the requirement of unconditional MFN impeded the more thorough reduction in intra-European tariffs to which the European countries would otherwise have consented. This disappointment with GATT results had a far-reaching consequence: it gave an additional impetus to the quest for intra-European solutions, a process which for political reasons came to focus on an already-established Western European institution, namely the relatively small European Coal and Steel Community (ECSC).

On 9 May 1950, the French Foreign Minister, Robert Schuman, had proposed a common market for coal and steel in Western Europe – mainly as a device to ensure some degree of international control over German coal and steel policy without having to deny to West Germany the degree of national autonomy enjoyed by other states. The ECSC was established in August 1952 by France, West Germany, Italy and the Benelux countries; the United Kingdom decided to abstain because of its opposition to the supra-national features of the ECSC.[72] In the following years, i.e. in the aftermath of the war in Korea, which had put the issue of a West German contribution to the defence of Western Europe on the agenda, politicians of the six ECSC countries worked out (i) statutes for a European Defence

---

[70] See Curzon (1965), pp. 87–100; Kock (1969), pp. 100ff.; Baldwin (1987), p. 42.
[71] Annecy 1949: 2 per cent; Torquay 1951: 3 per cent; Geneva 1955/6: 2 per cent. See Müller (1983), p. 57.   [72] Haas (1958), pp. 159–61.

Community (EDC) and a European Political Community (EPC), both of which implied a far-reaching transfer of powers to common institutions, and (ii) a plan for a customs union. After the rejection of the EDC and – implicitly – the EPC by the French National Assembly in August 1954, prominent supporters of European political unification changed their strategy. They now opted for an indirect approach: a customs union or – preferably – even a common market called the European Economic Community (EEC) was to become the nucleus of political integration.[73]

Although the United Kingdom participated in the expert committee that was to prepare the envisaged common market, it left the negotiations at an early stage because the British government resented even mild versions of supra-nationalism, i.e. of a transfer of political power to a common institution. More importantly, it did not take the talks very seriously in the first place. However, when the negotiations on an EEC made unexpected progress in early 1957, the British government presented the idea of an OEEC-wide free-trade area for non-agricultural goods as a substitute for, or at least a complement to, an EEC consisting of the six ECSC members only.[74]

The British counter-proposal helped to highlight the economic issues at stake. With some courageous simplifications, most of the differences between the various opinions voiced in the discussion can be attributed to a fundamental conflict between two concepts of integration for which Fritz Baade coined the terms 'liberal' and 'authoritarian'.[75]

The liberal position was based on the two tenets that progress towards global free trade was more important than the establishment of any narrow regional scheme and that government interference with economic affairs should be greatly reduced anyhow. Thus, if there had to be any special European arrangement at all, it should encompass the entire OEEC, and not only the ECSC six. The group should also reduce its barriers to trade and capital movements with non-member countries. Furthermore, the liberalization of markets need not and should not go along either with a harmonization of national laws and regulations or an integration of bureaucracies and a creation of powerful supra-national institutions.

The authoritarian position started from the belief that free competition between firms from different countries would produce desirable results only if it were not distorted by differences in the legal, institutional and social framework between the countries. Thus, common institutions to

---

[73] See Küsters (1982), pp. 64ff.; Dankert (1982), p. 6.   [74] See Küsters (1982), pp. 280–93.
[75] Baade (1957), p. 4; for an illuminating comparison of both positions, see Dicke (1987). In modern terminology, the authoritarian position may be labelled 'rational constructivist': Giersch (1988a), p. 5.

impose a harmonization of micro- and macro-policies were a prerequisite to the abolition of internal barriers to trade. Hence, the integration effort ought to be limited to those states ready to cede sufficient sovereignty to a supra-national, albeit democratically controlled, body. With its powerful High Authority that had the right to fix prices and quotas and to overrule national regulations, the ECSC was an embodiment of the authoritarian concept. On the other hand, the OEEC and the EPU were examples of comparatively liberal arrangements.[76] Because of the emphasis put on common institutions, advocates of the authoritarian approach to economic integration were natural allies of those European federalists who favoured a common market as a first step towards a political unification of at least parts of the continent.

In the academic and political debate within West Germany on the best ways towards the economic integration of Europe, the battle lines were not always drawn clearly. While Ludwig Erhard and some staunch free-market academics like Wilhelm Röpke (1958) presented the liberal position rather vocally, the more pragmatic Advisory Council to the Federal Minister of Economics pleaded for a mixture of authoritarian and liberal elements.[77] Both Röpke and the Advisory Council agreed that (i) a process of regional integration in Europe should not be confined to the ECSC six, that (ii) the introduction of currency convertibility was the key to all further liberalization efforts, and that (iii) the maintenance of currency convertibility at fixed exchange rates presupposed a coordination of policies in the member countries. Unlike Röpke, however, the Advisory Council saw a potential conflict between monetary discipline and other desirable targets of economic policy; monetary policy should serve both the maintenance of appropriate and stable (nominal) exchange rates and the preservation of a high level of employment by active demand policy. The scope for conflict between these two targets would increase with the degree of cross-border mobility of capital and goods. Therefore, the liberalization of markets necessitated a binding coordination of macroeconomic policies. Ultimately, the responsibility for macroeconomic policy should be handed over completely to a supra-national institution. To ensure that neither wage policy nor 'social policy' nor any other kind of microeconomic policy could run counter to the common macro-targets, the establishment of a strong European government was seen as both necessary and inevitable.

In the eyes of Röpke, the European (and worldwide) economic disintegration was a direct consequence of the turning away from liberalism towards interventionist and inflationary economic policies after

[76] Baade (1957).   [77] Wissenschaftlicher Beirat (1973), report of 1 May 1953, pp. 177–92.

the liquidity crisis of 1931 and especially in the aftermath of the Second World War – often in the name of macroeconomic stabilization.[78] If the interventionist majority of European countries liberalized their internal markets and adopted monetary discipline, there would be no further need for restrictions on currency convertibility and for import quotas. The most important problems of market reintegration would be solved, while the comparatively less damaging tariffs could be reduced in due course. In other words: if countries like France carried out liberal reforms, no European Economic Community was needed; if they did not, the establishment of an EEC would cause a further disintegration rather than an integration of markets in Europe. A centralization of wage bargaining and a harmonization of social policy would result in community-wide inflationary pressures, with inflation being the main obstacle to currency convertibility and trade liberalization. In the same vein, an institutional integration was bound to increase the average degree of harmful interventionism.

As far as trade policy is concerned, Röpke was afraid that – because of the 'additive character' of protectionist pressures in the member countries – the common external tariff would be higher than the average of the previous national import duties. Hence, the benefits from trade creation within a common market of the six ECSC members only would be smaller than the losses from trade diversion. Therefore, the idea of a 'little Europe' should be abandoned in the absence of a free-trade agreement between the six and the other OEEC members.[79]

So far, only opinions of professional economists have been presented and contrasted: that is views which, after all, might not carry any political weight. Theories of political economy suggest that organized interest groups matter much more in the political arena. Yet, the surprising fact is that the views of the two major non-agrarian interest groups were not far apart from those of academics: the position of the German Federation of Trade Unions (DGB) was to a large extent identical with the one expressed by the Advisory Council in 1953, while at least some influential industrialists shared Röpke's scepticism.

Prominent trade unionists regarded liberalization in general as an

---

[78] Röpke (1958), pp. 33ff.

[79] *Ibid.*, pp. 58ff. Röpke clearly equated trade diversion with disintegration. Although this is correct from a static point of view, it neglects the dynamics of trade diversion. Distortions to the detriment of outsiders might well provide the impetus for these countries to join the regional club, or at least to consent to a mutual abolition even of those trade barriers which they would otherwise not have been ready to reduce: Schmieding (1988), pp. 518–19. This effect, namely that a little European customs union might well serve as the catalyst for the economic integration of a greater OEEC Europe, was stressed by Giersch (1957), p. 615. Consequently, Giersch came up with a much less negative assessment of a common market originally confined to the ECSC six.

opportunity to raise productivity and thus real wages. None the less, supra-national institutions and international coordination of stabilization policies together with some planning of investment were held to be desirable not only for reasons of economic integration (the Advisory Council's view!) but also because they promised the opportunity to attain – via the European level – the influence on economic policy which had eluded the unions at home.[80] The unions were well aware that the adjustment process would imply a speeding up of structural change. However, the rapid growth of income and employment in the 1950s had encouraged them to call for state-subsidized retraining and further measures to enhance the mobility of labour rather than for the wholesale conservation of unprofitable locations.[81] The harmonization of social policy and social security systems was in general favoured by the unions, but this was seen as a long-term development rather than a prerequisite for the removal of trade barriers.[82]

While the trade unions by and large managed to present a common stance, industrialists (organized in the Federation of German Industry BDI) did not. Export-orientated industries, notably those selling a high share of production overseas – like the chemicals industry – shared the view of Röpke. Others, like the coal industry, which expected to come under increasing adjustment pressure, were far more inclined to endorse an EEC with strong supra-national institutions as eventual suppliers of subsidies and protection.[83]

Nevertheless, it is worth noting that neither trade unions nor industry in general favoured the 'little Europe' which finally materialized. Despite their differences with regard to integration concepts, both supported freeish trade, at least within the OEEC area and subject to some escape clauses. Thus, arguments of political economy alone cannot explain why Germany finally consented to the 'little European' solution. Politics played a decisive role.

A closer look at the attitude of Fritz Berg, president of the BDI from

[80] See Haas (1958), pp. 219 25.
[81] The only hint that the unions perceived some aspects of integration as a threat to the position of German labour as a whole was their initial reluctance to endorse the free movement of labour across national frontiers. In particular, the miners' union lobbied for rigorous standards of professional competence to slow down the influx of foreign workers from low-wage countries, mainly Italy; see Haas (1958), p. 221.
[82] Sure enough, the stance of the individual unions depended on the expected effects of liberalization on the competitive position of their industry. For instance, coal miners and metal workers emphasized the need to retain at least a 'modest level of protection': Friedrichs (1957), pp. 598–602. Still, the unions' main concern was not that liberalization could go too far. Rather, they were afraid that it might not go far enough, i.e. be confined to the ECSC six instead of encompassing the entire OEEC area or exclude agricultural products: see Kühne (1957), pp. 287–95; Riess (1955), pp. 105–7.
[83] See Haas (1958), pp. 219 25.

1951 to 1971, is quite revealing in this context. Berg was committed to the idea of close political cooperation between France and Germany, even if this implied some economic sacrifices. A free-trade agreement between the ECSC six and the rest of the OEEC, although economically desirable, should not be pursued if it jeopardized the political substance of the EEC and the Franco-German reconciliation.[84] This point exactly described the position which the West German representatives adopted in the negotiations on the founding of the EEC and the subsequent unsuccessful talks on an OEEC-wide free-trade agreement. Not Erhard, but Chancellor Adenauer and Hallstein, the top official in the Ministry of Foreign Affairs, determined the principal elements of the German bargaining position.[85] Adenauer was willing to disregard economics in order to further his political aims, the binding of West Germany to Western Europe in general and the promotion of Franco-German friendship in particular.

Because of West Germany's readiness to yield to French demands, French rather than German politics have to be put into focus in order to explain the course of events. The decisive years 1957 and 1958 were a time of political and economic crisis in France. Most non-agrarian lobbies were sceptical of trade liberalization: both industrialists and trade unions[86] emphasized that French industry would be at a competitive disadvantage through higher labour costs. Therefore, wage and non-wage labour costs should be harmonized before intra-European tariffs could be abolished. Furthermore, a preferential trade area should not be extended beyond the ECSC six (including colonies) in order to contain the threat to French industry.

To evaluate the attitudes of French industry and trade unions, two issues have to be clearly distinguished: (i) the issue of the overall cost level and (ii) the issue of structural change. If – at the going exchange rate – the overall level of production costs in one country is above that of its neighbours, a move towards free trade will induce a surge of imports which is not matched by a corresponding export growth – at least not until internal factor prices have fallen sufficiently. The current account will exhibit a substantial deficit. Clearly, French anxieties focussed on such a cost-level differential – i.e. a problem that could have been solved by a devaluation – and not on the genuine consequences of liberalization, i.e. the pressure for structural adjustment that would result from an increased intra-European division of labour.

In fact, the attitudes of French industry changed after de Gaulle had implemented the 'Plan Rueff', which included a devaluation of the franc

---

[84] Berg (1956), p. 397.   [85] Küsters (1982), p. 423.
[86] Haas (1958), pp. 176–93, 225–31.

by about 18 per cent in late 1958. From then on, opposition to the EEC weakened. Soon there were even hints that important parts of French industry were no longer opposed to a free-trade agreement encompassing Western Europe as a whole. Unfortunately, this change of attitude came much too late to affect the course of events. On 25 March 1957, representatives of the six ECSC states had already signed the Rome Treaties to establish the European Economic Community (and a European Atomic Energy Community, Euratom). According to these treaties, which came into force on 1 January 1958, the member states were (i) to abolish all restrictions on intra-union trade in industrial goods and services, (ii) to lift all restrictions on the free movement of capital and labour within the union, (iii) to organize a common market for agricultural products, the details of which were to be decided by 1962, (iv) to introduce a common external tariff,[87] and (v) to secure some harmonization of economic and social policy. These objectives were to be attained within a transition peri of twelve years – which could be prolonged by three years in case of difficulties.[88]

When the EEC integration commenced, the Community finally rejected the British proposal for an OEEC-wide free-trade zone for manufactures at the insistence of de Gaulle in November 1958. Unfortunately, the very politician who had finally removed the economic obstacles within France to freer trade in a broader framework preferred – for political reasons – a 'little Europe' without the United Kingdom. Consequently, the United Kingdom, three countries with close links to the United Kingdom (Denmark, Norway and Portugal) and three countries committed to political neutrality and thus unwilling to join the EEC (namely Switzerland, Austria and Sweden) formed the European Free Trade Association (EFTA) for non-agricultural products on 3 May 1960[89]. Thus, Western Europe was divided into two trading blocs.

All in all, the emergence of two separate regional clubs within Western Europe meant that a splendid opportunity for the mutual abolition of tariffs between all OEEC members had been missed. For West Germany, this was all the more unfortunate because of its proximity to major EFTA countries, notably Austria, Switzerland, Denmark and Sweden. Nevertheless, this relapse into a rather narrow kind of regionalism did not

[87] For most products the new duties were to be calculated as the arithmetic average of the 1 January 1957 tariff rates of the four customs areas within the EEC: high-tariff France and Italy, low-tariff Germany and Benelux. For some products, the duties were to be fixed closer to the original French rates.
[88] For a detailed account, see Küsters (1982), pp. 335–438.
[89] For a survey of what the EEC and the EFTA had in common and where they differed, see Krämer (1968).

constitute a genuine step back from West Germany's successful liberalization policy of the 1950s, as the essence of the progress made in the OEEC–EPU framework was not endangered. The real significance was that future progress was bound to be heavily skewed and constrained by the rules of the customs union. The abolition of the intra-EEC barriers to trade was to be the most notable achievement in the following decade. In the same vein, the introduction of a common external tariff implied that West Germany could no longer apply the successful recipe of the mid 1950s, namely the use of a unilateral liberalization as a means to fend off imported inflation and to enhance the elasticity of supply and hence widen the opportunities for a continuation of rapid and spontaneous growth.

4   1960–1973: towards managed growth

For most industrialized countries of the Western hemisphere, the 1960s and early 1970s were a golden age, with economic growth reaching its post-war peak. For West Germany, things look slightly different. As to unemployment the situation was very healthy, since a state of full or over-full utilization of the country's stock of capital and labour could be preserved for about one and a half decades – interrupted only by one major sharp recession in 1966/7. As for economic growth, however, the period looks more like a time of transition from the economic miracle of the 1950s to normal international standards and – from a historical perspective – to the secular growth slack of later years. The same holds true for the more qualitative category of structural change: while the economy still relied heavily on the successful export engine which had been at the heart of the German miracle in the 1950s, the need for structural adjustment away from the export orientation was increasingly felt all over the period.

That West Germany's economic transition went along with a gradual sociological and political transformation may be more than sheer historical coincidence: step by step the paternalistic conservatism of the Adenauer years gave way to a mixture of liberal openness and tolerance in lifestyle and a new wave of socialist thinking in intellectual discourse. Politically, the change of mood can be nicely read off the labels of successive federal governments: the decade began with a purely conservative government (until 1961), backed by an absolute majority in parliament; a centre–right coalition followed, but was replaced in 1966 by the so-called grand coalition, a government formed by the (conservative) Christian Democrats and the (left-wing) Social Democrats; the decade ended with a centre–left coalition which rose to power in 1969 and stayed in office throughout the 1970s until 1982.

In the following two sections, we shall review the main economic policy questions of this transition period. Again, we shall first examine major domestic issues, above all the persistent state of overemployment, the many attempts at smoothing the business cycle and the mounting supply-side pressures (Section A). We shall then turn our attention to those parts of the international economic scene which provided new chances and challenges for the small and open West German economy, namely the EEC-trade integration and the gradual erosion of the Bretton Woods system of international finance (Section B).

A   Overemployment at an undervalued currency

The overall macroeconomic picture of the West German economy in the period 1960–73 is characterized by one outstanding feature: the extremely low level of unemployment, the lowest of all peace-time periods of German economic history this century.[1] In twelve out of fourteen years (1960–1966; 1969–1973), the unemployment rate remained well below 1.5 per cent; in nine years (1961–6; 1969–71) it was even below 1 per cent. Only in the major recession of 1966/7, when the economy faced a (slightly) negative growth rate, did the unemployment rate rise to an annual average of 2.1 per cent, a level which at other times might have signalled a severe labour shortage.[2] These numbers suggest that the 1960s and early 1970s were a period of chronically tight labour-market conditions. Prior to any discussion of the policy debate of the time (which was mostly concerned with matters of short-term demand management), this basic long-term fact deserves careful examination.

1   Labour shortage – facts, causes and consequences

To begin with, the question arises whether the low unemployment of the time should be considered as an equilibrium phenomenon ('full employment'), with the labour market just clearing at the prevailing real wage level, or rather as a disequilibrium phenomenon ('overemployment'), with labour demand being rationed by labour supply. In answering this question two facts should be recognized (see Table 15): first, the period 1960–73 is unique in the sense that the level of vacancies persistently surpassed the level of unemployment, again with the exception of the recession year 1967. As we know from theoretical labour economics, both the number of unemployed and the number of vacancies depend on the optimal search behaviour of workers and employers respectively so that, even in labour-market equilibrium, one should not expect the two numbers to be equal.[3] Nevertheless, the sharp and durable changes in the level of both variables in 1959/60 and 1973/4 and the extremely high ratio of vacancies to

---

[1] See Paqué (1988), pp. 1–2.   [2] For statistical details, see *ibid.*, pp. 2–4.
[3] See, e.g., Jackman and Roper (1987).

Table 15. *Selected labour market statistics for West Germany 1950–89[a]*

	Unemployed persons (thousands)	Vacancies (thousands)	Share of foreign labour in total employment (%)	Change in employment over previous year (thousands)	
				Foreigners	Germans
1950	1,580	116	.		.
51	1,432	116	.	.	+612[b]
52	1,379	115	.	.	+468[b]
53	1,259	123	.	.	+590[b]
54	1,221	137	0.5	.	+624[b]
55	928	200	0.5	+ 7	+865
56	761	219	0.6	+ 19	+624
57	662	217	0.6	+ 9	+500
58	683	216	0.7	+ 19	+177
59	476	280	0.9	+ 40	+283
1960	271	465	1.4	+100[c]	+400
61	181	552	2.4	+228	+245
62	155	574	3.0	+122	+180
63	186	555	3.6	+144	+ 85
64	169	609	4.2	+129	+ 94
65	147	649	5.1	+217	+ 56
66	161	540	5.7	+125	−117
67	459	302	4.8	−230	−481
68	323	488	4.8	+ 5	+124
69	179	747	6.3	+347	+222
1970	149	795	8.1	+441	+ 53
71	185	648	9.4	+321	+ 38
72	246	546	10.0	+157	− 21
73	273	572	10.8	+213	+168
74	582	315	10.3	−117	− 69
75	1,074	236	9.2	−320	−249
76	1,060	235	8.6	−136	+181
77	1,030	231	8.3	− 53	+227
78	993	246	8.1	− 15	+290
79	876	304	8.2	+ 67	+444
1980	889	308	8.4	+ 94	+331
81	1,272	208	8.0	−106	−116
82	1,833	105	7.6	−125	−143
83	2,258	76	7.3	− 93	−253
84	2,266	88	6.9	− 85	+143
85	2,304	110	6.7	− 41	+249
86	2,228	154	6.6	+ 2	+349
87	2,229	171	6.5	+ 7	+224
88	2,242	189	6.6	+ 33	+190
89	2,038	251	6.8	+ 68	+325

Notes: [a] Annual averages and changes of annual averages respectively; from 1950 to 1959 excluding, from 1960 to 1989 including the Saar and Berlin; employment data excluding self-employed.
[b] Estimate assuming constant number of foreign employees.
Sources: Bundesanstalt für Arbeit and Statistisches Bundesamt; own calculations.

unemployed in the meantime – more than 3:1 in the years 1961–6 and 1969–71 – do point to some underlying regime shift from a buyers' to a sellers' labour market in the late 1950s, and vice versa in the mid 1970s.

Second, the period 1960–73 is characterized by a strong influx of foreign labour or *Gastarbeiter*, mainly from Southern Europe. From 1960 onwards, the share of foreign labour in total employment grew from about 1.4 per cent to 5.7 per cent in 1966, and then again from a sharply reduced level of 4.8 per cent in 1967 to 10.8 per cent in 1973, the highest reached so far; starting with the 1974/5 recession, the share gradually declined to 6.5–7 per cent by the mid 1980s, with only one slight recovery in the boom years of the late 1970s. Looking separately at the absolute annual change of employment of both Germans and foreigners, it becomes evident that from about 1963 until 1973 the influx of foreign labour was the main source of labour-supply elasticity. After the expellees from the former eastern provinces of Germany had finally been absorbed by the labour market in the late 1950s, a last surge of new 'German' employment (on balance one million new jobs) occurred in the boom period 1959–61, when the wave of refugees from East Germany reached its peak before the Berlin Wall was built. After this political caesura, the supply of German surplus labour dried up; with declining participation ratios (due to an unfavourable, war-distorted age structure) and with most other 'quiet reserves' (*stille Reserven*) mobilized, the West German labour supply turned inelastic and even began to shrink.[4] Hence, the business upswing of 1963–5 was the first one to rely mainly on the employment of foreign labour, with almost 70 per cent of the employment expansion due to the influx of foreign workers; in the long boom period 1969–73, when – on balance – 1.7 million new jobs were created, this share rose to 85 per cent. Similarly, the sharp recession of 1967 led to a net outflow of about 230,000 foreign workers (largely because of the fact that many foreign workers did not return to West Germany in 1967 after having spent the winter at home!) and virtually no net immigration in the following year, when the labour market still had to absorb the large number of Germans laid off during the recession.

These statistics clearly convey the picture of an economy on an overemployment growth path with no domestic labour reserves left over for exceptional boom periods. The labour shortage led to waves of foreign workers filling many, but by no means all, vacancies on offer. In the brief recession interlude of 1967, the labour supply of foreigners served as a

---

[4] On the elasticity of the domestic labour supply, see the annual reports of the Council of Economic Experts (Sachverständigenrat), 1964 and later years (chapters on supply constraints).

Table 16. *Change of employment by sectors 1960–73 and 1973–89*

	Absolute changes (thousands)		Relative changes (%)	
	1960–73	1973–89	1960–73	1973–89
Agriculture and forestry	− 1,635	− 933	−45.7	−47.9
Industry	+ 311	−1,812	+ 2.5	−14.1
Energy, mining	− 233	− 42	−31.2	− 8.2
Manufacturing	+ 302	−1,230	+ 3.1	−12.4
Construction	+ 242	− 540	+11.4	−22.8
Trade and transport	+ 191	+ 215	+ 4.0	+ 4.3
Insurance and banking[a]	+ 869	+1,750	+36.8	+54.1
Government	+1,275	+ 900	+60.8	+26.7
Private non-profit	− 8	+ 449	− 1.0	+59.4
All sectors	+1,003	+ 569	+ 3.8	+ 2.1
Private sector[b]	− 272	− 331	− 1.1	− 1.4
Private business[c]	− 264	− 780	− 1.1	− 3.4

Notes: [a] Including miscellaneous services.
[b] Including private non-profit organizations.
[c] Excluding private non-profit organizations.
Source: Statistisches Bundesamt; own calculations.

buffer stock which helped to alleviate the negative impact of the demand shortfall on the employment of domestic labour.

Of course, the labour shortage was not uniformly distributed across sectors of economic activity and regions, since structural change naturally leads to different degrees of labour scarcity. As to sectors, the general pattern of structural change in the period 1960–73 is apparent from Table 16: there was a dramatic drop of employment in agriculture and forestry as well as energy and mining, a moderate growth in manufacturing, construction, trade and transport, and a fast growth in most branches of services, above all the government sector. Compared to the time after 1973, two facts stand out: first, the particularly rapid shrinkage of the primary sector and second, the still significant growth of manufacturing and construction, which is unusual for a highly industrialized country like Germany in the 1960s. In this respect, the sectoral change of foreign workers' employment is most illuminating:[5] on balance, about 80 per cent of all foreign labour (about 1.4 million people) moved into manufacturing and construction; in both sectors foreigners apparently replaced Germans who switched to service sectors such as trade, banking and insurance and,

[5] For details, see Paqué (1988), pp. 7–9.

above all, to the government sector. In manufacturing, this substitution affected on balance about one million people in twelve years, leading to a share of foreigners in employment of almost 15 per cent in 1972.[6] This may help to explain why employment in services, which are less open to foreigners than manufacturing and construction because of the required language skills and institutional barriers, drastically increased at the expense of the primary, but not of the secondary sector.

As to regions, it was the southern industrialized areas of Hesse, Baden–Württemberg and newly rising Southern Bavaria which experienced the fastest employment growth and which sucked in the bulk of foreign workers: in 1972, the percentage of foreigners in employment was highest in Baden-Württemberg (16.7 per cent), followed by Hesse (13.7 per cent), Southern Bavaria (13.3 per cent) and highly industrialized North Rhine-Westphalia (10.9 per cent); it was lowest in the more rural areas of Lower Saxony/Bremen (6.0 per cent), Schleswig-Holstein/Hamburg (6.5 per cent), Northern Bavaria (7.0 per cent) and Rhineland-Palatinate/Saar (7.1 per cent).[7] Apparently, the labour shortage showed up most forcefully in the southern industrialized centres, and the mobile foreign workers willingly moved there to fill the emerging vacancies. In this sense, they served as a substitute for internal migration to alleviate interregional disparities. In fact, statistics on intra-national migration (see Table 6) indicate that the overall level of migration within West Germany declined sharply from the 1950s to the 1960s. Most visibly, the share of systematic interstate in total interstate migration (i.e., loosely speaking, the share of one-way migration between states) fell from above 30 per cent in the early and about 12 per cent in the late 1950s to 5.3–6.2 per cent in 1960–74; it did not rise again significantly until the 1980s. Hence, while the large regional disparities of the 1950s induced an extensive one-way migration from rural to urban centres, the – admittedly – less dramatic regional differences of labour shortage in the 1960s were mostly mitigated by the flexible supply of foreign workers who moved from abroad right into the southern industrialized centres.

To sum up, the 1960s and early 1970s were a period of general labour shortage or overemployment, with foreign workers figuring as the elastic part of the aggregate labour supply in times of both boom and recession. Structural change was accomplished by Germans moving from the primary

---

[6] See Bundesanstalt für Arbeit (1974), p. 15, Table 9. Within manufacturing, there were also significant differences between industries, with some branches having a share of foreigners close to 20 per cent (such as textiles and clothing). Viewed as a whole, however, the intra-sectoral differences were clearly less dramatic than the intersectoral ones.

[7] See Bundesanstalt für Arbeit (1974), p. 22. More detailed statistics show that the foreign workers were heavily concentrated in metropolitan areas, particularly in the southern ones (see Bundesanstalt für Arbeit (1974), pp. 25ff.).

and secondary into the tertiary sector, with foreign workers on balance filling the gaps left in manufacturing and construction, but not in agriculture and mining.

What were the causes of chronic labour shortage? Technically speaking, a non-cyclical state of overemployment can only persist if the marginal productivity of labour at full employment is and remains higher than the real wage, i.e. – roughly speaking – if real unit labour costs do not increase over the relevant period;[8] hence the term 'full employment' denotes a state in which the domestic (i.e. non-foreign) stock of labour is fully utilized, with no net inflow of foreign labour. The numbers in Table 17 show that – disregarding cyclical fluctuations – the ten years from 1960 to 1969 were a time of virtually constant aggregate real unit labour costs, with increases in 1960–3 and 1964–6 exactly compensated by the decreases in 1963–4 and 1966–9. Also, collective bargaining allowed for a substantial wage drift throughout the 1960s (see Figure 11): in all years between 1960 and 1970, effective wages rose faster than minimum contract wages, with the drift being particularly pronounced in the business upswings of 1963–5 and 1967–70. Hence, until the late 1960s, unions acted in collective bargaining as if they had an interest in the employment not only of West German union members, but also of potential foreign workers. Despite the early visible indications of a labour shortage and despite recurrent waves of immigration, they did not immediately press for a long-term real wage increase above productivity growth. Thus the labour shortage of the early 1960s was simply carried over to later years, with no substantial correction of real unit labour costs until the end of the decade. As actual labour productivity still grew fast – in 1960–9 by 4.4 per cent p.a., and in manufacturing by as much as 5.0 per cent p.a. – a drastic and, in absolute terms, increasing influx of foreign labour was the natural consequence. Not until 1969 did a wage explosion set in, with a hefty upward correction of real unit labour costs by about 1.6 per cent p.a. over five years (1969–74).

It is very difficult to answer the question why the union's wage policy tracked this kind of tortuous path; the issue will be taken up below when we turn to the sharply deteriorating supply-side conditions towards the end of the period. On the other hand, the fast growth of labour productivity is much easier to explain, at least with the benefit of hindsight. As in the 1950s, the key to it lies in booming exports and favourable investment

---

[8] The statement in the text is only correct if the relative change in average labour productivity is a good proxy for the relative change in marginal labour productivity. Whether this holds depends on the underlying production technology: the closer its parametric shape comes to a Cobb–Douglas technology, the better the approximation. In practice, the approximation appears to be good enough. See Bruno and Sachs (1985), Ch. 9, pp. 118–27.

Table 17. *The determinants of labour costs 1960–74*[a]

	(1) W	(2) LP	(3) PC	(4) PV	(5) PV/PC	(6) RULC
1960–61	10.2	3.2	3.4	4.7	1.3	2.0
1961–62	9.1	4.4	2.9	3.8	0.9	0.6
1962–63	6.1	2.5	3.0	3.1	0.1	0.3
1963–64	8.2	6.6	2.4	3.0	0.6	−1.5
1964–65	9.5	4.9	3.3	3.6	0.3	0.8
1965–66	7.6	3.3	3.5	3.3	−0.2	0.9
1966–67	3.3	3.2	1.8	1.4	−0.4	−1.3
1967–68	6.7	5.5	1.6	2.2	0.6	−1.0
1968–69	9.5	5.8	1.9	4.2	2.3	−0.6
1969–70	16.0	3.8	3.6	7.6	4.0	3.8
1970–71	11.6	2.5	5.6	8.0	2.4	0.9
1971–72	8.9	3.8	5.6	5.3	−0.3	−0.4
1972–73	11.6	3.6	6.3	6.4	0.1	1.3
1973–74	11.1	1.5	7.1	7.0	−0.1	2.3
1960–69	7.8	4.4	2.6	3.3	0.6	0.0
1969–74	11.8	2.7	5.6	6.9	1.2	1.6

Notes: [a] Average annual rates of change of selected variables (in per cent).
(1) W = wage level defined as average gross yearly earnings of employees (including social security contributions of employers); (2) LP = labour productivity defined as gross domestic product at constant prices divided by active labour force; (3) PC = private consumption deflator; (4) PV = deflator of value added (i.e. gross domestic product); (5) PV/PC = ratio of PV to PC as defined in notes to (4) and (3) respectively; (6) RULC = real unit labour cost defined as W/(LP·PV) as defined in notes to (1), (2) and (4) respectively.
Source: Statistisches Bundesamt; own calculations.

conditions: first, there was still plenty of scope for realizing productivity gains from international integration in the traded goods sector, i.e. mainly in manufacturing. Exports grew very fast in the period 1960–73, in real terms at a rate of 7.5 per cent p.a. compared to real domestic absorption, which increased by just 3.6 per cent p.a. The growth of exports was favoured by a series of steps towards trade liberalization within the European Community and by the apparent undervaluation of the West German currency in terms of domestic production costs which made the West German trade balance the only one of all industrialized countries that was in sizeable surplus throughout the period (Japan shared this distinction only later in the period).[9] Second, the capital stock grew very fast as well, in real terms at an annual rate of about 5.5 per cent, and in

[9] See Section B.1 of this chapter.

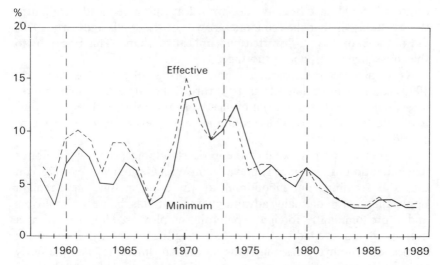

Figure 11. Contractual minimum and effective wages 1958–89.
Note: Average annual growth rate (in per cent) of index of hourly wage rate in industry.
Source: Statistisches Bundesamt: own calculations.

manufacturing at 6.5 per cent. By definition, capital stock growth is the result of net investment and thus depends on profit expectations; they, in turn, depend on the price of the complementary factors, notably labour, and the expected levels of future product demand (the accelerator principle). Apparently, there was reason for optimism in both respects: the longer labour restrained its wage demands, the more confident firms could be in expecting the celebrated social peace to continue without paying too high a price for it in terms of wage concessions; the longer the export surge continued in a rapidly expanding world market, the faster the future growth of the highly income-elastic demand for West German goods appeared to be. Hence, capital stock growth, which was largely taken for granted at the time, must itself be regarded as a function of the supply spurts initiated by the relatively low unit labour costs and the moves towards trade liberalization; by itself, it added a vigorous element of accelerator dynamics to the growth process which took on the features of a self-perpetuating virtuous circle, a straight – though somewhat moderated – continuation of what had happened in the 1950s. The virtuous circle was finally broken in the mid 1970s by the sudden and substantial revaluation of factor prices and the German currency which, with expectations still fixed on experiences of the happy past, drove the economy into a serious supply-side crisis. Whether this crisis and the later slackening of growth could have been avoided or at least mitigated leads straight to the question whether the economic growth of the 1960s and early 1970s did not already have a distorted and unhealthy shape. This brings us to the consequences of labour shortage.

As we have seen, the chronic labour shortage of the 1960s and early 1970s had two immediate effects: (i) it turned the domestic labour market into a sellers' market; and (ii) it induced a heavy influx of foreign labour. Both effects had far-reaching economic consequences which we have to consider separately.

(i) From a first-best welfare theoretic standpoint, a state of labour demand rationing, as it mostly prevailed in West Germany in 1960–73, can hardly be anything but suboptimal: at any point in time there remain opportunities for mutually advantageous contracts between employers and – predominantly foreign – potential employees. However, from a more pragmatic second-best stance featuring the growth dynamics of the domestic economy, things may look somewhat different: given the fairly rigid relative wage structure as it has traditionally prevailed across regions, economic sectors and industrial branches in West Germany, a less than equilibrium wage level may well yield better conditions than an equilibrium one to make market forces minimize frictions and mitigate structural distortions introduced by collective bargaining.

This is so for four basic reasons. First, more scope remains for a demand-induced wedge between the actual wage and the minimum wage set by collective agreements (i.e. wage drift) in a state of labour shortage than in a state of equilibrium. To the extent that the wage drift not only recoups the disequilibrium wedge, but also removes structural distortions through greater wage differentiation, there is an efficiency gain. As mentioned above, the 1960s were a time of large (temporary) wage drift (see Figure 11) which, in boom periods, helped to overcome severe bottlenecks in selected industries and regions.

Second, to keep labour motivated despite a relatively low minimum wage, employers will be inclined to be generous in granting fringe benefits as a partial substitute for pay increases; as fringe benefits are usually subject to fewer collective bargaining regulations than nominal wages, this is likely to add some flexibility to the labour market. In matters of labour mobility, this seems to be particularly important: incurring the cost of moving labour (including the provision of housing) is much more acceptable to the employer if the wedge between marginal labour productivity and the wage is not squeezed to zero by collective bargaining; to the extent that receiving the monetary equivalent of this cost as a pay increase is not a feasible alternative, labour will see its opportunity cost of moving reduced so that structural change can proceed with less friction without any socialization of mobility costs. There is no doubt that, in the 1960s and still in the early 1970s, employers were much more inclined to bear moving expenses for labour as a kind of ex-post compensation for wage moderation than in any other period.

Third, in a state of labour shortage employers have a strong incentive to take action to search for additional labour supplies, and workers can increasingly rely on them to do so. To the extent that employers have lower search costs than labour itself – and, because of their superior informational facilities, this is likely to be the case – one should expect the frictional costs of structural change to be further reduced. Obviously, the large-scale recruiting activities of West German firms in Southern Europe during the boom periods until 1973 are a good case in point.

Fourth, if labour mobility becomes a binding constraint, firms will be ready to move capital into structurally disadvantaged regions where the labour shortage still has the least dramatic dimension. Thus, a general labour shortage may become a private substitute for a government policy to promote backward regions. In fact, a good deal of the gradual reduction of regional imbalances which was observed in the 1960s and early 1970s may be due to such 'spillover effects', with the more rural areas of Lower Saxony, Rhineland-Palatinate and Northern Bavaria enjoying quite satisfactory employment growth in industry and services as compared to urbanized North Rhine-Westphalia;[10] this equilibrating mechanism might have worked even more effectively if there had not been the extremely elastic labour supply from abroad which was diverted mainly into the southern industrialized centres.

To sum up, the relatively low labour costs and the consequent labour shortage allowed placing the burden of structural adjustment mainly on the shoulders of the factors complementary to labour, i.e. on capital and on entrepreneurship. This, in turn, helped to preserve a climate of social peace in West Germany which was the envy of most other European countries. After all, fewer than two million working days were lost through strikes in the whole 1960–70 period.[11] These were very favourable conditions for a smooth and frictionless process of growth and structural change.

(ii) As to the long-term consequences of the labour influx from abroad, there were basically two distinct opinions among West German economists, namely

---

[10] In its annual report of 1965/6 (Ch. 4, Sec. III, pp. 153ff.) the Council of Economic Experts (Sachverständigenrat) provides some empirical evidence on the reduction of interstate disparities in income levels in the early 1960s. The Council explicitly argues that private firms were increasingly inclined to make investments in backward regions instead of industrial centres.   [11] See Langfeldt (1987), p. 28.

a positive one: meaning that foreign worker employment broke up important labour supply bottlenecks and smoothed the process of structural adjustment, thus improving the growth performance of the West German economy;[12] and

a negative one: meaning that foreign worker employment delayed structural adjustment and induced misguided investment, thus depressing growth in later years.[13]

Most proponents of the first view confined their argument to an elaboration of the fact that foreign labour served as a complementary buffer stock – something like the Marxian industrial reserve army – which flexibly alleviated the labour shortage whenever and wherever it showed up.[14] Although this appears to be an accurate picture, it does not imply that the influx of foreign labour was necessarily beneficial to long-term growth, since it is not clear what would have happened in the absence of an elastic labour supply. To make a sensible judgement one has to put the historical record against some relevant counterfactual development.

To do this, let us think of the West German economy of the 1960s as a stylized two-sector economy, with one sector being traded goods (called 'manufacturing') and the other being non-traded goods (called 'services'). Let us further postulate that, because of long-term income elasticities of product demand and irreversible shifts of the international division of labour, this economy moves away from the secondary to the tertiary sector in terms of both production and employment. For the time being, however, the economy is supposed to be in a process of rapid integration with other industrialized economies. On account of export-led growth at an undervalued currency within a rigid system of fixed exchange rates, this economy reaches its capacity limits in terms of labour and capital. Now, two polar scenarios are to be analysed, one with a virtually inelastic labour supply (the counterfactual) and the other with an almost completely elastic labour supply due to foreign worker immigration (the factual).

In the counterfactual scenario the labour shortage in manufacturing leads to a real wage push in this sector and – ceteris paribus – to a movement of labour back from services into manufacturing until the real wage increase has spread all over the economy. Clearly, this involves a

---

[12] See Sachverständigenrat (1964/5), para. 251; Kleemann (1965), pp. 82f.; Schmahl (1971), p. 62; Merx (1972), p. 14.

[13] See Harms (1966), pp. 277ff.; Rüstow (1966), pp. 35ff.; Föhl (1967), pp. 119ff., and, with a strong emphasis on structural change, Schatz (1974), pp. 205ff. The literature of the mid 1960s contains additional arguments against the employment of foreign workers (e.g., the need for additional infrastructure investment, the large transfers of income to the home country, etc.). As these arguments have no substantial bearing on matters of economic growth, we will not consider them here. For a summary statement see Merx (1972), Ch. 1.   [14] See above all the elaborate study by Merx (1972), Chs. 2 and 3.

structural shift against the long-term trend towards services. This shift will be all the more pronounced the less service producers are able to raise prices and, thus, to shift the burden of the labour-cost increase onto service consumers; if service demand is fairly price elastic, the structural backward shift may be quite substantial.

In the factual scenario the labour shortage in manufacturing is alleviated through an adequate influx of foreign workers; at the extreme, no wage increase is needed, so that there will be no structural backward shift from services into manufacturing either. Following the long-term trend, the domestic labour force moves into services (including the government sector), while foreign workers take jobs in manufacturing. As the wage level is kept relatively low, the profitability of investment in manufacturing will remain high, and so will the level of capital-widening investment.

This model can be realistically extended by adding a two-sector vertical structure of employment; in an extremely simplified picture of reality, we may distinguish between blue-collar and white-collar workers, with manufacturing being assumed to employ a much higher proportion of blue-collar workers than services. Long-term structural change naturally favours white-collar labour. Scenario I then implies an improvement of the terms of trade of blue-collar workers, which again runs counter to the long-term trend. Scenario II implies an undisturbed shift of the domestic labour force into white-collar employment, with foreigners taking over their blue-collar jobs. By this substitution, vertical mobility for Germans is achieved through an imported replacement supply of blue-collar labour.[15]

Given these scenarios, advocates of foreign-worker employment could legitimately conclude that importing foreign labour was the best feasible way out of a genuine dilemma between the demands of long-term structural change in favour of services and a medium-term expansion of manufacturing which was mainly due to the trade liberalization within the EEC and the undervaluation of the German currency. The influx of foreign workers allowed the domestic labour force to continue or even to accelerate its long-term shift into the service sector and into jobs requiring higher qualifications. Stopping the influx would have resulted in keeping German workers in the old business of manning the export machine without regard to their long-term comparative advantage.

Critics of the employment of foreign workers replied that this view underestimated the costs of the factual scenario. Their argument was threefold: the inflow of foreign workers led to a misguided process of

[15] The empirical results presented by Merx (1972), Ch. 2 on the use of foreign labour clearly point to strong replacement effects of this kind between Germans and foreigners, both horizontally across sectors and vertically across employment status.

capital widening in manufacturing, since it was precisely the newly created marginal jobs in mature industries like iron and steel, metal manufacturing, vehicles, textiles and clothing which had to be scrapped when competition from less developed countries (including the home countries of the foreign workers) increased.[16] Second, capital widening in manufacturing was particularly unjustified in the late 1960s and early 1970s since the German currency was undervalued in terms of production costs, so that a kind of monetary protection wall kept West German industry artificially competitive.[17] And third, the influx of foreign labour allowed too rapid an expansion of the public sector: with wages kept low through marginal foreign worker employment in industry, the opportunity cost for government to expand its administrative staff was below its true opportunity cost in terms of the value of domestic labour to the private sector. As long as wage increases remained moderate, the ensuing growth of public-sector employment seemed to be tolerable; however, given the high level of job security in the public sector, a dramatic increase of public spending was bound to occur as soon as wage demands picked up. This finally happened in the first half of the 1970s, just at the time when the growth of tax revenue slowed down because of the onset of a major recession.

From a long-term growth perspective, all these points against the influx of foreign workers are well taken, and they proved almost prophetic when the party was over in the mid 1970s. In a way, however, they miss the nature of the fundamental dilemma of the time, namely the conflict between the demands of long-term structural change within a worldwide division of labour and the medium-run boom in manufacturing. With all domestic resources fully utilized and the exchange rate fixed, it was hard to avoid some kind of misallocation of capital which could be identified as such later.

To sum up, the overemployment of the 1960s and early 1970s was a mixed blessing. It was a blessing in the sense that it allowed regional disparities to be minimized, frictional costs of structural change to be reduced and the German part of the labour force to be reallocated according to long-term comparative advantages. The blessing was mixed to the extent that it involved a substantial growth of government and a boom in manufacturing which was to come to an end as soon as factor

[16] See Schatz (1974), pp. 205ff. He shows that across industries the share of foreign worker employment in 1969 was somewhat negatively correlated with human capital intensity, i.e., on average, foreigners moved more into branches where one should not expect West Germany to have a long-run comparative advantage.
[17] See again Schatz (1974), p. 215.

prices and the exchange rate were adjusted and the dynamics of European integration came to a temporary halt.

2   The heyday of demand management

At no other time in West German post-war history was the economic policy debate so strongly focussed on demand-side issues as in the 1960s and early 1970s. There were basically two reasons for this, one economic and one institutional. Economically, the major supply-side deficiency of earlier years – capital shortage cum unemployment – had been overcome by the end of the 1950s; with labour now in chronically short supply, the attention of policy-makers quite naturally turned to curbing price inflation, to avoiding external imbalances and to fine-tuning the economy along a full or even overemployment growth path. Until the wage and oil price hikes in the first half of the 1970s, there were simply no obvious supply-side maladies to be put on the agenda. Institutionally, the early 1960s brought a major enlargement of professional macroeconomic policy counselling: in 1963, the West German parliament passed a law to establish an independent five-member Council of Economic Experts. It was assigned the task of periodically evaluating macroeconomic developments in the light of four objectives: price level stability, a high level of employment, external balance and steady and adequate growth. The task also included research into the formation and distribution of income and wealth and into the causes of so-called tensions between aggregate demand and supply which could endanger the simultaneous realization of the major macro-economic goals. Maladjustments were to be pointed out together with the means of avoiding or correcting them; however, the Council was explicitly denied the right to make specific policy recommendations, although, in practice, the difference between a 'legitimate' evaluation of different policy scenarios and an 'illegitimate' policy recommendation turned out to be largely academic. Unlike its American counterpart, the 1946-founded Council of Economic Advisors, it was designed as an advisory board independent of the government, so that a critical attitude towards the prevailing policy stance did not constitute a violation of its duties.[18]

The idea of establishing an expert council of this kind had first been floated by the Advisory Council to the Federal Minister of Economics in a report as early as 1956;[19] it then became the subject of long political deliberations which finally ended with the passing of the law in 1963.

---

[18] A detailed comparative account of the American Council of Economic Advisors and the West German Council of Economic Experts is provided by Wallich (1968).
[19] See Wissenschaftlicher Beirat (1973), pp. 291–320 (reports of 3 June and 8 July 1956).

From 1964 on, the Council was to deliver an annual report in November of each year and additional special reports whenever the macroeconomic situation called for a thorough analysis of some important policy issue. As it turned out, the newly founded Council quickly took over a major public role as a critical companion of government and central bank policies. On the other hand, the honeymoon of policy counselling might not have been possible without the receptiveness on the side of policy-makers. In particular, Karl Schiller – Minister of Economics from late 1966 to 1972 and himself a prominent economics professor – was ready to engage in a long-standing constructive dialogue with the Council of Economic Experts.

If one looks upon the years 1960 to 1973/4 as a kind of macroeconomic policy drama, one should divide the play into three acts: (i) the period 1960–3, a fairly quiet time of business consolidation after a powerful boom, but with no sign of a major contraction; (ii) the period 1963–9, covering one full business cycle, in which all fundamental issues of domestic demand management and corporatist coordination as well as internal and external stability came to the fore, and (iii) the period 1969–73, a time of an almost uninterrupted inflationary boom which provoked a fairly hectic crisis management of exchange-rate adjustments and stabil-ization measures. We shall now discuss the major macroeconomic events of these three acts.

(i) 1960–1963: consolidation at resilient inflation. By the turn of the decade, the West German economy grew extraordinarily fast, in 1959/60 at an annual rate of 8.6 per cent. With the unemployment rate converging to 1 per cent and price inflation beginning to accelerate, the Bundesbank tightened its monetary policy by a gradual increase of the discount rate from a low of 2.75 per cent in the first half of 1959 to 5 per cent in June 1960, accompanied as usual by a whole battery of complementary measures of credit contraction, above all an increase of minimum reserve requirements by about 55 per cent. The apparent drawback of this policy was a classical conflict between internal stability and external balance in a system of fixed exchange rates: given an export-led boom characterized by a substantial current account surplus, a tight monetary policy at home is bound to aggravate the external imbalance, because high interest rates simultaneously induce capital inflows and crowd out domestic absorption to the advantage of foreign demand, i.e. exports. This is precisely what happened in 1960: on top of the notorious West German current account surplus, the capital account balance turned into surplus for the first time since 1952, so that foreign exchange reserves swelled up dramatically. The obvious solution to the

dilemma – a revaluation of the German currency so as to redirect domestic and foreign absorption away from West German goods – was not yet considered. In November 1960, however, the Bundesbank eventually made a sharp policy U-turn by unambiguously giving priority to the external balance. To cut the capital account surplus, the restrictive monetary stance was abandoned: the discount rate was reduced by a full percentage point and – in two further steps in January and May 1961 – to a low of 3 per cent. Minimum reserve requirements were lowered by a total of about 35 per cent in nine stages in 1961. The risks for internal stability which these moves entailed were greatly mitigated through a revaluation of the West German currency by 5 per cent in March 1961. This parity adjustment was doubtless overdue. It received almost enthusiastic support from the Advisory Council to the Federal Minister of Economics: in its report of 4 March 1961, the Council fully endorsed the new policy mix of low interest rates and adjusted parities.[20]

For a while, this new policy mix did a remarkably successful job by pushing the economy closer to external balance: the current account showed a much lower surplus in the following years and even a slight deficit in 1962 and again in 1965; as the capital account returned to a deficit because of lower interest rates, the time of persistent West German external surpluses came to a temporary halt, which lasted to the second half of the 1960s. However, the price to be paid is likely to have been a creeping inflation: while the business climate cooled off in 1962/3, not least as a consequence of the revaluation, the inflation rate remained in the range of 2–3 per cent, a level which was still low by international, but not by West German standards of earlier years.[21]

All in all, the macroeconomic events of the period 1960–3 were anything but exciting. Even the moderate slack of growth in 1963 hardly raised tempers, simply because the unemployment rate remained persistently low and the utilization of the capital stock was not all that far below normal levels. Clearly, the miracle years of growth had passed, but this was now generally recognized and thus did not cause much political turmoil. In retrospect, the aftermath of the revaluation appears to be the last time for almost two decades to have a fairly calm and relaxed macroeconomic climate.

(ii) 1963–1969: curbing a boom and fighting a recession. In autumn 1963, the cyclical tide turned again: a new export-led upswing began and quickly gained momentum. In 1964, the growth rate of real GDP reached

---

[20] *Ibid.*, pp. 421–2 (report of 4 March 1961).
[21] On the details of monetary policy and its consequences in the years 1960–3, see Oberhauser (1976), pp. 615–21; on the revaluation of 1961, see Emminger (1976), pp. 503–9.

a respectable annual average of 6.7 per cent (after 2.8 per cent in 1963), and the first signs of an accelerated wage and price inflation became visible. This led the newly founded Council of Economic Experts to take up the fundamental question of how to solve the conflict between domestic price-level stability and powerful inflationary pressures from abroad in a world of fixed exchange rates. Using rigorous theoretical reasoning, the Council bluntly stated that, in these circumstances, price stability could only be maintained if exchange rates were sufficiently adjusted to neutralize the international inflation differential. This could best be achieved in a regime of flexible exchange rates as it ensured a continuous parity adjustment rather than the step-by-step changes which are characteristic of the fixed-parity framework provided by the Bretton Woods system.[22] This open plea for flexible exchange rates aroused a storm of protest from the public and a rather cold reply by the West German government in which a DMark revaluation and – a fortiori – a move towards exchange-rate flexibility were discarded as unrealistic and undesirable policy options. While the logic of the Council's points was not in any doubt, the government mainly relied on political and institutional counter-arguments: a fixed exchange rate was considered to be a precondition for international economic integration and political coordination, i.e. a kind of safeguard against the seductions of isolationism. In addition, the government still expressed the firm belief that it had enough effective internal policy instruments at hand to curb inflationary pressures.[23] The flat rejection of the Council's ideas indicates their political prematurity: the time was not yet ripe for a major public debate on exchange-rate regimes simply because the tensions in the Bretton Woods system still appeared to be quite manageable with a mixture of implicit international policy coordination and good luck. Less than a decade later, things looked altogether different.

As the Council had predicted in its first annual report, 1965 brought a significant worsening of the inflationary climate, with the annual rate of change of the consumer price index exceeding 3 per cent p.a. and with a further upward pressure of inflation towards 4 per cent being clearly detectable in the course of the year. For quite a long time, this trend did not lead to any major macroeconomic policy reaction. Fiscal policy had become increasingly expansionary throughout the first half of the 1960s: since 1961, public spending increased significantly faster than public revenues so that, by 1964, a budget deficit – albeit a small one (0.1 per

---

[22] See Sachverständigenrat (1964/5), Ch. 9, paras. 236–58. As early as June 1964, the Council had made a case for a revaluation in a confidential memorandum to the government. See Sachverständigenrat (1967/8), Appendix II, pp. 251–5.

[23] See Sachverständigenrat (1964/5), Stellungnahme der Bundesregierung, paras. 5–12.

cent of GNP)[24] – emerged for the first time since 1951. As federal parliamentary elections were due in September 1965, the usual wave of pre-election gifts and an income-tax cut swelled the public deficit to 1.4 per cent of GNP. In view of the booming economy at the turn of the year 1964/5, the obviously pro-cyclical fiscal stance became more and more of a political nuisance.[25]

As to monetary policy, the low level of interest rates in all major industrialized countries prevented the Bundesbank from taking any major contractionary steps: while minimum reserve requirements were increased by a small margin (10 per cent) in August 1964, the discount rate remained at its 3 per cent low – fixed in May 1961 – until January 1965, a record of 3.5 years of basically unchanged monetary conditions. After all, it was still the threat of rising external surpluses which restrained the Bundesbank from any more daring anti-inflationary moves. However, in 1965, this threat faded as the domestic boom eventually proved to be powerful enough to turn the balance of payments into a deficit and thus to remove the conflict between internal and external stability. Hence, the Bundesbank finally reacted – still somewhat cautiously – by raising the discount rate in two steps (in January and August 1965) from 3 to 4 per cent.

Against this background of mounting inflationary pressures and a slight external deficit, the Council of Economic Experts published its second annual report of November 1965 under the title *Stabilization without Stagnation*. In this report, the Council expressed deep concern about an emerging conflict between price stability and economic expansion which might eventually induce the monetary authorities to take more decisive action and thus to drive the economy into a sharp stabilization crisis. The core of the cyclical adjustment problem was located in inflationary expectations: with all contracts – including wage settlements – running on the presumption of a rate of 3–4 per cent price inflation, any sudden, non-anticipated monetary contraction would sharply reduce the scope of private firms to shift cost increases on to the shoulders of customers; thus any outright attempt to reduce price inflation would lead straight into a severe profit squeeze since contractual minimum wages and interest rates were fixed on the basis of prior inflationary expectations. To avoid these consequences, the Council recommended a gradualist strategy called 'Concerted Action'. Roughly, this amounted to a kind of social compact between all major agents in the corporatist play of macroeconomics,

[24] Figures for public budgets refer to the national accounts definition of the budget deficit (surplus) of all levels of government (federal, state, local) excluding the social security administration.
[25] For details of fiscal policy in 1965, see Fels (1988), pp. 8–10.

namely the government, the central bank and the so-called social partners, i.e. unions and employers' associations. The compact entailed a coordinated and step-by-step filtering out of all inflationary expectations in private contracts so that a – gradually tightening – monetary and fiscal policy could be carried out without a major stabilization crisis. In particular, the social partners should agree to a cost-neutral wage policy which confined the relative rise of the wage level to actual productivity growth plus a compensation for a 'minimal' price inflation rate, say, 2 per cent in the first and 1 per cent in the second year of the stabilization programme; the respective stability target would be credibly announced so that it could be taken into consideration in all credit contracts and thus gradually pull down the nominal interest rate. Hence price stability could eventually be achieved without a profit squeeze. Consistent with its prior position on the exchange-rate regime, the Council recommended complementing the gradualist Concerted Action by a revaluation of the currency to the extent that the international inflationary differential was widened through the domestic stabilization programme.[26]

This gradualist conception of stabilization without stagnation was received quite positively in two meetings of Council members with representatives of the government, the Bundesbank, the employers' associations and the unions.[27] However, in its official statement on the Council's report, the government expressed a clear-cut preference for fast, sharp and, by consequence, uncoordinated anti-inflationary measures.[28] This is in fact how policy proceeded in 1966: just two months after the federal elections in September 1965, the so-called *Haushaltssicherungs-gesetz* (Law for Securing Budget Balance) was passed and virtually all levels of government switched to a restrictive stance, mainly because – as often after elections – the consolidation of the government budget was temporarily considered to be the first and utmost priority. In addition, the Bundesbank put pressure on the federal government to support its own policy, which now became sharply contractionary: in May 1966, the discount rate was raised to 5 per cent and average yields of long-term bonds reached a high of 8.4 per cent. As usual in the late and inflationary stage of a boom, wages increased much faster than labour productivity, so that, in the prevailing circumstances, a marked profit squeeze became inevitable. The monetary policy of the Bundesbank came down to a deliberate demonstration of power to show that inflation would not be

[26] For the whole conception of Concerted Action, see Sachverständigenrat (1965/6), paras. 187–208.   [27] See Giersch (1977b), p. 136.
[28] See Sachverständigenrat (1967/8), para. 228.

allowed to surge out of public control. In this sense, the ensuing stabilization crisis was an almost classic example of a 'wanted recession'.[29]

From the expenditure side of national accounting, it is all too evident that the sharp cyclical downturn of 1966/7 had its roots in a contraction of domestic – not of foreign – demand: investment virtually stagnated in 1966 and sharply declined in 1967, while the growth of exports still accelerated in 1966 and slowed down just slightly in the recession year 1967. Right at the time of the steepest downturn – from the third quarter of 1966 to the second quarter of 1967 – investment collapsed, whereas exports – although slowing down – still grew vigorously.[30] Private business was badly hit by the rise of interest rates and labour costs, and the resulting profit squeeze cut heavily into investment plans. Although the Council of Economic Experts had warned of an incipient contraction due to the policy shock treatment, the sheer extent of the recession came as a surprise to everybody: after all, in its annual report of November 1966, the Council had still predicted a 2.5 per cent growth of real GDP for 1967.[31] Instead, real GDP actually shrank in that year (by 0.1 per cent), for the first time in post-war history. For the West German public, which had not lived through a major recession for almost two decades, this was a considerable shock, and many unduly anxious observers began to draw parallels with the gloomy days of the Great Depression, although the unemployment rate – at a peak of 3.1 per cent (!) in February 1967 and an average of 2.1 per cent in the same year – was still far lower than in the last ten years of the Weimar Republic.[32]

Unfortunately, the gloomy economic picture was temporarily complemented by a mood of political crisis: quite naturally, the incipient recession involved hefty public revenue losses, so that, despite all genuine efforts after the federal elections towards fiscal consolidation, the federal government failed to achieve its objective of balancing the budget in the fiscal year 1966. As the coalition parties of the government held different views on how to balance the books – broadly speaking, the conservative Christian Democrats favoured a surcharge on top of the income tax

---

[29] For details of monetary policy at that time, see Fels (1988), pp. 11–14, and Oberhauser (1976), pp. 624–5.

[30] For a precise quantitative picture, see Fels (1988), pp. 6–7. Seasonally adjusted, the growth rate of real gross investment in plant and equipment was 4.7 per cent in 1966 (I), −1.8 per cent in 1966 (II), −10.0 per cent in 1967 (I), and −4.0 per cent in 1967 (II); the growth rate of exports was 7.6 per cent in 1966 (I), 12 per cent in 1966 (II), 11.1 per cent in 1967 (I) and 4.8 per cent in 1967 (II). (I) and (II) denote the first and second halves of the year.

[31] See Sachverständigenrat (1966/7), Table 39. In its special report of March 1967 (see Sachverständigenrat (1967/8), Appendix V), this forecast was corrected downwards.

[32] For a general discussion, see Hildebrand (1984), pp. 203–5.

liability, while the liberals firmly pleaded for expenditure cuts – the government finally broke up and a grand coalition of Christian and Social Democrats came to power, with Kurt Georg Kiesinger replacing Ludwig Erhard as Chancellor. Despite the undeniable complexity of the political infighting leading to the fall of Erhard,[33] it is safe to say that, without the recession of 1966/7, his political survival would have been out of the question, at least for the time being. All this seemed to support the uneasy conclusion that political stability in West Germany was still heavily dependent on economic success, and that, if this success faded, the country might fall back into the bad old habits of the 1920s and 1930s.

As the economy visibly slipped into recession and the balance of payments returned to a healthy surplus, the Bundesbank released the monetary brakes a little: beginning in late 1966 and early 1967, reserve requirements and the discount rate were successively reduced, the latter from 5 per cent in the second half of 1966 in 0.5-percentage steps down to 3 per cent in May 1967. Given the extremely sharp business downturn, this looked very cautious indeed, and Karl Schiller, the new Minister of Economics, publicly complained about a policy of 'monetary trip steps'. Not before the last four months of 1967 did the Bundesbank engage in massive expansionary open-market operations, which helped to lower the long-term interest rate in capital markets by a significant margin.[34]

Fiscal policy shifted gears in January 1967: the government announced a public investment programme of 2.5 billion DMarks, which amounted to at least partial compensation for the strong pro-cyclical expenditure cuts in 1966. In addition, special depreciation allowances were granted for a limited period until October 1967. In view of the expert forecasts of about 2.5 per cent real GDP growth for 1967 which had still been made by the five leading research institutes and by the Council of Economic Experts in late 1966, the new fiscal stance looked adequate at first; as the recession quickly deepened, however, it soon turned out to be still too restrictive. In its special report on the state of the business cycle in March 1967, the Council of Economic Experts called for a second and more courageous fiscal programme featuring individual and corporate income-tax cuts, extended and still more generous depreciation allowances and another set of public investment projects to remove bottlenecks in infrastructure.[35] Three months later, in July 1967, the government in fact put up a second public investment programme, this time amounting to

[33] For the political details, see Hildebrand (1984), pp. 218–31.
[34] For details, see Oberhauser (1976), pp. 625–7.
[35] See Sachverständigenrat (1967/8), Appendix V. Note that these recommendations were made under the proviso that wage increases remained moderate to avoid endangering the modest yield of more price stability. As it turned out, the unions did in fact take a very cautious stance at the beginning of the recovery.

about 5 billion DMarks, which the Council of Economic Experts later explicitly endorsed in its annual report of November 1967.[36]

It is difficult to say whether and to what extent these Keynesian efforts really helped to overcome the recession. No doubt, the federal government deserves credit for changing the fiscal stance from restriction to (moderate) expansion; after all, the budget deficit increased from 0.1 per cent of GNP in 1966 to 0.9 per cent in 1967. On the other hand, the lower-level governments (states and municipalities) continued their fiscal consolidation and thus partly neutralized the expansionary impulse from federal spending.[37] In any case, most of the strong recovery dynamics of late 1967 and the whole of 1968 must be attributed to export growth: after a temporary slowdown in the course of 1967, exports increased sharply in the first half of 1968, with a seasonally adjusted growth rate of 8.4 per cent p.a. as compared to 3.3 per cent for private consumption, 0.3 per cent for public spending and 1.2 per cent for private investment in plant and equipment.[38] Hence, fiscal and – probably even more so – monetary policy may have prepared the ground for a recovery, but the major expansionary impulse came from exports.

Given this quite obvious fact, it is remarkable that, among the public, the fast recovery of the West German economy after the 1966/7 recession was widely attributed to the use of modern demand management techniques.[39] This conclusion was based on two particular political circumstances: first, the crisis management was handled by the brilliant Karl Schiller, who justly spread an aura of competence; this made it hard for any journalist to escape the impression that it was Schiller's magic tools of demand management (*Globalsteuerung*) which had pushed the economy back on to the growth track. Second, the recession trough nicely coincided with the passing of the so-called Law for the Promotion of Economic Stability and Growth (*Gesetz zur Förderung der Stabilität und des Wachstums der Wirtschaft*) of June 1967, which set a legal framework for the use of all standard counter-cyclical instruments to achieve simultaneously the three macroeconomic goals of price stability, full employment, and external balance at 'stable and adequate' economic growth. The stability law, as it was usually called, had been under parliamentary scrutiny for almost four years, and it only marginally enlarged the size of the macroeconomic policy tool-box.[40] In particular,

---

[36] See Sachverständigenrat (1967/8), paras. 244–5.   [37] See Fels (1988), pp. 17–19.
[38] See also *ibid.*, pp. 6–7.   [39] See, e.g., Hildebrand (1984), pp. 283–90.
[40] A summary of the provisions of the stability law is provided by Kloten (1976), pp. 643–5. The political discussion on a legal framework for stabilization policies had begun as early as 1956, when the Advisory Council to the Federal Minister of Economics wrote a long report on institutional provisions for macroeconomic policy. See Wissenschaftlicher Beirat (1973), reports of 3 June and 8 July 1956, pp. 291–320.

the government received a kind of emergency right – with a veto power reserved for the parliamentary bodies – to fight excess demand by limiting depreciation allowances and raising income taxes (up to 10 per cent for one year) and, conversely, to combat a recession by reducing taxes to the same extent and granting a tax credit on investment expenditure (up to 7.5 per cent). Despite its limited scope, the law was widely praised as the 'Magna Charta' of Keynesianism in a market economy, and this may at least partly explain why public opinion scored the victory over the recession as a first piece of empirical evidence on the power of demand management.

As by late 1967 the recovery had definitely set in, two macroeconomic issues moved into the foreground: (i) the optimal timing of the expansion and (ii) the revaluation of the West German currency.

(i) In its annual report of November 1967 and again in a special report of July 1968,[41] the Council of Economic Experts pleaded for a kind of intertemporal substitution of the cyclical expansion: with the capital stock still heavily underutilized in the early stages of the recovery, a hefty increase of production – preferably fuelled by another programme of fiscal expansion – did not run any great risk of rekindling inflation; in later stages, however, any boom was in danger of ending in an inflationary spiral, so that a timely shift to a more restrictive stance should ensure a soft landing. In the same vein, an early increase of wages, i.e. a shortening of the cyclical wage lag, was desirable to prevent an undue explosion of profits which would carry the risk of provoking high wage demands right at the boom peak and – if these were not accommodated by an inflationary monetary policy – a sharp recession. Conversely, wage restraint should be exercised in the later stages of recovery so as to ensure a non-inflationary phasing out of the boom. This whole strategy amounted to a common effort by all major agents in the corporatist game to smooth out the cyclical fluctuations; like the earlier proposals of the Council, it was firmly rooted in an optimistic spirit of what might be called corporatist gradualism.[42]

The concept of this strategy came close to ideas of the Minister of Economics, Karl Schiller, who had institutionalized the so-called Concerted Action in the form of regular meetings of representatives from the government, the Bundesbank, employers' associations, unions and the economics profession to coordinate expectations and plans in various fields of economic policy without in any way fixing mandatory rules for wage increases. Under Schiller's chairmanship, the first meeting of Concerted Action had taken place in February 1967, and many more

[41] See Sachverständigenrat (1969/70), Appendix IV.
[42] For a summary statement of the strategy, see Giersch (1977b), pp. 137–8.

were to follow. Naturally, the Council's proposed strategy could have given this institution another challenging macroeconomic task. As the cyclical upswing gained ground, however, the idea of another spending programme did not find much political support. Also, both employers' associations and the unions opposed the main thrust of the Council's ideas, the former because they naturally welcomed a steep increase of profits, the latter because they were afraid of becoming too constrained in their collective bargaining by informal wage guidelines.[43]

Even without a third public spending programme, the economic expansion of 1968 was faster than the Council (and other expert forecasters) had predicted late in 1967: real GDP grew by 5.6 per cent in 1968, with a marked acceleration in the second half of the year. Hence, in retrospect, the Council's forecast of 4 per cent growth was unduly pessimistic, and its call for another government programme somewhat misplaced. On the other hand, the Council's concern about an excessive surge of profits due to the particularly long wage lag proved justified (see Table 17): in the last three years of the 1960s, real unit labour costs declined quite sharply. While this clearly helped to pull the economy out of the recession, the concomitant profit explosion may well have contributed to the labour unrest which finally led to the dramatic upward shift of the wage level in the early 1970s.

(ii) With the current account surplus steadily rising and price stability increasingly endangered by imported inflation, the Council of Economic Experts argued strongly in favour of a drastic revaluation of the West German currency.[44] The Council was supported by the Bundesbank and by the Advisory Council to the Federal Minister of Economics.[45] In turn, a revaluation was forcefully opposed by West German industry, the Minister of Finance, Franz-Josef Strauß, and, most importantly, the Chancellor, Kurt Georg Kiesinger, who listened carefully to what industry had to say. The Minister of Economics, Karl Schiller, at first opposed a revaluation – at least in public;[46] from spring 1969, he firmly supported it. To accommodate political pressure from abroad, the cabinet finally agreed on a compromise solution in the form of a 'shadow revaluation', i.e. a scheme of taxing exports and subsidizing imports by a flat rate (4

---

[43] See Giersch (1977b), p. 137. For the details of the political controversy in the federal government, see Hildebrand (1984), pp. 294–6.

[44] See special report of 3 July 1968 in Sachverständigenrat (1968/9), paras. 197–282.

[45] See Wissenschaftlicher Beirat (1973), pp. 509–18 (report of 25 November 1967) and 535–44 (report of 1 February 1969).

[46] In private conversations with the authors, Karl Schiller has emphasized that, as an economist, he would have preferred the solution of a DMark revaluation as early as late 1968; as a politician, however, he had to make compromises and defend them in public, in particular to avoid destabilizing speculation in currency markets.

per cent) for a limited period of one and a half years. This happened in November 1968, but fairly soon, it proved to be an insufficient measure to drive the current account back into balance and to curb imported inflation. In May 1969, Schiller – by then openly advocating a revaluation – made an attempt to push the government into a change of parities; however, his proposals were blocked by the majority of the cabinet and the Chancellor. As a consequence, the question of revaluation became a major issue in the federal election campaign. This definitely proved to be to the advantage of the Social Democratic Party, since Schiller was able to transform this technocratic issue into a major campaign weapon to demonstrate the economic incompetence of the previous coalition partner, the Christian Democrats. In retrospect, it is clear that Schiller's campaign performance was of great help to the Social Democrats in overcoming their traditional image of being somewhat weak economists; it drove many middle-of-the-road voters into the arms of the (moderate) political left.

If one took a snapshot of the macroeconomic situation in the first half of 1969, the time of fastest growth throughout the recovery period after the 1966/7 recession, one would recognize the marked deviations from the ideal of stability which the Council of Economic Experts had in mind when making its policy proposals: the closer the economy moved towards full capacity utilization, the more momentum the upswing seemed to gain, reaching the highest growth rate since 1959/60 as late as 1969, the exact opposite of what the Council had argued was desirable; the current account remained in a persistent imbalance because of the equally persistent undervaluation of the German currency; and prices were clearly edging upwards. All in all, it seemed to be a far from perfect – though not altogether unsatisfactory – cyclical performance in a period when politicians and economists had been more concerned with questions of macroeconomic stability than ever.

(iii) 1969–1973: mounting inflationary pressures. The rapid recovery after the recession of 1966/7 passed into a boom which was exceptional in at least three respects. First, it was extremely powerful: in 1970, the degree of capital stock utilization reached the highest level since 1956 and the number of officially registered vacancies climbed to an all-time peak of 800,000 while unemployment was down to 150,000. Second, it was particularly long and sustained: after maximum growth in 1969 and maximum capacity utilization in 1970, the business climate cooled off slightly, but heated up again in 1973. As the short breathing space in 1971/2 can by no means be called a genuine recession, the period 1968/9–1973 figures as a kind of four-year marathon boom, the longest

since the first half of the 1950s. Third, the boom was markedly inflationary: after rising sharply in 1969/70, the rate of consumer price inflation remained at around 5–7 per cent throughout, with an upward trend even during the temporary slowdown of growth in 1971/2.

In the light of these facts, it is not surprising that the efforts of macroeconomic policy – both monetary and fiscal – concentrated almost exclusively on restraining an overbrimming aggregate demand and on controlling inflation which both originated in the US economy and swept across the whole industrialized world. Clearly, the main obstacle to setting up a watertight stabilization framework was – and remained – the rigid fixed exchange rates within the Bretton Woods system, which began to disintegrate but – after a first period of floating the DMark in 1971 – eventually survived until spring 1973. In retrospect, all domestic attempts by the Bundesbank and the government to reduce imported inflation look like desperate but futile emergency measures to stem a flood of US dollars which – in the prevailing institutional framework – simply dwarfed the power and scope of domestic policy instruments in a relatively small open economy. As the gradual breakdown of the Bretton Woods system will be dealt with in Section B of this chapter, we shall be brief on the domestic part of the macroeconomic turbulences, since they are mostly a mere reflection of what happened internationally.[47]

Until May 1971, the Bundesbank resorted to the standard tools of tight credit. At first, from March 1969 to March 1970, the discount rate was raised in steps from 3 per cent to the record level of 7.5 per cent, so that short-term interest rates shot up to well above 10 per cent. After the federal parliamentary elections, which brought about a new centre–left government favouring an adjustment of parities, the German currency was revalued by 8.5 per cent vis-à-vis the dollar in October 1969.

For a few months this gave the Bundesbank some relief, and the reserve requirements which had been raised before, more or less in step with the discount rate, were temporarily lowered. However, by 1970 this monetary honeymoon was over and the capital account turned into a huge surplus, mainly because of the inflow of short-term capital. All this looked like a replay of the events of 1960, albeit on a much more massive scale. As in 1960, the Bundesbank finally put considerations of external balance over the demands of internal stability, though with a somewhat different policy mix. Without a further currency revaluation, the discount rate was gradually reduced from its peak in March 1970 to 5 per cent in 1971; at the same time, reserve requirements were increased by almost 30 per cent

---

[47] A more detailed account of macroeconomic policies in this period is provided by Kloten (1976), pp. 652–73.

so as to tighten the liquidity of the banking system. In essence, these measures did not substantially help to curb either the capital inflow or inflationary pressures. Therefore in May 1971, the government went over to free floating, which proved remarkably successful as it led to a virtual stop of the capital inflow, a curbing of money-supply growth and a significant cooling of the economy: in the second half of 1971, investment stagnated and exports increased at a much slower pace than at any time since 1967.[48] The long-awaited – and certainly desirable – slowdown seemed to have arrived, and, towards the end of the year, the relevant forecasters predicted a moderate recession for 1972, with an annual growth rate of real GDP of just 1 per cent. After the currency realignment in December 1971, the Bundesbank again gave unambiguous priority to external over internal balance, though the cooling of the business climate made the choice look less of a dilemma than it did a year earlier: in the first two months of 1972, reserve requirements and the discount rate were reduced, the latter to a low of 3 per cent. By the middle of the year the temporary slowdown of growth had come to an early end and a new upswing set in. While the recovery gained momentum, the Bundesbank raised the reserve requirements and the discount rate, the latter from the 3 per cent low in October 1972 in various steps up to a high of 7 per cent in June 1973. As in March 1973 the Bretton Woods system gave way to a mixture of variable parities and block-floating, the Bundesbank finally gained more or less full control of the monetary expansion. In fact, the extremely tight monetary conditions – minimum reserve requirements had been raised by more than 50 per cent from the first half of 1972 to March 1973 – led to a drastic squeeze of liquidity in the banking sector and finally helped to stem the overbrimming boom.[49]

As to fiscal policy, the federal government made various attempts at counter-cyclical measures, most of them within the legal framework of the 1967 stability law.[50] Because of the usual political haggling, they were neither well timed nor particularly courageous in scope, at least if viewed against the background of the huge expansionary impulses coming from abroad. The following measures stand out: in mid 1969, the government decided to introduce a so-called cyclical fiscal reserve (*Konjunkturausgleichsrücklage*) of 3.6 billion DMarks and to enforce a temporary expenditure cut of 1.8 billion DMarks, which was later transformed into

---

[48] Seasonally adjusted and annualized, the growth rate of real gross investment in plant and equipment was 11.1 per cent in 1971 (I), but 1.9 per cent in 1971 (II); the growth rate of exports was 9.6 per cent in 1971 (I) and 3.7 per cent in 1971) (II). (I) and (II) denote the first and second halves of the year.

[49] For details, see Kloten (1976), pp. 658–62.

[50] For a summary of the measures, see Kloten (1976), pp. 654–7 and 662–6.

a permanent reduction. In July 1970, depreciation allowances were limited for almost seven months, and a temporary surcharge was imposed on top of the individual and corporate income-tax liability (to be repaid by June 1972). In May 1971 – parallel to the freeing of exchange rates – the government passed a stabilization programme involving expenditure cuts in the range of 1.7 billion DMarks. Finally, in 1973, two further stabilization programmes were passed, a minor one in February and a major one in May which entailed an 11 per cent investment tax, a limitation of depreciation allowances and a temporary 10 per cent surcharge on the income-tax liability. These measures read like a long list of cyclical activism, but their actual effect is difficult to appreciate. Certainly, the restrictive fiscal stance in the two boom years 1969 and 1973 broadly conformed to the requirements of the day, though gears were switched rather late in both cases. However, the bulk of the counter-cyclical fiscal work was probably done by the automatic stabilizer of the tax system, not by the discretionary spending and taxing provisions planted on top of it: drastic increases of regular tax revenues by more than 15 per cent p.a. in 1969 and 1973 helped to reach a more or less balanced overall budget of the public sector in both years. Hence, the contribution of discretionary fiscal policy to stabilization may well have been quite modest.

Throughout the period 1969–73, the ad hoc monetary and fiscal efforts to curb inflationary pressures met with criticism from many independent economists, in particular the Council of Economic Experts.[51] As inflation soared and proved increasingly stubborn, the Council's calls for drastic stabilization measures became more urgent and its prior strategy of gradualist smoothness faded somewhat into the background. The core of any stabilization programme was persistently seen in exchange-rate flexibility or at least a drastic revaluation of the German currency. Consequently, steps towards this goal – most importantly the first period of a floating DMark in 1971 ('singular floating') – were praised, and steps away from it – above all the Smithsonian realignment of December 1971 – in principle deplored.[52] All major domestic stabilization efforts both on the monetary and the fiscal side were supported, for example, in the Council's two special reports in May 1970 and May 1973, both published more or less at a boom peak; however, a fair amount of scepticism as to their chances of curbing inflation permeated the reports as long as a currency revaluation was out of reach.

[51] See the Council's annual reports for 1969–73 and the special reports of June 1969, September 1969, October 1969, May 1970, May 1971, July 1972 and May 1973, which are contained in the respective annual reports.
[52] See, in particular, the special reports of June and October 1969, May 1971 and July 1972, which all deal with the adjustment of parities.

If we look back over the whole drama of macroeconomic policy in the period 1960–73, an element of tragedy can hardly be dismissed: an impressive apparatus of policy counselling had been established and, at least in the eyes of the public, the door to a new era of demand management had been opened when the sharp and frightful recession of 1966/7 was overcome, seemingly through the magic tools of fiscal and monetary policy. Just as this optimistic belief in the power of government as a macro-economic manager reached its peak, an irresistible wave of inflation flooded through the channels of the Bretton Woods system. Soon, it became clear that under pegged exchange rates a relatively open economy like that of West Germany could not remain an island of stability, and the hopes pinned on the macroeconomic power of government were badly disappointed.

3   A deteriorating supply side

An economy-wide inflation is the result of a discrepancy between aggregate demand and supply: too much money chases too few goods. As we have seen, the most obvious source of inflation in West Germany during the late 1960s and early 1970s is to be located on the demand side, namely a fast liquidity expansion due to an undervalued currency in a fixed exchange-rate system. Of course, this sharp rise of aggregate demand could only be inflationary to the extent that the supply side was not elastic enough to transform the nominal demand increase into real growth. In fact, there are good reasons to believe that, towards the end of the period under consideration, the productive potential of the West German economy gradually lost much of its former exceptional elasticity. Three major reasons for this change stand out: (i) a drastic increase in labour costs; (ii) a virtual explosion of energy prices; and (iii) a creeping institutional change involving a fast growth of the government sector. We shall briefly review each of them.

(i) Increasing labour costs. Throughout the 1960s, the state of overemployment did not yet lead to anything like a sustained rise of real unit labour costs (RULC). Only cyclical changes of RULC are detectable (see Table 17): increases towards the end of boom periods as around 1960–2 and 1964–6, but also substantial downward corrections during upswings such as 1963/4 and 1967–9. Most unusual is the reduction of RULC in 1966/7, when the economy was sliding into recession: because of a very moderate nominal wage increase of 3.3 per cent, the private sector could be spared a cost push which might have worsened the chances for an export-led recovery as it actually took place in 1967–9.

The unions certainly showed a fair amount of social responsibility in this first major recession of West German post-war economic history.

To explain union restraint in the 1960s is very difficult. No doubt, the unions were rich and influential enough to take a more demanding and radical posture; after all, the unionization rate, which had been decreasing over the 1950s, now stabilized at about 35 per cent.[53] Given the extremely tight labour-market conditions prevailing after 1960 (with the exception, of course, of the 1966/7 recession), the time would have seemed to be ripe for a major redistributive effort. However, it is likely that a number of both political and economic circumstances helped to preserve the earlier spirit of moderation until almost the end of the decade.

Politically, the 1960s were a time of growing convergence of all major forces: after the Social Democrats had cast off their Marxist past in the celebrated Godesberg programme of 1959 and finally accepted the concept of a social market economy – albeit with a particularly strong dose of Keynesian demand management and public responsibility for growth and employment – the unions did the same with their Düsseldorf programme of 1963.[54] As the Social Democrats – by then unambiguously the party where union political interests had found their home – gradually gained ground in regional and federal elections throughout the 1960s, there seemed to be a reasonable chance that the unions could soon exert a much more powerful and decisive political influence through a Social Democratic federal government. Hence an unduly aggressive and uncooperative stance, which was unpopular among the general public, could have endangered the unions' fairly bright medium-term political prospects. With the grand coalition of Social and Christian Democrats coming to power in 1966, the general spirit of social partnership clearly called for a temporary suppression of rank-and-file instincts by union leaders. In actual policy practice, unions found themselves under persistent moral pressure to moderate wage demands so as to make an active contribution in the corporatist fight against price inflation. This pressure emanated above all from the authority of the Minister of Economics, the moral suasion of Concerted Action and the implicit, but widely perceived, policy recommendations of the Council of Economic Experts. Most calls for moderation were based on a characteristic vision of a major macroeconomic assignment problem:[55] while demand policies – both fiscal and monetary

---

[53] See Langfeldt (1987), p. 28.
[54] See Schwarz (1983), pp. 195–201, for the Godesberg programme and Flanagan et al. (1983), pp. 264–5 for the Düsseldorf programme.
[55] The notion of an 'assignment problem' – meaning the appropriate allocation of different policy instruments to different policy goals – goes back to Mundell (1962).

– were held responsible for the maintenance of full employment (and – nolens volens – external balance), wage policy was to determine unit labour costs and thus also the price level provided that the liquidity frame of the economy was large enough to allow private firms to shift the cost increases into prices by some kind of mark-up pricing rule. Hence, within the narrow bounds of the Bretton Woods system, a moderate wage policy would give the monetary authorities the leeway to pursue a stability-orientated policy without running the risk of a sharp recession.[56] For the time being, unions apparently took their assigned active role as a corporatist guardian of stability seriously enough to keep wage increases in check.

Economically, the moderation had the non-pecuniary rewards characteristic of a seller's labour market: employers voluntarily shouldering the costs of mobility and search, and immigrants taking inferior jobs at the contractual minimum wage so that German workers and employees had the chance of moving to better-paid and more respected positions. In this sense, even the large wage drift which prevailed during the 1960s with the exception of the cyclical trough years 1963, 1966 and 1967 (see Figure 11) had its positive side.

The spirit of wage moderation came to an abrupt end in autumn 1969, when a first wave of wild-cat strikes swept over West Germany, an immediate reaction of the rank-and-file to the enormous profit explosion and the soaring wage drift. The strike wave initiated a reopening of collective bargaining and, as a consequence, a dramatic increase in wages: for the first time since 1950, nominal wages rose at an annual rate of more than 15 per cent, and contractual minimum wages at a rate of 13 per cent. With profits high, the resistance of employers against wage demands was weak and, given the high level of liquidity in the economy, private firms were still able to shift part of the cost burden onto prices. However, in the following years, the wage pressure hardly abated, and so there was a fundamental upward shift of real unit labour costs: in four out of the five years from 1970 to 1974, nominal wages rose by at least 11.5 per cent p.a., and in just one year (1972) 'only' by 9.9 per cent p.a. Except in 1972, RULC increased by at least 1 per cent p.a., with the rise in 1970 (by 3.8 per cent) and in 1974 (by 2.5 per cent) being particularly dramatic. The politically most spectacular and economically most damaging bargaining round (popularly called the *Kluncker-Runde*) was staged in early 1974 when the union of public employees – traditionally more of a passive follower than of an active pacemaker in the annual process of wage determination – took an extraordinarily intransigent stance and, in

[56] For a detailed argument along these lines, see Sachverständigenrat (1964/5), paras. 248–9.

February 1974, negotiated an increase of contract wages by 11 per cent. This happened just a few months after the oil price shock and against the background of some clearly visible recession indicators; not surprisingly, the private sector followed suit, with the large and usually radical metal workers' union figuring as a kind of transmitter between the public and the private sectors of the economy.[57]

The sudden switch of union behaviour from moderation to aggressiveness in the late 1960s and early 1970s is unique in West German economic history and is therefore very difficult to explain. To be sure, it was a deliberate attempt to change the income distribution to the advantage of labour: in a projection of 1970, the unions' umbrella organization DGB envisaged an increase of the adjusted wage share in national income by 5.4 per cent in five years, which is, incidentally, more or less what took place afterwards.[58] Some reasons for this change of mood are identifiable. The Social Democrats had finally come to power in 1969, albeit with a liberal coalition partner and a Minister of Economics (Karl Schiller) who was by no means a union man. Hence, in the back of the union leaders' minds, the political rationale for restraint now began to fade away and among the rank-and-file the call for presenting the bill to the political friends certainly became louder. This can be seen most clearly in the public-sector wage round of 1974, when the Social Democratic Chancellor Willy Brandt was almost certainly much less able to resist union demands than a conservative would have been in the same circumstances. It is safe to say that the wage round seriously damaged the authority of the Chancellor and thus contributed to his resignation over the so-called Guillaume affair in April 1974.[59] Economically, the tremendous profit surge of the late 1960s and the consequent wild-cat strikes had taught union leaders the important lesson that the patience of the rank-and-file was definitely not unlimited. To regain members' confidence, a more aggressive bargaining style may have been the rational answer. As the membership statistics of the unions show, the new more radical posture was in fact popular: between 1969 and 1974, the unions gained one million members – after a decade of membership stagnation – and thus increased the unionization rate in the West German economy from 35 to about 39 per cent.[60] Finally, the persistently inflationary character of the late Bretton Woods system may also have contributed to the drastic change of wage policy: with accelerating price inflation becoming a lasting feature of the economy's performance, inflationary expectations began to play a par-

---

[57] For a detailed discussion of wage policy in the years 1969–74, see Flanagan et al. (1983), pp. 242–4.   [58] See Sachverständigenrat (1970/1), pp. 239–48.
[59] For a political interpretation of the 1974 wage round, see Bracher et al. (1986), pp. 110–12.
[60] See Langfeldt (1987), p. 28.

ticularly important part in wage bargaining and may at times have led to full or even super-indexation of nominal wage demands.

Whether all these plausible factors are really sufficient to account for the sharp rise of labour costs in the early 1970s remains open to doubt. Unions turned significantly more militant in virtually all European industrialized countries by the late 1960s, so that at least the specifically German factors may not have been decisive. After one or even two decades of unprecedented internationally synchronized growth dynamics, something like a qualitative shift away from efficiency to equity occurred everywhere, together with a general resurgence of more radical left-wing and Marxist ideas, in particular after the wave of student revolts in spring 1968 which swept over many countries of the industrialized world. Although the rediscovery of Marxism was basically an intellectual phenomenon confined to academics in universities with no strong ties to the more down-to-earth union membership, it may have had a hidden sociological impact on the inclination towards radicalism in the workplace; apparently, a new generation of young employees now took the high living standards for granted and simply asked for more, not realizing (or even not caring) that a basically pragmatic union stance was a precondition for growth and full employment in any economy with a strong element of corporatism.[61] However, all this remains a matter of speculation which, although no doubt fascinating, transcends the limits of our more narrowly economic account.

(ii) The first oil price shock. In the early 1970s, after a decade of stability, the prices of imported raw materials began to edge up. As a consequence of the political crisis in the Middle East, notably the Yom Kippur War in October 1973 between Israel and its Arab neighbours, this development took on dramatic dimensions: as the cartel of oil-producing and exporting countries (OPEC) drastically cut down the market supply of crude oil, the price of oil more than tripled within a few months around the turn of the year 1973/4. Other raw material prices followed suit, although not quite at the same pace.[62] In view of the sudden supply constraints and the uncertainty surrounding further possible measures by OPEC, the West German government passed an energy emergency law (Energiesicherungsgesetz) in November 1974 which provided a legal basis for various measures of supply rationing, including a general prohibition on driving motor vehicles on selected Sundays. For a few months in winter 1973/4, this prohibition was put into practice.

[61] For a detailed account of the resurgence of class conflict in the West European labour movement after 1968, see Crouch and Pizzorno (1978).
[62] See Sachverständigenrat (1974/5), p. 58.

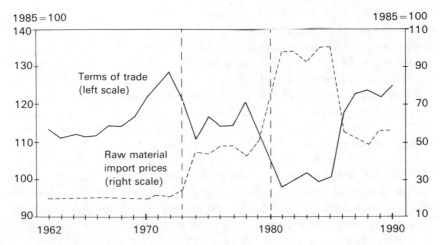

Figure 12. Terms of trade and raw material import prices 1962–90.
Source: Statistisches Bundesamt; own calculations.

Together with the then fashionable reading of the Club of Rome literature on the doomsday scenario of resource depletion,[63] these panicky measures helped to turn the public attention to the limits of economic growth and, as a by-product, to environmental pollution. For the first time in post-war history, these topics moved on to the centre stage of the policy debate.

Economically, the oil price shock resulted in a thorough worsening of West Germany's terms of trade (see Figure 12): as the price index of imported raw materials more than doubled from 1972 to 1974, the terms of trade turned down by almost 14 per cent in two years, by far the most dramatic change in external trade conditions since the late 1940s. Although the second half of the 1970s brought some temporary relief, economists at the time clearly recognized that the cost push of energy prices signalled a permanent change in the macroeconomic climate and in growth prospects: in the short and medium term, other factors of production – notably labour – were to curtail their demands so that the energy price hike did not translate into a disastrous profit squeeze, leading to a growth slack and unemployment. In the long run, a painful process of factor substitution would have to carry the economy on to a less energy-intensive growth path.[64]

[63] See Forrester (1971) and Meadows et al. (1972).
[64] See Sachverständigenrat (1974/5), pp. 183–98 (special report of 17 December 1973) and pp. 170–6.

(iii) The growth of the government sector. There is no doubt that government expanded fast in the 1960s and early 1970s, faster than the economy at large. This can be seen from all major macroeconomic indicators: as a percentage of GNP, total public spending went up from 32.9 per cent in 1960 to 42.1 per cent in 1973; if social security expenditures are excluded, the numbers are 23.7 per cent in 1960 and 29.2 per cent in 1973. The tax burden increased markedly: in 1960, taxes and social security contributions made up 35.9 per cent of GNP, and in 1973 43.3 per cent; taxes alone covered 25.8 per cent of GNP in 1960, and 29.0 per cent in 1973. Also, fiscal discipline suffered: an overall budget surplus of the public sector – in the late 1950s and early 1960s still the rule – became the boom-time exception and, after 1969, disappeared altogether, at least if social security contributions and benefits are excluded. Not surprisingly, it was in these years – to be precise in 1971 – that, for the first time in West German post-war history, a federal Minister of Finance resigned from office as he felt unable to take responsibility for the fiscal stance of the government.[65] As to employment in 1960–73, the public sector made a great leap forward, in absolute terms by 1.3 million people, and in relative terms by 60.8 per cent (see Table 16). The most rapid expansion took place in the first years of both the 1960s and the 1970s, whereas, in the time of and around the recession of 1966/7, public-sector growth slowed down significantly.

If one searches for the causes of government growth in the years from the early 1960s to the mid 1970s, one invariably ends up with a vague explanation in terms of *Zeitgeist*, i.e. the spirit of the times. After the economic miracle of the 1950s had done its excellent job of lifting West German living standards up to or even above the level of most other industrialized countries, a general consensus emerged that political and economic priorities ought to shift away from mere material progress to raising the quality of life and to achieving more social justice, whatever that meant in detail; on the instrumental level, extensive use should be made of the large tool-box of public planning and social engineering in all matters which seemed to transcend the competence of a narrowly profit-orientated private sector. Ideologically, these social aims have their traditional intellectual home on the political left, and in fact, the period 1960–73 can be characterized as a gradual advance of Social Democratic ideas into the forefront of political decision-making and of more general social and cultural thinking. In a way, the whole intellectual base-line moved a few steps to the left and stayed there until the economic slack

[65] See Bracher et al. (1986), pp. 49–50.

of the 1970s and 1980s greatly narrowed the financial leeway for any kind of social experimentation.

In a still cautious and ideologically restrained way, the new spirit appeared in Ludwig Erhard's concept of the *Formierte Gesellschaft* (the 'formed' society) which was developed in the years of his chancellorship (1963–6). Erhard – himself considered the father of the economic miracle – recognized the general need for a vision beyond the mainly economic dimension of Ordoliberal ideas prevailing in earlier times. He therefore postulated a programme of so-called *Gemeinschaftsaufgaben* (common tasks) like investments in infrastructure, education and culture which were to be genuine concerns of a responsible government in future years. At the same time, however, he strongly deplored the power of vested interests which persistently pressed the government towards granting favours to particular identifiable groups and thus abused the state for group egoistic redistribution. Thus Erhard quite explicitly opposed the kind of *Gefälligkeitsdemokratie* (democracy of favours) which had developed in the paternalistic spirit of the Adenauer years and which threatened to be expanded with the rise of Social Democratic ideals. Hence, his concept of the *Formierte Gesellschaft* was not just an attempt to widen the scope of government and thus to steal some Social Democratic clothes, but also – and maybe more importantly – to separate legitimate from illegitimate public goals and to build a solid defensive line against indiscriminate government growth.[66]

After the political fall of Erhard, this last defensive line was simply swept away. By its very nature, the grand coalition of Christian and Social Democrats did not have a coherent liberal philosophy of restraining government; on the contrary, it included very powerful wings of so-called socially minded politicians (the SOPOS, i.e. the *Sozialpolitiker* of both big parties) who formed a strong – though implicit – bipartisan faction in the cabinet and the parliament to defend the extension of the welfare state against all outside attacks.[67]

The centre–left coalition which came to power in 1969 began its work with an explicit programme of enlarging the scope of government in order to make society more democratic, to give new opportunities to socially disadvantaged groups, and to make public decisions more rational and 'scientific'. The public planning euphoria reached a clear peak in the early 1970s under the ideological guidance of the federal government. In virtually all spheres of public activity, medium- and long-term plans and projects were worked out, usually on the assumption that they could be

[66] For a thorough account of Erhard's concept, see Hildebrand (1984), pp. 160–70.
[67] For political details, see Hildebrand (1984), pp. 299–300.

financed out of tax revenues whose growth was simply extrapolated from prior experience. That the underlying premises concerning economic growth in the future could turn out to be much too optimistic was not yet taken seriously as a counter-argument against more public planning and spending. Note that, of course, this optimistic or even reckless spirit stretched well over the boundaries of political parties: while the federal government and the Social Democratic Party in particular figured as a kind of ideological pacemaker, many regional and local governments of different political colours had essentially the same outlook. Local communes constructed more administration buildings, public swimming pools, recreation areas, schools and the like in these years than in any other period of West German economic history after the Second World War.

If we summarize the main fields of public initiatives, the following picture emerges. In the years of the centre–right coalition until 1966, government growth proceeded within the traditional pattern of public activity laid out in the 1950s. Here and there, the coverage of the welfare state was marginally extended, but no fundamental reform took place. After all, Ludwig Erhard – Chancellor since 1963, but the Crown Prince long before that – had no zeal for pushing anything that could smack of welfarism. If he had any particular social concern apart from his vision of the *Formierte Gesellschaft*, then it was the promotion of a kind of 'people's capitalism', i.e. spreading the country's ownership of productive resources to as many hands as possible and thus turning workers and private households into responsible shareholders. With the partial privatization of publicly owned firms like Preussag (as early as 1959), Volkswagen (1961) and VEBA (1965) some steps in this direction had already been taken, but without any far-reaching consequences.[68]

In the three years of the grand coalition, some new instruments of economy-wide planning were introduced. In particular, the so-called medium-term planning of public finances (*mittelfristige Finanzplanung*) was to extend the horizon of fiscal projections beyond the narrow budgetary constraints of one year. As to the coordination between the various bodies of government from the federal down to the municipal level, special 'common tasks' (*Gemeinschaftsaufgaben*) were introduced which had to be carried out jointly by federal, state and possibly local authorities. In fact, this came close in spirit to Erhard's earlier ideas. Typical examples for common tasks were the building of new universities and public investments in the infrastructure of economically backward regions. As to taxes, the grand coalition did not refrain from closing the fiscal gap left in the course of the 1966/7 recession by introducing a

---

[68] For the details of the privatization initiatives, see Schwarz (1983), pp. 159–60.

surcharge of 3 per cent on the income-tax liability, confined to middle- and higher-income earners; ironically enough, this tax increase by any other name ran counter to the core of the tax reform of 1965 which had deliberately brought about a reduction of income-tax rates for the middle-income ranges.

In the first four years of the centre–left coalition, most sectors of the welfare state were enlarged in scope and financial underpinnings. In education, new laws provided for much higher grants to students in need and greatly extended the plans for university construction, both in view of a sharp increase in the number of students in the years to come. As to social security, the pension reform law of 1972 more or less guaranteed a minimum living standard independently of actual prior contributions to the system; in addition, virtually all benefits in the various branches of social security (especially health insurance) were substantially raised and usually extended in application. Many other ambitious public programmes were embarked on, whether in urban planning, in residential construction or, with increasing importance, in environmental protection, usually all with a substantial and lasting financial commitment by the government on all levels. On the revenue side, a number of minor tax reforms were carried out, the most important being the income-tax law of 1974, which, by and large, brought some relief for the low- and a somewhat heavier burden for the middle- and higher-income brackets.[69]

Whatever the merits or demerits of these reforms in any particular instance, there can hardly be any doubt that they created a considerable financial burden for the future. If the economy turned sour and if the expansion of the public sector proved irreversible, this would lead to a further drastic increase in the share of GNP absorbed by the government. In particular, the expansion of the welfare state with its usual ratchet effects created a major liability since it did not have the character of a genuine social investment which could be expected to increase future tax returns. In addition, many generous provisions of the welfare state may well have diminished the individual inclination to adjust to changes in economic conditions and thus, in the aggregate, reduced the elasticity of the economy's supply side. All these negative side effects were to show up earlier than even pessimists expected at the time.

All in all, it is undeniable that, by the mid 1970s, supply-side conditions had drastically worsened because of a wage revolution, an oil-price hike and a creeping but sustained government growth. Thus, a good part of the temporary stagflation and the chronic slack of growth which followed may have had their roots in earlier times.

[69] For the political details, see Bracher et al. (1986), pp. 139–40.

B   Coping with external constraints

In comparison with the rather turbulent period of the late 1940s and the 1950s, the development of West Germany's external economy in the 1960s and early 1970s may at first glance appear quite tranquil. Many of the major trends which had been discernible in the 1950s simply continued, albeit at a significantly slower pace. Taking the 1960s and the early 1970s as a whole, one may still say that exports remained a major driving force of West Germany's economic growth. The share of exports in GNP rose from 15.8 per cent in 1960 to 19.4 per cent thirteen years later.[1] Naturally, exports grew more slowly than in the previous decade: the annual average rate of export growth went down by almost half from 19.1 per cent in the 1950s to 10.6 per cent in the later period (see Table 18). By the late 1950s, West Germany had finally exhausted the scope for a seemingly effortless export surge which had been as much a mere reflection of its successful return to pre-war positions on the world market as the result of the country's internal supply elasticity and its comparatively liberal trade policies. Unlike in the 1950s, import values lagged only slightly behind (up 9.9 per cent p.a.), while – in volume terms – imports increased even marginally faster than exports (10.1 and 9.8 per cent p.a. respectively). In other words, West Germany owed its widening trade surplus mostly to the continuing improvement in its commodity terms of trade. This favourable development was achieved solely by the rapid increase in the prices fetched by German exports of finished manufactured goods in the world market relative to its respective import prices: while West Germany's terms of trade for all other categories of goods worsened between 1960 and 1973, the ratio of export to import prices for finished manufactures improved by 33 per cent.[2]

Yet, the seemingly satisfactory overall picture sketched above masks two serious asymmetries: (i) a significant divergence between the sub-periods 1960–5 and 1966–73 and (ii) a severe distortion in the regional profile of West Germany's foreign trade.

(i) Following the 5 per cent revaluation of the DMark in March 1961, the growth of imports outpaced that of exports by more than two percentage points p.a. in the first half of the 1960s (10.5 and 8.4 per cent respectively). Afterwards, exports soared ahead again with growth rates of 12.1 per cent p.a., while import growth slowed down to 9.5 per cent p.a. As a consequence, West Germany's trade surplus, which had first fallen to its lowest post-1952 level in 1965 (0.3 per cent of GNP) surged – amid cyclical fluctuations – to 2.3 per cent of GNP in 1970 and 3.6 per cent three years later. This is a clear indicator that, notwithstanding the

---

[1] See Figure 7 above.   [2] Statistisches Bundesamt; own calculations.

Table 18. *West Germany's foreign trade 1960–73*

	1960	1965	1970	1973	Average rate of growth[b]			
					1960–5	1965–70	1970–3	1960–73
Imports								
Values[a]	42.7	70.5	109.6	145.4	10.5	9.2	9.9	9.9
Volumes[c]	42.7	72.4	115.1	150.0	11.1	9.7	9.3	10.1
% of GNP	14.1	15.3	16.0	15.6				
Exports								
Values[a]	47.9	71.7	125.3	178.5	8.4	11.8	12.5	10.6
Volumes[c]	47.9	69.7	118.2	161.4	7.8	11.1	10.9	9.8
% of GNP	15.8	15.5	18.3	19.2				
Balance of trade[a]	5.2	1.2	15.7	33.0				
% of GNP	1.7	0.3	2.3	3.6				
Terms of trade	100.0	105.6	110.9[d]	113.6[d]				

Notes: [a] In billion DMarks.
[b] In per cent p.a.
[c] In 1960 prices.
[d] Original base: 1962 = 100.
Source: Statistisches Bundesamt; own calculations.

parity realignment of early 1961, the DMark had become significantly undervalued by the late 1960s.

Naturally, trade figures do not tell the entire balance-of-payments story. In the early 1950s, the current account surplus had considerably exceeded the trade surplus because of net earnings from services and transfers. From the late 1950s onwards, the effect of the widening gap between exports and imports on the current account was largely offset by net outlays for tourism as the *Wunderkinder* (children of the economic miracle) started to enjoy the fruits of their labour on holidays abroad, and for transfers, mostly development aid and remittances by foreign workers. As the integration of world financial markets was making substantial progress, investment decisions turned into a major determinant of the overall balance of payments. In the early 1950s, private capital flows had been all but negligible. Two decades later, between 1970 and 1973, capital inflows contributed twice as much to the growth in central bank reserves as the current account surplus. Note that the increasing importance of capital inflows does not weaken the argument that the DMark was undervalued. Quite the opposite: these inflows were an indicator that investors confidently expected a revaluation gain in the near future.

(ii) As far as the distortion in the regional pattern of West Germany's trade is concerned, a glance at some basic facts (Table 19) makes it plain

Table 19. *Regional structure of West Germany's foreign trade 1960–73*[a]

	1960	1965	1970	1973
Imports				
Western industrial countries	72.8	76.6	79.8	78.9
EC (6)	29.7	37.8	44.2	46.7
EFTA (7)	19.6	17.2	15.2	11.7
North America	16.0	14.3	12.7	9.5
Others	7.5	7.3	7.7	11.0
Eastern Europe	4.0	3.7	3.7	4.2
Developing countries	22.9	19.5	16.4	16.8
Asia	9.2	6.2	5.4	7.0
Exports				
Western industrial countries	76.3	81.5	83.6	82.2
EC (6)	29.5	35.2	40.3	39.9
EFTA (7)	28.0	27.0	22.6	22.7
North America	9.0	9.1	10.1	9.3
Others	9.8	10.2	10.6	10.3
Eastern Europe	3.9	3.3	3.8	5.5
Developing countries	19.5	14.9	12.4	12.0
Asia	8.8	7.1	5.5	5.5

Note: Respective share in per cent of total.
Source: Statistisches Bundesamt; own calculations.

that the continuing internationalization of West Germany's economy should rather be called a Europeanization in a pretty narrow sense. As West Germany conducted a rapidly increasing share of its external trade with its five immediate neighbours to the west with whom the European Economic Community had been formed as of January 1958, the relative importance of most of its other trading partners declined. The share of imports emanating from the US and the seven countries of the European Free Trade Area (EFTA) was particularly affected.

Below, we shall take a closer look at both of the policy-induced distortions of the otherwise fairly smooth development of West Germany's external economy. We shall start with an assessment of the EEC, i.e. of the major issue of trade policy, and then turn to monetary matters, i.e. to the exchange rate.

1   The economic division of Western Europe

(a) West Germany's integration into the Common Market. In many respects, the development of the EEC during the 1960s closely resembles the pattern of European integration efforts in the 1950s. Like

the vision of a European Defence and a Political Community in 1954, all ambitious plans for a political union failed. France was not ready to strengthen the supra-national character of the EEC; the German Bundestag (unlike Adenauer, who was Chancellor until October 1963) did not endorse de Gaulle's scheme for a close Franco-German cooperation, with its significant anti-Anglo-American features; and the smaller EEC states were afraid that a Franco-German coalition might by-pass their interests. Once again, the political emphasis was put on economic integration not merely as an end in itself, but rather as a necessary detour on the way to eventual political unification.[3]

Internally, the EEC kept a rough balance between the liberal and the authoritarian concepts of integration until 1967. The successive reduction of internal tariffs, which commenced in 1959, and the first major steps towards the free movement of labour and some forms of capital (mainly direct investments and trade credits) that were taken as early as 1960–2 were the most notable liberal achievements. However, after the 'Luxemburg compromise' of early 1966, which reinstated the unanimity requirement for all major decisions in the EEC Council of Ministers and after the fusion of the EEC Commission with the much more interventionist administrations of the ECSC and Euratom, the authoritarian approach gradually gained the upper hand. While the customs union was completed on 1 July 1968, i.e. eighteen months ahead of schedule,[4] further attempts to liberalize trade in services and capital movements remained largely unsuccessful. Instead, the markets were to some extent actually refragmented by non-tariff barriers to trade and an increase in national subsidies.[5] In addition, the EC Commission began to develop a common structural policy, a regional policy and an industrial policy which were neither explicitly mentioned in the Treaty of Rome nor necessary for an integration of markets.

Externally, the trade diversion to the detriment of EEC outsiders had a strong impact on European and American politics. Both the US and some non-EEC states of Europe launched initiatives to mitigate the effects of the EEC on their exports. Throughout the 1950s the US government had strongly encouraged various attempts at European economic integration. However, as the comfortable US trade surplus of the post-war years faded away in the late 1950s and early 1960s, US business began to view a European Economic Community as a substantial threat to its exports.[6] As a consequence, the US took the initiative in convening two

---

[3] See von der Groeben (1985), pp. 164ff.
[4] The remaining duties on intra-EFTA trade were abolished six months earlier than that.
[5] See Dicke (1988), p. 21.   [6] Von der Groeben (1985), p. 57.

GATT rounds of multilateral tariff reductions. In the Dillon Round (1961/2) the EEC agreed to lower the basis for the calculation of the common external tariff by 20 per cent for most industrial goods, while other participants were to reduce their tariffs on average by 7 per cent. The Kennedy Round (1964–7) was more successful. For the first time, the GATT members replaced the series of bilateral talks under the 'principal-supplier rule' by negotiations on a broad formula for tariff cuts. Although the final result fell short of the initially envisaged 50 per cent target, tariffs for industrial goods were – after lengthy discussions about exceptions from the rule – still reduced by 35–40 per cent on a mutual basis. Because of the Kennedy Round, the average 1972 tariffs on Germany's extra-EEC imports of manufactures were once again below their 1958 level (7.3 versus 9.0 per cent), down from 11 per cent in 1964.[7]

As early as mid 1961, the UK, Denmark and Ireland applied for entry into the EEC, followed by Norway in April 1962. Agriculture and the future trade relations between the UK and the Commonwealth were the most contentious issues in the negotiations.[8] However, when the talks with all four applicants were adjourned in January 1963, the reason was not an economic but a political one: de Gaulle saw the entry of the UK as a threat to his idea of close Franco-German cooperation. In spite of this setback, the same four countries renewed their applications four years later. Once again, de Gaulle forced the EEC to interrupt the negotiations without fixing a new date. In the early 1970s, de Gaulle's successor, Pompidou, finally agreed to the first enlargement of the EEC as of 1 January 1973.

From 1973 onwards, tariffs between the original EEC six and the EFTA seven[9] were gradually abolished, at least for manufactures, as all original EFTA members had either joined the Community (the UK and Denmark) or concluded parallel free-trade agreements for manufactures with the EEC. By mid 1977, the economic division of Western Europe finally came to an end.[10] Manufactured imports from the EEC and EFTA, which had been treated alike on the West German market until the late 1950s, were once again subject to similar, albeit by now much more favourable, conditions.

---

[7] Donges et al. (1973), pp. 23–6.
[8] See von der Groeben (1985), pp. 127–36.
[9] Unless stated otherwise, the term 'EEC' always refers to the original EEC six and the term 'EFTA' always to the original EFTA seven in this section.
[10] Incidentally, a few months after the two Western European trading blocs had started to fuse, the US proposed a new round of multilateral trade negotiations in the GATT framework (Tokyo Round, 1973–9). Kreinin (1979, p. 2) has suggested that the first EEC enlargement and the parallel free-trade agreements with the remaining EFTA countries should be viewed as the fusion of two trading blocs.

(b) The impact of 'little Europe'. Not surprisingly, the economic division of Western Europe into two trading blocs had a profound impact on trade flows. For all EEC and EFTA members, exports to and imports from their own trading bloc grew at a much higher rate than trade across the divide in the period from 1960 to 1972; the opposite holds for the following period from 1972 to 1980, i.e. during and after the fusion of the EEC and EFTA into one free-trade area for manufactures.[11] In the case of West Germany, the EEC member with the lowest share of imports from the Community and the highest share of imports from EFTA countries, the abolition of tariffs on intra-trade and the – albeit temporary – rise in duties on extra-EEC imports led to a particularly pronounced distortion of the regional composition of its imports. While the internationalization of the West German market continued, the bulk of the additional imports came from the EEC members. In 1960, 9.9 per cent of all manufactures[12] sold in West Germany had been imports; by 1972 this share had climbed to 17.1 per cent, with EEC suppliers accounting for four-fifths of the increase (from 3.9 to 9.4 percentage points). From 1973 onwards, the picture changed dramatically: whereas the overall share of imports in the West German market for manufactures rose to 29.4 per cent in 1987, the contribution of imports from the original EEC countries to this change was down to one-fifth.

A direct comparison of West Germany's manufactured imports from EEC and EFTA countries yields the clearest evidence of the impact of the economic division and subsequent reuniting of Western Europe. In 1960,[13] West Germany's imports of manufactures from the EFTA countries amounted to 72.1 per cent of those from the EEC. This ratio fell continually until it had more than halved by 1972 (31.8 per cent). From 1973 onwards, i.e. ever since the first steps towards a fusion of both trading blocs, the share rose again to 51.4 per cent in 1980 and 61.6 per cent in 1989 (see Figure 13). These numbers illustrate the extent of trade

[11] The only exception to this rule is the United Kingdom, whose exports to the EEC already grew slightly faster than those to EFTA members in the 1960–72 period. Obviously, this demonstrates a genuine trend away from long-distance trade with the UK's (former) colonies towards an increased division of labour with its immediate neighbours across the Channel. In 1960, the UK had sent a much smaller share of its manufactured exports to Europe and especially to its immediate neighbours than any other country in the sample. Schmieding (1988), p. 24.   [12] Excluding food processing and petrol products.
[13] Intra-EEC tariffs had been cut by 10 per cent on 1 January 1959, and by the same amount on 1 July 1960, compared to the January 1957 level. However, this implied no major change in German import duties, because West Germany had already reduced its tariffs unilaterally in mid 1957 for cyclical reasons. Discrimination between EEC and EFTA suppliers began in earnest on 1 January 1961, with a further cut in intra-tariffs by ten percentage points and the first step of the adjustment to the future common external tariff. For details, see Schmieding (1988), p. 22.

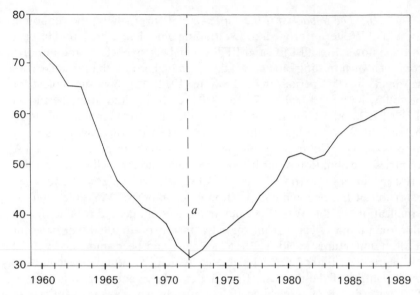

Figure 13. West Germany's EFTA and EEC imports 1960–89
(imports from EFTA as % of those from EEC).
Notes: Manufacturing only, excluding food processing and petrol
products; classification according to German production statistics;
EFTA seven, EEC six. [a] 1972: last year of full tariff discrimination
between EEC and EFTA suppliers.
Source: Statistisches Bundesamt; own calculations.

opportunities which European countries did forgo by not forming an
OEEC-wide free-trade area in the late 1950s in the first place.

Econometric estimates confirm that, without the economic division of
Western Europe, West Germany's 1972 imports from the EFTA countries
would have exceeded their actual level by roughly 7 billion DMarks, i.e.
about 50 per cent.[14] Obviously, most of the distortion in the regional
composition of West Germany's imports can be attributed to the tariff
wedge between EEC and EFTA suppliers. For all but one group of
manufactures, imports from the EEC rose faster than those from the
EFTA countries in 1962–72 and slower in 1973–84.[15] The distortion was

[14] Schmieding (1988), p. 32. Note that this number, based inter alia on actual domestic
absorption, is likely to underestimate the real losses incurred by EFTA exporters (and
West German consumers). Without the EEC–EFTA rift, growth in Western Europe might
have been faster, implying a higher level of domestic absorption in West Germany and
thus more West German imports from all countries including the EFTA seven.

[15] The odd industry out is the aircraft industry. Here, producers from the original EEC
gained market shares relative to their EFTA competitors even in the second period –
presumably a consequence of the heavy subsidization of just one multinational firm,
Airbus Industrie, which is still mostly a concern of some members of the original EEC six.

most pronounced for products for which EFTA and other non-EEC producers had faced comparatively high rates of effective tariff protection in 1972 (clothing, plastic products, petrol products, paper products). It was least pronounced for sectors with low rates of effective protection (stone goods, mechanical engineering, printing).[16]

Naturally, the gradual introduction of the EEC customs union altered the regional profile of West Germany's exports as well. In 1960, West German producers had sold more of their manufactures on the EFTA than on the EEC markets (28.4 as opposed to 25.7 per cent of West Germany's entire manufactured exports). During the following twelve years, the EEC share rose to 37.7 per cent, while the relative importance of the EFTA markets for West Germany declined to 23.5 per cent. Somewhat surprisingly, the share of West Germany's manufactured exports to the original EFTA countries increased only marginally thereafter (to 24.5 per cent in 1980), while the respective share of exports sold to the original EEC countries remained almost constant (37.1 per cent in 1980).[17] One reason for the comparatively sluggish growth of manufactured exports to the EFTA seven after the free-trade agreements of 1973 may be that many important EFTA countries had imposed only low import duties before these agreements in the first place (most notably Switzerland).

A closer look at West German exports and imports reveals that the EEC–EFTA rift distorted the commodity structure of trade in a very peculiar sense. While in 1960 the intra-industry share in Germany's trade with the EEC and EFTA had been about even, this share rose rapidly vis-à-vis the EEC and remained almost unchanged with regard to EFTA (see Table 20). Thereafter, the gap narrowed considerably. Clearly, the 'little European' customs union had accelerated the trend towards intra-industry specialization between West Germany and its partner countries in the EEC and delayed the same process vis-à-vis EFTA.

The establishment in 1958 of a 'little European' club called the EEC thus resulted in a severe distortion of trade flows within Europe. In comparison to an OEEC-wide free-trade area, one may well say that West Germany and other European countries paid a high economic price for the political option of a Gaullist Europe which – incidentally – did not even materialize. Nevertheless, the EEC did not bear out the worst fears of critics like Röpke (1958).[18] Instead of damaging GATT, the regional integration provided a new stimulus to multilateral liberalization efforts.

[16] Of course, there is no reason to expect a perfect correlation between tariffs and import growth rates, as the price elasticities of supply and demand may differ considerably between products.   [17] Schmieding (1988), p. 24.

[18] See Chapter 3, Section B.4 above.

Table 20. *Relative importance of intra-industry specialization in West Germany's foreign trade*

	Manufactures[a]			All commodities[b]		
	1960	1972	1980	1960	1972	1980
Share of intra-industry trade *in total trade (in %) with*						
EEC	62.3	75.8	81.3	59.8	71.6	72.9
EFTA	59.6	60.7	72.4	56.3	58.2	66.8
North America	48.5	57.5	66.9	39.4	45.6	50.2
World	55.9	68.6	74.0	46.4	58.6	66.0

Notes: [a] SITC-sections 5–8; two-digit level; number of industries 28.
  [b] SITC-sections 0–9; two-digit level except for SITC 0, 4, 9 (one digit level); number of industries 46.
Source: Schmieding (1988), p. 25.

While the abolition of internal tariffs benefited exporters in all member countries, the common external tariff also constituted a substantial import liberalization for high-tariff France and Italy, though not for West Germany. In other words, the customs union mattered more to France and Italy than to West Germany. In the 1950s, comparatively liberal West Germany had topped the European growth league.[19] It may be more than a mere coincidence that the erstwhile pacemaker for liberalization fell behind somewhat in the growth league in the 1960s and early 1970s as other countries caught up in terms of trade liberalization.

Note that the establishment of the EEC Common Market affected more than trade flows. In order to avoid a trade diversion to their disadvantage, firms from non-member countries resorted to acquiring existing or to establishing new production sites within the EEC. The inflow of foreign direct investment from the US was so pronounced as to be widely interpreted as 'le défi americain' ('the American challenge').[20] In the case of West Germany, the development of cross-border direct investment is especially remarkable: with the establishment of the EEC, it skyrocketed from 150 million DMarks in 1957 to a peak of 4.1 billion DMarks in 1966, of which one-third came from the US. The corresponding outflows merely increased from 400 million to 1.4 billion DMarks. Thereafter, foreign purchases of major stakes in West German firms or the setting

[19] Dicke et al. (1987), p. 15.
[20] Servan-Schreiber (1967).

up of foreign firms in West Germany respectively decreased at least relative
to GNP, while West German business ventured abroad more frequently.[21]

As the economic division of Europe did not turn out to be permanent,
the overall verdict on the 'little Europe' in which West Germany
participated for political rather than for economic reasons cannot be
entirely negative. However, there is one major sector of the economy
which turned into a liberal economist's nightmare under the auspices of
the EEC in the 1960s: agriculture.

(c) The case of agriculture. Both the West German and the
EEC-European agricultural policy may well serve as standard examples
for the conventional wisdom that early mistakes can give rise to grave
consequences by creating precedents and putting further development on
a wrong track. Traditionally, German governments since the days of
the Kaiser had been inclined to protect domestic farmers against
competition from abroad. During the post-war misery, however, the
comprehensive controls of agriculture had been deliberately geared
towards supplying consumers with food at artificially low prices. Hence,
when many of these controls were lifted in the two years after the currency
reform of June 1948, a large number of farmers may have been willing
to put up with genuinely free prices and at least freeish import competition.[22] Unfortunately, the government replaced the rigid regimentation of
markets not by free trade but by market orders relying on import quotas,
subsidies and buffer stocks for the stabilization of domestic prices.[23] Some
major prices, for instance, those for grain, continued to be fixed by the
state. In 1952, i.e. after the Korea boom had come to an end, world
market prices fell below the domestic level for major staple foodstuffs.
From then on, the market orders clearly served the interests of the
well-organized farmers at the expense of consumers; it had become too
late to gather sufficient political support for a liberalization. The farmers'
lobby skilfully used its political influence on the major governing parties,
the Christian Democrats and the liberals, both of which relied heavily on
their respective rural strongholds. The lobby managed to institutionalize
the special treatment of agriculture in the *Landwirtschaftsgesetz* of 1955
and to influence the negotiations about the emerging EEC.[24]

Besides the question whether there should be an exclusive 'little
European' club named the EEC at all, the talks about agriculture became

---

[21] The average annual net increase in foreign direct investment in West Germany was 3.6
billion DMarks compared to average outflows of 3.2 billion DMarks: Deutsche Bundesbank (1988), pp. 266f.   [22] Dicke (1987).   [23] Schmidt et al. (1984), pp. 165–6.
[24] Dicke (1987).

the most contentious bit of the entire EEC venture. These negotiations proceeded in three stages. Firstly, the commitment to establish a common market in agricultural products became part of the Treaty of Rome, with Article 40 listing common rules on competition, a compulsory coordination of the various market institutions of the member states and, least liberal of all, a European market organization as feasible institutional alternatives.[25] Secondly, the details of the Common Agricultural Policy (CAP) were to be fixed by the end of 1961. As was to become typical of EEC agricultural negotiations, the clock had to be stopped at the end of 1961 in order to meet the deadline for this stage. France insisted on taking the first steps towards a common market for agriculture by 1962, if possible coupled with a system of subsidies to be financed mainly by the richer member countries, while farmers and the government of West Germany wanted to preserve their comparatively interventionist national market orders (*Marktordnungen*) for as long as possible. The compromise reached in early 1962 was more or less the worst possible outcome. It provided for the gradual introduction of a common market with rigid market orders, politically determined prices as well as variable import levies and export subsidies for major products.[26] Thirdly, the common prices for major products were fixed in 1964, both as a step towards the integration of national markets during the transition period and as a preparation for the Kennedy Round of the GATT. While West Germany – with comparatively high national prices for cereals – consented to align these prices within the EEC as early as 1964, France agreed to fix the new common prices at almost the previous German level.

The EEC had thus succeeded in superseding many national regulations by a common institutional setting. However, the consequences of the CAP in the particular form in which it had emerged were grave. (i) Agriculture became hopelessly politicized, with international haggles constantly jeopardizing progress towards both the further economic integration of the EEC and the multilateral reduction of barriers to trade within the GATT framework. (ii) With the precedent of market orders for some products at hand, producers of other agricultural commodities succeeded in making the system spread to an ever-growing number of product groups. By 1968, 90 per cent of the European agricultural products were already supposed to be subject to common EEC policies, and by 1977, only five major products were not yet covered by EC regulations.[27] (iii) With internal prices frequently set far above the world market level – and shielded against import competition by variable border levies – EEC farmers were

[25] Von der Groeben (1985), p. 71.   [26] *Ibid.*, pp. 101–7.
[27] Europäische Gemeinschaften (1967), pp. 17ff.; (1978), pp. 4f.

encouraged to produce much more than they could sell on the market, with the EEC buying and hoarding the difference, which was ultimately destroyed or dumped on the world market at the expense of European taxpayers and to the detriment of foreign producers.[28] (iv) The system became increasingly expensive, not least through the growth of the agricultural bureaucracy in Brussels. EEC agricultural expenditures sky-rocketed from 115 million DMarks in 1962 to 1.5 billion in 1967 and 35.8 billion in 1972. In the 1970s, the major part of the entire budget of the European Communities was spent on agriculture (1970: 92.9 per cent; 1980: 69.5 per cent).[29] Furthermore, the national subsidies which were paid on top of the EEC outlays were not abolished. They increased from 1 per cent of West Germany's public spending in 1950 to 3 per cent in 1961 and 1970.[30] On account of the inherent waste of the system, only a fraction of the expenses eventually ended up in the pockets of the farmers themselves. In other words, a much smaller direct personal transfer to the farmers could have had the same impact on rural incomes. (v) In terms of a rational social policy, i.e. a redistribution from the wealthy to the needy, the CAP was also a disaster: the artificially high prices for foodstuffs hurt those consumers most who spend a comparatively large share of their income on food, i.e. basically the poor.

Nevertheless, neither the national nor the EEC agricultural policy could halt the structural change away from farming:[31] the share of agriculture in West Germany's gross value added declined from 10.7 per cent in 1950 to 6.3 per cent in 1960 and 3.1 per cent in 1973 (in current prices); its share in employment fell from 24.6 per cent in 1950 to 14.4 per cent a decade later and 7.2 per cent in 1973. The CAP could not even reverse the worsening of the terms of trade of agriculture. While the prices for agricultural commodities (as measured by the value added deflator) rose by an average of 1.9 per cent between 1950 and 1973, the overall prices increased at an average annual rate of 3.4 per cent.[32]

In the early 1970s, the negotiations on the first enlargement of the EC provided the last major opportunity for a thorough liberalization of agriculture and a switch towards direct income support. Unfortunately, the United Kingdom finally had to agree to adjust its more liberal system to that of the EEC because it did not find sufficient support among the old EEC members for a fundamental change in the CAP. Once on a

---

[28] As the economically wasteful overproduction was achieved in part by an excessive use of fertilizers and pesticides, the CAP turned out to be ecologically harmful as well, impairing the quality of drinking water and of some foodstuffs.
[29] Dicke et al. (1987), p. 102; Zijlmans (1970), p. 257; own calculations.
[30] Schmidt et al. (1984), p. 168.   [31] See Chapter 1, Section 2 above.
[32] Statistisches Bundesamt; own calculations.

wrong track, it turned out to be next to impossible to change the course of agricultural policy.

2   The erosion of the Bretton Woods system

The question of the appropriate external value of the DMark and of the optimal exchange-rate regime was the second major issue in West Germany's external economic policy throughout the 1960s and early 1970s. While a heated discussion about a minor revaluation of the DMark within the system of fixed parities marked the beginning of this period, the final breakdown of the post-war international monetary order marked its end.

Until the early 1970s, international monetary relations were – at least in theory – governed by the rules of the so-called Bretton Woods system. The ground-rules of this system had been laid down at a United Nations conference in a sleepy New Hampshire township in 1944 at the initiative of the United Kingdom and the US. The agreement required the signatories (i) to fix a parity at which their currency could be converted by central banks of other countries into dollars or gold and (ii) to make sure that the markets did not deviate from this rate by more than 1 per cent in either direction. Unfortunately, it was left unclear whether deficit or surplus countries should bear the burden of adjustment – a source of recurrent political quarrels throughout the lifespan of the scheme. Furthermore, the agreement called for the liberalization of payments for current account transactions. The parities, the remaining restrictions on currency convertibility and a common fund for balance-of-payments assistance were to be supervised by the International Monetary Fund, which came into being in March 1947. In case of a 'fundamental disequilibrium', a country could adjust the parity of its currency after consultation with the International Monetary Fund (IMF).

As only the dollar was to be freely convertible into gold at the official rate upon the request of a central bank, the arrangement de facto assigned the US money the role of the reserve and intervention currency. This gave the US the privilege of covering eventual balance-of-payments deficits in its own money. Yet, the obligation to keep the dollar price of gold stable at 35 dollars per ounce looked like a strong anti-inflationary anchor for the entire system. On the plausible assumption that the law of one price holds for tradables in the medium run, the system of fixed exchange rates was meant to ensure that, at any given state of restrictions on international trade and payments, all member countries would either have a similar and, thanks to the gold-anchor, low rate of inflation for tradable goods or would have to adjust parities vis-à-vis the dollar.

After the devaluation of most European currencies in late 1949, in which the fledgeling IMF had played hardly any role at all, the system supervised by the Washington-based Fund enjoyed a comparatively calm and successful time during the 1950s, although it still had to rely on far-reaching restrictions of international currency transactions. In the late 1940s and early 1950s, the gross overvaluation of their currencies against the dollar (the 'dollar gap') had forced European governments to prop up the external value of their moneys by discriminating thoroughly against transatlantic trade and payments and to devise the EPU and its precursors as regional clearing mechanisms. As the special post-war needs to import food and advanced machinery from the US diminished over the course of the 1950s, these restrictions could gradually be lifted. By and large, the inherent values of European currencies came to fit their official parities.

In 1957 and 1958, i.e. in the aftermath of the cyclical boom of the mid 1950s, the West German authorities came under pressure for the first time to revalue the DMark. However, as the Advisory Council to the Federal Minister of Economics pointed out,[33] the underlying problem of the trade imbalances and the speculative capital inflows was – at that time – not a genuine strength of the DMark against the dollar but rather a weakness of other European currencies vis-à-vis both the DMark and the dollar. West Germany was running a huge trade surplus with Europe and a small deficit with the rest of the world, while the other OEEC members combined had massive deficits vis-à-vis both Europe and the rest of the world. Hence, the two devaluations of the French franc in 1957 and 1958 and the cyclical downturn in Europe and the US, which reduced the demand for West German exports, made it possible to weather this storm without a DMark revaluation.

When a new export-led boom commenced in mid 1959, the situation was different from that of two years earlier. This time, the speculation in the foreign exchange markets clearly focussed on the DMark–dollar rate, not on intra-European parity misalignments. In the eighteen months from September 1959 to early March 1961, the currency reserves of the Bundesbank jumped by 70.7 per cent from 16.7 to 28.5 billion DMarks, an increase tantamount to 3.9 per cent of GNP in 1960.[34] Initially, the Bundesbank had tried to hold the line.[35] To counter the inflow of short-term capital, interest payments on foreign deposits were prohibited in June 1960. However, by late 1960, the Bundesbank had to recognize that, despite its legal autonomy from the West German government, ultimately it could not control the money supply and thus inflation. The

---

[33] Wissenschaftlicher Beirat (1973), report of 30 April 1957, pp. 333–45.
[34] Deutsche Bundesbank, *Monatsberichte* (December 1961), p. 90; own calculations.
[35] For a detailed account, see Emminger (1976), pp. 504–9.

exchange-rate policy and hence the influx of reserves were determined by the government in Bonn, not by the central bank in Frankfurt. In early March 1961, the accelerating inflation finally convinced the government[36] to agree to a 5 per cent revaluation (from 4.20 to 4.00 DMarks per dollar).

In the following seven years, the problem seemed to have been solved. According to some calculations, the revaluation reduced West Germany's propensity to export by 10 per cent.[37] In the years from 1961 to 1965, the growth of imports outpaced the rise in exports by more than two percentage points (10.5 and 8.4 per cent respectively); the current account even exhibited slight deficits in two years (1962 and 1965); and from 1961 through to 1967, the foreign exchange reserves – amidst some fluctuations – on balance even decreased marginally. Thus, the arduous breakdown of the Bretton Woods system of fixed parities which commenced in 1968 and finally became official in early 1973 took many politicians by surprise, despite some early warnings by academics.[38]

As in the late 1950s, the turbulences were heralded by intra-European foreign exchange imbalances, with the DMark being the preferred currency for investors shying away from the British pound and the French franc. The pound was already devalued by 14.3 per cent in 1967. After the student revolts in France in May 1968 and the 15 per cent wage hike granted by the French government afterwards, a massive capital flight from the franc into the DMark put pressure on both parities. In November 1968, when the cautious Bundesbank already advocated a revaluation of the DMark in combination with a devaluation of the French franc, the German foreign exchange market was closed for three days to give the authorities a breathing space. Still reluctant to change the parity, the Bonn government opted for a 'shadow revaluation' in the shape of a 4 per cent export tax and import subsidy.

Once again, a measure turned out to be futile. With the West German current account surplus rising from 1.7 billion DMarks in 1966 to 13.2 billion two years later and with the turn of the US monetary policy towards an inflation financing of President Johnson's 'Great Society' programme and the Vietnam War effort after 1967, the foreign exchange markets obviously expected a DMark revaluation. After a net outflow of reserves in early 1969, the Bundesbank had to cope with an influx of some 7 billion DMarks each in the second and third quarter of 1969. In the two working days before the parliamentary elections in September 1969,

---

[36] The desire to divert public attention from an embarrassing ruling of the Constitutional Court on one of the government's internal pet projects was reported to be more on the mind of Chancellor Adenauer than the economic rationale of this move.
[37] Spittäler (1970), pp. 110–23; Deppler (1974), p. 623.
[38] See Chapter 4, Section A.2.

the foreign exchange markets were closed again; immediately afterwards the DMark was allowed to float for one month for the first time.[39] On 24 October the new parity for the DMark was fixed at 3.66 DMarks per dollar, a revaluation by 9.3 per cent.[40] At first sight, this seemed the final solution to the currency problem. In the last quarter of 1969, the Bundesbank gladly lost a record 22.2 billion DMarks in foreign reserves as speculative capital flowed out of the country, with investors, for whom the whole affair had been a straight one-way bet, happily pocketing the revaluation gain.

The period of respite was rather brief. As the US Fed resumed a policy of cheap money to counter the first signs of an imminent recession, the Bundesbank tried to reassert its control over the domestic money supply at the peak of the 1970 cyclical boom by raising the discount rate to 7.5 per cent in March. Although West Germany, with an inflation rate of 3.8 per cent in 1970 and 5.2 per cent in 1971,[41] had ceased to be a haven of monetary stability, investors reacted to the international interest-rate differential.[42] In 1971, despite a current account surplus that was down to an almost negligible 2.5 billion DMarks, the capital inflow actually boosted the exchange reserves by slightly more than had been withdrawn from the country in late 1969. When the flood swelled in early 1971 (by 19.6 billion DMarks in the first five months, i.e. a sum equal to 6.5 per cent of West Germany's GNP in these months),[43] the West German government decided to let the DMark float, with the Dutch guilder following suit. In a way, the floating of the DMark – to which the other EEC countries had consented after a heated discussion in Brussels – represented a breakthrough. It established the principle that the relative values of currencies need not be fixed by the state. The growth of the West German money supply slowed down considerably, dampening the boom and easing inflationary pressures.

In mid August 1971, US President Nixon formally renounced the gold convertibility of the dollar – which had already been suspended in 1968. The Bretton Woods system was severely battered but not yet dead. On 18 December 1971 the governments of major Western countries tried to re-establish a system of fixed parities (now rechristened 'central rates'). In this 'Smithsonian realignment', named after the Washington museum where the representatives had met, the new dollar parity of the DMark

---

[39] For details see Sinn (1988), p. 78.
[40] The French franc had already been devalued by 12.5 per cent in August.
[41] Consumer price index, Sachverständigenrat (1972/3), p. 35.
[42] See Emminger (1976), pp. 515ff.
[43] For the figures on the influx of reserves, see Deutsche Bundesbank, *Monatsberichte*, various issues.

was fixed at 3.22 (up 13.6 per cent vis-à-vis the 1969 rate), the price of gold was fixed at 38 dollars (a largely symbolic move, as the US did not reintroduce the gold convertibility of its currency), and the permissible range for currency fluctuations was broadened from 1 per cent to 2.25 per cent in either direction.[44]

As if history had yearned to repeat itself, even this new and ambitious arrangement broke down within fifteen months. After a short-lived alleviation of currency tensions in late 1971 and early 1972, money started to pour into West Germany as investors once again lost confidence in the dollar. From January 1972 through to March 1973, an influx of 27.8 billion DMarks from abroad swamped the West German money supply. In mid 1972, Karl Schiller, the most prominent economist of the Social Democrats and by then West Germany's *Superminister* of Finance and Economics, resigned in protest at the strict controls on capital inflows which the government introduced to stem the flood.[45] Neither this administrative emergency action nor the last desperate measure, namely a further devaluation of the dollar by 10 per cent in mid February 1973, had any lasting effect. After the Bundesbank had been forced to defend the newly fixed parity by buying dollars worth 7.5 billion DMarks on a single day (1 March 1973), the foreign exchange markets in West Germany and several other countries were closed down.[46] When they reopened two weeks later, the valuation of the DMark vis-à-vis the dollar was finally left to the market, with some other European currencies being tied to the DMark in the 'currency snake'. The introduction of this European 'bloc floating' marked the end of the Bretton Woods system.

At first glance, the answer to the question why the Bretton Woods system collapsed seems fairly easy. Sure enough, the notorious West German surpluses on current account triggered most of the crises described above. These surpluses reached their peaks in 1957, 1960 and 1968 (with 3.0, 1.9 and 2.4 per cent of GNP respectively), i.e. at the onset of the major turbulences.[47] Furthermore, it seems obvious that inflation-rate differentials between stability-orientated West Germany and its less disciplined partners are to blame for these surpluses and hence the

---

[44] For a detailed account, see Emminger (1976), pp. 523–6.
[45] The relation between Schiller and other cabinet members had already been strained by his insistence on expenditure cuts in the continuing boom.
[46] Emminger (1976), pp. 530–3.
[47] In the early 1970s, with an increasing mobility of financial capital, the mere attempt by the Bundesbank to tighten the monetary reigns sufficed to induce major disturbances. If the central bank had been successful, this would have reduced the growth of domestic absorption and thus have made more room for a higher surplus on current account. In spite of a still rather small current account surplus, the interest-rate differential drew in enough capital to make the parity untenable.

breakdown of the system of fixed parities. From 1960 to 1973, the West German producer price index rose by 30.1 per cent as opposed to 42.9 per cent in the US and 49.6 per cent in other major industrial countries.[48] Note, however, that the inflation-rate differentials vis-à-vis other European countries could have been corrected by devaluations like those of sterling (1967) and the French franc (1968) without repercussions on the DMark–dollar rate, i.e. the rate on which the monetary turbulences ultimately focussed. Thus, a closer look at US–German price differentials is warranted.

Somewhat surprisingly, the inflation rates had not differed all that much. The entire divergence in the producer price indices until 1973 could have been offset by a DMark revaluation from 4.02 (1961) to 3.68 DMarks per dollar in 1973. Instead, the dollar tumbled to 2.66 DMarks in 1973 once floating was introduced. The development of nominal unit labour costs in manufacturing, i.e., broadly speaking, the tradables sector, is even more puzzling: US costs[49] went up by less then West German costs, so that, in order to re-establish labour-cost parity for manufactures, the DMark should even have been *devalued*.

A second look at the supposedly dull period which started with the revaluation of March 1961 and lasted until early 1968 confirms the suspicion that mere price comparisons may not tell the whole story. From 1960 to 1967, US producer prices and unit labour costs were admirably stable (plus 0.8 and 0.5 per cent p.a. respectively), while West German prices and costs (plus 1.1 and 3.1 per cent p.a.) increased somewhat faster, adding to the relative cost advantage which the US had gained by the German revaluation. Seemingly in line with these developments, the mere balance-of-payments figures do not point towards a problem of a DMark undervaluation in this period.

However, appearances may deceive. In spite of these US cost advantages, the system of fixed parities already had to be buttressed artificially both by West Germany and the US. At the height of the currency crisis in 1960, West Germany had – at the insistence of the US – initiated its first major programme of aid to developing countries as a means of easing the balance-of-payments strain.[50] These official capital exports were continued and stepped up thereafter. In mid 1961, West Germany prematurely repaid 3.1 billion DMarks of its foreign debt; in March

---

[48] Belgium, France, the UK, Italy, the Netherlands, Canada, Japan, Switzerland; average weighted with 1970 shares in German exports; Sachverständigenrat (1979), pp. 238f., own calculations.

[49] The comparisons of US and West German unit labour costs and prices are based on United States, *Economic Report of the President* (1989); Sachverständigenrat, various issues; own calculations.   [50] See Emminger (1976), p. 505.

1964, the Bundesbank started to subsidize capital exports by offering favourable terms for hedging against exchange-rate risks for West German buyers of US treasury bills;[51] in April 1964, interest payments on foreign time deposits in West Germany were prohibited, and at the same time a 25 per cent 'coupon tax' on interest payments accruing to foreign holders of German bonds was announced; it went into force in March 1965.

On their side, the US started to introduce capital controls in 1963. As the major European countries had made their currencies freely convertible for domestic holders (for current account purposes at least) by 1961 – West Germany in late 1958 – the 'success period' of the Bretton Woods system in terms of a high degree of currency convertibility at stable exchange rates thus lasted only two years.[52] At first, an 'Interest Equalization Tax' was levied on foreign asset incomes; in February 1965, the 'Voluntary Foreign Credit Restraint Program' required US banks and firms to restrict their capital exports; in January 1968, the 'Foreign Direct Investment Program' put ceilings on US direct investments abroad and – for the time being – even prohibited further net direct investments in European industrial countries.[53]

Although US producer prices rose by 5.2 per cent p.a. in the 1967–73 period, i.e. by two percentage points p.a. more than West German ones, the official parity realignment of the Smithsonian Agreement was more than sufficient to close this gap. Yet the agreement broke down within fifteen months. What had gone wrong?

So far, the discussion has been restricted to asking which changes in nominal exchange rates would have been warranted to offset price differentials so that the real exchange rate would remain stable. However, a constant real exchange rate was not in fact a feasible target. In the 1950s, when US and West German prices had developed roughly in line, West Germany had been able to close the 'dollar gap' at stable nominal and real exchange rates simply by regaining its pre-war export capacity and by improving the technological quality of its products vis-à-vis those from the US. In other words, West Germany enjoyed a revaluation of its underlying (i.e. undistorted) real exchange rate. While the DMark–dollar exchange rate had originally been fixed too high and thus had to be supported by an initial infusion of US aid and by trade and payments controls, it was possible for these restrictions to be lifted gradually up to late 1958.

After that, the same process continued. As there was little scope for a

[51] See Scheide (1988), p. 66.
[52] Glismann et al. (1982), p. 234.
[53] For brief summaries of these measures, see Scheide (1988), pp. 66–7.
[54] See Sachverständigenrat (1964/5), pp. 18–22.

further liberalization of German commercial imports and capital exports and as the nominal revaluation of 1961 was rather small, the underlying trend towards a DMark revaluation in real terms had to be countered by the new restrictions on capital flows from the US to West Germany described above. Policy-makers failed to understand this development. As the actual parity realignments were always discussed in terms of and geared towards offsetting cumulative inflation-rate differentials, they were invariably too small to accommodate the underlying trend towards a dearer DMark in real terms.

There were two causes for the divergence of real and nominal exchange rates, both directly linked to West Germany's catching-up process. First, poorer regions are cheaper regions in terms of the prices for non-tradables, while tradables, abstracting from transport costs and artificial distortions, are subject to the law of one price. As West Germany managed to narrow the income gap vis-à-vis the US throughout the 1950s and 1960s, the prices for West German non-tradables had to increase relative to those in the US, implying a real revaluation of the German currency.[54] Second, the spectacular improvement in the West German terms of trade for manufactures testifies to the improving quality of West German exports relative to those of other countries; it enabled German firms to demand higher prices and bear higher unit labour costs and to gain market shares at the same time. West Germany had successfully specialized in investment goods with a high income elasticity of demand, i.e. in goods for which world demand increased even faster than world income.

Despite the surge in US inflation in the late 1960s and early 1970s, the breakdown of the Bretton Woods system thus cannot be simply blamed on a lack of monetary discipline on the part of the post-war hegemon, the United States. While the rather modest US inflation rates may eventually have made an adjustment in the official dollar price of gold inevitable, the real flaw was that, given the need for real exchange-rate adjustments, the system could only have survived if countries such as West Germany had been willing to accept a much higher rate of overall inflation than the US. West Germany by and large tried to stick to an exchange-rate target most of the time; it thus had to accept a fair amount of imported inflation. Nevertheless, the Bundesbank and the Bonn government were ultimately not willing to sacrifice internal price stability to the extent necessary to keep the nominal external value of the DMark stable.

Because of a reluctance to adjust the fixed parities as frequently and to the degree that would have been required, the Bretton Woods system

[54] See Sachverständigenrat (1964/5), pp. 18–22.

was but a 'fair-weather' system, working reasonably smoothly just for comparatively short periods in which foreign demand for German exports was low for cyclical reasons. In all DMark–dollar crises, the actual revaluations came too late to prevent an outburst of price and wage inflation in Germany. In all cases, the money supply had already expanded rapidly in the previous futile attempts to defend the external value of the currency. This had created a scope for a substantial erosion of the internal value of the DMark.

To sum up, two institutional constraints induced a twofold distortion of West Germany's external economy during the 1960s and early 1970s. In the realm of trade policy, the economic division of Western Europe led to a rather skewed regional structure of West Germany's exports and – to an even larger extent – of her imports. In the monetary domain, the emerging undervaluation of the DMark in the Bretton Woods straitjacket gave an artificial boost to the level of exports and jeopardized internal price stability at the same time. By early 1973, the stage seemed to be set for a change for the better. The economic division of Western Europe was coming to an end, at least for trade in manufactures, and the external value of the DMark was allowed to adjust, by and large, in line with demand and supply oh the foreign exchange markets. Nevertheless, the problems that were to beset West Germany's internal and external economy in the years to come were to dwarf all the predicaments of the 1960s and early 1970s.

5   1973–1989: facing the slowdown

The year 1973 marks a watershed in the economic history of most industrialized countries: for at least one and a half decades to come, economic growth did not recover its prior speed, and unemployment became a persistent rather than a merely cyclical feature of the macroeconomic picture. For West Germany, the time after 1973 was a particularly bitter period of awakening: until the early 1970s, the country had been spared any major economic crisis, and the only sharp recession, in 1966/7 – albeit frightening – had seemingly been cured with a strong dose of Keynesian medicine. Although everybody knew that the happy days of the German miracle had passed long ago, the macroeconomic performance – especially the state of overemployment – still looked quite satisfactory by the international standards of the day. Clearly, warning voices from academia could be heard early on, but the public was not yet ready to listen. All this changed dramatically after 1973: as all could now see, West Germany gradually turned into a laggard in the international growth race, with the lowest real GDP growth of the six largest industrialized countries. While the unemployment record remained better than in most other economies of Western Europe, the shift from general labour shortage in the 1960s and early 1970s to chronic labour surplus thereafter was very disquieting.

In the following two sections, we shall ask which economic forces can be held responsible for this change for the worse, and what economic policy did about it in the past and could do about it in the future. As we thus move very close to the present, our account will cover policy issues which are still hotly debated. The tone will therefore become less historically detached and a bit more theoretically involved than in previous parts of this book. Again, we shall deal first with the domain of domestic policy issues (Section A) and then move on to the realm of international trade and finance (Section B).

A   **Persistent unemployment and the growth slack**

In the period 1973–89, there were two major recessions that hit the West German economy: in 1974/5 and 1981/2. After both of them, economic recovery was disappointingly slow and unemployment hardly declined. As a consequence, the focus of the economic policy debate began to move beyond short-term cyclical demand-side issues to more fundamental long-term questions of supply-side growth and of the fight against chronic unemployment. Below, we shall first sketch the path of cyclical macro-economic events and policies (Section 1); we then turn to the more basic questions of the causes and policy consequences of persistent unemployment (Section 2) and of sluggish growth (Section 3).

1   The demand side: a tale of two cycles

The period 1973–89 covers two full business cycles, the first one from the cyclical peak in 1973 through the trough in 1975 to the peak in 1979/80, the second one from the peak in 1979/80 through the trough in 1982 to the end of the 1980s. Both cycles were extraordinary, although for a slightly different combination of reasons: the business downturn of the mid 1970s was unusually sharp and deep, and the one of the early 1980s unusually long and sustained. On the other hand, the two cycles have important similarities: both were worldwide phenomena, both were preceded by a hefty raw material price shock, and both entailed a fairly slow recovery.

(i) The cycle of the 1970s. After the breakdown of the Bretton Woods system in spring 1973, the Bundesbank used its newly gained degree of freedom and switched to a very tight monetary policy so as to cut consumer price inflation, which was running at an annual rate of about 7 per cent in 1973 and still 6.2 per cent in 1974. From June 1973 to late October 1974, the discount rate stood at 7 per cent, and the free liquidity reserves of the banking system were squeezed down close to zero. Interest rates shot up to post-war peaks, both at the short and the long end: the prime rate for daily money reached an average of 10.2 per cent in 1973, and the long-term rate in the capital market climbed to record levels of 9.5 per cent in 1973 and 10.6 per cent in 1974. By itself, the tough monetary stance could have provoked a marked cooling of the business climate, and in fact, most experts at the end of 1972 foresaw a deceleration of annual GDP growth from almost 5 per cent in 1973 to 2.5 per cent in 1974. However, things got much worse: with two major supply-side shocks around the turn of the year 1973/4 – the oil-price hike

and the wage push – a much more dramatic profit squeeze appeared unavoidable if the Bundesbank did not provide the monetary leeway to accommodate the shocks. In fact, monetary policy stayed on course, at least until late 1974, when it became obvious that the peak of price inflation had been left behind. In turn, fiscal policy gradually moved towards expansion: in December 1973, the previous stability programme of May 1973 was mostly cancelled and, at various times in 1974, a number of special investment and employment programmes were initiated. All in all, these programmes amounted to close to 10 billion DMarks, i.e. roughly 1 per cent of GNP; they entailed substantial tax incentives to stimulate private investment as well as additional public expenditures, partly targeted at those regions and sectors which were hit hardest by the recession.[1]

By and large, both the restrictive monetary policy and the expansionary fiscal stance were supported by academic economists. Notably, the Council of Economic Experts endorsed the monetary policy as an unpleasant but necessary step towards breaking inflation and towards demonstrating to the public that excessive wage increases would not be given the monetary leeway to be shifted on to prices.[2] As to fiscal policy, the Council was much less enthusiastic: it welcomed some selective fiscal measures to support those industrial branches – above all construction – which suffered most from high interest rates; however, it warned against any indiscriminate deficit spending which, in a tight money and capital market, would only crowd out private investment and endanger the long-term prospect of fiscal consolidation.[3]

As in the earlier recession of 1966/7, the economic downturn originated at home, not abroad: while exports grew at annual rates above 10 per cent in both 1973 and 1974, investment began to stagnate in the second half of 1973 and sharply contracted by almost 10 per cent in 1974.[4] Apparently, the increase in the costs of the major factors of production – capital, labour and raw materials – cut heavily into profits and investment plans and thus pushed the economy into recession. It is worth noting, however, that the true extent of the downturn was underestimated for

---

[1] For details of the programmes, see Sachverständigenrat (1974/5), paras. 198–218, and Jäger and Link (1987), p. 16.
[2] See Sachverständigenrat (1974/5), paras. 30*–33*; characteristically, the 1973/4 report of the Council of Economic Experts – published a few months after the onset of the Bundesbank's restrictive course – had the title *Mut zur Stabilisierung (Courage to Stabilize)*.
[3] See Sachverständigenrat (1974/5), paras, 25*–27* and 50*–56*.
[4] The precise numbers from the national accounts statistics are: private investment in real terms (excluding inventories) shrank by 0.3 per cent in 1973, 9.6 per cent in 1974 and 5.3 per cent in 1975; in turn, the export volume still grew by 10.1 per cent in 1973 and 12.1 per cent in 1974, but collapsed in 1975 (−6.7 per cent).

quite a long time: professional forecasters at the end of 1974 – after a full year of largely unexpected stagnation of economic activity – predicted a growth rate for real GDP of 2–2.5 per cent for 1975. Apparently, they assumed that the trough of the cycle was over.[5]

Again, expectations were badly frustrated: in 1975, a worldwide recession set in and, as a consequence, the volume of West German exports declined sharply (by 6.7 per cent) for the first time in any single year since the currency reform. With investment continuing its collapse throughout the year, the recession trough was not yet reached before the middle of 1975. By then, monetary policy had turned from sharp restriction to cautious expansion: within twelve months (from October 1974 to September 1975), the discount rate was successively cut from 6.5 to 3.5 per cent. Also, something like a paradigm shift took place in the monetary philosophy of the Bundesbank: vaguely impressed by the monetarist gospel of a stable long-term relationship between the growth of the money stock and the increase of aggregate spending, the Bundesbank decided to announce annual targets for the change in central bank money, beginning in late 1974 with a target for 1975. Originally, an increase of 8 per cent was envisaged, but – with the economy approaching rock bottom – the actual growth rate turned out to lie around 10 per cent; with inflation still running at 6 per cent p.a., this could be classified as moderately expansionary. In turn, fiscal policy continued its counter-cyclical course: when the recession proved deeper and longer than predicted, a further investment programme of 5.75 billion DMarks was decided upon in late August, after the Council of Economic Experts had explicitly supported the idea of another fiscal push in its special report of 17 August.[6] With the tax revenue drastically reduced by the recession, the overall deficit of the public sector (excluding social security administration) reached a record high of 5.4 per cent of GNP in 1975. More than ever before, the counter-cyclical activism on top of the sustained government growth was to leave a heavy need of fiscal consolidation for the future. All in all, the macroeconomic picture of the year 1975 was by far the worst since the early 1950s: an unemployment rate of 4.7 per cent, the highest since 1955, an inflation rate of 6.2 per cent, higher than in any year between 1950 and the time of the first oil-price shock, and a decline of real GDP by 1.6 per cent, the worst peace-time performance since the Great Depression.

Yet a recovery took shape towards the end of the year. It quickly gained momentum and encouraged hopes that a forceful export-led upswing was

---

[5] See Sachverständigenrat (1974/5), Table 24 and Arbeitsgemeinschaft (autumn 1974), p. 14.
[6] See Sachverständigenrat (1975/6), Appendix IV.

in the making: in 1976, exports grew by almost 10 per cent and, after more than two years of decline, private investment rose by 3.6 per cent. Note that the upswing was not fuelled further by monetary and fiscal impulses: the central bank money stock rose by 9 per cent – just above the 8 per cent target announced in late 1975 – which was clearly not imprudently expansionary at the beginning of a recovery. Fiscal policy turned towards 'consolidation': the *Haushaltsstrukturgesetz* (law to adjust the structure of the budget) of January 1976 provided for a broad array of expenditure cuts and reductions of tax concessions.[7] This was generally welcomed by economists as a first step towards cutting the budget deficit, which in fact came down from 5.4 per cent of GNP in 1975 to 3.5 in 1976, but it was obvious that more unpopular spending cuts would be needed in due course.[8]

However, the expansionary momentum did not last long: 1977 brought a flattening out of the investment and export surge and a disappointing real GDP growth of just 3 per cent. With the number of unemployed still above the magic one million threshold in the second year of the upswing, calls from the public for more expansionary measures became louder. At first, monetary policy barely reacted at all: the growth rate of the central bank money stock was kept close to the target of 8 per cent for most of the year. However, in late 1977, the Bundesbank made a sharp U-turn: to slow down the accelerating revaluation of the DMark vis-à-vis the dollar on the foreign exchange markets, the discount rate was further reduced to 3 per cent, quite a bold move in view of an inflation rate which was just beginning to fall below 3 per cent p.a. As to fiscal policy, some minor investment and employment programmes were introduced, with the focus gradually shifting from global demand increases towards facilitating structural adjustments in the labour market. As time went by, West Germany's trading partners – notably the United States – began to join the chorus calling for a more drastic expansion: West Germany was seen as running an unduly large surplus on trade and current account which, in the name of international coordination of macroeconomic policies, should be cut down through an increase of domestic absorption. In this sense, West Germany was urged to take over the role of a cyclical demand locomotive to pull other countries out of their apparent growth slack.[9]

At the Bonn economic summit of July 1978 the government gave way to these foreign demands and announced a reflation of the West German

---

[7] For details see Sachverständigenrat (1976/7), para. 206* and Table 25.

[8] See *ibid.*, paras. 87*–90*.

[9] For an extensive analysis of the so-called locomotive strategy, see Gebert and Scheide (1980), and Section B.2 of this chapter.

economy by a fiscal demand push amounting to one per cent of GNP. In at least two respects, this political decision and the following so-called locomotive experiment involved an important policy innovation. (i) For the first time in post-war history, the West German government and the Bundesbank[10] engaged in a deliberate expansionary policy at a moment when all the indicators of the business cycle showed a normal, not a depressed, level of economic activity and capacity utilization. This marked a break with the staunch anti-inflationary orientation which had established the reputation of the West German economy as a haven of stability. (ii) Also for the first time in post-war history, the West German government responded on a grand scale to urgent calls for expansion from abroad, notably the United States. Having leaned for years against the international inflationary wind in the Bretton Woods straitjacket, the West German economy was now to play the role of a demand (and possibly inflation) leader. This new philosophy carried the stamp of Helmut Schmidt, Chancellor of the centre–left coalition since 1974 and himself an economist. As a firm adherent to the idea of international coordination of macroeconomic policies, he accepted that the 'big' West German economy had a special responsibility to ensure a more 'balanced' flow of goods and capital between nations. In the mercantilist language of the day, this meant a lower West German trade and current account surplus to be achieved through a policy-incited rise of internal absorption. Politically, this prominent role for West Germany helped to build up a high profile for the German Chancellor, most impressively visible at the Bonn summit, which in many ways marks a peak of Schmidt's popularity and international standing.[11] Obviously, the whole approach rested on the dubious premise that a deliberate demand push would not soon meet serious supply-side constraints and thus fuel inflation; it implicitly assumed that the productive potential could still be made to grow at the high rates of the 1960s and early 1970s.

The actual fiscal measures taken consisted of additional expenditures of 11.1 billion DMarks and reductions of tax revenue by about 16 billion DMarks, all spread about evenly over 1979 and 1980.[12] Thus the public budget became heavily expansionary: the positive fiscal impulse on aggregate demand measured as a percentage of the production potential was raised from 0.3 per cent in 1977 to 1.5 per cent in 1978, 2.5 per cent in 1979 and 2.8 per cent in 1980, which – at a boom peak – came very

[10] Note, however, that the Bundesbank had already switched gears in late 1977, i.e. well before the Bonn summit.
[11] For the political details of the summit meeting, see Jäger and Link (1987), pp. 286–90.
[12] For a detailed survey of the measures, see Sachverständigenrat (1978/9), paras. 173–200 and Table 22.

close to the record high of 3.3 at the trough year of 1975.[13] As a complement to the fiscal impulses, monetary policy stayed on the expansionary course of late 1977, at least for the time being: in 1978, the prior growth target of the central bank money stock of 8 per cent was overshot by a flat 3 percentage point margin; the discount rate remained at its low of 3 per cent. The switch of fiscal policy gears was accompanied by many sceptical comments by academic economists, notably the Council of Economic Experts: in its special report of 19 June 1978, issued immediately after the Bonn summit, a case was made against further deficit spending which could endanger the 'consolidation' of public finances and crowd out private investment. However, in so far as the expansion involved tax reductions favouring investment, the Council took a more positive view.[14]

There is no doubt that the bold policy shift gave the economy a kind of second wind and pushed the growth rate of real GDP to a respectable 4.2 per cent in 1979. Because of the sharp increase of domestic absorption, the current account went into deficit for the first time since the mid 1960s; it amounted to 0.7 per cent of GNP in 1979 and 1.7 per cent in 1980. Unfortunately, the inflationary overheating took place much sooner than supply-side optimists had expected: the consumer price level rose by almost 4 per cent in 1979 and as much as 5.8 in 1980 after the temporary low of 2.8 per cent in 1977. Although employment growth picked up for a while, the jobless rate could not be pulled below 3.8 per cent in both 1979 and 1980, by earlier West German standards clearly no signal of full employment. Apparently, the core of the labour surplus had other causes than a lack of aggregate demand.

As had been feared by pessimists, events took a turn for the worse. With inflation gaining speed, the Bundesbank began to make a sharp policy U-turn by stepping on the monetary brakes: from March 1979 to May 1980, the discount rate was successively raised from 3 to 7.5 per cent, a post-war high which had only been reached once before in spring 1970. The growth of the central bank money stock was kept at the lower limit of the announced targets, which were 6–9 per cent in 1979 and 5–8 per cent in 1980. As in the mid 1970s, interest rates soared: the prime rate for daily money reached an average of 9.1 per cent in 1980 and 8.6 per cent in 1981, and the long-term rate an average of 10.6 per cent in 1981. In carrying out the two-year programmes decided upon in 1978, fiscal policy remained outright expansionary, which looked increasingly pro-cyclical and ill-timed.

[13] See Sachverständigenrat (1982/3), Table 22. The fiscal impulse is calculated within the theoretical framework of a cyclically neutral public budget; for details see Sachverständigenrat (1982/3), Appendix V.D.
[14] See Sachverständigenrat (1978/9), Appendix IV, paras. 8–14.

If one takes a macroeconomic snapshot of West Germany at the turn of the decade and compares it with the picture around 1973, it becomes all too evident that the old problems still existed and that new ones had been added: as in 1973/4, inflation and interest rates moved up, but in addition, there was more unemployment, a high 'structural' (i.e. non-cyclical) deficit of the public budget and – less frightening – a deficit in the current account. Hence there can be no doubt that the cyclical activism of the years after the first oil-price shock did not have any tangible macro-economic benefits, at least not in the relevant medium run. On top of this thoroughly unsatisfactory performance came the second oil-price shock at the turn of the decades.

(ii) The cycle of the 1980s. In many respects, the worldwide cyclical downturn in 1981/2 had a macroeconomic genesis very similar to the one of the 1974/5 recession: a deliberate and sharp U-turn of monetary policy towards restriction, a worldwide oil-price hike and a concomitant worsening of the terms of trade (see Figure 12). The déjà vu experience helped economic observers to make fairly accurate forecasts of an incipient profit squeeze and a deep recession as early as the second half of 1980, when the growth of investment and export demand began to slow down. For 1981, both the Council of Economic Experts and the Working Group of the German Economic Research Institutes expected the economy to stagnate at a growth rate of real GDP in the range of 0–0.5 per cent. When the downswing set in, the same observers retained their gloomy outlook and predicted just 0–1 per cent growth for 1982 and 1983, which turned out to be close to the mark.[15] This is worth noting, since the extent of the two previous major recessions in 1966/7 and 1974/5 had not been forecast with any degree of precision.

Despite the early visible signs of a downturn, the Bundesbank kept its monetary policy on an extremely tight rein until 1982, when the recession trough had been reached or even passed; thereafter, the discount rate was lowered step by step from 7.5 per cent in 1981/2 to 4 per cent in spring 1983. The target range for the growth rate of central bank money was held at 4–7 per cent throughout 1981–3, with the actual growth rate gradually rising from the lower limit of 4 per cent in 1981 to the upper one of 7 per cent by 1983. All this added up to an even more consistent fight against inflation than in the period 1973–5.

The reasons for this apparent return to a more traditional 'German-style' stability orientation were probably twofold. First, the – essentially

[15] For the relevant forecasts, see Sachverständigenrat (1980/1), Table 39; (1981/2), Table 32 and (1982/3), Table 31; Arbeitsgemeinschaft (autumn 1980), p. 19; (autumn 1981), p. 21 and (autumn 1982), p. 17.

monetarist – lesson had by now been learned that half-hearted measures do not really help to knock out inflation for more than a very short period. True, a gradualist approach might have required fewer sacrifices in terms of real output losses and unemployment, and some experts with monetarist leanings made a strong plea for a smooth filtering out of inflationary expectations.[16] However, with the experience of the 1960s and 1970s in mind, a gradualist strategy began to look like nothing more than a remote academic first-best solution. And once the process of driving down inflation was on its way, a premature turn of monetary policy back towards expansion, as in the locomotive experiment of the 1970s, would have clearly endangered the long-term gains of disinflation. Thus, although Keynesian demands for expansion could be heard – above all from union leaders and some related economists – public opinion and the vast majority of academic economists, including the Council of Economic Experts,[17] supported the Bundesbank's line, if only because there seemed to be no realistic alternative. Second, with the current account deficit reaching a peak of 1.7 per cent of GNP in 1980, a general lament set in that the country was living beyond its means and that the West German traded goods sector had lost much of its legendary competitiveness. Of course, these fears were ill founded, because – per se – a current account deficit says almost nothing about how profitably the imported resources are used and how competitive the domestic export industry happens to be. Nevertheless, the deficit alarmed politicians as well as the Bundesbank and helped to make the public vaguely ready for some sort of economic 'consolidation'.

As to fiscal policy, the turn towards contraction came rather late. When the economy slipped into recession by late 1980, the government did not have the financial leeway for any substantial counter-cyclical measures in the style of the 1970s. Moreover, because of the usual pro-cyclical fluctuation of tax revenues, the public deficit rose to almost 4 per cent of GNP by 1981 and 1982, the highest level in the whole post-war period except for the dismal year 1975. Despite the cyclical downturn, the centre–left coalition in power made some attempts at cutting the deficit of the federal budget.[18] These efforts turned out to be much too cautious, and the general public gradually began to lose confidence in the ability

---

[16] See Arbeitsgemeinschaft (autumn 1979), pp. 16–17, where the Kiel Institute of World Economics held the minority opinion that, given the sharp incipient monetary contraction, a deep recession would be unavoidable. For a detailed account of the Kiel Institute's gradualist policy stance, see Boss et al. (1979).

[17] See Sachverständigenrat (1979/80), paras. 29*–36*; (1980/1), paras. 36*–39* and (1981/2), paras. 48*–49*.

[18] For the details of the measures, see Sachverständigenrat (1981/2), paras. 223–33 and Table 24.

of a government led by Social Democrats to make the necessary spending cuts and to revive the economy through other – notably supply-side – means. Eventually, the question of fiscal consolidation led to a government crisis and a change of coalition – popularly called the *Wende* (the turnaround):[19] in autumn 1982, the centre–left government was replaced by a centre–right one under Chancellor Helmut Kohl, who embarked on the campaign for the early federal elections in spring 1983 with an explicit austerity programme. Remarkably enough, the centre–right coalition gained a comfortable majority in parliament and could thus cut expenditures straight away and move the federal budget closer towards balance.[20] By the mid 1980s, the deficit was reduced to 1–2 per cent of GNP, about the level of the late 1960s and early 1970s.[21]

From 1983 on, a gradual business recovery set in and was to last – more or less without interruption – up to 1990/1. By the historical standards of earlier periods, this recovery was slow, with the annual growth of real GDP hovering around 2 per cent and only in 1988–90 accelerating to 3.5–4 per cent. Capital-stock utilization reached normal levels by the middle and very high levels by the end of the 1980s. The great macroeconomic achievement of the period was price level stability (see Figure 5): from its peak of 6.2 per cent in 1981, consumer price inflation gradually slowed down to a low of 0.6 per cent in 1987 and 1.3 per cent in 1988, with the brief price-level decline of 1986 being a mere transitory phenomenon due to a sharp drop in oil prices and the simultaneous sudden improvement of the terms of trade (see Figure 12). With the economy overheating somewhat in the late 1980s, inflation picked up again, but still remained in ranges which look moderate compared to earlier periods. The dark spot of the macroeconomic picture remained unemployment: in the period 1983–9, the annual average number of jobless did not fall below the 2 million threshold level (see Table 15).

In matters of counter-cyclical demand policy, one is tempted to say that the time after the 1981/2 recession was exceptionally boring, since both the Bundesbank and the government followed a wholly undramatic steady course with only very modest counter-cyclical elements. As to monetary policy, the discount rate was kept at 4–4.5 per cent over the years 1983–5. Thereafter, with inflation and long-term (nominal) interest rates coming down, the rate was successively cut to 2.5 per cent by

[19] For the political details, see Jäger and Link (1987), pp. 234–51.
[20] For the measures taken in 1982 and 1983, see Sachverständigenrat (1982/3), paras. 165–77 and Table 23; (1983/4), paras. 217–29 and Table 28.
[21] For the details of the fiscal consolidation by the centre–right coalition, see Hellwig and Neumann (1987), pp. 132–7.

December 1987. This was the lowest level in the whole post-war period. It was reached when the much-dramatized worldwide stock market crash in October 1987 induced the Bundesbank to open all available liquidity channels temporarily to avoid anything smacking of a banking crisis. From 1984 onwards, the target growth rate of the central bank money stock was fixed in the range of 3–6 per cent. Only until 1985 did the actual growth rate remain within these bounds; thereafter, with rapidly declining inflation and a growing current account surplus, the upper limit was usually surpassed by a margin of 1–3 percentage points. Not before the second half of 1988 did the Bundesbank tighten credit conditions again by raising the discount rate.

As to fiscal policy, the government generally succeeded in keeping the public deficit below 2 per cent of GNP, with minor variations being mainly due to cyclical fluctuations of the tax revenue. After the main consolidation packages had been passed, the government turned its attention to a tax reform to improve supply-side conditions. Only in the temporary growth slack of 1987 did the government put on a fairly modest counter-cyclical investment programme for 1988–90.[22]

All in all, demand management virtually disappeared from the policy agenda in the West Germany of the 1980s. By the middle of the decade, this passivity began to arouse a storm of protest from abroad, since the emerging record current account surplus of the West German economy seemed to give the monetary and fiscal authorities enough leeway for another locomotive experiment in the spirit of the late 1970s. However, after the bad experience with the Keynesian programme of the Schmidt era, both the West German government and the Bundesbank by and large stuck to their course. While they paid lip-service to the idea of internationally coordinating macroeconomic policies, their actual policy stance remained fairly steady and reliable.

2   The nature of unemployment

After the mid 1970s, one major macroeconomic deficiency overshadowed everything else: persistent unemployment. In this respect, the West German economy was no exception in Europe, as most of the non-communist industrialized countries of the old continent faced the same problem at about the same time. Naturally, theories of European (or for that matter, West German) unemployment proliferated throughout these years. Two kinds of theories may be distinguished: those inquiring why unemployment has been so high at a given trend growth of output, and

[22] See Sachverständigenrat (1988/9), Table 19.

those asking why the trend growth of output and – as a mere consequence – of employment was too slow to allow for a reintegration of the jobless. We shall deal below exclusively with the first group of theories; the important second one will be implicitly taken up in Section 3, when we discuss the reasons for the poor growth performance of the West German economy since 1973.

There are four paradigmatic theories of unemployment which figured as the main landmarks of the European economic policy debate, namely the theories of (i) a Keynesian demand gap, (ii) a neoclassical wage gap, (iii) a hysteretic labour market and (iv) structural rigidities. Leaving aside technical details, we shall evaluate their explanatory power for West German unemployment since 1974/5.[23]

(i) Keynesian demand gap. When assessing the (traditional) Keynesian view that a lack of aggregate demand is the main explanation for West German unemployment, one has to distinguish between two alternative meanings of the term 'explanation'.

If 'explanation' means a historical account of the emergence of unemployment, then the Keynesian view has some appeal. Clearly, a new dimension of unemployment was reached in 1974/5 and 1981–3 in the course of a demand contraction which was the immediate result of deliberate policy shifts of the West German Bundesbank towards stabilizing the price level and – at least in the early 1980s – of the government towards reducing the public budget deficits. The relevant macro statistics are broadly consistent with this view; econometric evidence supports it.[24] After all, this is not surprising: the historical record shows that drastic upward shifts in the unemployment rate usually occur via a stabilization crisis; in post-war West Germany, this was so in 1948–50 after the currency reform, but also in 1974/5 and again in 1981–3. If 'explanation' means a genuine diagnosis of unemployment as it persisted at a rate of about 4 per cent by the late 1970s and about 8 per cent by the late 1980s, the traditional Keynesian view is hardly compatible with the facts, since the relevant economic indicators show that, from 1977 to 1980 and again from 1985 to 1990, the West German economy did not suffer from a general demand slump involving underemployment of both capital and labour. By 1979 and again by 1989, capacity utilization in industry – however measured – had reached peak levels comparable to the boom year 1973 or even 1970 (see Figure 3).

[23] Much of the reasoning which follows derives from the more extensive treatment in Paqué (1989b,c), where the technical details of the relevant empirical studies are dealt with.

[24] See, e.g., Bruno (1986). Similar results for West Germany have been obtained with different econometric techniques by, Layard and Nickell (1985); Layard, Nickell and Jackman (1985); Franz and König (1986) and Gordon (1988).

(ii) Neoclassical wage gap. The traditional neoclassical diagnosis of West German unemployment states that the *level* of real unit labour costs has been too high for full employment to be achieved. The only straight way to test this hypothesis comes down to comparing the actual level of real unit labour costs at a hypothetical state of full employment with a base level at some time in the past when full employment of labour and capital actually prevailed. The difference between these two levels – expressed as a share of the base level – is then called a wage gap.

Wage-gap estimates[25] for West Germany give a quite uniform picture: for the manufacturing sector,[26] they indicate substantial wage gaps of around 20 per cent in the late 1970s and early 1980s, with only a rather recent downward trend. Of course, these numbers may be misleading, as manufacturing has a share of no more than 35 per cent of total employment in West Germany. Estimates for the entire West German economy point to much smaller gaps since the mid 1970s, peaking at around 10 per cent in the mid 1970s and early 1980s and then falling to levels around 7 per cent in 1986 and – as a first guess – around 5–6 per cent in 1988/9.[27] Also, intertemporal patterns are remarkable: while the wage gap in manufacturing reached a new dimension in the second half of the 1970s, it levelled off in the economy as a whole, with only a very modest increase from the mid 1970s to the early 1980s. Table 21 gives a clue to the structural forces behind this well-confirmed empirical picture: in the early 1970s, all sectors – including both manufacturing and services – were hit by a hefty rise of nominal labour costs which was mainly due to an increase of the wage level (see Table 17). Yet, throughout the 1970s, producer prices (and thus also the value added deflator) increased much faster in the service sector than in manufacturing. Technically speaking, the intersectoral terms of trade between services and manufacturing moved in favour of the former, so that, by the middle of the decade, real unit labour costs in services began to decline again while employment continued to grow; not so in manufacturing, where it took two recessions with a net loss of more than 1.5 million jobs to achieve the required cost adjustment by the late 1980s (see Table 22). Apparently, import competition from newly industrialized countries finally squeezed the manufacturing sector down to a competitive size with a better product mix to halt a further change of the intersectoral terms of trade relative to the advantage of the service sector.

[25] Many serious technical difficulties are involved when calculating a wage gap. For details of the concept, see Artus (1984), pp. 256–61, Bruno and Sachs (1985), pp. 179–83, and Paqué (1989b), pp. 13–18.

[26] See especially Burda and Sachs (1987) and Paqué (1989b). Using data up to 1984, Gordon (1988) finds no wage gaps at all for the West German economy in the early 1980s. For a critique of Gordon (1988), see Vaubel (1989).

[27] See Paqué (1989b,c). Technical details are discussed in Paqué (1989b).

Table 21. *Determinants of labour costs in manufacturing and the service sector (average annual change, in %)*[a]

	1969–74	1974–80	1980–9
Value added deflator			
Manufacturing	6.0	3.3	3.2
Services	8.1	4.7	2.6
Labour productivity[b]			
Manufacturing	3.4	2.9	1.4
Services	2.4	2.3	2.1
Nominal wages[c]			
Manufacturing	11.8	7.6	3.9
Services	9.9	5.7	3.3
Real unit labour cost[d]			
Manufacturing	2.0	1.2	−0.7
Services	−0.1	−1.0	−1.5

Notes: [a] The service sector includes trade and transport, banking, insurance and miscellaneous services.
[b] Value added at constant 1980 prices divided by employment (including self-employed).
[c] Average gross yearly earnings (including employers' social security contributions) of employees (excluding self-employed).
[d] Nominal wage (as defined in note *c*) divided by the product of the value added deflator and labour productivity (as defined in note *b*).
Source: Statistisches Bundesamt; own calculations.

In fact, in the 1980s, manufacturing even managed to accomplish a slight intersectoral terms-of-trade gain which translated into a marked reduction of real unit labour costs.

Given this distinct pattern of structural change between two major sectors of the West German economy, it would be misleading to infer from a large manufacturing wage gap that, by the late 1980s, the level of unit labour costs was on average 'too high' in the economy as a whole and thus – per se – could explain the persistence of unemployment.[28] As the relatively small wage gap for the total economy indicates, a good part of the manufacturing wage gap is likely to be due to intersectoral terms-of-trade effects. By themselves, these effects raise important issues of intersectoral wage rigidity. Nevertheless, they speak against the simple neoclassical wage-level diagnosis.

(iii) Hysteresis. The failure of the (traditional) Keynesian paradigm to explain the European unemployment record in the 1980s led

[28] This inference pervades much of the argument by Burda and Sachs (1987).

Table 22. *Change of employment by sectors in selected periods (in 1,000)*

	1973–6	1976–80	1980–3	1983–9
Agriculture and forestry	− 329	− 214	−123	− 267
Industry	−1,403	+ 316	−879	− 154
Energy, mining	− 17	− 4	+ 9	− 30
Manufacturing	−1,034	+ 202	−715	+ 317
Construction	− 352	+ 118	−173	− 133
Trade and transport	− 63	+ 145	−133	+ 266
Insurance and banking[a]	+ 295	+ 442	+210	+ 803
Government	+ 271	+ 285	+125	+ 219
Private non-profit	+ 45	+ 124	+ 71	+ 209
All sectors	−1,184	+1,098	−729	+1,384
Private sector[b]	−1,455	+ 813	−854	+1,165
Private business[c]	−1,500	+ 689	−925	+ 956
Labour force	− 399	+ 914	+657	+1,174

Notes: [a] Including miscellaneous services.
[b] Including private non-profit organizations.
[c] Private sector excluding private non-profit organizations.
Source: Statistisches Bundesamt; own calculations.

Blanchard and Summers (1986; 1988) to formulate a theory of hysteresis which takes explicit account of the asymmetry of this record. Briefly summarized, the theory states that, after the long and severe recessions of 1974/5 and 1981–3, a dual labour market developed with two kinds of workers: those who remained employed throughout or became re-employed after a brief jobless spell, and those who remained unemployed. For the latter group, the opportunities for re-employment subsequently worsened for two main reasons: (i) an effective depreciation of their human capital due to the lack of work experience, demotivation and demoralization and the potential employers' inclination to take the length of a spell of unemployment as a negative indicator for the expected productivity of a job applicant; and (ii) the nature of the wage-setting process, where the interests of (employed) insiders are much better represented than the interests of (unemployed) outsiders.

Does this theory stand up to the facts of the West German economy in the recovery periods 1976–80 and 1983–90? A straight empirical implication of a process of hysteresis is that, in the aftermath of a recession, the share of long-term unemployment in total unemployment rises. In fact, this is broadly what happened in West Germany in the 1980s: the share in total unemployment of those who had been out of work for more than one year rose from 13.0 per cent in 1981 to over 24.9 per cent in 1983 and 32.6 per cent in 1988 (end of September in each case). A similar process of hysteresis took place in the recovery years of the second half of the 1970s, with the share of long-term unemployment (unemployment lasting a year or more) increasing from low levels of about 5 per cent in 1971–3 to 14.5 per cent in 1979.[29] Hence hysteresis seems to have been a general characteristic of the two extended recovery periods after the slowdown of trend employment growth some time in the mid 1970s.

As is well known, the hysteresis theory has far-reaching macroeconomic implications for the intertemporal pattern of wage inflation: whenever unemployment becomes hysteretic, recession-induced wage moderation fades away as soon as laid-off workers lose their market clout while they slide into long-term unemployment. Theoretically, this means that the non-accelerating inflation rate of unemployment (NAIRU) is no invariable 'structural' constant all through the cyclical history, but rather dragged along the actual unemployment rate, maybe with a lag of a few years.[30] Macroeconometric studies of nominal wage behaviour in the West German economy give quite unanimous support to the (hysteresis) view that wage moderation is of a cyclical nature and thus fades away rather quickly – after three to four years at the latest – in the process of economic recovery, no matter how large and persistent the remaining sediment labour surplus turns out to be.[31] Together with the macro statistics on long-term unemployment, this points to an increasingly dualized labour market as postulated by the hysteresis theory, both in the late 1970s and the 1980s.

Nevertheless, the question remains which economic forces are responsible for the hysteretic macro picture. A casual glance over some aggregate statistics shows that structural factors like age, qualifications, health and region play an important part in West German long-term unemployment. In September 1988, 74.5 per cent of all long-term unemployed (people out of work for more than one year) were either over fifty-five and/or had impaired health and/or no vocational qualifications; the corresponding share of short-term unemployment of this group was 56.8 per cent. If the large group of unemployed persons without vocational qualifications is excluded – it alone comprises about 50 per cent of all the unemployed – these shares drop to 42.5 per cent and 20.7 per cent respectively, i.e. more than 40 per cent of all long-term unemployed persons are either unlikely to find a job because of their age or are in an economically relevant sense 'disabled'.

On the whole, these data support the view that – given the high level

---

[29] As the method of computing long-term unemployment was changed slightly in 1983 (for details, see Paqué (1989b), p. 32, n. 30, and Werner (1987a), pp. 41–2), the share given for 1971–3 is an estimate by the authors; the share for 1979 is an ex-post recomputation by the Bundesanstalt für Arbeit.

[30] On the NAIRU, see Dornbusch and Fischer (1987), pp. 549–58.

[31] See, inter alia, Blanchard and Summers (1986a), Coe (1985, 1988) and Paqué (1989b,c).

of protection against dismissal which West German labour law and collective agreements grant to any worker under normal business-cycle conditions[32] – the cyclical downturns of 1974/5 and 1981/2 were taken by firms as a chance to cut their labour costs by laying off the least productive workers. From the start, laid-off workers with some 'structural handicap' (lack of qualifications, impaired health and, above all, age) were at a disadvantage in seeking work, since – given the quite rigid structure of wages negotiated by collective bargaining – there was little chance for them to offer a permanent compensatory wage cut for their particular handicap. Hence, in the course of economic recovery, they were left untouched as a sediment of long-term unemployment.

(iv) Structural rigidities. A structural explanation of West German unemployment is clearly limited in one important dimension: by its very nature, it cannot account for the sudden bursts of unemployment in the mid 1970s and early 1980s, which must no doubt be attributed to cyclical forces. It can only deliver a set of microeconomic reasons why irresistible long-term forces loomed behind these short-term bursts, and why after the bursts, a core of long-term unemployment remained even in the course of a pronounced recovery. In this respect, both the sectoral and the regional components of structural change are relevant.

As to sectors, we must remember that, since the mid 1970s, the growth of the wage gap has predominantly been a structural phenomenon, with manufacturing – and not the modern service sector – bearing the main share of the burden. The question then is whether a 'structural' wage gap can explain aggregate unemployment. After all, the net loss of about 2 million jobs in the recessions of 1974/5 and 1981–3 was almost exclusively due to the shrinkage of industrial – above all manufacturing – employment, while the moderate employment gains in the recovery periods 1976–80 and 1983–9 were mostly – though not exclusively – made in service-sector employment (see Table 22).[33] A tentative answer to the question lies in a comparison of the West German case with a country which experienced a rapid structural change between sectors without persistent unemployment, namely the United States. Between 1973 and 1988, American manufacturing employment (excluding self-employment) shrank slightly

---

[32] For a summary of employment protection in West Germany, see Soltwedel (1980), pp. 185ff, and Paqué (1993a), pp. 227–8. In general, West German labour law requires that any dismissal must be 'socially justified', with by far the most important case of justification being urgent business requirements. This condition is most likely to be met in times of recession. By a more liberal permission of fixed-term employment labour contracts, the 1985 employment promotion law (Beschäftigungsförderungsgesetz) led to some de-facto lessening of employment protection in recent years. The economic effects of this change will be discussed below.   [33] See also Glyn and Rowthorn (1988), p. 146.

(by 3.7 per cent), while private service-sector employment grew by a hefty 65.0 per cent (i.e. a rate of 3.4 per cent p.a.), which amounts to a net gain of about 24.8 million service-sector jobs, with the growth proceeding at a fairly constant rate throughout cyclical booms and recessions; in the same period, West German service-sector employment (also excluding self-employment) grew by just 24.8 per cent (1.5 per cent p.a.), i.e. by about 1.6 million jobs in the course of fifteen years.[34] The American employment success story had its counterpart in a marked increase of intersectoral wage dispersion between manufacturing and services which also finds no parallel in West Germany, where the dispersion remained roughly constant. Apparently, intersectoral wage flexibility allowed a rapid expansion of employment in the United States which intersectoral rigidity prevented in West Germany. As a consequence of the fast service-sector expansion, the labour productivity growth throughout the economy slowed down much more dramatically in the American than in the West German service sector.[35] Also, a good part of the exceptionally bad overall productivity growth of the US economy in the last two decades and the disproportionally large increase in low-wage employment may be explained by this rapid structural change.[36]

With the West German manufacturing sector bound to shrink because of a high wage gap and, on top of that, two sharp recessions, the private service sector was about to absorb the labour load. Thus, in the 1970s and 1980s West Germany faced a dilemma: either it imitated the United States by allowing some more intersectoral wage flexibility to give service-sector employment an additional boost above its trend growth, or it imitated its own past in the early 1960s, when the relatively low wage level allowed structural change to proceed in a state of overemployment.[37] Note that both courses would have amounted to a reduction of labour costs at least somewhere in the economy to compensate for the employment effect of the wage gap in manufacturing. Hence, if one is ready to assign explanatory power to the vast difference between the experiences of the two countries in question – and it would be hard not to do so – then a structural wage gap combined with a fairly rigid wage structure between sectors may well explain a good part of the persistent unemployment in West Germany.

[34] Note that the sectoral classification schemes are somewhat different in the US and West Germany. However, this does not lead to any serious distortion of the empirical picture. See Hoffmann (1988) for details.

[35] For a detailed comparison of intersectoral wage flexibility and productivity growth in the US and West Germany, see Burda and Sachs (1987), pp. 27–31.

[36] See Bluestone and Harrison (1988), Freeman (1988), and *The Economist* of 12 November 1988, 'America's Shrinking Middle'.   [37] See Chapter 4, Section A.1 above.

As to regions, there is no doubt that the emerging labour surplus was distributed quite unevenly in the last fifteen years: by 1988, a clear-cut north–south divide had emerged, with the three northern regions being hit much harder by unemployment than the southern ones. This corresponds to the sectoral incidence of job creation: the regions with a concentration of modern service and industrial sectors (above all Baden–Württemberg, Hesse and Southern Bavaria) took the lead in overcoming unemployment, while the main steel-producing, coalmining and/or ship-building regions (Schleswig-Holstein, Lower Saxony, North Rhine-Westphalia and – to some extent – Rhineland-Palatinate/Saar) fell behind. While all the northern regions faced a further rise in their unemployment rates in the recovery period 1983–8, all the southern regions managed to achieve a reduction.[38]

Viewed as a whole, the composition of long-term unemployment, the sectoral employment growth pattern and the regional imbalances do point to an important structural dimension of the West German unemployment malaise. If one further recognizes the fact that, in the late 1980s, official estimates put the number of vacancies at around 600,000,[39] a level not reached since the early 1970s at a time of extreme labour shortage, there is little doubt that the core of the problem as it has evolved since the mid 1970s is structural.

What was done and what could have been done about structural (long-term) unemployment at a given trend growth of output? The use of three major policy tools has repeatedly been proposed by economists: (a) wage differentiation, (b) active labour-market policies, and (c) the liberalization of labour-market regulations.

(a) Wage differentiation. Theoretically, any large differences in value productivity between workers of different ages, health status and qualifications call for wage differentiation. In an extreme case – abstracting from actual institutional constraints – anybody with some 'structural handicap' could offer his labour at a wage corresponding to his/her marginal value productivity as seen by any potential employer. As a consequence, the type of heterogeneity in the labour force which is most relevant for re-employment prospects could enter wage formation and thus open up additional submarkets for 'structurally handicapped labour'.

In West German practice, any reform along these lines would boil down

---

[38] For a detailed empirical analysis of regional unemployment in West Germany, see Paqué (1988a,b, 1990).
[39] See *Handelsblatt* of 12 April 1989, 'Experten halten die Zahl von einer bis 1,5 Millionen offener Stellen für unrealistisch.'

to removing all contractual minimum wage restrictions as they traditionally apply in West Germany's collective bargaining system.[40] This, in turn,
would require a major overhauling of the tightly knit social net. At present,
unemployment support of 63 per cent of the last net wage (68 per cent if
the person has at least one child) is paid on an insurance basis for a
limited period, mostly 12–24 months, depending on age and other factors;
thereafter means-tested unemployment aid of 56 per cent or 58 per cent
is paid indefinitely out of taxpayers' money.[41] Clearly, an offer of a job
paying, say, 50 per cent of the unemployed person's last net wage means
a net income loss. Traditionally, West German law gives an unemployed
person the right to decline a job offer without losing his claim to benefit
if the job would significantly worsen his long-term chances of returning
to the kind of work he did before or to a job of comparable professional
status.[42] In the case of many low-wage offers – at least to persons over a
certain age or in bad health – this condition would be met. Hence, once
mass unemployment was there, a generous social minimum standard has
become the ultimate obstacle to an adjustment of the wage structure.

   In West Germany, the most widely discussed type of structural wage
differentiation is that between regions. Economically, its main task would
be that of compensating inherent differences in local conditions which, in
the eyes of potential investors, make the expected value productivity –
though mostly not the expected physical productivity – of the same kind
of work differ between regions. In an ideal setting, the perfectly mobile
factor capital moves to the place where the profitability of investment is
highest because of a whole range of diverse local conditions, including
labour costs and property prices. If labour is an essentially immobile
factor – a quite realistic assumption for West Germany in the 1970s and
1980s[43] – wages have an important function for the allocation of capital
in space: when wages are kept the same everywhere, capital moves ceteris
paribus to the regions with the highest value productivity of labour, with
the load of price adjustment being exclusively on property; thus regions

---

[40] In West Germany, collective agreements usually fix minimum wages for different types
of skilled and unskilled labour at industry level. As about 80 per cent of all industrial
firms employing about 90 per cent of all industrial workers are members of employers'
associations, the vast majority of all wage contracts are subject to collective bargaining
restrictions. Under certain circumstances, collective agreements can even be declared
binding for all firms and workers in a region. For details, see Soltwedel and Trapp (1988),
pp. 194–205.

[41] In recent years, there have been some minor changes in the legal basis of unemployment
benefits. However, they are irrelevant for the question at hand.

[42] See §103 of the *Arbeitsförderungsgesetz* (AFG) and §2 of the *Zumutbarkeits-Verordnung*.

[43] See Table 6, which shows that most standard measures of migration indicate a sharp
decline of the migration propensity from the early 1970s onwards.

with a locational disadvantage forgo investment and become depressed areas with low property prices, but high unemployment.

All the relevant statistics show that both the minimum wages as fixed by collective agreements for different labour categories and the respective effective wages as actually paid have always had a very low spread across regions, with a coefficient of variation mostly around 5 per cent. More important still, the regional pattern has been quite uniform and stable over time, with the urbanized states Hamburg, North Rhine–Westphalia, Hesse and Baden–Württemberg in the lead, and the rural states – especially Bavaria – lagging behind. Obviously, this rigid structure does not reflect the changes in labour-market and general economic conditions like the emerging north–south divide in West Germany in the 1970s and 1980s, which can be read off the statistics on property prices.[44] Hence, on economic grounds, more regional wage differentiation would have been warranted.[45]

(b) Active labour-market policies. Theoretically, the employment effects of wage differentiation can also be achieved by manipulating the relevant unit labour costs through appropriate labour-market policies. Within the standard arsenal of labour-market policy instruments which are all commonly applied in West Germany,[46] the most important ones are wage subsidies and qualification measures.

According to the West German Labour Promotion Act (*Arbeitsför-derungsgesetz*) in its current form, any firm employing a long-term jobless person over fifty may receive wage subsidies amounting to 50 per cent in the first year, decreasing to 30 per cent in the third year of a new (unlimited-term) employment contract. In addition, in 1989 the West German Labour Ministry initiated a more broadly based programme to support the reintegration of all types of long-term unemployed persons

---

[44] See Deutsche Bundesbank (1989), p. 39, where it is shown that, in 1988, property prices were on average about 40 per cent higher in cities of southern than of northern Germany.

[45] Major studies on wage differentiation in West Germany are Bell and Freeman (1985), Gundlach (1986), Koller (1987), Hardes (1988), Soltwedel (1988) and Bellmann and Buttler (1989). There has been a somewhat curious economic debate about the extent and development of interregional wage differentiation in West Germany. Too much attention has been directed to differentials in actual earnings, which are heavily influenced by regional differences in the sectoran and industrial structure of economic activity. Typically, urbanized regions with a high concentration of modern industries and services have a particularly high value productivity and wage level per worker. However, for locational investment decisions, this information is only of minor interest. Relevant instead are comparative wage levels in the one particular sector of economic activity where investment ought to take place. Hence, only a sector-by-sector comparison – preferably on a very low level of aggregation – has any substantial bearing on the issue at hand.   [46] See Werner (1987b) for a summary.

by granting wage subsidies of up to 80 per cent over one year for employment contracts of unlimited duration;[47] for this purpose an additional 1.5 DMarks was supplied by the West German government. Although these provisions and programmes look generous in scope and well targeted, their beneficial effects are hampered by the – unavoidably – temporary nature of subsidization: for a firm, a temporary cut in labour costs at the early stage of a new contract may not outweigh the long-term disadvantage of being stuck with a low-productivity worker, at least as long as there are plenty of superior alternatives in the market because of a fast growth of the labour force as a consequence of large-scale immigration from Eastern Europe. After all, the generous provisions for subsidizing the employment of elderly persons in recent years have not noticeably slowed down the emergence of a dual labour-market structure.

As to qualification measures, there was quite a boom in the 1980s: the amount spent by the West German labour administration on supporting vocational training doubled in the period 1983–8, from 5.4 to 10.7 billion DMarks.[48] To smooth structural adjustment by facilitating occupational, sectoral and also regional mobility as a partial substitute for wage differentiation, this makes good economic sense, although the actual returns of this kind of public investment are not well known. However, as an initiative targeted at long-term unemployment, it may simply miss the core of the problem. Most qualification measures naturally involve not training, but rather some sort of retraining. Hence, the more than half of all long-term unemployed persons who have no qualifications in the first place hardly profit from the additional options. To a large extent, this conclusion also applies to the other major fringe groups of long-term unemployment: obviously, the main structural handicap of older or chronically ill persons is not having the wrong qualifications, but age or bad health. Thus, after all, labour-market policies may not figure as more than mere supplementary measures which alleviate the problem somewhat, but are no significant step towards its solution.

(c) Liberalization of labour-market regulations. By international standards, the West German labour markets are and have always been heavily regulated, with the complex framework of protection against dismissal being the main legal constraint.[49] By passing the Employment Promotion Act (Beschäftigungsförderungsgesetz (BeschFG)) in 1985, the West German legislator made a first move towards liberalization: inter

---

[47] See, inter alia, Wirtschaftswoche of 9 June 1989, 'Langzeitarbeitslosigkeit – Neuer Anlauf'.
[48] See Lampert (1989), p. 187.
[49] See Emerson (1988), who reports employers' relative evaluations of different regulatory systems of labour markets in EEC countries.

alia, the period for which fixed-term contracts are generally permitted was extended from 6 to 18 months (and in special cases to 24 months). Thus private firms were given the opportunity to circumvent at least the cost of long-term dismissal protection when engaging new workers.

By the time of its passing, the law was the object of fierce political debate, with the front line running along the familiar union/Social Democratic versus liberal/conservative boundaries. By now, a fairly detailed statistical stock-taking by the Wissenschaftszentrum, Berlin shows that the law has been a success, albeit by no means a spectacular one.[50] All in all, the Employment Promotion Act has added a significant element of flexibility to West German labour-market regulations. Nevertheless, the core of the employment protection laws has been left untouched; as these laws apply most forcefully to the labour-market fringe groups which are also hit hardest by long-term unemployment, they figure as a persistent impediment to employment growth, at least as long as a compensatory wage differentiation is not feasible.

To sum up, the economic leeway for reducing unemployment on the micro level of the labour market is very limited within West German corporatist and institutional constraints. On the other hand, removing or at least substantially lifting these constraints would be no less difficult, simply because they have become the backbone of a social consensus which transcends the boundaries of all major political parties. Hence, in practice, the only way to reduce unemployment is to return to growth rates of the economy's production potential – above all the capital stock – which allow for a full absorption of the labour force.

3   Roots of the growth slack

Since the mid 1970s, the causes of sluggish growth have become a perennial topic of the macroeconomic policy debate. For a while, the monetary and/or fiscal contractions which invoked the two sharp cyclical downturns in 1974/5 and 1981/2 were made responsible for the unsatisfactory growth performance. With cyclical recovery gaining ground, this position lost much of its intellectual appeal and gradually degenerated into a relic for a heretical group of economists with strong ties to unions or the more extreme political left.[51] The opposite view, that the growth slack had its roots on the supply side, was at first a minority standpoint held by German

---

[50] Büchtemann (1989). The law was originally intended to expire in 1990, but it was extended to apply for another five-year term. Although the net employment effect of the BeschFG is naturally very difficult to calculate, a tentative estimate in the range of 170,000 new employees in two years, with about 90,000 more permanent jobs, looks quite reasonable. For details, see Büchtemann (1989), Ch. 4.

supply-side economists, mostly scholars with a strong neoclassical background and ideological ties to liberalism.[52] As time went by, its main diagnostic gospel became something of a consensus view, although opinions continued to differ as to the extent of reforms required to initiate a new growth spurt.

By definition, the trend of supply-side growth may decelerate for three reasons: namely (i) a slowdown of capital formation, (ii) a slowdown of labour-supply expansion and (iii) a slowdown of joint factor productivity growth. In the case of West Germany, all three variants are relevant, albeit to different degrees, and we shall deal with each of them successively.

(i) Capital formation. There is no doubt that capital formation has been exceptionally weak since the mid 1970s (see Figure 14): gross investment in plant and equipment stagnated at around 20 per cent of GNP as compared to 25 per cent in the 1960s and early 1970s. The development of net investment was even worse: as a share of GNP, it followed a steady decline from about 15 per cent before 1973 to a low of 7 per cent in the second half of the 1980s, with a brief cyclical recovery at the turn of the decade. As a consequence, capital stock growth slowed down significantly, from a high of 6.1 per cent p.a. in 1960–73 to 3.8 per cent in 1973–80 and 2.8 per cent in 1980–9.[53] If one further recognizes that the sharp increase in labour costs in the first half of the 1970s is likely to have given the technology embodied in the new capital equipment a pronounced labour-saving bias,[54] then the balance of capital formation looks all the more unsatisfactory.

The probable major reason for this poor performance can be read from Figure 15: a commonly used measure of the rate of return on capital

[51] See above all the so-called *Memorandum zur Wirtschaftspolitik* (*Memorandum on Economic Policy*) which, from 1975 on, was published annually as an explicit academic and political counterweight to the annual reports of the Council of Economic Experts. All the memorandums were signed by a large group of professional economists and union members, mostly of the political left. They stuck to an orthodox demand-side interpretation of the growth slack which was explicitly embedded in a strongly interventionist and socialist policy framework with increasingly ecological undertones. By and large, the deliberate ideological bias of the authors and the lack of any serious attempt at presenting a detached economic analysis based on a clear-cut theoretical framework and on empirical evidence disqualified these reports from the outset. In public discussion, they played only a very minor fringe role.

[52] For a collection of fairly radical supply-side views on a long list of matters relevant to growth and structural change, see Giersch (1983), which contains contributions from prominent liberal-minded economists. For somewhat more moderate views of this kind, see virtually all reports of the Advisory Council to the Federal Minister of Economics (Wissenschaftlicher Beirat (1987)), and the annual reports of the Council of Economic Experts (Sachverständigenrat, various issues).

[53] See Table 2.   [54] See Giersch (1983), pp. 10–11.

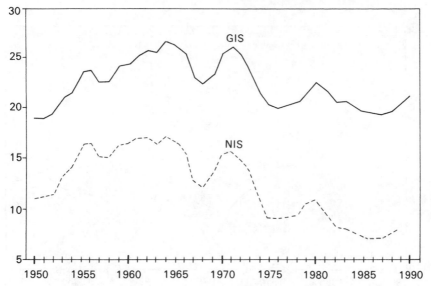

Figure 14. Share of investment expenditures in GNP 1950–90 (in per cent).
Notes: GIS: share of gross investment expenditures (excluding inventories) in gross national product; NIS: share of net investment expenditures (net of depreciation, excluding inventories) in gross national product.
Source: Statistisches Bundesamt; own calculations.

shows that, from the early 1970s until the second half of the 1980s, the profitability of investment was much lower than in earlier periods.[55] However, while the temporary improvement in the late 1970s was merely cyclical, the revival of profitability towards the end of the 1980s looks much more sustained and may signal a change for the better. Note that more recently (since about 1988) the investment performance has also improved substantially.

Why did the return on capital remain so low for about one and a half decades? Two reasons stand out. First, it took no less than fifteen years until the increase of labour costs in the early 1970s (see Table 17) was finally reversed (see Table 23). While wage pressure abated early enough to allow for some reduction of real unit labour costs (RULC) in the recovery period 1976–9, the worsening of the terms of trade due to the second oil-price shock set the economy back again. Only after a prolonged period of wage moderation in the 1980s could a substantial improvement

---

[55] Basically, the rate of return on capital used in the text and the table is defined as operating surplus (net of the costs of all factors of production including interest costs and depreciation) divided by the value of the capital stock.

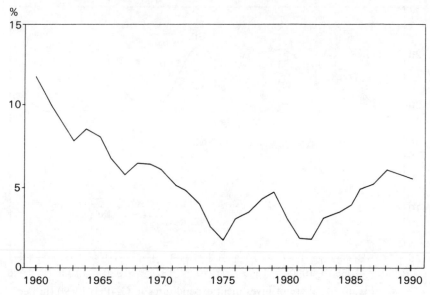

Figure 15. Rate of return on capital 1960–90.
Source: Sachverständigenrat (1990/1), p. 90.

be achieved. Second, however measured, real interest rates turned out to be significantly higher in the 1980s than in the 1970s (see Table 24), and thus temporarily prevented reductions of other factor costs from being translated into a rise in the rate of return on capital. Why this was so is one of the great economic puzzles of the last decade and deserves a somewhat more detailed – albeit far from exhaustive – discussion.[56]

In the 1970s, the inflationary climate had prevented real interest rates from converging to their (Wicksellian) natural level: monetary policy led either to artificially depressed rates – as in the final Bretton Woods years until 1973 and during the locomotive experiment as in 1978 – or to sharp and steep rises as in the cyclical downturn of 1973–5. Given the contractionary monetary stance in the early 1980s, inflationary expectations were successively driven down, so that – at least until 1983/4 – a very high level of real interest rates could perhaps best be explained as the by-product of stabilization, i.e. as an essentially monetary phenomenon. Note that this process was accompanied by a new valuation of the country's capital stock: all those manifold investments – above all in property and housing – which had served as hedges against inflation

---

[56] For a more comprehensive account, see Giersch (1985), pp. 420–3, and Schmieding (1989b), pp. 67–71.

Table 23. *The determinants of labour costs 1974–89[a]*

	(1) W	(2) LP	(3) PC	(4) PV	(5) PV/PC	(6) RULC
1974–75	6.9	1.1	5.8	6.0	−0.2	−0.2
1975–76	7.3	6.0	4.1	3.6	−0.5	−2.3
1976–77	6.3	2.8	3.6	3.7	0.1	−0.3
1977–78	5.5	2.0	2.7	4.3	1.6	−0.9
1978–79	5.4	2.4	4.0	4.0	0.0	−1.0
1979–80	6.6	−0.2	5.8	4.8	−1.0	1.9
1980–81	4.5	0.3	6.2	4.0	−2.0	0.2
1981–82	3.4	0.6	4.7	4.4	−0.3	−1.5
1982–83	3.6	3.0	3.2	3.3	0.0	−2.6
1983–84	3.3	2.7	2.5	2.0	−0.6	−1.3
1984–85	3.0	1.2	2.1	2.2	0.2	−0.5
1985–86	3.5	0.9	−0.5	3.1	3.6	−0.5
1986–87	3.0	1.0	0.6	2.0	1.4	0.0
1987–88	3.0	2.9	1.2	1.6	0.4	−1.5
1988–89	2.8	1.9	3.2	2.6	−0.6	−1.6
1974–80	6.3	2.3	4.4	4.4	0.0	−0.5
1980–89	3.3	1.6	2.6	2.8	0.2	−1.0

Notes: [a] Annual average rates of change of selected variables (in per cent).
(1) W = wage level defined as average gross yearly earnings of employees (including social security contributions of employers); (2) LP = labour productivity defined as gross domestic product at constant prices divided by active labour force; (3) PC = private consumption deflator; (4) PV = deflator of value added (i.e. gross domestic product); (5) PV/PC = ratio of PV to PC as defined in notes to (4) and (3) respectively; (6) RULC = real unit labour cost defined as $W/(LP \cdot PV)$ as defined in notes to (1), (2), and (4) respectively.
Source: Statistisches Bundesamt; own calculations.

without adding much to the economy's productive potential lost their rationale and were drastically devalued. Thus, the 1980s brought the most sustained crisis in housing and the construction industry in the post-war period.

For the time after 1983, however, a standard liquidity theory is insufficient to explain the persistently high level of real interest rates; apparently, shifts of the demand and/or supply curves for savings had brought about a fundamental upward movement of the natural rate of interest in the market for long-term capital. As this has been a worldwide phenomenon, any attempt at explanation should also have an international dimension.

Basically two factors come to mind. First, as to the supply of capital,

Table 24. *Nominal and real interest rates 1955–89*

	Interest rate (% p.a.)		
	Nominal	Real	Real
	(1)	(2)	(3)
1955–59	6.4	4.1	4.0
1960–64	6.1	3.1	2.6
1965–69	7.1	4.7	4.2
1970–74	8.9	3.3	2.0
1975–79	7.4	3.3	3.1
1980–84	8.8	4.3	5.1
1985–89	6.4	5.1	4.1

Notes: (1) Defined as average bond yield in long-term capital market.
(2) Defined as (1) minus average annual rate of change of consumption deflator.
(3) Defined as (1) minus average annual rate of change of value added deflator.
Sources: Deutsche Bundesbank and Statistisches Bundesamt; own calculations.

there is a general consensus that in all industrialized countries savers became more 'interest conscious': after more than a decade of price instability, the sensitivity of savers towards inflation may have risen so that the slightest reawakening of inflationary expectations was bound to drive up interest rates more than it did before. Second, as to the demand for capital, there has been a transatlantic crowding out of investment through the peculiar policy mix of the early Reagan administration: after the American Tax Reform Act of 1981, the sharp rise of the US budget deficit caused a high current account deficit, a surge of interest rates and also – temporarily – a drastic appreciation of the US dollar. On the other hand, US firms were heavily favoured by the newly implemented tax cuts and investment subsidies; thus, they did not face a rise of capital costs despite the increase of real interest rates. In West Germany (and also in continental Europe in general), no comparable changes in the tax legislation took place, so that firms there could not escape the pressure of capital costs.[57] Note that, on this view, the US budget deficit by itself cannot be considered the reason for the crowding out; in the last resort the main cause lies in a 'transatlantic tax-reform gap' which – at a given interest rate – raised the profitability of investment in the US, but not in Europe. In addition, the transatlantic gap of labour-market flexibility as

[57] For a detailed description of this transatlantic crowding-out hypothesis, see Fitoussi and Phelps (1988), pp. 89–94.

described in Section A.2 of this chapter is likely to have pulled in the same direction, since the high degree of wage rigidity in Europe prevented firms from having access to a pool of relatively cheap labour as was available in the US.

Apart from the low rate of return on capital, there were other important, though hardly quantifiable, factors which created a relatively bad West German investment climate in the fifteen years after 1973. Two stand out: (a) a worsening of industrial relations, and (b) high levels of subsidization and regulation as impediments to structural change.

(a) Prima facie, it looks inappropriate to claim that industrial relations worsened at a time when wage demands were clearly not outright aggressive. Nevertheless, most observers of the West German economic scene diagnosed a fading away of the general spirit of constructive cooperation between labour and capital which had its heyday in the 1960s. After all, the two most strike-intensive years in West German post-war history (1978 and 1984) were in the period under consideration.[58] While, by international standards, the West Germany of the later 1970s and the 1980s may still have appeared to be an island of labour tranquillity, the outstanding appeal of German-style social peace was gradually lost through a deep-seated sociological and economic transformation.

A symbolic but nevertheless highly significant sign of this climatic turn to the worse was the unions' quitting of the Concerted Action in 1977. Established by Karl Schiller ten years earlier, the regular round-table meetings of union leaders with representatives of the employers' associations and public authorities had long degenerated into a fairly ineffective exchange of ideas. In the public mind, however, they had still featured as the visible incarnation of a constructive working spirit of corporatism. The immediate reason for the unions' quitting was itself characteristic of the change in atmosphere: after long political deliberations going back to the early 1970s, a new co-determination law had been passed in 1976 which was to enforce labour participation on the board of directors of all larger firms outside heavy industry. In principle, the law provided for a parity of capital and labour representation; however, as one member of the labour side was required to be a white-collar managerial employee (*leitender Angestellter*) who could well be expected to identify more with the interests of capital owners than with those of blue-collar workers, a slight but decisive dominance of capital was preserved. Politically, this hybrid form of co-determination emerged as a compromise between the Social Democrats, who traditionally favoured a strongly syndicalist model with full parity, and their coalition partner, the liberals, who were ready

[58] See Langfeldt (1987), p. 28.

to extend co-determination beyond the framework provided by the 1952 company statute law,[59] but insisted on keeping it well short of full parity.[60] Nevertheless, the employers' associations went as far in their protest as initiating a suit against the new law in the Supreme Court which was finally turned down in 1979. For the unions, this suit gave a signal – possibly not an unwelcome one – not only to quit the Concerted Action, but also to take a tougher stand on some major issues which gradually began to move on to the bargaining table as a partial substitute for wage demands. Given the high level of unemployment, an openly aggressive wage policy as in the early 1970s would have met with strong resistance from the general public. The focus therefore shifted to broader 'social issues', above all to the introduction of new technologies and the shortening of the working week.

As to the implementation of new technologies in the workplace, an almost paradigmatic controversy arose in spring 1978: the traditionally radical printers' union demanded severe restrictions on the use of new electronic printing and typing techniques so as to preserve jobs which would otherwise become obsolete. After six weeks of bitter industrial conflict with strikes and lock-outs, a compromise was struck which – though not preventing the introduction of the new techniques – provided an extensive social cushioning in the form of quasi-job guarantees to the printers at firm level. More important than the actual costs of this outcome for one single and small industry was the economy-wide psychological effect of the conflict: for the first time in West German post-war history, a union had deliberately blocked an obviously profitable labour-saving innovation which could be expected to sweep over the whole industry within a few years. West Germany – once a pacemaker in the modernization of capital equipment – suddenly looked set to become a laggard. In fact, with unemployment remaining high, the issue of allegedly 'social rationalization investments' became a recurrent theme among the public and at the bargaining table, just as in the late years of the Weimar Republic, when a protracted controversy about the extent of technological unemployment had taken place. As in the 1920s, the unions rejected the argument of economists that labour-saving investments and a low labour intensity of production were themselves a direct consequence of the wage pressure of earlier times.

To be sure, the main thrust of anti-technology feeling which gained ground by the late 1970s came from outside the unions, namely from the

[59] That law assigned one-third of the seats in the supervisory board of directors to labour. See Chapter 3, Section A above.
[60] For a summary of the poiitical debate on co-determination, see Bracher et al. (1986), pp. 127–9.

rapidly growing ecological movement. It reached a first climax in the staunch resistance against the construction of nuclear power plants: in 1977, a heated public debate and huge demonstrations around the construction site of the projected nuclear reactor at Brokdorf (to the north of Hamburg) indicated that, to a growing section of the West German population, previously uncontroversial technologies were simply not acceptable any more. The core of the anti-nuclear feeling was a mixture of perfectly rational concerns about safety and a romantic longing for a post-industrial paradise of modesty and self-sufficiency. Needless to say, a similar technological scepticism arose in other parts of Europe – notably the Protestant northern belt from the Netherlands to Sweden – but in West Germany, the whole movement had a particularly emotional and quasi-religious flavour which signalled the revival of the seemingly forgotten traditions of German romanticism. More than in other countries, this was in particularly sharp contrast to the consensual social climate of the 1950s and 1960s, with its down-to-earth materialistic value orientation. Naturally, the unions did not go so far as joining the ecological chorus, since far too many jobs seemed to depend on those technologies which were now under heavy attack. However, with an eye to new popular themes, they began to take a more critical attitude towards the ecological costs of industrial and post-industrial society.

Step by step, the main new issue of collective bargaining became the shortening of working time, in particular the introduction of the thirty-five-hour working week. From 1977 on, it was widely discussed as a measure against unemployment; and in 1978, the unions' umbrella organization DGB established it as a major programmatic medium-term aim. The two largest industrial disputes in West Germany's post-war history – the steel workers' strike in winter 1978/9 and the metal workers' strike in 1984 – were basically fought over moves towards this end. Although the first cuts into the forty-hour working week were not achieved before the mid 1980s, the persistent public discussion about the general issue of working hours did not die down again after 1978. Economically, a flat shortening of the working week was clearly a blunt weapon with which to fight unemployment, even if it came without the so-called 'full wage compensation', roughly meaning a reduction of working hours without a corresponding reduction of gross income per worker. At best, it would be a redistribution of labour, not a genuine creation of jobs; at worst it would merely create more acute sectoral, professional and regional shortages and thus raise new impediments to economic growth. Therefore, almost unanimously, economists pleaded for (and employers' associations in fact offered) more flexible working hours which might in sum be shorter, but take account of emerging structural imbalances and the wishes of individual workers. However, to preserve centralized control over working conditions, unions mostly resisted a general flexibility and quite stubbornly stuck to their idea of an across-the-board reduction. Thus the whole controversy began to degenerate into a kind of ideological struggle: as the Social Democrats took over the demand for the thirty-five-hour working week in their programme for the first elections to the European parliament in 1979, the issue was explicitly politicized and thus removed from the comparatively innocent range of compromise in collective bargaining. More than ever before, the unions merged their ideas with Social Democratic thinking and, as a consequence, identified with just one political party, again a tendency which endangered the consensual pillars of corporatism.[61]

All this happened in a period when a visible change of generations took place in the ranks of the union leadership: highly respected 'elder statesmen' who had been in charge throughout the early post-war reconstruction and the years of overemployment in the 1960s now retired and were replaced by new types of functionaries who lacked the experience of successful pragmatism and were thus inclined to use a much sharper rhetoric and to take a more radical left-wing political stance. At the same time economic realities ran counter to apparent union interests: persistent structural unemployment called for less centralization and more differentiation of wage demands; new technologies and the structural change away from heavily unionized industry reduced the weight of the classical union clientele, i.e. blue-collar workers; and, a specifically German phenomenon, a long series of management scandals in union-owned firms – notably the Neue Heimat, which owned a large chunk of tax-favoured social residential construction (*Sozialer Wohnungsbau*) – undermined the moral authority and social aspirations of the whole union movement.[62] The unions were therefore economically and morally on the defensive, and tried to regain lost ground by broadening their scope as a political voice beyond the collective bargaining table. On the whole, this strategy restrained outright wage demands somewhat; however, it did not help people to react flexibly to the new demands of an increasingly post-industrial economy, and it is likely to have contributed to the erosion of a social consensus which, in earlier times, had preserved a favourable investment climate.

(b) Although public subsidization and heavy legal regulation of economic activity had always been a significant feature of the West German economy, they took on a new qualitative dimension in the 1970s and 1980s. Since 1973, subsidies – i.e. cash grants and tax incentives – have amounted to 4–5 per cent of GNP, with no downward trend in the 1980s,

[61] For an account of the political orientation of the unions since the mid 1970s, see Jäger and Link (1987), pp. 173–83.   [62] For details, see Jäger and Link (1987), pp. 181–3.

despite a centre–right government which placed a high priority on 'fiscal consolidation'. The degree of effective subsidization – a measure analogous to the degree of effective protection[63] – stood at about 7 per cent throughout. These aggregates hide an extremely unequal distribution, with the bulk of public support falling on structurally weak sectors such as agriculture, mining, shipbuilding and, after the recession of 1981/2, iron and steel.[64] Only one modern industry – the aircraft industry – enjoyed a higher degree of subsidization than the average for the whole economy, although there was substantial indirect public support for research and development in all branches with a significant share of high-technology products.[65] Most subsidy programmes are based on very poor welfare-theoretic reasoning, and it has hardly been controversial in academia that most of them should be removed, at least in the medium and long run. In fact, many were originally designed as strictly temporary measures to ease the adjustment of ailing industries and to save capital and jobs from immediate scrapping but not from eventual obsolescence. Because of the successful lobbying of industry pressure groups and unions, however, most of them have become permanent, thus taking on the character of welfare provision rather than adjustment support.

Economists agree that the persistence of subsidization not only involved heavy static welfare losses but, even more importantly, reduced the growth dynamics of the West German economy: capital and labour were channelled into sectors of economic activity which, in the long run, could not stand the competition from newly industrialized and less developed countries. Agriculture, mining and shipbuilding thus became permanent subsidy recipients, with no great chance of recovery except for short-term cyclical reasons. Naturally, all the resources retained in structurally weak sectors were lacking in those branches – mostly high-tech industries and modern services – which could be expected to have a bright future in a world of free trade and free capital movements.

The second large array of impediments to structural change lies in the regulation of large areas of the West German economy, above all the modern service sector: retail trade, banking, insurance, communications, transportation and utilities have always been and still are heavily regulated branches. As at least some of them are also sectors with a very high growth potential in advanced industrialized countries, there can be hardly any doubt that opportunities for investment were sacrificed through the straitjacket of public restrictions. Most German economists now agree that many of these regulations are more the accidental result of history

[63] See Donges, Schmidt et al. (1988), pp. 147, 206–8.
[64] See ibid., 145–58, 216 (Table A6) and unpublished data provided by the Kiel Institute of World Economics.   [65] See Donges, Schmidt et al. (1988), pp. 159–66.

or of explicit lobbying efforts of established firms than of any rational economic or social argument. As long as West Germany could rely on the expansion of its export machine of industrial output as the main engine of growth, the high level of regulation may have been just a nuisance, but no serious impediment to growth. However, since the early 1970s, the need for change has become more pressing and may at some stage become a matter of economic survival in the small league of rich nations. For these reasons, other countries – notably the United States, the United Kingdom and the Netherlands – have made quite courageous attempts at liberalization in many of these fields since the late 1970s. While there has been some deregulation in West Germany as well – most of it in financial markets – the balance looks modest by international standards. At any rate, a whole agenda of deregulation remains to be tackled.[66] The long and tortuous political discussion on the almost trivial matter of liberalizing the rigid West German shopping hours has become something of a paradigmatic example of Teutonic inflexibility: it took years of extensive public debate, with the relevant union leading the status quo lobby, until a law was passed which allowed shops to extend their opening hours beyond the standard 6.00 or 6.30 to 8.30 p.m. on one single day of the week!

(ii) *Labour supply*. There are at least three good reasons to believe that, despite chronic unemployment, there were also supply-side constraints to economic growth from the labour side. First, to a large extent, unemployment was structural, and a shortage of skilled labour in expanding sectors and regions became visible in the recoveries of both the 1970s and the 1980s. Second, from 1973 onwards, the influx of foreign workers came to a virtual halt; thus, for the first time in post-war West German economic history, no mobile 'industrial reserve army' could be made available to smooth the frictions of structural change, a role which expellees and refugees had played in the 1950s and foreign workers in the 1960s and early 1970s.[67] Note that the youngsters of the large baby-boom generation who entered the labour force were less than a perfect substitute in this respect, since they were not regionally mobile enough to remove the labour-demand overhang wherever it showed up. Only more recently, in the years 1988–90, did the sharp increase of immigration from East Germany and Eastern Europe mark a return to the favourable labour-supply conditions of earlier times. Third, and maybe most importantly, the system of income and payroll taxation is likely to have had a noticeable disincentive effect on work effort, especially for middle- and

[66] See the detailed account of both the extent of regulation and proposals for deregulation by Soltwedel et al. (1986).   [67] See Chapters 3.A and 4.A of this book.

higher-income earners who make up the bulk of skilled labour. From the mid 1970s until the late 1980s, the public-sector share in GNP varied between 45 and 50 per cent, after less than 30 per cent in the 1950s and 30–40 per cent in the 1960s; excluding social security, the share was lower, but the upward trend until the mid 1970s equally unmistakable. A growing part of public revenue came from direct taxes, notably from progressive income tax. As ever more middle-income earners moved into the higher tax brackets – partly because of genuine income increases, partly because of the 'bracket creep' of inflation – supply-side economists repeatedly warned of a gradual worsening of the incentive structure and called for a bold overhaul of the system.[68] In fact, after 1983, the centre–right government put much effort into drafting an income-tax reform aimed at lowering the marginal tax burden. After long and painful political struggles, not least within the federal government itself,[69] a step-by-step tax reform was introduced which provided for tax reductions in three successive steps to take place in 1986, 1988 and 1990. Only the last step was to lead to a substantial reduction of marginal income-tax rates for the vast majority of taxpayers, above all in the middle-income ranges; the top marginal rate was only slightly reduced from 56 to 53 per cent, which amounted to no more than a return to the pre-1975 state of affairs. Compared to tax reforms in other countries – notably the United Kingdom and the United States – the achievement looked modest indeed.[70]

As to payroll taxes, the situation became even more critical: as a share of GNP, social security contributions had risen from 8–10 per cent in the 1950s and 10–12 per cent in the 1960s to more than 17 per cent throughout the 1980s. For different reasons, the burden of the three major payroll tax components increased sharply: the contributions to unemployment insurance because of the rise of the unemployment rate; the contributions to the pay-as-you-go old-age insurance because of a worsening of the age structure, i.e. a rising share of retired people in the population; and the contributions to health insurance because of the soaring costs of medical treatment. In many respects, these difficulties could be considered the logical consequence of the principles on which the system was constructed, and they had in fact been foreseen for a long time. To the extent that individuals regarded the rising burden of social security contributions as a straight increase in taxation, negative supply-side effects were to be expected.

[68] See, for example Engels (1983).
[69] Notably the left wing of the Christian Democratic Party was lukewarm at best vis-à-vis the tax reform, which received the strongest political backing from the liberals and the business wing of the Christian Democrats.
[70] For the details of the tax reform, see Sachverständigenrat (1985/6), Table 25 and (1987/8), Table 30.

As old-age and health insurance make up the bulk of the payroll tax burden, political reform efforts naturally focussed on these two items.[71] At first, only very minor corrections of benefit schemes were made, such as postponing the annual adjustment of pensions or adjusting the coverage of the public health insurance scheme here and there. After protracted political debates, the federal government finally made some more drastic benefit cuts and structural changes which are suited to reducing the financial burden of the system in the long run. As the respective laws were passed towards the end of the 1980s, their main effects will have to be awaited. In any case, the basic structure of the compulsory public insurance schemes has been preserved and the measures taken are at best ad hoc adjustments to obtain some breathing space in the medium run, not fundamental reforms which might help to rule out future crises.

(iii) Joint factor productivity. Apart from all the specific factor constraints which may have slowed down supply-side expansion from the mid 1970s up to the late 1980s, it is unquestionable that, in West Germany, trend productivity growth itself, i.e. trend growth at given factor inputs, was much slower after than before the time around the first oil-price shock in 1973. The economic blessings of technical progress were somehow harder to discern than in the two decades before. The reason for this is very much a matter of speculation, although a tentative 'catching up' hypothesis does not look implausible.[72]

Until the early 1970s, the driving force of West German economic growth was certainly its manufacturing industry, which had a great potential for achieving fast productivity gains through the installation of the most modern capital equipment. Although the economy of West Germany (and, for that matter, other continental European countries) was already one of the most industrialized in the world, a technological gap with the United States remained and was gradually closed in the course of rapid trade integration which favoured the profitability of investment in manufacturing. By the early 1970s, this catching-up process had finally run its course, and the first oil-price shock dealt a severe blow to the further growth of manufacturing. With a few other countries, West Germany was now at the top of the technological league of nations; its 'natural' productivity growth fell to the levels which had long been common in the United States. As there, the less export-orientated service

---

[71] Supply-side economists had consistently called for reforms of the social security system. See Boss (1983), Knappe (1983) and Sachverständigenrat (1986/7), paras. 307–28.
[72] A more comprehensive account of the reasons for the productivity slowdown is provided by Giersch and Wolter (1983).

sector had to become the growth locomotive. Although, in the 1980s, labour productivity grew somewhat faster in services than in manufacturing (see Table 21), it never reached the dimensions of industrial productivity growth in earlier periods. In the long run, this may change as the rise of modern computer technology has been revolutionizing not only industrial, but also clerical and administrative work; however, in the short and medium run, even this very promising technological breakthrough may have slowed down productivity growth temporarily since the transition period of implementing a new technology across a whole economy is typically a time of extensive learning on the job, with great frictions which are not conducive to the efficiency of production processes. With something like full computerization being reached by the late 1980s, there is reason to hope that this transition period is now coming to an end and that the full productivity scope of computer technology will soon show up in the statistics.

All in all, the slack of supply-side growth in the 1970s and 1980s is an economic phenomenon of considerable complexity which defies any straight account in terms of some easily identifiable or even quantifiable variables. Ex-post, the factors discussed above add up to a plausible picture of an economy with an all too low rate of capital formation, with constricting structural bottlenecks in the labour market and with too slow a speed of 'autonomous' productivity growth in a qualitatively new stage of structural change. Nobody can say with any degree of precision whether this picture comes close to the whole truth or whether some deeper sociological reasons loom behind the lack of growth dynamics, but remain invisible to the economist's eyes.

B   **Painful adjustment to external challenges**

1   *Protectionist temptations*

In retrospect, the quarter-century 1948–73 appears to have been a golden age for West Germany's tradable goods sector. The rewards of a rapidly intensifying international division of labour were huge and obvious, while the concurrent pains of adjustment hardly mattered at all. For a variety of reasons, the general structural change had not been marred by severe frictions: first of all, the intensification of trade had occurred mainly vis-à-vis traditional industrial countries in Western Europe and North America. This had been helpful because the growing share of intra-industry trade with comparatively similar countries in overall cross-border exchanges eases the burden of adjustment, since a part of the necessary relocation of factors of production may take place within firms or at least industries.[1] Furthermore, West Germany had been catching up technologically with North America throughout the period, putting pressure on its competitors rather than being challenged itself. More importantly, the macroeconomic conditions were extremely favourable. The high rates of growth ensured that structural change implied no significant threat of medium- or long-term unemployment, as people laid off in declining industries had good prospects of finding new and ultimately even better-paid jobs elsewhere. And the undervaluation of the DMark since the late 1950s contributed to the emergence of a somewhat oversized manufacturing sector, so that even industries in which West Germany had lost a previous comparative advantage did not have to shrink all that drastically.

This happy state of affairs had made it easy for West Germany to live up to its reputation as a relatively free-trading country. However, the golden age came to an end in the early 1970s. Wage hikes, oil-price increases, a sharp revaluation of the DMark and the concurrent deterioration of the general macroeconomic climate in West Germany and most other industrial countries brought the problems of adjustment to a changing pattern of world trade to the fore. Instead of being a challenger to technologically more advanced countries like the US, West Germany had to face challenges from below, namely the rise of Japan and various developing countries whose emergence had been observable as early as the 1960s but which had been much less noticeable at that time. The combined share of West European and North American suppliers in West Germany's

[1] See Giersch (1986), p. 12.

manufactured imports[2] dropped from 87.1 per cent in 1965 and 84.5 per cent in 1973 to 77.9 per cent in 1988. At the same time new suppliers gained ground.

The threat to the established position of West German industries in the international division of labour was by no means uniform. As to the regions from which the pressure to adjust emanated, one may broadly distinguish between three waves of what in German are aptly called *Aufholländer* (catching-up countries): first the Japan of the late 1950s, second the so-called newly industrialized countries (NICs) proper,[3] which gained market shares from the mid 1960s onwards, and third a further generation of mostly Asian developing countries such as Thailand and Malaysia which adopted an outward-orientated development strategy in the 1970s and 1980s. The share of Japanese goods in West Germany's manufactured imports[4] jumped from 1.4 per cent in 1962 to 3.5 per cent in 1973 and 8.1 per cent in 1989 (see Table 25). After a comparatively disappointing performance by the later NICs in the early 1960s, the rapid rise of this group of countries began in earnest in the late 1960s and early 1970s. In 1973, they took as much as 3.9 per cent of the West German import market for manufactures as compared to 2.1 per cent in 1965. They further enhanced their position to 6.0 per cent in 1989.

More important than the overall level of exports to West Germany was the concentration of the new competitors on certain product groups. Broadly speaking, one may say that Japan and the NICs proper went through three stages, with the mostly Asian newcomers of the late 1970s and the 1980s (i.e. the third generation of catching-up countries) probably set to follow suit in the near future. Initially, the emphasis was on low-quality and labour-intensive consumer goods, soon to be supplemented by capital-intensive intermediate goods and steel-based investment goods. Ultimately, both Japan and the NICs proper upgraded the quality and the product mix of their exports to West Germany to such an extent that they gained sizeable shares of the markets for skill-intensive investment and consumer goods. Part of this apparent success of the second- and even the third-generation NICs on the West German market may, however, be attributable not to a genuine technological catching up but rather to their role as attractive locations for the labour-intensive assembly

[2] Excluding petrol products, food, beverages and tobacco: Statistisches Bundesamt; own calculations.

[3] I.e. Argentina, Brazil, Hong Kong, India, Iran, Israel, Mexico, Singapore, South Korea and Taiwan.

[4] Excluding petrol products, food, beverages and tobacco: Statistisches Bundesamt; own calculations.

Table 25. *Share of non-traditional suppliers in West Germany's manufactured imports[a] (in %)*

	1962	1965	1973	1979	1989
Japan					
Manufactures	1.43	2.15	3.50	4.26	8.10
Intermediate goods	0.61	1.22	2.12	1.69	2.65
Investment goods	1.33	2.41	6.76	8.56	14.79
Consumer goods	3.22	3.69	2.33	1.59	1.74
Developing countries					
Manufactures	6.65	6.49	6.33	8.18	8.92
Intermediate goods	8.89	8.24	5.83	5.27	6.48
Investment goods	0.34	0.38	1.84	4.32	6.26
Consumer goods	9.91	10.57	13.29	17.95	18.32
of which:					
Newly industrialized countries[b]					
Manufactures	2.42	2.09	3.92	5.21	6.01
Intermediate goods	1.59	1.48	1.31	1.26	2.76
Investment goods	0.18	0.28	1.61	3.70	5.35
Consumer goods	6.86	5.57	11.02	12.97	12.30
of which:					
'Four Little Dragons'[c]					
Manufactures	—	0.92[d]	2.22	3.39	4.25
Intermediate goods	—	0.13[d]	0.33	0.41	0.71
Investment goods	—	0.18[d]	1.20	2.85	4.61
Consumer goods	—	3.42[d]	6.46	8.33	8.74

Notes: [a] Excluding petrol products, food, beverages and tobacco; classification according to the West German production statistics.
[b] Argentina, Brazil, Hong Kong, India, Iran, Israel, Mexico, Singapore, South Korea, and Taiwan.
[c] Hong Kong, Singapore, Taiwan and South Korea.
[d] Without Singapore.
Source: Statistisches Bundesamt; own calculations.

of high-tech goods or the capital-intensive manufacturing of new products which had been developed elsewhere.[5]

    Traditional factor-proportion models of international trade predict that, in the course of intensifying exchanges with less advanced and hence comparatively labour-abundant regions, it is those sectors of industrialized countries which make the least efficient use of labour that have to bear the brunt of the burden of adjustment. The facts roughly fit these models. Among the seven manufacturing sectors with the lowest level of labour

[5] See Klodt (1990b).

productivity in West Germany[6] were five in which the position of Japanese exporters on the West German market was particularly strong in 1965.[7] Testifying to the spectacular upgrading of Japanese exports, only one of these still played a major role in West Germany's imports from Japan in 1989.[8] As far as the NICs proper are concerned, five of these sectors were among their export strengths in 1973 and 1989.[9] Not surprisingly, the five low-productivity sectors in which the NICs had gained a sizeable market share in 1973 were among the fastest-shrinking branches of West German manufacturing throughout the 1965–89 period.

Detailed studies for the early 1970s confirm that low-wage countries exerted considerable adjustment pressure on industries with a high share of low-skill employment and on industries concentrated in comparatively backward regions of West Germany.[10] In other words, the challenge was most pronounced for those branches exhibiting features similar to those prevalent in the developing countries themselves. The natural export emphasis on low-productivity industries displayed by Japan in the late 1950s and the 1960s and then by the NICs and other developing countries in the 1970s and beyond aggravated the adjustment problem in three interrelated ways. First, it implied a general pressure on one particular factor of production, namely unskilled labour. Unfortunately, the relatively sharp increases in wages for unskilled labour in West Germany in the early 1970s worsened the employment prospects for this category of workers, making the competition from the Far East and the South appear even more threatening. Second, the adjustment to the typically inter-industry type of trade with developing countries calls for a comparatively high degree of inter-firm, inter-industry and inter-regional mobility.[11] Third, increasing external competition for sectors that are declining anyway means that these branches will have to shrink rather fast. As a consequence, both workers and capital owners have a stake in trying to prevent the decline of their industry by clamouring for external protection and internal subsidies.

The question whether West Germany did in fact turn protectionist cannot be answered easily. First of all, the country is not autonomous in

---

[6] Fels (1974), p. 39; sectors classified according to value added per employee in 1970, excluding electrical engineering, an increasingly high-tech sector with labour-intensive assembly processes.

[7] Clothing, leather processing, precision ceramics, precision mechanics/optics, musical instruments/toys, with a strong position being defined as a share in West German manufactured imports in this category at least 40 per cent above the average of all sectors: Statistisches Bundesamt; own calculations.   [8] Precision mechanics/optics.

[9] Clothing, shoes, leather processing, textiles, musical instruments/toys.

[10] See Fels (1974), pp. 24ff.; Wolter (1980), p. 23; for a survey see Giersch (1981).

[11] See Krugman (1981).

its decisions: it is a contracting party to the General Agreement on Tariffs and Trade (GATT) and, more importantly, a member of the European Community, to which the authority for external trade policy had formally been delegated in the process of the completion of the customs union. Because of the successive enlargements of the EC by the United Kingdom, Denmark and Ireland in 1973, by Greece in 1981 and by Spain and Portugal in 1986 and because of the free-trade agreements for manufactures with EFTA members (1973), roughly two-thirds of West Germany's external trade in manufactures have no longer been subject to tariffs and most other traditional border instruments of protection at all since the late 1970s. Only manufactured imports from beyond Western Europe meet with the full height of the external trade barriers.[12] Nominal tariff protection of industry, which had first gone up in the early 1960s as German tariffs were gradually raised towards the EC average, went down by roughly one-third until the early 1970s as a result of the Kennedy Round (1964–7). After protracted negotiations, the participants in the subsequent Tokyo Round of the GATT (1973–9) agreed to cut their industrial tariffs by a further one-third until 1988, with above-average tariffs being subject to above-average reductions according to the 'Swiss formula'. As the EC implemented the new tariff schedule as of 1 January 1985 the nominal tariff protection of West German industry (vis-à-vis non-members of the EC and EFTA) had come down to 5.2 per cent in 1985 from 11.0 per cent in 1964 and 7.3 per cent in 1972.[13] A successful completion of the Uruguay Round would reduce tariffs even further.

These achievements are in stark contrast to the development of other import impediments less subject to the international GATT discipline. While border duties came down, governments increasingly resorted to non-tariff barriers to trade (NTBs) which, in the case of the EC members, left more leeway for purely national as opposed to Community objectives.[14] The shift from assistance to industry by means of trade barriers to domestic subsidies and tax allowances had started in the 1960s.[15] This trend continued in the following decades, together with a proliferation of typical NTBs such as import quotas and so-called voluntary export restraint agreements (VERs). By 1982, 11.7 per cent of West Germany's imports in the mining and manufacturing sectors were subject to quotas and VERs,

---

[12] Because of the many restrictions and built-in safeguards, the further trade preferences granted to developing countries were largely ineffective. For an assessment of the Generalized System of Preferences for developing countries within the GATT framework see Langhammer and Sapir (1987); for an analysis of the somewhat more generous EC trade preferences vis-à-vis a wide range of states in Africa, the Caribbean and the Pacific (mostly former colonies of EC members) see Amelung and Langhammer (1989).

[13] Dicke et al. (1987), p. 26; because of a different weighting of sectors, Weiss et al. (1988), p. 18, come to the slightly different result of 6.3 per cent for 1985.

[14] See Weiss et al. (1988), p. 2.   [15] See Fels (1974), p. 3.

and 2.5 per cent to anti-dumping duties and investigations which became increasingly fashionable in the EC in the 1980s.[16] An inventory of subsidies in the entire West German economy reveals that these handouts, including tax allowances, increased from an already quite sizeable 7.0 per cent of value added in 1973 to 9.9 per cent by 1980 and 9.7 per cent four years later.[17]

The rise of internal subsidies as a substitute for external protection is hardly surprising. Subsidies offer protection even to firms whose major competitors come from within the reach of the EC's external border. As this border shifted outwards with the establishment and the enlargements of the EC, external protection by border instruments was bound to become less important relative to subsidies, which, incidentally, may benefit exporters as well as merely import-competing firms.

Within the EC, however, West Germany tended to be in the liberal camp, at least with regard to manufactured imports. In the intra-EC quarrels which prevented an effective inclusion of NTBs in the Tokyo Round negotiations of the GATT, West Germany had opposed French demands for far-reaching selective safeguards; when the rather protectionist EC stance for international talks on the conclusion and the three subsequent prolongations of the Multi-Fibre Arrangement was formulated, French interventionism rather than West German objections was decisive.[18]

The national policy stance came out most clearly in the number of cases in which an EC member applied to exempt goods from Community treatment, i.e. for permission to inhibit the free movement of a third-country import within the EC. Without such an exemption an EC member could not successfully erect barriers against third-country imports that are higher than those of the Community at large. While the overall number of such exemptions according to Article 115 of the Treaty of Rome rose from 34 in 1973 to 237 in 1979 (159 and 125 in 1983 and 1985 respectively), West Germany hardly resorted to national treatment at all, with 13 instances in 1977, 21.6 per cent of the EC total of that year, being the most noteworthy exception to the rule.[19]

Table 26 presents estimates of the effective rates of assistance to West German companies in 1958, 1970, the mid 1970s and the mid 1980s, including subsidies and major NTBs.[20] The most notable feature is the sectoral selectivity, with a limited number of mostly rapidly shrinking

---

[16] The numbers refer to the percentage share of affected tariff lines: Weiss et al. (1988), p. 13; for an estimate of the import values affected see Nogues et al. (1985), pp. 16, 58; on the EC's anti-dumping policy see Messerlin (1989).   [17] Weiss et al. (1988), p. 22.
[18] See Dicke et al. (1987), p. 29.   [19] Ibid., p. 31.
[20] Some of the differences between the estimates for 1970 and the mid 1970s may be attributable to methodological changes and a somewhat broader coverage of subsidies in the latter period; on the methodology see Weiss et al. (1988), pp. 5–28.

Table 26. *Effective rates of assistance in West Germany*

	Effective rate of assistance (%)						Growth rate of employment (% p.a.)		
	1958	1970	mid 1970s Total	of which subsidies	mid 1980s Total	of which subsidies	1965–73	1973–9	1979–87
Agriculture			497.9	201.1	347.6	198.6	−4.90	−4.27	−1.51
Mining	0.8	102.1	96.7	35.9	262.3	97.0	−5.86	−1.82	−1.54
Coal mining	0.1	111.0	109.0	38.7	316.7	116.5	−5.73	−1.61	−1.53
Other mining	5.4	2.5	12.6	16.7	2.0	6.0	−7.20	−4.21	−1.55
Manufacturing							−0.25	−1.59	−0.98
Intermediate goods	23.5	19.4	13.3	2.4	16.3	4.8			
Stone goods	1.6	4.4	8.1	0.3	5.2	0.3	−1.22	−3.24	−2.90
Iron and steel	33.3	23.8	−2.1	1.0	65.2	24.4	−3.87	+1.95	−4.68
Foundries	13.4	18.7	11.9	1.3	5.4	1.0	−2.21	−2.22	−2.39
Drawing mills	12.3	10.3	8.1	0.4	−1.4	0.6	−0.95	−0.95	−0.71
Non-ferrous metals	32.2	32.1	14.4	3.6	12.2	2.8	−0.14	−2.92	−0.33
Petroleum refining	—	168.4	16.4	5.7	15.7	5.0	+2.40	−7.30	−0.78
Chemicals	18.0	16.0	17.1	2.0	11.0	2.4	+0.79	−0.24	−0.26
Wood	15.9	13.1	23.3	1.8	18.6	2.9	−1.98	−3.39	−2.46
Pulp, paper, paperboard	51.3	42.1	20.5	2.1	14.3	1.2	−2.34	−3.26	0
Rubber goods	27.8	15.7	14.6	2.9	10.8	3.8	+0.55	−2.56	−0.64
Investment goods	5.5	7.4	10.1	3.2	8.2	3.1			
Structural engineering	0.6	3.0	6.9	2.1	0.4	1.7	−1.61	−1.90	−1.16
Mechanical engineering	0.8	3.7	4.8	2.2	3.7	3.1	+0.85	−1.45	−0.46
Road vehicles	11.0	9.4	11.3	1.3	12.5	1.8	+2.05	+1.12	+0.41
Shipbuilding	—	—	2.6	9.8	19.9	24.6	−1.48	−3.31	−5.15

Aircraft, aerospace	—	—	60.6	45.0	34.9	20.8	+2.83	+3.79	+2.93
Electrical engineering	5.1	8.1	12.3	3.7	8.2	3.4	+1.40	−1.61	+0.37
Precision mechanics, optics	3.2	6.3	8.8	1.6	7.4	2.3	+1.48	+0.76	−0.74
Metal products	8.4	11.0	9.3	1.5	4.4	1.7	−0.37	−2.10	−0.58
Data processing equipment	—	—	13.8	5.8	11.2	2.1	+4.42	−5.19	+3.19
Consumer goods	20.4	20.6	28.8	1.9	25.0	2.3	−1.86	−2.34	−2.29
Precision ceramics	9.5	18.7	8.9	1.7	8.3	2.8	+0.78	−2.51	−2.05
Glass, glass products	16.7	15.1	11.8	1.4	10.0	2.4	−1.46	−1.07	−3.15
Wood products	23.1	17.5	12.0	0.9	7.0	1.3	−1.32	+0.17	−1.60
Musical instruments, toys	6.3	10.6	9.1	1.0	9.8	1.3	+0.32	−3.30	−1.41
Paper products	29.7	27.4	29.3	1.9	23.2	3.7	+0.23	−3.22	−1.00
Printing	4.3	8.3	5.9	3.9	5.3	4.5	+5.10	+0.48	+2.52
Plastic products	8.8	9.5	17.0	1.8	8.4	1.9	−5.06	−4.46	−4.89
Leather, shoes	22.0	15.2	9.2	0.5	7.7	0.9	−3.07	−5.40	−3.92
Textiles	24.9	25.6	57.4	1.9	50.4	2.4	−3.01	−4.63	−4.15
Clothing	20.9	25.1	86.5	2.5	73.8	2.8			
Food, beverages, stimulants	—	—	51.2	3.6	34.3	3.1	−0.46	−0.73	−1.73

Sources: Donges et al. (1973), p. 80; Weiss et al. (1988), p. 26; Statistisches Bundesamt; own calculations.

industries being heavily protected. Within manufacturing the sectoral structure of protection remained fairly constant throughout these periods. Producers of investment goods, West Germany's major strength in the international division of labour,[21] received comparatively little assistance. This group of industries, however, includes one which does not fit the overall pattern: the aircraft and aerospace industry is West Germany's only sunrise branch that enjoyed sizeable government assistance, an expression of Western Europe's heavily subsidized Airbus challenge to Boeing. The rather different case of shipbuilding is also of interest. Because of import barriers against typical inputs, the effective protection of this industry by means of trade barriers was negative at any time. As shipyards came under increasing pressure from Japanese, South Korean and Taiwanese competitors in the 1970s and 1980s, employment shrank rapidly while subsidies pushed the overall rate of assistance from 2.6 per cent of gross value added in the mid 1970s to 19.9 per cent a decade later.

In the consumer goods industries, textiles and clothing are the classic examples of sunset branches that had to face fierce import competition from more labour-abundant countries and managed to elicit sizeable assistance, largely in the form of non-tariff barriers to trade under the successive international textiles and multi-fibre arrangements. However, being challenged in this way is no guarantee of lasting protection. In the leather, leather goods and shoe industry, which is in a roughly comparable position to textiles and clothing, the rate of assistance even declined as nominal tariff cuts were not compensated by major NTBs.

In the intermediate goods industries, the originally high levels of protection for non-ferrous metals, for pulp, paper and paperboard products and for plastics were reduced in the entire period. Initially, the protection of the iron and steel industry went down as well. However, the severe adjustment crisis which this sector faced in the first half of the 1980s on account of a general slack in world demand and the emergence of new competitors led to a dramatic reversal of the trend. By the mid 1980s, iron and steel was, besides clothing, the sector most effectively shielded against external competitive pressures.

All in all, the sectoral profile of assistance to West German manufacturing reveals a significant bias in favour of major sunset industries, which are often identical with those under competitive pressure from newly industrializing countries. If the analysis is broadened to include mining and agriculture, the bias of industrial policy towards conserving unprofitable and hence declining activities becomes even more obvious. In both

---

[21] Investment goods accounted for more than half of West Germany's exports in the 1960s, 1970s and 1980s: Statistisches Bundesamt; own calculations.

coal mining and agriculture, labour had been shed at an extraordinarily rapid rate between 1965 and 1973. In both sectors, the effective rate of assistance surpassed 100 per cent in the mid 1970s and mid 1980s. In other words, gross value added per unit of output at internal prices was at least twice what it would have been if world market prices for inputs and outputs had in fact prevailed.

As West Germany's external protection is widely differentiated between branches, it is well suited to test two common views on the determinants of the structure and the level of protection.[22] The first view, brandnamed 'the political economy approach', attributes the sectoral profile of import impediments to the interplay of domestic interest groups and politicians on a 'market for protection'.[23] The alternative view maintains that the scope for protection is given by the outcomes of international negotiations and emphasizes the link between trade and foreign policy and the particular interests of the dominant 'hegemonic' country.[24]

According to the political economy interpretation, protection flourishes in sectors where the respective domestic agents have both a pronounced interest in state interventions and the means of making politicians and bureaucrats heed their demands. The urge to be shielded against import competition is in general strongest in the least competitive sectors of the economy, where free imports would accelerate the decline and thus harm the immobile or locked-in factors of production, be it through the debasement of activity-specific skills and fixed capital or – in the case of agriculture – a reduction in the value of land on top of the loss of the owner's job. In stable or growing branches, rent-seeking is less profitable because rents will be eroded by the entrance of new suppliers. And in order to impress their views on politicians and bureaucrats, the beneficiaries of the socially harmful trade restrictions need to represent a sizeable voting power and/or be comparatively effective lobbyists.

An econometric analysis of the changes in the absolute level of effective total protection across West Germany's industries between 1978 and 1985 by and large vindicates the political economy interpretation.[25] Sectors with a large number of employees – as a proxy for voting power – and with high degrees of firm concentration and of regional concentration, both as proxies for the ease with which workers and firms can agree on collective action, have been able to elicit protection more successfully than others. The opposite holds for branches with a high human capital intensity – a rough measure of the international competitiveness of the respective industries. Physical-capital intensity per se seems to induce higher pro-

---

[22] See Weiss (1989).   [23] See Magee (1984, 1987) and the literature cited there.
[24] See Keohane (1984).   [25] Weiss et al. (1988), pp. 67ff.

tection. The latter tendency is quite understandable as, in industries under pressure, the more physical capital there is, the more would have to be written off prematurely if firms had to close down.

The alternative approach stresses the incentives to observe the rules of the international trading system. As long as a hegemon is strong and committed enough to lend credible support to a liberal and ultimately mutually beneficial trading system, other nations will not want to be singled out as major offenders threatened with retaliation. In its pure form, the hegemonic cooperation approach thus states that the post-war progress towards freer trade was possible because the US took the lead, whereas the rise of the new protectionism in the 1970s testifies to the hegemon's diminishing influence.[26] With their remaining political clout and their own trade policy, the Americans were merely able to ensure the functioning of the well-established mechanism for the reduction of industrial tariffs, but they had become much too weak to check the proliferation of the new non-tariff interventionism. In a more refined version, the approach purports to show that the new protectionism blossomed mainly in those sectors where the hegemon had himself set an early precedent by bending or amending the rules or had at least explicitly tolerated departures from the original GATT discipline.[27]

A look at the institutional setting of four of the most highly protected sectors of West Germany's economy is quite illuminating in this respect. Until the late 1950s, West Germany and other European countries had justified their remaining quantitative restrictions on clothing and textile imports from Japan with the GATT-proof argument of 'balance-of-payments problems' (Article XII), although in the face of West Germany's mounting trade surpluses, this was no longer accepted by other GATT members and the OEEC. Unfortunately, the Americans themselves signed a voluntary export restraint agreement in textiles with Japan in 1957 which was to become a precedent[28] for the following Short-Term Arrangement and the later Long-Term Agreement on cotton textiles. With the natural tendency under protectionist regimes for restrictions on some products to spread to close substitutes, more and more of world trade in textiles and clothing came under tight control under the subsequent multi-fibre arrangements, be it in the form of VERs or bilateral quotas.

In the case of agriculture, the theories of hegemonic cooperation seem to miss the point from the outset. The US, a major agricultural exporter, consistently tried to push the European Community towards a more liberal policy in the 1960s and afterwards, although it did not succeed in putting

---

[26] See Keohane (1984).   [27] See Weiss (1989).   [28] See Yoffie (1983).

agriculture firmly back on the GATT agenda until the recent Uruguay Round. Nevertheless, the US had itself set important precedents by unilaterally restricting imports of dairy and other agricultural products in 1950 and 1951. These actions were eventually sanctioned by a GATT waiver according to which future measures were exempted from the GATT discipline as well.[29] The US had thus critically weakened its bargaining position on agriculture precisely at a time when West Germany among others was establishing its own and rather protectionist agricultural regime, many features of which were to become a model for the EC Common Agricultural Policy later on.[30]

In the case of coal and steel, the founding of the European Coal and Steel Community (ECSC), which became effective in 1952, had put both sectors out of the normal institutions governing world trade.[31] Until 1958, internal trade barriers were mostly abolished while at least external tariffs were harmonized. Over the course of the 1960s, when cheap oil and less expensive American coal put pressure on West German pits, the European coal policy was de facto renationalized. Local demand for West German coal was propped up by the so-called *Jahrhundertvertrag* ('century contract') worked out in 1966. According to this contract, the steel industry would use German coal only under the condition that the government subsidized the price of German coal for industrial users (and for exports to other EC members) down to the world market level.[32] Similarly, West Germany's coal-fired power stations agreed to buy fixed quantities of German coal, and were granted a fixed mark-up on the state-controlled electricity prices in return.

Unlike coal mining, the steel industry remained essentially under the auspices of the European Commission. EC steel protectionism commenced with an increase in tariff and non-tariff restrictions on third-country imports in 1963 and the negotiation of a VER with Japan in 1967. By the mid 1970s, Euro-protectionism flourished in the form of minimum prices and further VERs. In the early 1980s with the steel industry in a deep crisis, the European steel market was transformed into an outright cartel in which Brussels determined capacities, set internal sales quotas and supervised the massive subsidization of firms. As a consequence, the share of West German steel imports originating in Western Europe went up from 76 per cent in 1979 to 81 per cent eight years later. As West German suppliers were among the most competitive at least within the EC, the internal production quotas prevented them from gaining market

---

[29] See Weiss (1989), pp. 8–10; Winham (1986), pp. 152ff.   [30] See Chapter 4, Section B.1.
[31] This section draws on Weiss (1989), pp. 11–15.
[32] An amendment of 1985 put quantity ceilings on the volume of coal to be subsidized in this way: Weiss et al. (1988), p. 55.

shares in Western Europe. After a slashing of capacities and a revival in world demand for steel, these quotas were abolished in 1986, although much of the external protection remained in place. Nevertheless, at least West Germany's steel producers appear to be in good shape. They have apparently gone through a quite successful restructuring, which – by the late 1980s – makes them look highly competitive in market niches that remain out of the reach of the developing countries in years to come.

All in all, both the political economy approach and the refined theory of hegemonic cooperation roughly fit the West German facts. Fortunately, the two explanations are not mutually exclusive. The analysis of the international institutional setting shows which sectors were permitted to be exempted from standard and hence more liberal procedures. This scope for non-tariff protectionism was granted long before the advent of the adjustment crises of the 1970s and 1980s. The extent to which West Germany, or the European Community respectively, actually used this leeway for discrimination of foreign suppliers in individual sectors can still be attributable to some internal market for protection. Furthermore, the fact that the US set early protectionist precedents or at least tolerated gross departures from free-trade principles in sectors that were to come under severe adjustment pressure in West Germany and the EC later on is no mere coincidence. In the case of textiles and clothing, for instance, the US administration yielded to protectionist demands from its own declining industries. As a more advanced country, at least in the 1950s and 1960s, the US experienced some of the structural changes and hence the concurrent adjustment problems somewhat earlier than West Germany. By assisting its own declining industries the US opened up loopholes in some of those sectors in which West Germany's organized interest groups were to clamour loudly for state assistance in later times.

Although the new non-tariff protectionism did in fact flourish in response to the challenges for adjustment in the 1970s and 1980s, the overall verdict on West German and EC-European policy-makers cannot be entirely negative. Between 1973 and the early 1980s, employment went down in almost every branch of West German manufacturing as well as in mining and agriculture. Given the size of the structural adjustment problem in times of macroeconomic slack and high unemployment – to which the microeconomic rigidities fostered by internal subsidies and external barriers to trade contributed significantly[33] – it is remarkable that policy-makers did at least prevent the outbreak of international trade wars. The nature of West Germany's corporatism helps to explain why the overall level of industrial protection did not get out

[33] See Giersch (1985).

Table 27. *Employment in major protected sectors (% of total employment)*

	1960	1965	1973	1979	1989
Agriculture	13.7	10.7	7.2	5.3	3.7
Mining	2.1	1.6	1.0	0.9	0.7
Iron and steel	1.8	1.8	1.3	1.2	0.8[a]
Textiles	2.8	2.3	1.8	1.3	0.9[a]
Clothing	2.1	2.1	1.7	1.3	0.9[a]

Note: [a] 1988.
Source: Statistisches Bundesamt; own calculations.

of hand. Because of the comparatively strong influence of the quite comprehensive umbrella organizations of employers and workers, namely the Federation of German Industry (BDI) and the German Federation of Trade Unions (DGB), protectionist demands by particular industries were somewhat mitigated by broader considerations of national welfare within the corporatist set-up. Even in major branches of industry in which protection increased considerably in response to the challenges from newly industrializing countries, namely textiles, clothing and – most importantly – steel, West Germany usually was in the comparatively liberal camp within the EC. The two really dark spots are the protection of agriculture and coal mining, two natural-resource-based sectors in which West Germany – on top of supporting protectionist approaches on the EC level – granted generous national subsidies to stop or at least mitigate the decline of employment. Politically, both sectors may be classified as especially sensitive as they are traditional strongholds of the two major political parties, namely the CDU/CSU in the case of agriculture and the SPD in the case of coal mining. By supporting major sunset branches of the economy, policy-makers impaired the flexibility of the entire economy at a time when external challenges required a pronounced readiness to adjust. Nevertheless, structural change away from these major resource-based activities continued throughout the 1970s and 1980s, albeit at an artificially reduced pace.[34] Hence, while the adjustment to a new international division of labour was delayed and made unnecessarily painful by artificial rigidities, it did proceed, even during the times of crisis (see Table 27). With part of the adjustment process completed and in view of the general improvement in the macroeconomic situation in the second half of the 1980s, the protectionist tide seems now to be turning. The

[34] See Klodt (1990a), pp. 29–32.

liberalization of the much leaner and more competitive steel industry has begun. And even in the notorious case of agriculture, the gap between internal and world market prices for major foodstuffs has narrowed recently.

2   The current account debate

Remarkable as the comparatively liberal stance of West Germany's overall trade policy may have been, it did not make the country look like a major exception by international standards. The aspect of West Germany's external economy to catch the attention of foreign policy-makers was the behaviour of its current account. In the 1960s, the current account had usually exhibited a mild surplus, disregarding two minor deficits in 1962 and 1965 and two years of notable surpluses in 1967 and 1968, i.e. at the end of the 1967 cyclical slump. After a decline in the first half of the 1960s, the balance of trade (measured in per cent of GNP) had started to rise again after 1965 in line with the emerging undervaluation of the DMark. Nevertheless, the growing net outlays for tourism and transfers, particularly development aid, contributions to the EC budget and remittances of foreign workers, had kept the current account balance on average below the level of the 1950s.

With regard to the current account in the 1973–89 period, it is not the levels themselves but rather the violent swings which are the most outstanding feature. Initially, the surplus soared to 2.8 per cent of GNP in 1974, the highest level since 1958 (see Table 28). Afterwards, the surplus dropped. From 1979 to 1981, West Germany experienced its only period of major and protracted current account deficits. As if this experience had been traumatic, the current account balance rose to a record high of 4.4 per cent of GNP in 1986 and stayed at almost that level until German unification in mid 1990.

Table 28 shows that the current account had largely been driven by the trade balance. As the balance of transfers and services had oscillated around −2.3 per cent of GNP between 1973 and 1982, the development of exports and imports accounts for the massive swings in the current account balance. However, it is worth noting that the particularly rapid improvement in the current account from 1983 to 1985 can partly be attributed to the service balance.

In the context of the balance of trade, the oil import bill is of particular interest. Until 1973 West Germany's fairly satisfactory growth performance had been fuelled by cheap oil. Its oil consumption had soared from 0.6 per cent of real GDP in 1950 to a record high of 4.8 per cent in 1973.[35]

[35] In 1980 prices: Sachverständigenrat (1989/90), p. 324.

Table 28. *West Germany's balance of payments 1950–90[a]*

	Current account					Capital account[b,c]			Change in foreign exchange reserves[d]
	Total	Trade	Services Total	of which tourism	Transfers	Total	Long term	Short term	
1950	0.3	−3.1	0.7	0.1	2.1	0.6	0.5	0.2	−0.6
1951	2.1	−0.1	1.0	0.1	1.3	−0.4	−0.1	−0.4	1.7
1952	2.0	0.5	1.4	0.0	0.1	0.0	−0.3	0.3	2.1
1953	2.8	1.7	1.5	0.0	−0.3	−0.5	−0.3	−0.2	2.5
1954	2.5	1.7	1.2	0.1	−0.3	−0.4	−0.3	−0.2	1.9
1955	1.5	0.7	1.4	0.2	−0.5	−0.4	−0.2	−0.2	1.0
1956	2.5	1.5	1.8	0.2	−0.6	−0.1	−0.2	0.1	2.5
1957	3.0	1.9	2.1	0.2	−0.9	−0.8	−0.2	−0.6	2.4
1958	2.8	2.1	1.8	−0.1	−0.9	−1.2	−0.6	−0.6	1.5
1959	1.9	2.1	1.3	−0.2	−1.3	−2.5	−1.4	−1.1	−0.7
1960	1.9	1.7	1.3	−0.3	−1.2	0.7	−0.0	0.8	2.6
1961	1.2	2.0	0.7	−0.4	−1.3	−1.5	−1.2	−0.3	−0.7
1962	−0.2	1.0	0.5	−0.6	−1.4	−0.2	−0.1	−0.1	−0.2
1963	0.5	1.6	0.4	−0.6	−1.3	0.2	0.5	−0.3	0.7
1964	0.4	1.4	0.4	−0.5	−1.3	−0.3	−0.2	−0.1	0.1
1965	−1.1	0.3	0.1	−0.6	−1.4	0.8	0.2	0.5	−0.3
1966	0.4	1.6	0.2	−0.7	−1.3	0.0	−0.1	0.1	0.4
1967	2.3	3.4	0.3	−0.6	−1.3	−2.4	−0.6	−1.8	−0.0
1968	2.4	3.3	0.5	−0.6	−1.3	−1.1	−2.0	0.9	1.3
1969	1.5	2.6	0.4	−0.7	−1.5	−3.1	3.9	0.7	−2.4
1970	0.7	2.3	0.1	−0.8	−1.4	2.5	−0.1	2.6	3.4
1971	0.4	2.1	−0.3	−1.0	−1.4	1.2	0.8	0.3	1.5
1972	0.5	2.5	−0.5	−1.1	−1.5	1.3	1.9	−0.6	1.8
1973	1.5	3.6	−0.7	−1.2	−1.5	1.2	1.4	−0.2	1.8
1974	2.8	5.2	−0.8	−1.3	−1.5	−2.9	−0.6	−2.3	−0.9
1975	1.0	3.6	−0.8	−1.4	−1.7	−1.2	−1.8	0.6	0.3
1976	0.8	3.1	−0.6	−1.2	−1.6	−0.1	−0.1	0.0	0.1
1977	0.8	3.2	−0.9	−1.3	−1.5	0.1	−1.1	1.2	0.2
1978	1.4	3.2	−0.5	−1.4	−1.4	0.5	−0.2	0.7	0.9
1979	−0.7	1.6	−0.8	−1.4	−1.5	0.7	0.9	−0.2	−0.5
1980	−1.7	0.6	−0.7	−1.5	−1.6	0.0	0.4	−0.4	−1.7
1981	−0.5	1.8	−0.7	−1.5	−1.6	0.4	0.5	−0.2	0.1
1982	0.8	3.2	−0.9	−1.5	−1.6	−0.2	−0.9	0.7	0.2
1983	0.8	2.5	−0.4	−1.4	−1.5	−1.1	−0.4	−0.7	−0.1
1984	1.6	3.1	0.3	−1.3	−1.7	−2.1	−1.1	−1.0	−0.1
1985	2.6	4.0	0.3	−1.3	−1.6	−3.0	−0.7	−2.3	−0.1
1986	4.4	5.8	0.1	−1.3	−1.4	−4.3	1.7	−6.0	0.1
1987	4.1	5.9	−0.2	−1.4	−1.4	−1.9	−1.2	−0.8	1.6
1988	4.2	6.1	−0.4	−1.4	−1.5	−6.0	−4.1	−1.9	−1.5
1989	4.6	6.0	0.3	−1.3	−1.5	−5.7	−1.0	−4.7	−1.0
1990[e]	4.0	5.6	0.2	−1.2	−1.7	−5.0	−4.2	−0.8	0.4

Notes: [a] Annual averages in per cent of GNP at current prices.
[b] Minus figures: capital exports.
[c] Excluding errors and omissions.
[d] Net of de-/revaluation of previous holdings.
[e] January–June.
Source: Deutsche Bundesbank.

The twin oil shocks of 1973/4 and 1979/80 pushed up the Rotterdam spot market price for crude oil by a factor of 12.8 in dollar terms. Interestingly, these price movements did not translate themselves fully into changes in West Germany's import prices for oil. Mainly through the appreciation of the DMark vis-à-vis the dollar, West Germany's actual import prices for crude oil rose merely by a factor of 5.3 between 1973 and 1980. Thereafter, the reverse happened as the DMark lost ground against the dollar. Whereas the dollar price on the spot market decreased by 24 per cent between 1980 and 1985, West Germany's DMark import prices kept rising by a total of 38 per cent in this period.

The price increases left their mark in West Germany's oil bill.[36] If oil imports are deducted from the trade and current account balance, the general picture described above changes somewhat. First of all, the trade and current account surplus of 1974 looks all the more remarkable as it happened while the oil bill had risen by two percentage points from 1.3 per cent of GNP in 1972 to 3.3 in 1974.[37] With oil imports excluded, the 'underlying' trade surplus took its biggest quantum leap ever from 3.7 to 8.4 per cent of GNP in these two years, with two-thirds of the swing falling in the second year (see Figure 16). On the other hand, the rising oil bill helps to explain roughly half of the reduction of the trade surplus in 1979–81 and hence of the current account deficit of these years. Still, even adjusted for oil, West Germany's current account balance in 1980 was 1.3 percentage points below the 1975–8 average.

More importantly, the look at oil imports helps to put the extraordinary trade and current account surpluses of the late 1980s into perspective. With the oil bill declining from 4.6 per cent of GNP in 1981 to 3.8 in 1985, both the trade and the current account surplus had gone up to a level which was quite high (4 and 2.6 per cent of GNP respectively), albeit not out of touch with the current account surpluses experienced in 1974, 1967/8 and throughout most of the 1950s. In 1986 a third oil shock hit the economy. This time, though, it came as an extremely positive surprise. While the dollar price per barrel on the Rotterdam spot market almost halved, the concurrent rise of the DMark against the dollar ensured that the DMark import price index for crude oil was cut by two-thirds by 1988. Because of the remarkable drop in oil consumption,[38] West

[36] Imports of crude oil and petrol products per unit of GNP in current prices.
[37] Sachverständigenrat (1989/90), p. 324.
[38] Responding to higher energy prices, the country's energy intensity (primary energy consumption in per cent of GDP at constant prices), which had risen marginally from 8.5 Petajoule per billion DMarks in 1960 to 8.7 in 1973 improved substantially to 7.7 in 1980 and a mere 6.4 in 1989. At the same time, West Germany substituted other energy sources, mainly natural gas and nuclear energy, for oil. The share of oil in West Germany's primary energy consumption had jumped from barely 4.7 per cent in 1950 and 21.0 per

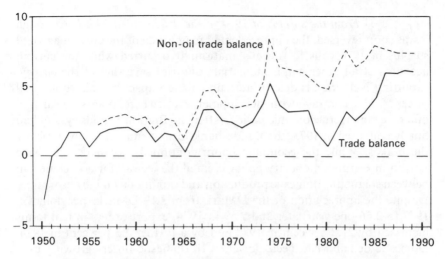

Figure 16. Oil imports and the balance of trade (per cent of GNP).
Sources: Deutsche Bundesbank; Sachverständigenrat (1990), p. 428;
own calculations.

Germany's oil import bill in 1989 was even significantly below that of 1973 (1.3 per cent of GNP as opposed to 1.6 per cent in 1973).[39] The drastic fall in the oil bill by more than two percentage points from 1985 to 1986 and the further improvement by 0.4 percentage points until 1989 entirely account for the record level of West Germany's current and trade account surpluses in the late 1980s. The underlying current account surplus even declined slightly after 1985. Excluding oil, the surpluses – while still noteworthy – do not look all that extraordinary any more. In other words, West Germany had gradually adapted to the higher price for oil to such an extent that, by the mid 1980s, the country was once again able to run current account surpluses of the magnitude attained in some earlier years – and could then unexpectedly cash in the windfall benefit of cheaper oil in the second half of the 1980s.

While it does explain a fair share of the major upheavals, the oil bill is by no means the sole cause of the swings in the current account balance in the late 1970s and the 1980s. In particular, (i) the changes between 1974 and 1981 and (ii) the persistently high levels after 1984 deserve further attention, all the more since the German current account became a major focus of a lively international debate from the mid 1970s onwards.

cent in 1960 to 55.2 per cent at the advent to the first oil crisis in 1973. By 1980, the share had come down again to 47.6 per cent and decreased further to 40.0 per cent in 1989. Sachverständigenrat (1989/90), pp. 247, 321; own calculations.
[39] All figures in this paragraph: *ibid.*, pp. 237, 324; own calculations.

(i) From the surplus of 1974 to the deficits of 1979–81. Although it was soon reversed, the unprecedented magnitude of the current account surplus in 1974 calls for an explanation. It occurred while the current accounts of all other major industrial countries save that of the energy-exporting Netherlands deteriorated under the impact of quadrupling oil prices.[40] The contrast with developments elsewhere points towards a difference in macroeconomic policy. After the Bretton Woods system had finally collapsed in 1973, the Bundesbank lost no time in firmly applying the brakes. While the economic boom continued elsewhere, the sharp U-turn in German monetary policy created the leeway for a sizeable gap between stagnating domestic production and rapidly shrinking absorption. Despite the appreciation of the DMark from 3.19 DMarks per dollar in 1972 to 2.66 one year later and 2.59 in 1974, export orders in real terms increased by 27.2 per cent in 1973 and by a further 4.3 per cent in 1974. Domestic demand had been slower, with domestic orders growing by a mere 7.0 per cent in 1973 and declining by 8.8 per cent in the following year. In 1975, when the recession hit West Germany's export markets as well, the reverse happened. While local orders were flat in real terms (-0.2 per cent), export orders slumped (-15.4 per cent).[41] At the trough of the recession in 1975, the current account surplus thus normalized to 1.0 per cent of GNP. In the following two years it fell further to 0.8 per cent. By West German standards, these surpluses on current account were rather unimpressive. To the surprise of the country's politicians, foreign government officials and academics increasingly urged West Germany to do something about this imbalance.

Quite understandably, the severe recession that afflicted all major industrial countries in 1974/5 initiated a search for feasible remedies. At the time the standard interpretation of insufficient growth and persistently high unemployment was lack of aggregate demand rather than a need to adjust to new relative prices and a changing international division of labour. Hence, an expansionary macroeconomic policy seemed to be the obvious answer. Unfortunately, the oil-price increase had pushed the current accounts of many would-be expansionary countries like Britain, France and Italy into the red, preventing them from taking up the supposed slack of their economies by unilateral action.

As early as 1975, the OECD proposed a way out that became known under the brandname of 'the locomotive concept'.[42] Notwithstanding the great variety of versions being propagated and discussed by academics

---

[40] Sachverständigenrat (1989), p. 230.   [41] *Ibid.*, pp. 285, 304.
[42] OECD, *Economic Outlook* (December 1975), p. 9; (July 1976), pp. 126–52; (December 1976), pp. 11–12; (July 1977), pp. 11–12.

and politicians in the following years,[43] the basic idea was straightforward: a coordinated and differentiated demand management should serve to relax the external constraint for deficit countries and impart tailor-made macroeconomic stimuli to everyone. So-called 'strong' countries, i.e. those with comparatively low rates of inflation and sizeable current account surpluses, were supposed to adopt a more expansionary fiscal stance. While part of the stimulus would boost their own rates of growth and bring down unemployment at home, the rise of domestic absorption and hence imports would benefit those 'weak' countries which, because of their current account deficits, their precarious fiscal deficits and their high rates of inflation, could not step up demand for their products themselves.[44] Like a locomotive, strong countries would thus pull weaker ones out of their difficulties.

In essence, the concept was simply an application of the standard Keynesian multiplier-analysis, but with one difference: the import-leakage (the marginal propensity to import rather than to absorb domestically produced goods) that reduces the domestic multiplier of additional government expenditures was not seen as a nuisance but rather as the desirable means of transmitting a stimulus abroad. Although the danger of rekindling inflation was not completely ignored,[45] both the standard approach of taking unemployment as a proof of a general underutilization of capacities and hence of a scope for a non-inflationary expansion of demand and the short-term bias of most of the models backing up the arguments[46] made proponents of the locomotive concept argue that the effects of expansion would show up in volumes rather than prices. Frequently, monetary policy was not discussed at all, the reasoning obviously being based on the implicit assumption that it would be accommodating to prevent a rise in interest rates.[47]

Monetarist opponents differed from the Keynesian supporters of the locomotive strategy in both diagnosis and policy prescription.[48] According to the monetarists, the high levels of unemployment were attributable to a rise in the natural rate, caused by supply problems such as distortions in relative prices and the need for structural adjustment, rather than by a shortfall in aggregate demand. As capacity was thus utilized to the extent that it could be gainfully employed at given relative prices, a mere

---

[43] See, for example, Cooper (1976), p. 47, and Kindleberger (1978), p. 285; for an in-depth treatment, see Gebert and Scheide (1980).

[44] Supporters of differential demand management usually neglected the fact that a demand stimulus transmitted from abroad would be as inflationary as one generated at home. This point was raised by Giersch (1977a), p. 248.

[45] See OECD, *Economic Outlook* (December 1976), pp. 5ff.

[46] For a survey, see Gebert and Scheide (1980), pp. 149–57.

[47] See Gebert and Scheide (1980), p. 5.   [48] Gebert and Scheide (1980); Vaubel (1983).

fiscal expansion would only serve to crowd out private demand while a monetary expansion would clearly jeopardize the hard-won gains in the fight against inflation. As far as the international transmission of demand was concerned, there would either be a transfer of monetary purchasing power and hence inflation between countries if countries sought to stabilize exchange rates or – if exchange rates were left to adjust freely – the participants would be largely insulated against the effects of foreign demand policies. Hence, each country should rather put its own house in order.

Initially, the US and West Germany were singled out as the major locomotives, with France, the United Kingdom and Italy being classified as 'weak'. Over the course of time, the concept and the role assigned to individual countries changed. With declining rates of inflation in the weak countries, the pure locomotive concept was modified in the sense that even these countries, instead of doing nothing or even pursuing an anti-inflationary policy, were to expand to the extent that the differentiated stimulus would leave their current account balance unchanged ('convoy strategy'). As the US current account turned from a surplus of 18.1 billion dollars in 1975 into a deficit of 14.5 billion dollars two years later, the international and by now especially the American demands for taking the lead in expansion increasingly focussed on West Germany (and Japan).

By early 1978, West German policy-makers – exasperated by the repeated pressure from abroad and wondering whether some fiscal stimulus might not indeed be helpful – started to heed these demands. While previous world economic summits, instituted as annual events between the leaders of the seven major industrial countries in 1975, had produced few tangible results, the Bonn summit of July 1978 became the most serious and successful effort at international macroeconomic coordination to date, at least with regard to the fact that detailed agreements were reached, not necessarily with regard to the eventual effects of these policies.

The Bonn summit ended with four major results: (i) West Germany pledged to augment internal demand by a fiscal stimulus worth 1 per cent of GNP; (ii) Japan repeated its previously stated willingness to gear its fiscal policy towards the ambitious 7 per cent growth target for 1978; (iii) the US promised to restrain its exorbitant internal demand for oil, which was still being fuelled by fixed and artificially low prices;[49] (iv) the participants agreed to conclude the Tokyo Round of GATT trade

---

[49] Although President Carter first had to resort to administrative import restrictions to meet this rather unpopular commitment in the run-up to the 1979 elections, oil prices were finally decontrolled in 1980. For a survey and assessment of all world economic summits until 1986, see Putnam and Bayne (1987).

negotiations by mid December. The latter target can be interpreted as a major supply-side achievement of the Bonn summit. Like the other targets, it was in fact met, although – in this case – a Franco-American quarrel delayed the signing of the trade agreement until mid April 1979.[50]

While the Bonn summit provided for an explicit coordination of fiscal policies, an implicit coordination of monetary policy between the US and West Germany had been going on for some months already. The US had indeed pursued a kind of monetary locomotive concept since mid 1976. High rates of US monetary growth fed through into first creeping and then accelerating inflation[51] and a rapid fall of the dollar from 2.51 DMarks in 1976 to a 1.81 DMarks four years later. Worried about the effects of a soaring DMark on the competitiveness of Germany's tradable goods sector, the Bundesbank abandoned monetary restriction in late 1977 and started to intervene massively in support of the dollar.[52] Hence, the fiscal stimulus agreed upon at Bonn met with an amply expanding money supply.

As the West German economy was already approaching the peak of the 1976–9 cyclical boom, the timing of the combined monetary-fiscal expansion could hardly have been worse. For West Germany the results were a short-lived acceleration of real GDP growth in 1979, rising rates of inflation even before the second oil shock in 1979/80, high budget deficits at the time of a cyclical peak, and the first sustained period of current account deficits ever in the history of the Federal Republic.[53] Hence, West Germany was uniquely ill equipped for the severe slump that was to come in the early 1980s.

(ii) The surpluses of the 1980s. The outbreak of inflation after the abortive attempt at demand management on an international scale heralded the end of the age of purely Keynesian policy prescriptions, at least until 1985. The international paradigm shift towards a kind of monetarism had been discernible in academia for some time already. Between 1979 and 1981, politicians and central bankers in the major industrialized countries followed suit, putting the fight against a further

[50] See Putnam and Bayne (1987), pp. 87–8.
[51] 1977: 6.5 per cent; 1978: 7.7 per cent; 1979: 11.3 per cent: Sachverständigenrat (1980), p. 14.
[52] Interestingly, more than half of the entire improvement in West Germany's current account in 1978 (1.4 per cent of GNP as against 0.8 per cent in 1977), which had been taken as proof of still overly restrictive policies, was caused by a surge in net receipts of interest payments from abroad as the falling dollar and the Bundesbank's monetary expansion had pushed German interest rates far below the international level (short-term rates: 3.7 per cent in West Germany and 7.2 per cent in the US; long-term rates: 5.7 per cent and 7.9 per cent respectively: Sachverständigenrat (1989/90), p. 224).
[53] Note, however, that the deficits of 1979–81 can to some extent be attributed to the rise in the oil bill (see above) and to the preceding real revaluation vis-à-vis the dollar. Sachverständigenrat (1981/82), p. 81.

erosion of the value of money at the top of the policy agenda. The sharp U-turn in monetary policy on both sides of the Atlantic triggered the recession of 1980–2.

Although both the US and West Germany first suffered from the slump of 1980–2 and then enjoyed a recovery from 1983 onwards, their external balances behaved rather differently in the first half of the 1980s. The US current account moved from a small surplus (0.1 per cent of GNP) in 1980 to a deficit of 2.8 per cent of GNP five years later, while the German balance of visibles and invisibles improved from −1.7 to 2.6 per cent of GNP in the same period, a development that was paralleled by Japan (from −1.0 to 3.7 per cent). When US growth started to slow down in 1985, West Germany and Japan found themselves in a situation reminiscent of that in 1977/8. Once again, a period of strong growth in the US had led to a massive inflow of capital and hence to huge current account deficits; and once again the economies of West Germany and Japan – with less buoyant domestic demand in the previous years – exhibited large current account surpluses and very low rates of inflation.

Prominent US politicians[54] and many academics from both sides of the Atlantic took these surpluses as evidence of exaggerated macroeconomic restriction on the part of West Germany and Japan and started to call for a more expansionary fiscal stance. In the following years, economists and politicians went through a replay of the coordination debate of the late 1970s. Yet the experiences of the previous decade had left their traces. (i) This time advocates of coordination devoted a great deal of attention to explicit theoretical reasoning why coordination is per se desirable for all prospective participants, as opposed to merely stating that expansionary policies are good for one's weaker neighbours.[55] (ii) Current account imbalances were not merely interpreted as an indicator of an economy's 'weakness' or 'strength' and hence its suitability as a prospective demand locomotive; rather, they were seen as problems in themselves as they might give rise to unwarranted corrective swings in exchange rates or even prompt a new wave of protectionism on the part of the major deficit country, i.e. the US.[56] These two points will be considered in turn.

(i) Theoretically, the case for coordination is based on the assertion that – in an increasingly interdependent world – the economic policies pursued by one country create spillover effects on other countries. As in the case of microeconomic externalities, the overall efficiency could be enhanced if these effects were explicitly taken into account. Hence sovereign policy-making should give way to coordination, which, in the ideal case, would lead to a full internalization of these external effects. For example, consider a country which in its own best interests should relax its fiscal stance to combat Keynesian unemployment. Given the transmission of a demand stimulus abroad via a rise in imports, either a government would be discouraged from going ahead – or it could be tempted to go too far in an attempt to raise demand for domestically produced goods despite the import leakage. And in the field of monetary policy, any single country aiming for a thorough reduction in the rate of inflation could tighten its monetary stance to such an extent that its currency would appreciate markedly. While the resulting fall in import prices would constitute a fast and easy windfall gain in the fight against inflation at home, other countries would have to put up with a devalued currency and higher import prices. If all countries tried to import price stability via a real appreciation of their currencies at the same time – which is logically impossible – the result could well be a competitive and hence unnecessarily pronounced tightening of monetary policy. This could in turn push the world economy into a severe recession. To avoid such harmful competition, policies should be coordinated internationally – to the benefit of all.

Just like the advocates of coordination, opponents of international demand management focus on a competition between governments, though on a rather different one. In their view, government policies are one of the main factors which determine the attractiveness of a country for internationally mobile factors of production, most of all for capital and highly skilled people. Countries offering an attractive mix of macro- and microeconomic policies would be rewarded by an inflow of these increasingly footloose factors, while others would eventually have to adjust their policies in order to halt the drain. As this competition between governments would eventually lead to better policies in all countries concerned, the process should not be disturbed by any cartel-like collusion called 'coordination'.[57]

(ii) With regard to West Germany, the international debate clearly focussed on the current account. By definition, a current account surplus arises if domestic production exceeds domestic absorption or – from a different angle – if investment lags behind saving in the domestic economy. Naturally, the two national accounting identities are logically equivalent; nevertheless, the choice between the two terminologies tends to be closely linked to fundamental differences in diagnosis and policy prescriptions. In the standard Keynesian interpretation, a current account surplus figures as a gap between demand and supply that could and – in most cases –

[57] See Vaubel (1985), pp. 223ff.

should be corrected by an expansion of domestic demand. In the supply-side interpretation, the same surplus is taken as evidence that a country saves more than it deems profitable to invest at home. As long as all resources of a country are gainfully employed, such a surplus is no reason for concern; however, if parts of the labour force are unemployed, supply-sided conditions ought to be improved so that savings are invested at home in order to provide domestic workers with jobs.

By and large, both neo-Keynesians and supply-siders agreed that the emergence of West Germany's current account surplus in the early 1980s was at least to some extent linked to developments in the US. At first glance, transatlantic policy differentials seem to back the standard Keynesian interpretation: while monetary policy had been fairly anti-inflationary in both the US and West Germany, the US budget[58] had moved deeply into the red (from −1.3 per cent of GNP in 1980 to −3.3 in 1985). On the other hand the West German fiscal stance had tightened (from −3.1 in 1980 to just −1.1 five years later).[59] Hence, divergent fiscal policies seemed to be the cause of the current account imbalance. (The same argument holds for Japan, where the budget deficit had been reduced from −4.2 per cent of GNP in 1980 to −0.8 in 1985.)

Supply-side orientated economists read the same evidence somewhat differently. According to them, it was not the difference between the level of US government expenditures and tax receipts but the way the budget deficit arose which was the essence of the 'Reagan recipe': the sizeable tax incentives to invest which had been introduced in 1982 and the general improvement of the microeconomic efficiency of the US economy due to deregulation, which had already set in under President Carter, had made the US a particularly attractive place in which to invest.[60] The rapid recovery of the US economy from the slump of 1982 was in fact driven by investment, with the share of gross fixed investment in GNP (in 1980 prices) rising from 14.4 per cent in 1982 to 19.1 per cent two years later. At the same time West German investment had remained flat (20.6 and 20.5 per cent of GNP respectively).[61] The surge of the dollar from 1.82 in 1980 and 2.56 in 1982 to a peak of 3.50 in February 1985 supports the view that a genuine attractiveness of the US for foreign capital as opposed to a mere rise in the budget deficit caused the net capital inflow and hence its logical counterpart, the US current account deficit. In Keynesian-style

[58] Federal, state and local government, including the social security system.
[59] Sachverständigenrat, various issues; own calculations.
[60] Note that German supply-siders in general do not adhere to a 'Laffer curve' concept, i.e. the proposition that taxes have already impaired the growth performance of the economy to such an extent that, after a reduction in tax rates, income would soar and hence augment the tax base sufficiently to boost tax receipts even above their previous level quite quickly.   [61] Sachverständigenrat (1989/90), pp. 221, 227; own calculations.

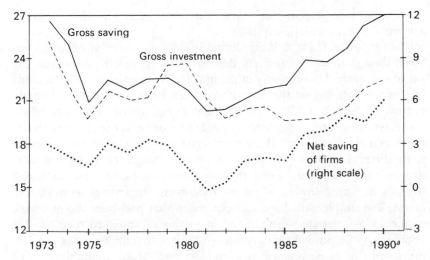

Figure 17. The gap between saving and investment 1973–90 (per cent of GNP at current prices).
Note: [a] January–June only.
Source: Statistisches Bundesamt: own calculations.

language one may say that, because of the healthy state of the US economy, the US budget deficits and the concurrent rise in interest rates did not depress domestic investment; the crowding out took place across the Atlantic instead.

An analysis of West Germany's saving–investment balance corroborates the supply-side interpretation. Despite a quite satisfactory growth of exports by 15.3 per cent in real terms between 1982 and 1985 and despite a marked improvement in the domestic rate of return on capital,[62] gross investment hardly recovered until 1988 from the trough of 1982. At the same time, gross saving increased from 20 per cent of GNP in 1982 to 22 per cent in 1985 and to 27 per cent in the first half of 1990 (see Figure 17). Note that it is the rise in net saving ratio of private firms (excluding the financial sector) that accounts for almost the entire net increase in the propensity to save,[63] with the changes in the saving propensity of households, the public sector and financial institutions[64] roughly offsetting each other. The asymmetry between the recovery in export demand, profits and business saving on the one hand and the slack in domestic investment on the other hand indicates that until 1988 investors did not take the cyclical upswing in the West German economy as evidence of a lasting

[62] Sachverständigenrat (1989), pp. 71, 304.   [63] Schmieding (1989b), p. 65.
[64] Plus private rented sector.

improvement in supply-side conditions and hence in the country's attractiveness for mobile capital.

The further increase in West Germany's current account balance after 1985, though it was exclusively due to the drop in oil prices, and the slowdown of the US economy in the mid 1980s gave rise to new demands for fiscal expansion on the part of West Germany (and Japan). In spite of their fundamental differences on the vices and virtues of coordination, neo-Keynesians and supply-side orientated economists sometimes joined forces in these years. While the former urged the West German government to cut direct taxes mainly as a (macroeconomic) means of raising domestic demand, the latter advocated the same measure as an important step towards an improvement of the microeconomic incentives to work and invest. The simple calls for fiscal expansion that had been the hallmark of the 1975–9 debate were shelved in favour of so-called 'two-handed approaches';[65] acknowledging supply-side impediments to faster growth, proponents of expansionary fiscal policies now urged a combination of macro-expansion and micro-deregulation to enhance the responsiveness of aggregate production to demand stimuli. Yet the West German authorities stuck to their cautious position. While some laws to tackle major supply-side deficiencies and to ease the burden of direct taxes were in fact introduced for internal reasons, the government did not heed the repeated calls for bolder measures, notably for carrying the 1988 and 1990 tax cuts forward in time. Nevertheless, the gap between the US and the West German budget deficits vanished in the second half of the 1980s. By 1988, government expenditures exceeded revenues by 2.1 per cent of the respective GNP in both countries. The concurrent dollar devaluation from a peak of 3.50 DMarks in February 1985 to an average of 1.75–1.85 in 1987–9 and to 1.50 in early 1991 did not fail to boost US exports. And as the US propensity to invest normalized after its extraordinary 1984 peak in the second half of the 1980s, the US current account deficit and hence the country's capital imports started to shrink from 3.6 per cent of GNP in 1986 to 2.1 per cent of GNP in 1989. Hence, the calls for a deliberate fiscal expansion by West Germany (and Japan) to the presumed benefit of the US and other countries with current account deficits finally abated by late 1988.

Looking back over the entire forty years of West Germany's economic history from 1950 onwards and abstracting from short-term fluctuations, one may say that sustained current account surpluses in the range of 1.5 to 2.0 per cent of GNP have become typical for the country.[66] Does this

[65] See Blanchard et al. (1985); Drèze et al. (1987); and the EC Commission's 'Cooperative Growth Strategy for More Employment', in: Commission of the European Communities (1985), pp. 5–80.   [66] See Figure 6.

mean that West Germans are less prodigal than people elsewhere and blessed with a government and a central bank which deliberately restrain demand in a permanent mercantilistic attempt to boost exports at the expense of domestic absorption? Not quite. While it is true that West Germany's propensity to save is higher than America's, it is much lower than, for instance, Japan's. More importantly, a look at savings does not answer the question why the resources are not put to good use at home. As far as macroeconomic policy is concerned, one cannot dispute the inclination at least of the central bank to tighten the reins whenever a current account deficit seems to indicate that the country is 'living beyond its means'. This has definitely been of short-term importance after the deficits of 1949/50, 1965 and 1979–81, but it remains an unconvincing long-term explanation. In the end, any persistent attempt to create otherwise unwarranted surpluses would finally be rendered meaningless by the currency appreciation which the resulting large-scale inflow of foreign exchange would be bound to bring about. Hence, one ought to leave such mercantilist notions behind and take a bird's-eye view of West Germany's position in the international division of labour.

By and large, West Germany's sustained mild current account surpluses roughly fit what factor-endowment theories of international transactions would predict. As a comparatively capital-rich country, West Germany is predisposed to be a net exporter of capital[67] and, immigration laws permitting, a net importer of labour as long as pure exchanges of goods and services do not suffice to equilibrate real (expected) factor earnings around the globe. Abstracting from temporary fluctuations, this is exactly the position which West Germany held most of the time.

As to the above-average surpluses of the 1950s, one has to bear in mind that the Federal Republic had come into being with no foreign exchange reserves at all and with a foreign debt which it could not even serve until the burden was cut by half in early 1953. Furthermore, most private financial assets had been wiped out by the war and the currency reform of 1948. Hence, it is not altogether surprising that in the early years the central bank as well as ordinary citizens used the rapid growth of their revenues and incomes in part as an opportunity to replenish their net foreign assets. In the 1960s, the import of foreign labour was to some extent substituted for capital exports, thus contributing to the comparatively low surpluses at least in the first half of the decade. In the late 1960s and early 1970s, the DMark had become so undervalued that external surpluses started to rise again in spite of a continuing inflow of foreign

[67] On the role of rich countries as exporters of capital, see Giersch (1980), pp. 306–8. For a similar explanation of West Germany's position as a structural exporter of capital, see, for example, Wallich and Wilson (1979), p. 489.

workers. Under the impact of two oil-price shocks, a thorough appreciation of the DMark in real terms and an ill-timed demand boost
('locomotive experiment'), the surplus for once became a noticeable deficit
by the turn of the decade. As has been described above, the following
rise of the surplus to a level somewhat above average in 1985 can be
attributed to a shortfall in domestic investment, whereas the further hike
to particularly high surpluses was caused exclusively by the unexpected
reduction in the country's oil bill. All in all, West Germany's current
account surpluses are no miracle. With the soaring budget deficits that
the unification of Germany in 1990 brought about and given the needs
and opportunities to invest substantial amounts of capital in the former
East Germany, the pan-German current account is highly unlikely to
exhibit major surpluses in the 1990s.

3   International monetary coordination

With regard to international macroeconomic cooperation, the 1980s differ
markedly from the late 1970s. At the famous Bonn summit in mid 1978,
the fiscal policies of the major participating countries had been tuned
explicitly to the perceived needs of demand-led growth without external
constraints. Monetary policies on both sides of the Atlantic were coordinated only implicitly in the sense that the Bundesbank reacted to the
inflation-induced slide of the dollar by relaxing its monetary stance
considerably for roughly one year (late 1977 to early 1979) as well. In the
1980s, policy-makers opted for the reverse: while summit meetings had
little influence on national fiscal policies, some coordination of monetary
policies via exchange-rate targeting went on throughout most of the
decade. At the international level, West Germany played an active role
in the concerted effort to stop the post-1985 decline of the dollar; within
Western Europe, the Bundesbank gradually assumed a leading role within
the European Monetary System of fixed – though readily adjustable –
exchange rates.

(i) *Transatlantic monetary cooperation.* As to the DMark–dollar
parity in the system of flexible exchange rates, politicians and central
bankers had more or less passively watched the dollar rise to its peak in
early 1985. With the advent of the second Reagan administration in 1985,
benign neglect of currency movements gave way to a renewed US interest
in managing the parity. At their meeting in New York's Plaza Hotel on
2 September 1985, the finance ministers and central bank governors of
the Group of Five industrial countries[68] stated that the dollar should come

---

[68] G5: the US, West Germany, Japan, France and the UK.

down, a signal which the markets had obviously not needed as the dollar was already declining. The U-turn in US monetary policy towards expansion at the end of 1984[69] as well as the calming down of the investment-led boom in the US economy after 1984 had made the dollar appear overvalued. With investors losing a good deal of their confidence in the American economy, a large-scale capital inflow into the US could only be achieved through a sharp devaluation of the dollar. When the dollar approached 1.80 DMarks in early 1987, the finance ministers and central bank governors of the G6 (G5 plus Canada) committed themselves in the Louvre Accord of 22 February to keeping the dollar stable at roughly that rate, a pledge which they (plus their Italian colleagues) confirmed at a second meeting at the Louvre in late December of the same year.

In one respect, this effort at exchange-rate management was surprisingly successful: abstracting from occasional fluctuations of roughly 10 per cent in both directions, the DMark–dollar parity actually stayed close to the 1.80 DMarks per dollar level throughout the late 1980s. However, the Bundesbank initially went to great lengths to stick to the policy of exchange-rate targeting. In both 1986, when the German central bank had tried to mitigate the decline of the dollar, and in 1987, the year of the Louvre Accord, the actual rate of monetary growth exceeded the pre-announced target by some 2.5 percentage points.[70] Because of the interventions to support the dollar, the West German official foreign exchange reserves increased by an equivalent of 1.6 per cent of GNP in 1987.[71] Fortunately, the externally motivated expansion did not trigger a major bout of inflation – as it had in the late 1970s. While the second oil-price shock had added to the inflationary pressures in 1979 and beyond, the decline in the DMark price of oil by almost two-thirds between 1985 and 1988 now helped to keep inflation at bay. As it turned out, the above-target increases in the money supply in 1986 and 1987 did no major harm. Instead, they may even have created the monetary leeway for the acceleration of real GNP growth in the final years of the decade.

(ii) The European Monetary System. With regard to monetary cooperation within Western Europe, a close coordination of monetary policies has been an explicit goal of the EC members for a long time. At their summit at The Hague in December 1969, the heads of the (still six) EC governments had in principle endorsed the so-called 'Werner Plan',

---

[69] On the influence of US monetary and fiscal policy on the decline of the dollar see Scheide (1987b); and Kauffmann and Scheide (1989), pp. 20–1.

[70] For a comparison of the Bundesbank's monetary targets and the actual growth of the money supply in the late 1980s see Sachverständigenrat (1987/8), pp. 81–9; (1988/9), pp. 74–84; (1989/90), pp. 82–8, 280; (1990/1), p. 119.   [71] See Table 28.

which provided for the establishment of a monetary union by 1980.[72] However, this ambitious project did not survive the currency turbulences of the early 1970s. Yet, still inspired by the idea of closer intra-European cooperation, the EC governments (including those of the would-be members the United Kingdom, Denmark and Ireland, plus non-EC Norway) agreed in spring 1972 to keep the fluctuations of their currencies within narrower ranges than allowed by the Smithsonian realignment.[73] When the Bretton Woods system finally fell apart in early 1973, a European 'snake' was retained so that the participating currencies floated jointly vis-à-vis the dollar and other non-member currencies. However, the snake could hardly be called a happy creature. The British pound and the Italian lira left the arrangement almost immediately after its birth, and the French franc followed suit in early 1974, only to join the snake again for a second brief spell from the end of 1975 to 1977. On top of the changes in membership, the internal parities had to be adjusted frequently, in most cases to allow for the DMark appreciation demanded by the markets.

To the amazement of many observers, the European Council (i.e. the regular summit of the EC heads of governments) decided at its Bremen meeting in mid 1978 to replace the snake by the more ambitious European Monetary System (EMS). Dismayed by the continuing decline of the dollar at that time and by the lack of effective US action against this slide, the West German Chancellor, Helmut Schmidt, had made the EMS his pet project, finding immediate support from the French President, Giscard d'Estaing.[74] Politically, the EMS was supposed to be a further step on the way towards an eventual economic and political unification of Western Europe; economically, the EMS was the attempt of the EC to create a zone of monetary stability conducive to the growth of intra-European trade. The EMS provides for fixed but adjustable currencies and covers an area with which West Germany conducts some 50 per cent of its foreign trade.[75] As in the snake, the margins for deviations from the bilateral parities were set at 2.25 per cent in either direction,[76] but unlike the snake, the EMS was organized around an 'invented composite currency',[77] namely the European Currency Unit (ECU), i.e. a basket of the EMS currencies.

[72] The plan was named after the politician who headed the preparatory committee. For a more detailed account, see Zis (1984), pp. 48ff.   [73] Sarcinelli (1986), p. 60.

[74] Note that this decision was taken ten days before the Bonn world economic summit: Putnam and Bayne (1987), p. 76; for a detailed account of how the EMS came into being, see Ludlow (1982).

[75] Including Austria and Switzerland, which unilaterally tie their currencies to the DMark without being members of the EMS; with the participation of the United Kingdom and Spain, this share has risen to roughly 60 per cent.

[76] They were set at 6 per cent in the case of high-inflation Italy.

[77] Artis (1987), p. 177.

Note that the United Kingdom, although formally a member of the EMS, did not participate in the exchange-rate mechanism until late 1990.[78]

In contrast to the expectation of its critics,[79] the EMS survived throughout the 1980s. After a stormy initial period in which the parities had to be realigned seven times within less than three years,[80] the system worked quite smoothly, although the scope for market pressure on the parities remained limited by the continuation of severe convertibility restrictions, most of all by Italy and France. All in all, the EMS could weather major upheavals in the international economy like the second oil-price shock and the recession of 1981/2 because it was handled much more flexibly than the Bretton Woods arrangement. Most notably, the parities were changed frequently enough to prevent the system's collapse. Over the course of the eleven realignments that were undertaken up to the end of the 1980s, the DMark was revalued by a total of 38 per cent against the average of the other participating currencies and even by 45 per cent vis-à-vis the French franc.[81]

Because of its very resilience, the EMS is frequently regarded as an example of successful coordination. In fact, the EMS countries have done quite well in terms of the scheme's purpose of creating a zone of monetary stability. Compared to the fluctuations of say the DMark–dollar rate, the intra-EMS parity changes were rather small. As to the internal value of the currencies, inflation rates within the EMS declined markedly after 1980.[82] Most notably, the prestige-laden objective of avoiding frequent and embarrassing devaluations played some role in bringing French and Italian monetary policies and inflation rates closer to the German ones. In the event, the one major breach of EMS discipline, namely the French attempt at unilateral reflation in 1981/2 under the newly elected socialist President Mitterrand, had to be abandoned soon, since despite several devaluations, the French currency reserves were running out.[83]

Nevertheless, the EMS cannot be hailed convincingly as a decisive cause of the return to comparatively low levels of inflation in Western Europe: non-members achieved roughly the same feat.[84] The system simply

[78] Hence, the EMS initially linked the DMark to six other currencies only, namely the French franc, the Italian lira, the Belgian–Luxemburg franc, the Dutch guilder, the Danish krone, and the Irish punt; in mid 1989, the Spanish peseta joined the arrangement, while the currencies of the two further EC newcomers, i.e. the Greek drachma and the Portuguese escudo, stayed outside.

[79] For a thoroughly sceptical initial assessment see Vaubel (1979); see also Lehment (1978).

[80] For an account of all currency realignments see Deutsche Bundesbank, *Monatsberichte* (November 1989), pp. 30–8.   [81] *Ibid.*, p. 32. ˙

[82] From an average of 14 per cent to slightly above 3 per cent in 1988: *ibid.*, p. 34.

[83] For a critical assessment of the Mitterrand experiment see Trapp (1982).

[84] For a summary of the evidence see Belongia (1988); note that the judgement whether EMS members or non-members were on average slightly more successful in bringing down inflation depends critically on the weight attached to the individual countries.

operated at a time when the fight against inflation had become or was about to become the top priority in most industrial countries anyway. Note, however, that the time-profile of disinflation and the concurrent increase in unemployment differs between members and non-members, at least on average: unburdened by the constraints of semi-fixed parities, non-members like Britain and the US opted for a comparatively sharp 'disinflation cum recession', while the same process, including the rise in unemployment, typically took longer in the EMS member countries.[85] The reason is simple: if a country's currency is allowed to appreciate substantially in real terms against (most) other currencies, a sufficiently thorough monetary restriction shows quick results via reduced import prices and an immediate squeeze of the tradable goods sector. Hence, fixed exchange-rate regimes have a built-in bias towards a more gradual and less front-loaded approach to disinflation.

Unlike the dollar-based Bretton Woods regime, the EMS does not assign any currency a special role. In fact, the EMS was explicitly supposed to replace the perceived asymmetry of the snake by a strictly symmetrical arrangement in which the burden of adjustment would have to be borne by surplus as well as by deficit countries. For intervention purposes, central banks can draw on generous intra-EMS credit facilities. Nevertheless, as these credits have to be repaid within nine and a half months,[86] a deficit country is still under much more pressure to adjust than a surplus country, which could simply continue to intervene in its own currency and pile up foreign exchange reserves. As the central bank with the best record of monetary stability, the Bundesbank gradually assumed a leading role within the EMS.

To sum up, the international monetary arrangements after the break-down of the Bretton Woods system have made it possible for the Bundesbank to pursue a low-inflation policy, be it unilaterally or in concert with other central banks. In spite of some periods when West Germany's monetary policy was guided by an exchange-rate target rather than by considerations of internal price stability, the Bundesbank by and large used the autonomy it enjoyed in the framework of flexible exchange rates to keep the domestic rate of inflation almost consistently below the average of the other industrial countries. And even the European Monetary System did not restrain the Bundesbank's freedom of movement very severely, because the system was handled flexibly and, more importantly, because the other participating countries did more or less adopt the anti-inflationary stance of West Germany's central bank. As long as the reduction of inflation topped the economic agenda, the Bundesbank's

[85] See de Grauwe (1989).   [86] Bofinger (1988), p. 321.

leading role was accepted by other central banks, as they could benefit from the credibility of the Bundesbank by pegging their currencies to the DMark.[87] When inflationary dangers receded into the background and attention once again turned towards reducing unemployment from the mid 1980s onwards, the de facto leading role of the Bundesbank was increasingly questioned, in particular by the French. Hence – supported by the French government – the president of the European Commission, Jacques Delors, put the issue of a European Monetary Union firmly on the agenda again. It remains to be seen whether Western Europe will actually achieve this oft-cited goal in the 1990s.

[87] See Eggerstedt and Sinn (1987).

6   Two cheers for German unification

Up to this point, this book has dealt exclusively with the history of economic policy in West Germany, i.e. in one of the two separate states which had emerged from the ashes of the German Reich after the Second World War. Because of the virtual absence of economic exchanges between the eastern and the western part of the divided country from 1945 to late 1989, comparatively small East Germany has hardly been worth mentioning at all in this context. In late 1989, however, the peaceful revolution in East Germany paved the way for the most joyful event in the history of twentieth-century Germany: economic and political unification. West Germany's currency and its economic order were introduced in East Germany on 1 July 1990; political unification followed shortly afterwards, on 3 October. Since then, the devastating heritage which the demise of the Soviet-type command economy had left behind in the East has become a major challenge and concern for economic policy in the new Germany. In the following three sections, we shall briefly summarize what the heritage of the communist command system was for the East German economy by the time when the Berlin Wall came down (Section 1), how economic unification between the two German states was actually carried out and which consequences it had in the short run (Section 2), and what will be the long-run prospects of the eastern German economy in a re-united country (Section 3).

1   *The heritage of a command system*

In the aftermath of the Second World War, Germany – and Europe – had been divided into a communist East and a democratic and market-orientated West. The very failure of the communist regime in the East testifies to the superiority of the West's political and economic order. Before the war, those regions of East-Central Germany that were to become the Soviet zone of occupation (1945–9) and subsequently the Soviet satellite state called the German Democratic Republic (1949–90) had been roughly on a par with the Western parts of the German Reich in terms of per capita GDP and the level of industrial development. In the first three years after the war, the process of post-war reconstruction had proceeded at a similar snail's pace in both East and West Germany. In mid 1948, however, the liberal reforms initiated the celebrated economic miracle in the West. Interestingly, the Soviet occupation authorities copied the currency reform in essence a few days later in their zone: they removed the monetary overhang by a drastic devaluation of money assets and replaced the debased Reichsmark by a new currency (the Mark). Nevertheless, East Germany started to fall behind the West from 1948 onwards. The reason for this is simple: West Germany had linked the currency reform to a return to a market economy; in East Germany the absurdly controlled economic system which all occupying powers had maintained in the first post-war years remained intact; it was gradually transformed into a Soviet-type command economy by successive waves of expropriations and some modifications in the planning mechanism.

A description of the East German economic system prior to 1990 reads like an economist's nightmare. Political and economic decision-making was centralized at the top, the major means of production including all industrial firms were owned by the state, a rigid plan guided the allocation of inputs and the distribution of outputs, and investable funds were collected by the one-tier system of state banks and channelled to the firms according to rather arbitrary priorities. Furthermore, the fixed prices did not convey any reliable and relevant information about true economic scarcities. To firms, these prices were little more than book-keeping entries.

Externally, foreign trade was conducted by a government monopoly. The exchange of goods with other socialist countries mostly took the form of outright bilateral barter; firms exporting to the West were not confronted with a uniform exchange rate but with a system of product-specific and firm-specific rates (*Richtungskoeffizienten*) supposed to equate the production costs in local currency to the world market price. Because of these differential exchange rates and the state monopoly on foreign trade, there was no direct link between East Germany's comparative advantage in production and its export structure. The bulk of exports (61 per cent) went to the European members of the Council for Mutual Economic Assistance (CMEA). Hence, these exports were not subject to noticeable competition from other suppliers. To make matters worse, the structure of specialization within the CMEA was determined by a political bargaining process, not by a market-based assessment of economic viability.[1]

In the absence of private ownership, the managers of firms were not driven by self-interest to make profits in an economically meaningful sense; they merely strove to achieve (or to pretend successfully to achieve) the prescribed targets. As firms could not go bankrupt, they had little endogenous incentive to

[1] See Stehn and Schmieding (1990).

improve their efficiency. Instead, they faced what Janos Kornai (1980) aptly christened a 'soft budget constraint'. When the financial situation became precarious, the state-owned firms could rely on the state banks to supply them with the needed funds to pay their bills; when the price competitiveness of exporters to the West was endangered by either lower prices for their goods or an increase in their production costs, they had the easy option of asking for a simple adjustment of the *Richtungskoeffizient*. There was no strong incentive to keep costs in check or to restructure the output mix. The better the managers of a firm were at influencing political decision-making, the easier they made life for themselves and the workers in their factory.

Except for some minor allowances for tourists, the East German currency was completely inconvertible into foreign money, at least officially. Even 'internal convertibility', i.e. the opportunity to exchange money for goods at home, was rather limited. Many important goods, including some essential inputs for industrial firms, were not available in sufficient quantities through official channels. In any case, deliveries could hardly be stepped up when – through unforeseen circumstances – a producer needed more than the pre-planned quantity of a specific input to meet the plan. Hence, firms frequently had to resort to barter trade or to payments in hard currency to get hold of the needed inputs.

All in all, the East German economy of the 1980s exhibited the following major structural deficiencies:

(1) Most economic activities were organized as state monopolies. Almost all of the roughly 8,000 firms were grouped together into 316 vertically and horizontally integrated conglomerates (*Kombinate*). Only 4.4 per cent of all industrial workers were employed in small firms with fewer than 100 employees (West Germany: 17.6 per cent), while the bulk of industrial employment (73.2 per cent) was concentrated in firms with more than 1,000 employees (West Germany: 39.8 per cent).[2]

(2) Compared with Western enterprises, East German firms employed far too many workers, who frequently did not have very much to do most of the time. Hence, a switch towards a more efficiency-orientated economic system was bound to reveal a considerable amount of hidden unemployment.

(3) Firms tended to keep huge inventories of raw materials and semi-finished goods as buffers against unexpected and unplanned developments. Similarly, industrial efficiency was severely impaired by a tendency towards self-production of inputs. Firms forfeited the benefits both of an inter-firm division of labour according to their specific comparative advantages and of economies of scale. Moreover, each of the conglomerates attempted to be almost autarkic with regard to services that in the West are normally contracted out. For

---

[2] Institut für angewandte Wirtschaftsforschung (1990b), p. 8.

instance, the *Kombinate* – and in many cases even the plants within them – usually had their own departments for the construction of premises and the production of capital goods, for maintenance work and repairs, for transport and even for child care. The inherent bias against a rational division of labour between firms was even fostered by deliberate policy: the conglomerates in the investment goods industries were required to produce consumer goods worth at least 5 per cent of their total output. For instance, a Dresden firm specializing in X-ray equipment and transformers had to devote some of its skills and resources to the production of special frying pans (raclette sets) for East German consumers!

(4) The tendency towards underspecialization was visible in foreign trade as well. Under market conditions, East Germany, with a population of only 16.4 million, should have had a significantly higher share of imports and exports in GNP than much larger West Germany, with its 62 million people. Nevertheless, the East German export quota (roughly 21 per cent) was far below the West German one (29 per cent) and less than half the Dutch one (58 per cent), although the Netherlands have a population of comparable size. According to one calculation, the East German metal manufacturing industry produced 65 per cent of the range of goods in this category in the world, but its much more specialized counterpart in the much larger Federal Republic only 17 per cent.[3] Once again, the bias against a rational division of labour was in part the consequence of a deliberate policy aimed at a high degree of self-sufficiency in most products.

(5) As the behaviour of firms was controlled neither by private owners nor by a capital market, managers had no strong incentive to keep the physical capital stock intact. In a market economy, a systematic neglect of the physical assets would show up in a declining stock market value of the firm; under the conditions of central planning, state ownership of the means of production and a soft budget constraint, neither managers nor workers have a well-defined interest in safeguarding and augmenting the future productive potential of the firm. For similar reasons, new technologies were introduced only slowly and reluctantly in East Germany. By 1989, only 27 per cent of the equipment in industry was less than five years old; 50.6 per cent was older than a decade. In comparison, 39.3 per cent of all industrial equipment in West Germany has been installed in the last five years, and 69.7 per cent in the last ten years.[4] In short: the East German capital stock was to a large extent technologically outdated and physically run down; a considerable part of it was economically obsolete.

(6) The centralization of the major investment decisions at the top resulted

---

[3] Institut für angewandte Wirtschaftsforschung (1990a), p. 33.
[4] Institut für internationale Politik und Wirtschaft (1990), Table 7.

in a significant bias towards a few large-scale projects. To reduce the dependency on oil imports from the USSR after the oil-price shocks of 1973/4 and 1979/80, the East German leadership embarked upon an economically wasteful and ecologically disastrous programme of extracting and burning domestic lignite to generate power for electricity and heating. And to tackle East Germany's technological backwardness, resources were channelled on a grand scale into microelectronics without paying proper attention to opportunity costs. Not surprisingly, the attempt to reinvent ultramodern technology which already existed in the West turned out to be a major economic failure.

(7) Because of the traditional neglect of the tertiary section by socialist planners, the sectoral structure of the East German economy differed noticeably from the more advanced and less distorted West German one. In 1989, 47.2 per cent of total East German employment was in agriculture, energy, mining and manufacturing as opposed to only 37.0 per cent in West Germany. Modern non-government services such as banking played only a minor role in the East. Moreover, East German employment was heavily concentrated in sectors and branches that declined rapidly in the West in recent decades. In 1989, agriculture, forestry and fishery, mining, and clothing and textiles together accounted for 16.2 per cent of the East German labour force as opposed to merely 6.2 per cent in West Germany.[5]

A few numbers reveal how bad East Germany had fared under its inflexible system of economic planning. Forty years after the formal establishment of the two separate German states in late 1949, East Germany's per capita GDP was below 40 per cent (see Table 29), and labour productivity in the tradable goods sector reached less than 30 per cent of that in West Germany; like the capital stock, major parts of the infrastructure and the stock of buildings were run down. In many regions of the country, the ecological situation was desperate: for example, East Germany emitted about twenty-five times more sulphur dioxide per unit of GDP than West Germany.

From the late 1940s onwards, the political repression in the East and the growing gap in living standards between the two German states had caused a swelling flood of migrants to the free and prosperous West. In mid 1961, the East German regime could avert its collapse only by building the infamous Berlin Wall, that is by closing the last loophole in the iron curtain. For the following twenty-eight years German unification seemed to be no more than a distant dream. Not before the democratic revolution that swept East-Central Europe in 1989 did unification become a subject for practical policy again.

With the example of both a greater freedom to express dissident opinions (*glasnost*) and some political and economic reforms (*perestroika*) in the Soviet

[5] Siebert (1990), p. 35; own calculations.

Table 29. *On the eve of unification – East and West Germany 1989*

	West Germany	East Germany	Ratio East to West (%)
Area (1,000 sq km)	249.0	108.0	43.4
Population (million)	61.8	16.4	26.5
GDP (billion DM)	2,236	230[a]	10.3
GDP per capita (1,000 DM)	36.2	14.0	38.7
Employment (million)	27.6	9.3[c]	34.9
Agriculture[e]	3.9	9.9	
Energy and mining[e]	1.7	3.2	
Manufacturing[e]	31.4	34.1	
Construction[e]	6.6	6.1	
Trade[e]	13.0	7.8	
Banking and insurance[e]	3.1	0.7	
Government, other services[e]	41.3	38.4	
Exports (billion DM)[d]	649.1	48.3	7.4
of which to CMEA[b]	5.8	61.8	
Imports (billion DM)[d]	513.7	49.2	9.6
of which from CMEA[b]	6.3	56.2	
Households with[b,e]			
Automobiles	97.0	52.0	53.6
Colour televisions	94.0	52.0	55.3
Telephones	98.0	9.0[f]	9.2

Notes: [a] Estimate.
[b] In per cent of total.
[c] Excluding apprentices.
[d] Including intra-German trade.
[e] 1988.
[f] 1984.
Source: Statistisches Bundesamt; own estimates.

Union, and with the emancipation of other East-Central European states from Soviet hegemony, the dogmatic Stalinist leadership of East Germany came under increased pressure for domestic reforms from both their fraternal parties in Eastern Europe and their own population in the late 1980s. When Hungary, which was still communist, started to take down the barbed wire at the border to Austria in spring 1989, many East Germans gladly took the long escape route from East to West Berlin via Budapest and Vienna. And when the Soviet President Gorbachev visited East Berlin on the occasion of the fortieth anniversary of the GDR's existence in early October 1989, he gave the final signal for popular revolt. Exasperated by fruitless discussions with the elderly East German leaders, he reminded them publicly of the Russian proverb 'He who comes too late will be punished by life.' East Germans interpreted this as a hint that Soviet tanks would not interfere with changes in East Germany – as they had done bloodily in 1953 – and took to the streets to topple not only their government but also the entire political and economic order of East Germany.

2   Unification and its immediate aftermath

On 9 November 1989 the Berlin Wall and the equally brutal intra-German border were breached. For the first time ever all East Germans had the chance to see not only on television but also for themselves how superior the results of a free economic and political order really are. The end of East German statehood was nigh. In early December 1989, West Germany's Chancellor Helmut Kohl – who had sometimes been portrayed as a hopeless blunderer before – skilfully seized the initiative, proposing a confederation of the two German states as a first step to unification. When the situation in East Germany became increasingly unstable in early February 1990, he advocated an immediate currency union as a first practical stage to unification, in fact the decisive step which would make the process of unification irreversible and even more popular with the East German population. Although many economists warned against the economic hazards of a premature currency union between the advanced West and the comparatively poor East and especially against a currency union at terms which would make East German goods uncompetitive, political rationality prevailed over economic logic.[6] On 1 July 1990, East Germany, still nominally independent, was incorporated into the West German economy.

Until the collapse of communism, the East German economy was no special case in communist East-Central Europe. In terms of most socio-economic indicators, the level of economic development, the state of the infrastructure and the extent of environmental damage, East Germany was roughly comparable to the Czech part of Czechoslovakia. In 1990, however, East Germany became a place apart. Compared with the other states of East-Central Europe – and with West Germany in 1948 – East Germany appeared to be in a uniquely favourable position for the transition to a market economy. It had the opportunity to make use of one fundamental advantage: West Germany.

In comparison to West Germany, with its well-established and advanced market economy, East Germany was rather small (26.5 per cent in terms of population, roughly 10 per cent in terms of GDP: see Table 29). Hence, regardless of the details of the policies adopted, German unification meant from the outset that the pains of political and economic transformation in the East were to become mere regional problems of a much larger unit whose overall stability would be only marginally affected by whatever difficulties the switch to a market economy in the eastern part would entail.

---

[6] See Hoffmann (1991).

By virtue of German unification, East Germany could import the proven political stability and legitimacy of the Federal Republic.[7] In a similar vein, the German Economic, Monetary and Social Union (GEMSU) meant that the regime switch in East Germany was absolutely credible and definitely irreversible. Furthermore, East Germans gained access to the highly developed social security system of the West, so that real adjustment costs would be cushioned by transfers from the West. These factors were not only advantages per se; they also seemed to imply far greater freedom to conduct first-best economic policies than in all other post-socialist countries. In Hungary, Poland, the CSFR and beyond, the short-term repercussions of potentially painful economic policies on the fragile body politic had to be one of the major concerns of the reformers. As the elections of 18 March 1990 in East Germany had revealed overwhelming support for rapid political and economic unification with the West, decisions could be taken swiftly and implemented instantaneously.

The *macroeconomic problems* of the late GDR were de facto solved with GEMSU. On 1 July 1990, West Germany's DMark, which had long been an unofficial and illegal parallel currency in East Germany, became the sole legal tender in East Germany, with the Bundesbank as the sole monetary authority. Most domestic financial assets and liabilities were converted at a rate of 2 East Mark = 1 DMark. The exception was the savings of GDR residents. Up to certain limits (M 2,000 per capita for those under 14 years of age, M 4,000 for those between 14 and 58 and M 6,000 for older people) they were revalued at the preferential rate of 1:1. On average, a rate of 1.8:1 applied to monetary assets. Recurrent payments such as rents and wages were converted at the rate of 1:1.

With the DMark replacing the East German Mark, the accumulated East German monetary overhang was spread over a much larger currency area. This diminished the threat of a surge of inflation after price liberalization.[8] East German fiscal problems were greatly eased by unification. Even to the extent that East German budget deficits were not directly financed by Western transfers, East German public authorities benefited from the creditworthiness of the West because lenders could confidently assume that these credits were implicitly guaranteed by the federal German government.

---

[7] For details, see Schmieding (1991).
[8] With the currency union, the DMark quantity of money (M3) increased by 14.5 per cent (Deutsche Bundesbank, *Monatsberichte* (1990), p. 4*), while the productive potential of the DMark currency area was enlarged by roughly 8 per cent. The difference constitutes a potential for pan-German inflation, although a manageable one. The Bundesbank partly succeeded in neutralizing this unwarranted surge in the money supply by an appropriate restrictive monetary policy. Furthermore, the very fact that German unification led to an exceptionally severe adjustment crisis induced East Germans to keep a part of their involuntarily accumulated money balances as voluntary savings.

Because of GEMSU, the basic *microeconomic reforms* needed for the regime switch from central planning to a coordination of economic activities via markets could be introduced in one stroke; only some sectors (housing, public services) were exempt from deregulation. With regard to *external economic relations*, the problem of the former GDR's foreign debt de facto vanished for East Germany by courtesy of unification. The incorporation into the European Community amounted to a dramatic liberalization of almost all external transactions. And with West German banks rapidly establishing branch offices east of the Elbe, East Germans gained unrestricted access to the world capital market. All in all, the internal and external liberalization of the East German economy in mid 1990 was much more sweeping than West Germany's economic reforms forty-two years earlier. In the late 1940s and the early 1950s, the restrictions on external trade and payments had been relaxed only gradually.

Drawing on the successful outcome in West Germany of the reforms of 1948, many people had hoped that the regime switch in East Germany would initiate a speedy upswing. However, the short-run result was a decline in production and employment of unprecedented proportions. In the six months after the currency reform in West Germany in 1948, industrial production *rose* by more than 50 per cent. In East Germany in 1990, it *fell* by more than 50 per cent. Without substantial subsidies for many firms, the decline would have been even more pronounced. With a minus of roughly 30 per cent in 1990, the slump in East German GDP was not as bad as that of industrial production. The major reason for this divergence is that one big sector of the economy – government services – was almost completely financed by transfers and transfer-like credits from the West and thus could even expand slightly in the second half of 1990.

With the usual delay, employment followed suit. Between autumn 1989 and early spring 1991, it declined by 30 per cent.[9] A growing number of people started to commute to the West, including West Berlin. Unlike employment, living standards were completely divorced from the short-run slump in domestically generated output. Nominal consumption was 3–8 per cent higher in the fourth quarter of 1990 than in the fourth quarter of 1989. In addition, the consumption figures significantly understate the actual rise in real living standards, as they do not capture the effect that East German consumers largely switched from substandard East German products to cheaper and far superior Western tradables (for instance, to a Volkswagen Golf instead of East Germany's famous little Trabant).

Reflecting its completely different starting position, post-unification

---

[9] Half of the workers who benefited from the generous provisions for short-time work in East Germany are counted as employed in this calculation.

East Germany was never likely to undergo an exact repetition of the 1948 experience.[10] As has been pointed out in Chapter 2, Section 1 above, favourable conditions for economic recovery had already existed in 1948. War damage aside, the stock of capital, technology and labour of West German companies had changed little from four years previously. Nevertheless, industrial production in early 1948 was less than one-third of that at the beginning of 1944. When the straitjacket of economic controls was removed in mid 1948, production became profitable again. Relatively modest investment in repairs sufficed to reactivate substantial parts of the capital stock – together with a quite modern infrastructure. To a considerable extent, the first two to three years of the West German 'economic miracle' thus represented simply a speedy return to normality, made possible by the unleashing of market forces.

In this respect, one point was of crucial importance. During the twelve years of economic planning after 1936, when Nazi centralization took hold, West Germany had preserved the institutional infrastructure of a market economy, notably private property, suitable laws, rules and common practices, as well as institutions and qualified staff to do the administrative and legal work. The private-sector legal code (*Privatrechtsordnung*) had been retained and the administrative system had not lost touch with the market completely. In 1990, however, as the reform states of Eastern Europe struggled to adapt to life after communism, helpful continuity with market-conformable practices had long been lost.

Yet, even with regard to the institutional infrastructure, East Germany was in a special position in 1990. While other post-socialist countries had to build most of this legal and administrative framework from scratch, East Germany simply adopted the well-established laws and regulations of West Germany, which did not even need to be translated. Together with the establishment of the West German judicial system in the East, this meant that the most fundamental basis of capitalism, i.e. private property rights, would be fully and lastingly respected. Hence, the uncertainty of property rights boiled down to the question whether previously expropriated owners would be reinstituted or merely compensated financially. Many West German institutions extended their reach to East Germany, and many Eastern institutions could be remodelled on the Western image. Some transfers of human capital and other kinds of technical assistance were supposed to facilitate the implementation of the institutional reforms and the application of the new rulebook. The cultural proximity to West Germany and the fine net of contacts between East Germans and their Western brethren were likely to make it comparatively easy for East Germans to get used to the rules of the market quickly.

Furthermore, political stability, generous social security provisions,

[10] See Schmieding (1991).

unrestricted access to the world capital market and the transfer of administrative know-how made the East German privatization process look much easier than elsewhere in East-Central Europe. And by virtue of German unification, the pool of talents from which new managers for private enterprises and state firms can be drawn is much larger.

Given these favourable starting conditions vis-à-vis the other ex-socialist countries, the depth of East Germany's slump cannot be attributed solely to the unavoidable problems brought on by switching from a socialist to a free-market system. In spite of East Germany's apparent advantages and the massive subsidies to firms, the decline of production in East Germany was much more pronounced than in other regions of post-communist Europe. A comparison with Poland's radical reforms of January 1990 is rather telling. For both Poland and East Germany, some drop in output was to be expected for two reasons. (i) Some of the goods produced under socialist conditions (notably many investment goods) had no positive added value at world market prices; unless generous subsidies were paid to maintain this absurdity, the switch to a market economy would give rise to welfare-enhancing cuts in these value-distracting production activities. (ii) The regime switch induced a crisis of adjustment and reorientation which became evident in a temporary decline in production. East Germany and Poland differed in two important respects: on the one hand, Poland had to eradicate hyperinflation at the beginning of 1990, while in mid 1990 East Germany imported the macroeconomic stability of the Federal Republic. As drastic stabilization programmes tend to go along with a deep recession, the drop in production was likely to be more severe in Poland. On the other hand, the greater degree of liberalization in East Germany should have made the East German crisis more front-loaded. Taken together, the starting conditions did not point to a decisive East German disadvantage. Yet, the short-term fall in output was more than double that observed in Poland after its switch to a market economy in 1990.

The answer to the question why East Germany's short-term performance was so much worse lies largely with the rise in local production costs. Based on what is admittedly only an imperfect yardstick – the measured competitiveness of East German exports to the West – the former East German Mark was worth only 23 West German Pfennigs (the foreign currency coefficient which indicates the value of domestic input in East Marks needed to earn one DMark in exports stood at 4.4 in 1989). Hence, the 1:1 conversion rate for current payments in the replacement of the East Mark by the DMark on 1 July 1990 brought a dramatic overvaluation of East German economic output.

Furthermore, fostered by the political promise to narrow the gap in living standards between the two parts of Germany, East German nominal wages (on the basis of 1 East Mark = 1 DMark) rose by more than one-third over the course of 1990, while at the same time production collapsed. Whereas Poland had levied punitive taxes on wage increases in state-owned firms exceeding the rate of inflation (or a certain percentage of price-level increases), there were no constraints on collective agreements in East Germany. In this type of setting, it may well be that, ceteris paribus, similar unrealistic wage levels would soon have been agreed upon between trade unions and employers even if the initial wage had been set lower, for instance, with a conversion rate of 2:1 for current payments.[11] In any case, the actual development of wages cannot be interpreted as the outcome of a market process or of 'autonomous' collective bargaining. Wage increases were in most cases granted by managers of state firms who had no strong incentive to care about the profitability of their firm and who – because of their past role as members of the ruling elite (the nomenclatura) – could not count on much political backing for a tough stance against excessive wage demands.[12] In addition, both employers and employees had good grounds for assuming that, for political reasons, the firms would operate under an extraordinarily soft budget constraint so that excessive cost increases would be compensated by additional subsidies. At the beginning of 1991, those East German workers who were still fully employed earned roughly eight times as much as their Czechoslovakian counterparts and six times as much as Polish workers.

The East German cost explosion wiped out the opportunities for profitable production in most existing plants with the given physical and institutional infrastructure. Although it continued to exist in physical terms, much industrial capacity had been made economically obsolete. Because of the cost hike, investments to improve existing East German plants could hardly succeed in quickly attaining the high level of productivity that corresponded to the inflated level of wage costs. Hence, the modernization of the East German economy was bound to take place via the lengthy and costly route of rebuilding the major part of production capacity almost from scratch.

From the beginning of the reforms in East Germany, it was widely perceived that the economic transformation could not proceed swiftly unless large parts of the East German capital stock were privatized in a reasonable period of time. As early as March 1990, the GDR government had established a holding company of virtually all East German state-owned enterprises, the so-called Treuhandanstalt, which was to become the decisive agent in the subsequent process of privatization. Practically, it started its work after German political unification on 3 October 1990 when it was assigned three major tasks, namely the restructuring, the privatization and the de-monopolization of existing firms.

---

[11] A conversion rate of 2:1 for stocks and flows had been proposed by Schmieding (1990) and subsequently – in a slightly modified form – by the Deutsche Bundesbank.

[12] Similarly, those Western investors who set up new production plants in the East had little reason to oppose such wage rises, as – after a period of retraining – the workers they selected were likely to reach the same productivity levels as their Western counterparts.

To be sure, the legal task assignment did not provide any guidance with respect to the hierarchy of aims; in particular, there was no explicit priority given to privatization. Therefore, in practice, much depended on the strategy of the Treuhand's management and its supervisory board as well as the government, most of all the federal minister of finance who set the frame in which the Treuhand was to receive government subsidies, credits and credit guarantees. The federal government also had a major influence on the selection of the members of the Treuhand's supervisory board. Thus, although legally no political institution, the Treuhand was bound to be subject to the political will of the government and to all standard political pressures from outside lobby groups.

Given this institutional framework, the Treuhand's subsequent record looks remarkably successful. The privatization of small firms and shops in the service sector had nearly been completed by the end of 1991. From the stock of roughly 13,000 larger firms – most of them in industry – about 58 per cent had been privatized or re-privatized by late 1993, 2 per cent had been taken over by local government and about 24 per cent had been put on the way towards liquidation. A large part of the remaining 16 per cent had been dismembered into about 7,000 units that were then privatized separately. Only 7 per cent of all enterprises remained Treuhand property. In terms of jobs, Treuhand firms provided no more than about 200,000 jobs by late 1993, i.e. less than 4 per cent of total employment in eastern Germany. Even in manufacturing, i.e. in the sector where privatization was most difficult, the respective share was still below 11 per cent.[13]

At least for large parts of industry, this privatization record could only come about because the federal government gave the Treuhand the financial leeway to sell existing plants even if their market value was actually negative; in fact, a considerable part of the eastern German industrial capacity was privatized with a 'golden handshake'. Early forecasts of the privatization receipts turned out to be much too optimistic, and it is highly unlikely that, in the end, the process of privatization will have generated a positive fiscal balance.

If one takes a bird's-eye view of German economic unification and its immediate aftermath including the privatization efforts, the sheer speed and extent of the transformation are impressive; in no other post-communist economy of central and eastern Europe has the institutional break with the past been so complete and the building-up of new institutions so rapid as in eastern Germany. In this respect, German unification was certainly successful. However, whether this fast transformation was successful in the broader sense of supplying the basis for a sustained future growth remains an open question.

---

[13] See Treuhandanstalt (1993).

3   The prospects of the eastern German economy

By the early 1990s, it is still impossible to make any firm conjecture on whether German economic unification may some day be called a success or not. What one can do, however, is to identify certain traces and patterns of adjustment that will not fade away in the near future and thus figure as medium- and long-term landmarks for the prospective economic development of eastern Germany. In this respect, three major points should be recognized.

First, the eastern German economy has gone through a process of de-industrialization which may be historically unique both in its extent and its depth. By early 1992, when the trough of industrial production was reached, output and employment in manufacturing had contracted to roughly one third of its level in the first half of 1990. To be sure, non-manufacturing industries, above all construction, had a somewhat better record, but their relatively good performance depended to a large extent on strong government demand, notably on the heavy public investment in infrastructure which will be substantially reduced as soon as the most urgent reconstruction and modernization needs are met. Thus there is hardly any doubt that the industrial base from which future growth in eastern Germany is to start has become very small indeed.

Second, the structure of this industrial base has a marked bias towards non-traded goods because the shock of price liberalization in the wake of German economic unification led to the most pronounced worsening of market conditions in those branches of manufacturing that happen to be most thoroughly exposed to international competition. Thus large parts of the investment goods industry covering mechanical and electrical engineering, the production of motors, vehicles, machine tools, etc., were affected most badly by the adjustment pressures; some branches of industry virtually disappeared within a few months (such as the production of business machines). Along with the chemical industry, which also suffered badly, these investment goods branches correspond exactly to those parts of the West German economy that had been the traditional backbone of its international competitiveness and the driving motor of the spectacular export-led growth in the 1950s. Ironically, they had also been the pride of the GDR-economy over four decades, providing its main export products within the heavily distorted division of labour in communist eastern Europe. On the other hand, the non-traded goods sectors of the economy – notably a large part of private services (e.g. wholesale and retail trade, finance, transport, etc.) and some selected industrial branches (e.g. printing, stone and minerals, the food industry) – survived quite well, either because they supply local markets only and/or because they involve bulky, heavy or perishable products that are very expensive to transport over long distances so that there is a kind of natural protection. Typically, however, these are not the branches which are dynamic enough in the longer run so as to figure as a growth motor for any larger economy.[14]

Third, the process of de-industrialization has left deep traces in the eastern German labour market: by 1992, the official unemployment rate had risen to about 15 per cent, and the degree of effective underemployment, if the non-working status of people in short-time work, re-qualification and work-creation programmes as well as early retirement schemes was properly included, came close to 30 per cent.[15] This is a degree of underemployment which has no parallel in post-war German economic history. It indicates how challenging the task of returning to a more or less full utilization of the labour supply really is. In fact, to reach anything close to full employment within a decade, employment growth in eastern Germany would have to be even faster than it was in West Germany during the miraculous 1950s, when the number of jobs increased by a remarkable 24 per cent.

Such were the starting conditions at about the trough of the eastern German transformation crisis. All in all, one may say that the conditions of unification and its aftermath – notably the sharp rise of eastern wages – made the eastern German economy shrink to a competitive core which is small by all standards. Only if this core is supplemented in due course by massive investments in new capital equipment can there be a realistic chance of making the eastern German economy viable and competitive at roughly the same level of income per capita as the western part of the country. However, this capital gap will only close if eastern Germany can attract substantial 'direct' investment, be it from the western part of the country or from the rest of the world. The government has done much to make this possible, though not always in a consistent policy framework. There have been vast public investments to improve the physical infrastructure (roads, railroad tracks, communication networks, etc.) and the efficiency of public administration; and there has been (and there still is) a long array of different investment subsidy schemes that, as a rough guess, lower the cost of investing in eastern Germany by about 20–30 per cent.[16] While one may wonder whether such a heavy subsidization does not put future growth onto a too capital-intensive track – thus creating not enough jobs per unit of investment outlay[17] – the measures do certainly contribute to a re-industrialization of eastern Germany. Rebounding from an extremely depressed level of production, the eastern German economy in fact reached respectable GDP

---

[14] On the differential growth of the various branches of economic activity, see Deutsches Institut für Wirtschaftsforschung, Institut für Weltwirtschaft (1993), pp. 6–40.

[15] For various extended measures of underemployment in eastern Germany from 1990 to 1992, see Klodt and Paqué (1993), pp. 14–16, and Paqué (1993b), pp. 1–4.

[16] For a survey of the various schemes as of 1991, see Deutsches Institut für Wirtschaftsforschung, Institut für Weltwirtschaft (1991), pp. 30–3.

[17] See, e.g. Giersch (1992); Paqué (1993b).

growth rates in the range of 6–10 per cent in the years 1992 and 1993. Much of this growth was fuelled by the massive public transfers from the West, but the share of commercially viable eastern German production appears to be on the rise as well. Nonetheless, a gap of approximately DM 200 billion remains between domestic absorption and production in eastern Germany, which is still largely financed by the western taxpayer. As eastern German absorption is likely to keep growing, it will take many more years of real GDP growth rates well above 5 per cent until the gap between production and absorption will narrow significantly, perhaps some time around the turn of the century.

In any event, there are good reasons to remain sceptical whether this will be enough to bring down the unemployment rate to western standards within a reasonable period of time. If anything, the recent experience with massive investment aid has shown that, at equal prospective labour costs between West and East in the future, it is much more difficult than anticipated to make western firms re-orientate their investment plans by shifting from a prospective location in the industrial heartlands of the West to eastern regions, which still lack the dense network of trade and communication links that make up viable agglomerations of economic activity. In addition, the parallel – though much slower – transformation of the economies of central and eastern Europe implies that those western firms that want to profit from low-production costs are likely to shift their investments directly to Poland, the Czech Republic, Slovakia or Hungary, where wages are only a fraction of the level in Germany, both East and West. Hence, although eastern Germany is not badly located at the cross-roads of two parts of Europe which will gradually grow together, it has been deprived of the opportunity to become the extended workbench of western firms.

Thus the most likely prospect for eastern Germany may well be to have something like a dual economy, at least in the medium run. On the one side, there will be a growing modern latest-vintage capital stock which allows a part, but only a part, of the active labour force to reach or even surpass western labour productivity levels. Besides, however, there will be a high degree of open unemployment or hidden underemployment, which may well remain higher than the levels that prevail in those regions of the West that experienced the most severe industrial crises in the 1970s and the 1980s. Of course, it would be presumptuous to call such an outcome an outright failure or an outright success because, as usual, the counterfactual for such a judgement remains poorly specified. Those who regard the option of keeping real wages significantly lower in the eastern than in the western part of the country as unrealistic will be inclined to call it a success because, given the historical and political circumstances and constraints, not much could have been done differently; they will also point to the fact that the approach chosen has caused a rapid surge in eastern German productivity and consumption levels. Those who hold that, with some more common sense in collective wage bargaining, a good deal of the subsequent dualization could have been avoided, will lean towards a more negative judgement, maintaining in particular that more could have been achieved at much lower social costs.

In any event, German unification is likely to have quite profound long-run consequences for the institutions of collective bargaining. With unemployment remaining at high levels in a relatively large part of the united country, the pressures of outsider competition in the labour market may become more virulent and may induce ever more firms to leave employers' associations and to put together a workforce at subcontractual conditions. Thus there may be more and more elements of flexibility injected into the traditionally rigid wage structure, and this may well spill over to the western parts of the country. In the end, the traditional system of collective bargaining may be undermined, and the labour market in united Germany may increasingly resemble that of the United States. To be sure, this kind of institutional erosion will be a long-drawn-out process going well beyond the medium run of reconstructing and modernizing the eastern German economy. But it may finally turn out to be the most sustained impact of German unification on the 'social market economy'.

7   A new miracle?

At least in its first five chapters, this book has told the story of a fading miracle. The main economic messages of this story may be summarized as follows:

(i) After three dismal years of central administration by the Allied authorities, the West German economy was subjected to a shock therapy of radical monetary reform and price liberalization. This combined treatment proved extraordinarily successful: it unleashed supply-side forces and allowed for a very fast reconstruction and a thorough structural adjustment of the economy's productive potential within about two years. Because of the strict stability orientation of monetary and fiscal policy, an initial surge of corrective price inflation could be kept at bay without any major macroeconomic disruptions.

(ii) In the 1950s, the early momentum of reconstruction became a genuine growth miracle. Given the ample supply of highly mobile and well-trained surplus labour, the only temporary impediment to high growth and the reduction of unemployment was the shortage of capital. This could be overcome mainly through high business profits, which were heavily favoured by tax exemptions to give firms the financial leeway to carry out the necessary investment projects, despite a still very narrow capital market. Foreign aid – notably US aid through the European Recovery Program – was only of minor economic importance for the process of capital formation, although it may well have been a very important political indicator for the American presence in Europe, which raised private investors' confidence in political stability and thus facilitated the reintegration of West Germany into the world economy.

(iii) At least four major fortuitous economic factors helped to initiate and sustain a kind of virtuous growth circle in the 1950s. First, the Korea boom gave the West German economy an unexpected head start, which paved the way for a viable process of export-led expansion, above all of investment goods industries. Second, after just one short-lived balance-of-payments crisis, West Germany ran a persistent current account surplus, piled up currency reserves and thus quite naturally became a pacemaker of trade liberalization.

Third, monetary and fiscal policy refrained from any cyclical activism, at least until the second half of the 1950s, when the first significant inflationary pressures emerged; given the comfortable external position of the West German economy, any sign of cyclical overheating could be taken as a strong case for further steps towards import liberalization. Fourth, through a variety of complex reasons – most of all the persistently underestimated speed of the advance of productivity – unions turned out to be relatively moderate in their wage demands, so that the scope for supply-side growth and the rapid reduction of the remaining unemployment was not diminished through an undue rise in labour costs.

(iv) By the 1960s, the performance of the West German economy had normalized to the international standards of the time. Externally, the rapid integration into the world economy continued, albeit with a pronounced bias towards intra-EEC trade and with heavy protectionism in agriculture and mining. Internally, the undervaluation of the West German currency led to a state of persistent overemployment and a growing influx of foreign labour, which had positive and negative consequences. On the positive side, the increasing employment of foreign workers reduced the frictions of structural change and thus made for an exceptionally peaceful industrial climate, with the unions being quite cooperative in the fight against inflation and the macroeconomic policy efforts to overcome the 1966/7 recession. On the negative side, the currency undervaluation prevented an early structural change away from industry to the modern service sector; in the late years of the Bretton Woods system, it even paved the way for severe inflationary pressures, in terms of both prices and wages.

(v) In the early 1970s, supply-side conditions worsened, mainly because of a drastic rise of labour and energy costs. After the breakdown of the Bretton Woods system, the tough monetary stance of the Bundesbank prevented the wave of unfavourable supply-side shocks from accelerating price inflation. As a consequence, the West German economy stumbled first into a severe recession and then into a vicious circle of slow growth and high unemployment. While the immediate cause of the stagnation lay in a policy-induced shortfall of aggregate demand in the course of a major recession, the deeper reasons must be located on the supply side, most of all in a slack of investment.

(vi) In brief, there are three sets of factors which can be made responsible for the slow pace of capital formation in the fifteen years after 1973. First, because of the sharp rise in labour costs, two oil price hikes – in 1973/4 and 1979/80 – and a drastic increase of real interest rates by the early 1980s, the rate of return on capital remained chronically low, significantly lower than in earlier periods. Only the deliberate demand push ('locomotive experiment') in the late 1970s could pull it up for a brief period, but only at the cost of another wave of inflation and a temporary 'twin' deficit of the public budget and the current account, which triggered a new round of severe monetary contraction and fiscal consolidation. Second, sharply rising competitive pressures emanating from newly industrialized countries forced major traditional industries such as textiles, clothing, shipbuilding and iron and steel into painful adjustments to a new international division of labour. In part, these challenges led to a viable process of slimming down to a competitive size; in part, however, they invoked a revival of protectionism. Third, a cluster of diverse institutional character-istics reduced the scope for promising investments: a deterioration of industrial relations, the heavy subsidization of ailing industries, undue regulation of the service sector, and a fairly rigid labour market which hindered the reintegration of the unemployed into the labour force and accentuated structural imbalances. Worse still, West Germany lagged well behind the Anglo-American world in its efforts to give its economy a more supply-friendly incentive structure through tax reform and a less stifling system of regulations. Thus the persistent surplus on current account became an indicator of unattractiveness for foreign capital far more than of German-style export performance and sound macroeconomic policies.

By and large, this was the picture of the West German economy until well into the second half of the 1980s. There was no longer any doubt that the German miracle had faded away in every relevant respect and that, economically, West Germany had become just another part of Europe, with its fair share in all positive and negative characteristics of the old continent. In terms of its stability orientation – both fiscal and monetary – it remained ahead of most other EC countries, although the difference had greatly narrowed in recent years; also, the unemployment balance looked slightly better than elsewhere, though by itself clearly not satisfactory. Yet, in terms of growth dynamics, West Germany had become a laggard and was widely perceived as remaining so for quite a while. Therefore it is hardly surprising that, as quoted at the beginning of this book, a British weekly was to portray the West German economy as rich, saturated and stodgy, as an ageing *Wunderkind* with not much of a future in terms of growth dynamics.[1]

This was in May 1988, but since then, the ageing *Wunderkind* has passed through a powerful cycle of boom and gloom in the course of business fluctuations which took many observers by surprise, at least with respect to the scale of the amplitudes. At first, i.e. in the years 1988–1990/1, the ageing *Wunderkind* proved that there was more vitality left in its seemingly saturated body than most sceptics were inclined to believe. Yet in the subsequent sharp recession, it turned out that the prior expansion was at least partly unsustain-able. Both stages of this business cycle must be seen against the background of structural improvements and newly emerging problems.

[1] See *The Economist* of 7 May 1988, 'Wunderkind at 40'.

By the late 1980s, there were at least three major reasons to justify a new optimism over the prospects of the German economy. The first reason was that supply-side conditions had – after all – markedly improved. Most importantly, the rate of return on capital had finally climbed back to levels not reached since the late 1960s, mainly because of a sharp decline in imported raw material prices by 1986 and the sustained reduction of real unit labour costs. In addition, the last step of the tax reform coming into effect in 1990 brought the first sizeable reduction of marginal income tax rates since the mid-1950s. And structural labour shortages could be partially mitigated through a large influx of ethnic German immigrants from the Soviet Union, central and eastern Europe and East Germany who, in many economic respects, resembled the expellees and refugees of the 1950s. Hence, despite the lack of any really fundamental reform to unbound supply-side forces, the macroeconomic picture lost a good deal of its gloom. Actually, the years 1988–90 brought an average real GDP growth of 3.9 per cent p.a., a rate not known since the late 1970s, with price inflation far less of a threat than at that time. Most importantly, investment in plant and equipment picked up again and reached a growth rate of 6.8 per cent p.a. in 1988–90, more than in any three consecutive years since the early 1970s. In these three years, employment increased by a respectable total of 1.4 million jobs, which led to a fairly easy absorption of immigrant labour and to a reduction of the unemployment rate by almost two percentage points; although the core of long-term unemployment largely remained untouched, a new dynamics of the labour market became visible.

The second reason for optimism lay in the European Community's 'Project 1992'. In late 1985, the EC had set itself the task of completing the internal market within seven years: by the end of 1992, all remaining impediments to free trade in goods and services and to the free movement of capital and labour were to be removed. This meant in particular that all elements of hidden protectionism in product norms, service regulations, public procurement, tax and border formalities, etc., were to disappear. Although the Community was not quite able to meet this ambitious deadline – even by 1993/4, the project has not been fully completed – progress was clearly visible in the late 1980s and an EC-wide growth push could be expected in the long run because of static and dynamic productivity gains stemming from a more efficient international division of labour.

For West Germany, the 1992-project offered a unique opportunity to expose its heavily regulated service sector to a new wave of competitive pressures. This was especially important for those services such as insurance and transport for which countries like Britain and the Netherlands had traditionally provided a much more liberal legal environment and proved more successful internationally. Of course, these opportunities were only to be seized if the level of EC-wide regulation did not converge to the German level through a political process of deliberate ex-ante harmonization. Fortunately, Germany has not (yet) been able to push its EC partners into accepting the high and stifling standards of German regulatory practices; hence a fair amount of overall liberalization in the service sector has been achieved by the early 1990s. Naturally, this liberalization may provoke temporary adjustment crises in service branches that had previously been shielded from outside competition; as usual, however, the medium- and long-term productivity gains from trade should outweigh the costs of such temporary frictions.

The third reason for growth optimism – and maybe the most important one – lay in the dramatic events which were reshaping the political and economic landscape of central and eastern Europe from 1989 onwards. In essence, they came down to a wholesale demise of communist ideology, including the central administration and planning of a tightly controlled economy. Even nowadays, it is still not clear whether all member countries of the former Soviet bloc will be able to transform their mismanaged command systems into genuine market economies in a reasonable period of time. In this mammoth task, they face much more difficulties than West Germany at the threshold of its liberal reforms in 1948, although the West German example might give them some important hints about how to overcome a capital shortage and how to reintegrate into the world economy. If they are successful – and, at least outside the erstwhile Soviet Union, there has been some reason for optimism all along – they will add important elements of dynamics to economic growth in Europe just as EC integration did two decades earlier. Located right at the centre of Europe, Germany will be well placed to take full advantage of this growth spurt; in particular, new and fast-growing export markets may open for its manufacturing, most of all its investment goods industries, and profitable opportunities for direct investment may emerge. Until the collapse of communism, the share of West German exports going to the CMEA countries including East Germany amounted to less than 5 per cent, a very low level in the light of the countries' size and geographical proximity to West Germany. Hence, there is a large potential ready to be tapped, and it may in the end lead to a quite radical enlargement and reshaping of the intra-European division of labour.

One major stage of the reintegration of eastern and western Europe is already past: the economic and political unification of the two German states, or, in other words, the end of a separate West German economy. Because of the overriding importance attached to political considerations, the economic terms of German unification were less than fortunate. Motivated by the wish to narrow the sizeable gap between living standards in the East and in the West, the external value of East German wages and, hence, production costs rose dramatically, with West Germany footing the bill. The immediate effect was a collapse of tradables production in the East; at the same time, unification brought a huge deficit-financed demand boost for the West which, in 1990 and 1991, prolonged a forceful business upswing that had already given way to a downturn or even an outright recession in most other western countries.

In some respects, the subsequent sharp recession in 1992/3 has been a quite natural consequence of a prior boom that had been artificially extended by a thorough demand stimulus plus a politically fuelled unification euphoria which apparently left its traces even in sober business minds. With inflationary pressures mounting and wages edging up faster than at any time since the late 1970s, a downward correction was overdue, not least because the wave of pent-up eastern German demand for consumer durables reached a first stage of saturation. But, just as in the mid-1970s and early 1980s, the cyclical downturn only overlapped a deeper structural adjustment crisis arising from competitive pressures from the newly industrializing parts of the world: with eastern Asian and now also central and eastern European economies improving their export mixes and raising the technological standards of their products, the evidence became stronger that a new phase of shrinking rents from technological leadership had been reached. This trend hit the economies of all advanced industrialized countries, but those economies that have traditionally relied most heavily on exports of custom-made, high-quality products seemed to suffer most badly. In fact, what had been the great advantage of countries like Sweden, Switzerland and Germany for over four decades, notably the excellent reputation of their engineering workforces which had its counterpart in a high labour productivity and a high real wage level, now seemed for the first time to be devalued most dramatically by the onslaught of foreign competition.

To be sure, the adjustment to these new pressures is fully underway in Germany (and also in countries like Sweden and Switzerland). It takes many forms: a wave of productivity-enhancing investments focusing on new forms of work organization ('lean production'), a genuine attempt to make working conditions (working time, remuneration, etc.) substantially more flexible on the plant level and a temporary moderation of wage demands in collective bargaining. It remains to be seen whether this will be enough to restore the potential of dynamics that is required to take advantage of the many options that the new geographical position of Germany in the centre of a non-divided Europe can offer. As to the long run, there is reason to remain basically optimistic, not least because, in the end, a new international division of labour including such population giants as China and India will open up opportunities for beneficial trade and investment that are likely to provide net benefits well above the costs of adjustment. Nevertheless, the process of adjustment may be protracted, leading to a further rise of unemployment and thus dominating the public discussion well into the first years of the next century.

On top of these adjustment pressures that originate in the changing international division of labour, the German economy will have to digest the long-term fiscal burden of German unification. In essence, this burden will consist of three parts, namely (i) a higher level of taxation, notably of value added and of gasoline taxes as well as, from the mid-1990s, a surcharge on individual income taxes; (ii) a higher level of social security contributions, to both the old-age pension scheme and the unemployment insurance system; and (iii) a higher level of public debt, which is likely to stabilize at a new plafond of around 60 per cent of GNP by the second half of the 1990s, compared to roughly 40 per cent in the pre-unification 1980s. To what extent this additional burden will become a brake on growth is largely a matter of speculation; at least the factual rise of income and payroll taxation may well involve growth-impeding disincentive effects. In a more complete empirical evaluation of the government's role in German unification, however, one would have to balance any of these disincentive effects against the additional supply potential of the German economy as a whole that will be created through the public investments in the eastern part of the country. If such a cost-benefit analysis could be made – unfortunately, it cannot, at least not at this early stage – the picture might turn out to be not so bad after all.

References

Abelshauser, Werner (1975). *Wirtschaft in Westdeutschland 1945–1948*. Stuttgart.
(1979). 'Probleme des Wiederaufbaus der westdeutschen Wirtschaft 1945–1953'. In: Heinrich Winkler (ed.), *Politische Weichenstellungen im Nachkriegsdeutschland 1945–1953*. Göttingen, pp. 208–53.
(1989). 'Zur Funktion des Marshallplans beim westdeutschen Wiederaufbau', *Vierteljahreshefte für Zeitgeschichte*, Vol. 37, No. 1, pp. 85–113.
Agartz, Viktor (1955). 'Lohn, Arbeitszeit und Produktivität', *Gewerkschaftliche Monatshefte*, No. 6, pp. 347–53.
Agency for International Development (AID) (1971). *U.S. Economic Assistance Programs Administered by the Agency for International Development and Predecessor Agencies, April 3, 1948–June 30, 1970*. Washington, D.C.
Albrecht, Gerhard (ed.) (1951). *Die Problematik der Vollbeschäftigung*. Verhandlungen auf der Tagung des Vereins für Socialpolitik in Bad Pyrmont, 13–15 October 1950. Berlin.
Amelung, Torsten, and Rolf J. Langhammer (1989). *ACP Exports and EC Trade Preferences Revisited*. Institut für Weltwirtschaft, Kiel Working Paper No. 373, May.
Arbeitsgemeinschaft deutscher wirtschaftswissenschaftlicher Forschungsinstitute (1950). *Lebensfähigkeit und Vollbeschäftigung*. Bonn.
Die Lage der Weltwirtschaft und der westdeutschen Wirtschaft, autumn 1974, autumn 1979, autumn 1980, autumn 1981, autumn 1982.
Artis, Michael J. (1987). 'The European Monetary System: An Evaluation', *Journal of Policy Modeling*, Vol. 9, No. 1, pp. 175–98.
Artus, Jacques R. (1984). 'The Disequilibrium Real Wage Rate Hypothesis. An Empirical Evaluation', *IMF Staff Papers*, Vol. 31, pp. 249–302.
Baade, Fritz (1957). *Deutschland und die europäische Integration: Vortrag und Diskussion*. Wirtschaftswissenschaftliche Informationen No. 3, Berlin (DDR).
Balabkins, Nicholas (1964). *Germany under Direct Controls*. New Brunswick, N.J.
Baldwin, Robert E. (1987). 'Multilateral Liberalization'. In: Michael J. Finger and Andrzej Olechowski (eds.), *The Uruguay Round*. Washington, D.C., pp. 37–44.
Bandow, Doug (ed.) (1985). *U.S. Aid to the Developing World – A Free Market Agenda*. Washington, D.C.
Bank deutscher Länder. *Geschäftsberichte für die Jahre 1950–1958*. Frankfurt-on-Main (from 1957 onwards: Deutsche Bundesbank).
Monatsberichte 1949–1957. Frankfurt-on-Main, various issues.

Bank for International Settlements (1959). *Germany – Monetary and Economic Situation 1950–1959*. Basle.

Bank für Internationalen Zahlungsausgleich (Bank for International Settlements, BIS), *Jahresberichte (Annual Reports)*. Basle, various issues.

Barnikel, Hans-Heinrich (1959). *Der westdeutsche Arbeitsmarkt 1945–1956 unter besonderer Berücksichtigung regionaler Verhältnisse dargestellt am Beispiel Nordbayerns*. Bamberg.

Bell, Linda A., and Richard B. Freeman (1985). *Does a Flexible Industry Wage Structure Increase Employment?: The U.S. Experience*. NBER Working Paper No. 1604.

Bellmann, Lutz, and Friedrich Buttler (1989). 'Lohnstrukturflexibilität – Theorie und Empirie der Transaktionskosten und Effizienzlöhne', *Mitteilungen aus der Arbeitsmarkt- und Berufsforschung*, Vol. 22, pp. 202–17.

Belongia, Michael T. (1988). 'Prospects for International Policy Coordination: Some Lessons from the EMS', *Federal Reserve Bank of St. Louis*, July/August, pp. 19–29.

Berg, Fritz (1966). *Die westdeutsche Wirtschaft in der Bewährung: Ausgewählte Reden aus den Jahren 1950 bis 1965*. Hagen.

Blanchard, Olivier, et al. (1985). *Employment and Growth in Europe: A Two-Handed Approach*. CEPS Papers, No. 21, Brussels.

Blanchard, Olivier, and Lawrence H. Summers (1986). 'Hysteresis and the European Unemployment Problem', *NBER Macroeconomics Annual*, Vol. 1, pp. 15–78.

Blattberg, Robert C. (ed.) (1976). *The Economy in Transition*. New York.

Bluestone, Barry, and Bennett Harrison (1988). 'The Growth of Low-Wage Employment: 1963–86', *American Economic Review, Papers and Proceedings*, Vol. 78, pp. 124–8.

Bofinger, Peter (1988). 'Das europäische Währungssystem und die geldpolitische Koordination in Europa', *Kredit und Kapital*, No. 3, pp. 317–45.

Borchardt, Knut, and Christoph Buchheim (1987). 'Die Wirkung der Marshall-plan-Hilfe in Schlüsselbranchen der deutschen Wirtschaft', *Vierteljahreshefte für Zeitgeschichte*, Vol. 35, No. 2, pp. 317–48.

Boss, Alfred (1983). 'Reform der Alterssicherung'. In: Herbert Giersch (ed.), *Wie es zu schaffen ist: Agenda für die deutsche Wirtschaftspolitik*. Stuttgart, pp. 278–96.

(1987). *Incentives und Wirtschaftswachstum – Zur Steuerpolitik in der frühen Nachkriegszeit*. Institut für Weltwirtschaft, Kiel Working Paper No. 295, August.

Boss, Alfred, et al. (1979). 'Vor einer Stabilisierungsrezession', *Die Weltwirtschaft*, No. 2, pp. 19–43.

Bothe, Adrian (1987). *Leistungsanreize und Wachstumsdynamik – Die Sozialpolitik in den westlichen Besatzungszonen bzw. der Bundesrepublik Deutschland 1945–1957*. Institut für Weltwirtschaft, Kiel Working Paper No. 293, July.

Bracher, Karl-Dietrich, et al. (1986). *Republik im Wandel 1969–1974: Die Ära Brandt. Geschichte der Bundesrepublik Deutschland*, Vol. V (1), Stuttgart/Wiesbaden.

Braunthal, Gerard (1965). *The Federation of German Industry in Politics*. Ithaca, N.Y.

Bruno, Michael (1986). 'Aggregate Supply and Demand Factors in OECD Unemployment: An Update', *Economica*, Vol. 53, No. 210, pp. S35–S52.

Bruno, Michael, and Jeffrey D. Sachs (1985). *Economics of Worldwide Stagflation*. Cambridge, Mass.

Buchheim, Christoph (1988). 'Die Währungsreform 1948 in Westdeutschland', *Vierteljahreshefte für Zeitgeschichte*, Vol. 36, 189–231.

(1990). *Die Wiedereingliederung Westdeutschlands in die Weltwirtschaft 1945 bis 1958*. Munich.

Büchtemann, Christoph F. (1989). *Befristete Arbeitsverträge nach dem Beschäftigungsförderungsgesetz (BeschFG 1985)*. Forschungsbericht (Sozialforschung) 183, Wissenschaftszentrum Berlin, Berlin.

Bundesanstalt für Arbeit (1974). *Ausländische Arbeitnehmer 1972/73*. Nuremberg.

Bundesanzeiger of 3 November 1949, ed. Bundesminister der Justiz, Bonn.

Bundesminister für Vertriebene (1953). *Vertriebene, Flüchtlinge, Kriegsgefangene, heimatlose Ausländer 1949–1952*. Bonn.

Bundesministerium der Finanzen (BMF) (1951). *Zolltarifgesetz vom 16. August 1951 und Gebrauchszolltarif mit Anhang*. Bonn.

Bundesverband der Deutschen Industrie (BDI) (Federation of German Industry). (1950–9). *Jahresberichte (Annual Reports)*, 1949/50–1958/9. Cologne.

Burda, Michael C., and Jeffrey D. Sachs (1987). *Institutional Aspects of High Unemployment in the Federal Republic of Germany*. NBER Working Paper No. 2241, Cambridge, Mass.

Clay, Lucius D. (1950). *Decision in Germany*. Garden City, N.Y.

Coe, David T. (1985). *Nominal Wages, the NAIRU and Wage Flexibility*. OECD Economic Studies No. 5, pp. 85–126.

(1988). 'Hysteresis Effects in Aggregate Wage Equations'. In: Rod Cross (ed.), *Unemployment, Hysteresis and the Natural Rate Hypothesis*. Oxford, pp. 284–305.

Colander, David C. (ed.) (1984). *Neoclassical Political Economy*. Cambridge, Mass.

Commission of the European Communities (1985). Annual Economic Report 1985–86, *European Economy*, No. 26.

Cooper, Richard N. (1976). 'Turbulence and Interdependence in the World Economy'. In: Robert C. Blattberg (ed.), *The Economy in Transition*. New York, pp. 29–49.

Cowen, Tyler (1985). 'The Marshall Plan: Myths and Realities'. In: Doug Bandow (ed.), *U.S. Aid to the Developing World – A Free Market Agenda*. Washington, D.C.

Cross, Rod (ed.) (1988). *Unemployment, Hysteresis and the Natural Rate Hypothesis*. Oxford.

Crouch, Colin, and Alessandro Pizzorno (eds.) (1978). *The Resurgence of Class Conflict in Western Europe since 1968*, Vol. I: *National Studies*; Vol. II: *Comparative Analyses*. New York.

Curzon, Gerard (1965). *Multilateral Commercial Diplomacy*. London.

Dankert, Pieter (1982). 'The European Community – Past, Present and Future', *Journal of Common Market Studies*, Vol. 21, pp. 3–18.

Deppler, Michael C. (1974). 'Some Evidence on the Effects of Exchange Rate Changes on Trade', *IMF Staff Papers*, Vol. 21, No. 3, pp. 605–36.

Deutsche Bundesbank (1976). *Währung und Wirtschaft in Deutschland 1876–1975*. Frankfurt-on-Main.

(1988). *40 Jahre Deutsche Mark, Monetäre Statistiken 1948–87*. Frankfurt-on-Main.

Monatsberichte. Frankfurt-on-Main, various issues.

Deutscher Bundestag (1953–7). *Verhandlungen,* II, *Wahlperiode 1953–1957.* Stenographische Berichte, Bonn.

Deutscher Gewerkschaftsbund (DGB). (1951–8). *Gewerkschaftliche Monatshefte.* Cologne, various issues.

Deutsches Institut für Wirtschaftsforschung, Institut für Weltwirtschaft (1991). *Gesamtwirtschaftliche und unternehmerische Anpassungsprozesse in Ostdeutschland.* Zweiter Bericht. Institut für Weltwirtschaft, Kiel Discussion Paper No. 169. June.

(1993). *Gesamtwirtschaftliche und unternehmerische Anpassungsforschritte in Ostdeutschland.* Neunter Bericht. Institut für Weltwirtschaft, Kiel Discussion Paper No. 218/19. October.

Deutsche Zeitung und Wirtschaftszeitung of 26 September 1951, 'Verschätzte Lohn- und Gewinnquoten – I. Gesetzliche und freiwillige Sozialleistungen gehören zur Lohnquote'.

of 29 September 1951, 'Verschätzte Lohn- und Gewinnquoten – II. "Gewinnquote" und Verteilung des Einkommens'.

of 24 October 1951, 'Verschätzte Lohn- und Gewinnquoten – Eine Stellungnahme aus gewerkschaftlicher Sicht'.

of 18 October 1952, 'Liberalisierungsschaukel'.

Dicke, Hugo (1987). 'Grenzen der Liberalisierung – Zur ordnungspolitischen Sonderstellung der Landwirtschaft'. Paper presented at the seminar 'Anatomie eines "Wunders" – Die westdeutsche Wirtschaftspolitik in der frühen Nachkriegszeit', Institut für Weltwirtschaft, Kiel, 25–7 February, mimeo.

(1988). 'Der Wandel des Integrationskonzepts in der EG'. Paper presented at the seminar 'Die sechziger Jahre – Zeit des wirtschaftspolitischen Umdenkens', Institut für Weltwirtschaft, Kiel, 24–6 February, mimeo.

Dicke, Hugo, et al. (1987). *EG-Politik auf dem Prüfstand: Wirkungen auf Wachstum und Strukturwandel in der Bundesrepublik.* Tübingen.

Donges, Juergen B., et al. (1973). *Protektion und Branchenstruktur der westdeutschen Wirtschaft.* Tübingen.

Donges, Juergen B., Klaus-Dieter Schmidt et al. (1988). *Mehr Strukturwandel für Wachstum und Beschäftigung.* Tübingen.

Donovan, Robert J. (1987). *The Second Victory – The Marshall Plan and the Postwar Revival of Europe.* New York.

Dorn, J. A., and W. A. Niskanen (eds.) (1989). *Dollars, Deficits and Trade.* Dordrecht.

Dornbusch, Rüdiger, and Stanley Fischer (1987). *Macroeconomics,* 4th edition. New York.

Dreißig, Wilhelmine (1976). 'Zur Entwicklung der öffentlichen Finanzwirtschaft seit dem Jahre 1950'. In: Deutsche Bundesbank (ed.), *Währung und Wirtschaft in Deutschland 1876–1975.* Frankfurt-on-Main, pp. 691–744.

Drèze, Jacques, et al. (1987). *The Two-Handed Growth Strategy for Europe: Autonomy through Flexible Cooperation.* CEPS Papers, No. 34, Brussels.

Economic Cooperation Administration (ECA) (1951). *Thirteenth Report to Congress of the Economic Cooperation Administration for the Quarter Ended June 30, 1951.* Washington.

The Economist of 2 October 1948, 'Western Germany on its Feet'.

of 11 March 1950, 'Economic Dogmatism in Germany'.

of 10 February 1951, 'Trade Union Triumph in Germany'.

of 18 October 1952, 'The German Economy – Divided it Stands'.

of 14 August 1954, 'Strike and Boom in Germany'.

of 16 August 1958, 'Germany's Syndicalist Experiment'.

of 15 October 1966, 'The German Lesson'.

of 7 May 1988, 'Wunderkind at 40'.

of 12 November 1988, 'America's Shrinking Middle'.

The Economist (ed.) (1985). *Economic Statistics 1900–1983*. London.

Eggerstedt, Harald, and Stefan Sinn (1987). 'The EMS, 1979–1986: The Economics of Muddling Through', *Geld und Währung*, No. 3, pp. 5–11.

Ehmann, Georg (1958). *Entwicklung und Erfolg der westdeutschen Außenhandelsliberalisierung*. Nuremberg.

Ehret, Rolf G. (1959). *Der Weg zur Vollbeschäftigung in der Bundesrepublik Deutschland – Eine Studie über die Problematik der Vollbeschäftigung unter Berücksichtigung sowohl der theoretischen als auch der politisch-historischen Aspekte*. Winterthur.

Emerson, Michael (1988). 'Regulation or Deregulation of the Labour Market: Policy Regimes for the Recruitment and Dismissal of Employees in the Industrialized Countries', *European Economic Review*, Vol. 32, pp. 775–817.

Emminger, Otmar (1976). 'Deutsche Geld- und Währungspolitik im Spannungsfeld zwischen innerem und äußerem Gleichgewicht'. In: Deutsche Bundesbank (ed.), *Währung und Wirtschaft in Deutschland 1876–1975*. Frankfurt-on-Main, pp. 485–554.

Engels, Wolfram (1983). 'Steuerreform'. In: Herbert Giersch (ed.), *Wie es zu schaffen ist: Agenda für die deutsche Wirtschaftspolitik*. Stuttgart, pp. 153–75.

Erhard, Ludwig (1953). 'Die deutsche Wirtschaftspolitik im Blickfeld europäischer Politik'. In: Albert Hunold (ed.), *Wirtschaft ohne Wunder*. Zurich, pp. 128–57.

(1954). *Deutschlands Rückkehr zum Weltmarkt*, 2nd enlarged edition. Düsseldorf.

(1957). *Wohlstand für Alle*. Düsseldorf.

Eschenburg, Theodor (1955). *Herrschaft der Verbände?*. Stuttgart.

(1983). *Jahre der Besatzung 1945–1949. Geschichte der Bundesrepublik Deutschland*, Vol. I, Stuttgart/Wiesbaden.

Eucken, Walter (1948). 'Die soziale Frage'. In: E. Salin (ed.), *Synopsis, Festgabe für Alfred Weber*. Heidelberg, pp. 111–13.

(1952). *Grundsätze der Wirtschaftspolitik*, edited by E. Eucken-Erdsieck and P. K. Hensel. Bern/Tübingen.

Europäische Gemeinschaften (1967). *Agrarmarkt und Agrarmarktpolitik in der EG*. Gemeinsame Veröffentlichung der Sprechergruppe und des Presse- und Informationsdienstes der Europäischen Gemeinschaften. Brussels.

Europäische Gemeinschaften – Generaldirektion Information (1978). *Mitteilungen zur gemeinsamen Agrarpolitik, Auszug aus dem Bericht über die Lage der Landwirtschaft in der Gemeinschaft im Jahre 1977*, Sonderausgabe. Brussels/Luxemburg.

European Payments Union. *Annual Reports 1950/51–II/1958*. Paris, various issues.

Eymüller, Theo (1950). 'Radikale Lohnforderungen', *Der Volkswirt* of 11 August 1950.

Fels, Gerhard (1974). *Assistance to Industry in West Germany*. Institut für Weltwirtschaft, Kiel Working Paper No. 14, March.

Fels, Joachim (1987). 'The European Monetary System 1979–1987: Why has it worked?', *Intereconomics*, September/October, pp. 216–22.

(1988). *1966/67 – Anatomie einer Rezession*. Institut für Weltwirtschaft, Kiel Working Paper No. 320, February.

Financial Times of 26 August 1948, 'Recovery in Western Germany – Currency Reform Succeeds in its Two Main Objects'.

of 21 July 1952, 'German Labour in Management'.

Finger, J. Michael, and Andrzej Olechowski (eds.) (1987). *The Uruguay Round*. Washington, D.C.

Fitoussi, Jean P., and Edmund S. Phelps (1988). *The Slump in Europe – Reconstructing Open Economy Theory*. Oxford.

Flanagan, Robert J., et al. (1983). *Unionism, Economic Stabilization, and Incomes Policies – European Experience*. The Brookings Institution, Washington, D.C.

Föhl, Carl (1967). 'Stabilisierung und Wachstum bei Einsatz von Gastarbeitern', *Kyklos*, Vol. 20, pp. 119–46.

Forrester, Jay W. (1971). *World Dynamics*. Cambridge, Mass.

Frankfurter Allgemeine Zeitung of 18 July 1954, 'Expansive Lohnpolitik heute?'.

Franz, Wolfgang, and Heinz König (1986). 'The Nature and Causes of Unemployment in the Federal Republic of Germany since the 1970s: An Empirical Investigation', *Economica*, Vol. 53, pp. S219–S244.

Freeman, Richard B. (1988). 'Evaluating the European View that the United States has No Unemployment Problem', *American Economic Review, Papers and Proceedings*, Vol. 78, pp. 294–9.

Friedman, Milton (1953). 'The Case for Flexible Exchange Rates'. In: Milton Friedman, *Essays in Positive Economics*. Chicago, pp. 157–203.

Friedrichs, Karl-Heinz (1957). 'Wirtschafts- und Konjunkturpolitik im Gemeinsamen Markt', *Gewerkschaftliche Monatshefte*, Vol. 8, pp. 598–602.

Gebert, Dietmar, and Joachim Scheide (1980). *Die Lokomotiven-Strategie als wirtschaftspolitisches Konzept*. Kiel.

Giersch, Herbert (1957). 'Einige Probleme der kleineuropäischen Zollunion', *Zeitschrift für die gesamte Staatswissenschaft*, Vol. 133, pp. 602–31.

(1977a). 'Comments'. In: Paul McCracken et al. (eds.), *Towards Full Employment and Price Stability – A Report to the OECD by a Group of Independent Experts*. Paris, June, pp. 247–8.

(1977b). *Konjunktur- und Wachstumspolitik in der offenen Wirtschaft – Allgemeine Wirtschaftspolitik*, Vol. II. Wiesbaden.

(1979). 'Aspects of Growth, Structural Change and Employment – A Schumpeterian Perspective', *Weltwirtschaftliches Archiv*, Vol. 115, pp. 629–52.

(1980). 'Die Rolle der reichen Länder in der wachsenden Weltwirtschaft', *Schweizerische Zeitschrift für Volkswirtschaft und Statistik*, Vol. 116, No. 3, pp. 301–20.

(1981), 'Problems of Adjustment to Imports from Less-Developed Countries'. In: Sven Grassman and Erik Lundberg (eds.), *The World Economic Order: Past and Prospects*. London, pp. 265–88.

(ed.) (1983). *Wie es zu schaffen ist. Agenda für die deutsche Wirtschaftspolitik*. Stuttgart.

(1985). 'Perspectives on the World Economy', *Weltwirtschaftliches Archiv*, Vol. 121, pp. 409–26.

(1986). *Liberalisation for Faster Economic Growth*. Seventeenth Wincott Memorial Lecture, IEA Occasional Paper 74. London.

(ed.) (1987). *Free Trade in the World Economy: Towards an Opening of Markets.* Symposium Kiel 1986. Tübingen.

(1988a). *Der EG-Binnenmarkt als Chance und Risiko.* Institut für Weltwirtschaft, Kiel Discussion Paper No. 147, December.

(1988b). 'Liberal Reform in West Germany', *ORDO*, Vol. 39, pp. 3–16.

(ed.) (1988c). *Macro and Micro Policies for More Growth and Employment.* Symposium Kiel 1987. Tübingen.

(1992). *The German Economy 1945–1995. What went Right, What is Going Wrong?* Massachusetts Institute of Technology, World Economy Laboratory, Working Papers 92-12. Cambridge, Mass.

Giersch, Herbert, and Frank Wolter (1983). 'Towards an Explanation of the Productivity Slowdown: An Acceleration–Deceleration Hypothesis', *Economic Journal*, Vol. 93, pp. 35–55.

Glismann, Hans H., et al. (1982). *Weltwirtschaftslehre – Eine problemorientierte Einführung*, 2nd edition. Munich.

Glyn, Andrew, and Bob Rowthorn (1988). 'West European Unemployment: Corporatism and Structural Change', *American Economic Review, Papers and Proceedings*, Vol. 78, pp. 194–9.

Gordon, Robert J. (1988a). 'Wage Gaps versus Output Gaps: Is There a Common Story for All of Europe?'. In: Herbert Giersch (ed.), *Macro and Micro Policies for More Growth and Employment.* Symposium Kiel 1987. Tübingen.

Grassman, Sven, and Erik Lundberg (eds.). 1981. *The World Economic Order: Past and Prospects.* London.

Grauwe, Paul de (1989). *The Cost of Disinflation and the European Monetary System.* University of Louvain and Centre for European Policy Studies, International Economics Research Paper No. 60, April.

Groeben, Hans von der (1985). *The European Community – The Formative Years, The Struggle to Establish the Common Market and the Political Union (1958–66).* The European Perspectives Series. Brussels/Luxemburg.

Gundlach, Erich (1986). 'Gibt es genügend Lohndifferenzierung in der Bundesrepublik Deutschland?', *Die Weltwirtschaft*, No. 2, pp. 74–88.

(1987). *Währungsreform und wirtschaftliche Entwicklung: Westdeutschland 1948.* Institut für Weltwirtschaft, Kiel Working Paper No. 286, April.

Haas, Ernest B. (1958). *The Uniting of Europe.* London.

Handelsblatt of 17 December 1959, 'Vor Welle neuer Lohnforderungen'.

of 12 April 1989, 'Experten halten die Zahl von einer bis 1,5 Millionen offener Stellen für unrealistisch'.

Hardes, Heinz-Dieter (1988). 'Vorschläge zur Differenzierung und Flexibilisierung der Löhne', *Mitteilungen aus der Arbeitsmarkt- und Berufsforschung*, Vol. 21, pp. 52–73.

Harms, Uwe (1966). 'Wirtschaftliche Aspekte des Gastarbeiterproblems', *Hamburger Jahrbuch für Wirtschafts- und Gesellschaftspolitik*, Vol. 11, pp. 277–83.

Hartog, Joop, and Jules Theeuwes (eds.) (1993). *Labour Market Contracts and Institutions. A Cross-National Comparison.* Amsterdam.

Hayek, Friedrich A. von (1944). *The Road to Serfdom.* London.

Hellwig, Martin, and Manfred J. M. Neumann (1987). 'Economic Policy in Germany: Was There a Turnaround?', *Economic Policy*, Vol. 5 (October), pp. 105–40.

Hentschel, Volker (1983). *Geschichte der deutschen Sozialpolitik, 1880–1980, Soziale Sicherung und kollektives Arbeitsrecht.* Frankfurt-on-Main.

Heuser, Carl Otto (1955). 'Droht uns ein großer Katzenjammer?', *Handelsblatt* of 23 September.

Hildebrand, Klaus (1984). *Von Erhard zur Großen Koalition 1963–1969. Geschichte der Bundesrepublik Deutschland*, Vol. IV. Stuttgart/Wiesbaden.

Hoffmann, Edeltraud (1988). 'Beschäftigungstendenzen im Dienstleistungssektor der USA und der Bundesrepublik', *Mitteilungen aus der Arbeitsmarkt- und Berufsforschung*, Vol. 21, pp. 243–67.

Hoffmann, Lutz (1991). 'Preise, Politik und Prioritäten', *Frankfurter Allgemeine Zeitung* of 2 February 1991.

Hunold, Albert (ed.) (1953). *Wirtschaft ohne Wunder*. Zurich.

Institut für angewandte Wirtschaftsforschung (1990a). *Ursachen der Wirtschaftskrise in der DDR, Schlußbilanz einer verfehlten Wirtschaftspolitik*. Berlin.

(1990b). *Grundzüge einer marktwirtschaftlich ausgerichteten Strukturpolitik in der DDR und Anforderungen für die Arbeitsteilung im europäischen Raum*. Kolloquium, Berlin, 25 April.

Institut für internationale Politik und Wirtschaft (1990). *Die marktwirtschaftliche Integration der DDR – Startbedingungen und Konsequenzen*. Berlin.

Jackman, Richard A., and Steven Roper (1987). 'Structural Unemployment'. *Oxford Bulletin of Economics and Statistics*, Vol. 49, pp. 9–36.

Jacobsson, Per, and Alec Cairncross (1950). *The Position of Germany in the European Payments Union* (Report by the Managing Board of the EPU to the Council of the Organization for European Economic Co-operation). 13 November.

Jäger, Wolfgang, and Werner Link (1987). *Republik im Wandel 1974–1982: Die Ära Schmidt, Geschichte der Bundesrepublik Deutschland*, Vol. V (2). Stuttgart/ Wiesbaden.

Jerchow, Friedrich (1979). 'Außenhandel im Widerstreit: Die Bundesrepublik auf dem Weg in das GATT 1949–1951'. In: Heinrich Winkler (ed.), *Politische Weichenstellungen im Nachkriegsdeutschland 1945–1953*. Göttingen, pp. 254–89.

(1982). 'Der Außenkurs der Mark 1944–1949', *Vierteljahreshefte für Zeitgeschichte*, Vol. 30. pp. 256–98.

Joint Export–Import Agency (JEIA) (1948–9). *Report of the Month*. Frankfurt-on-Main.

Kaplan, Jacob J., and Günther Schleiminger (1989). *The European Payments Union – Financial Diplomacy in the 1950s*. Oxford.

Kauffmann, Barbara, and Joachim Scheide (1989). *Die amerikanischen Defizite im Kreuzfeuer der Kritik*. Institut für Weltwirtschaft, Kiel Discussion Paper No. 150, March.

Keohane, Robert O. (1984). *After Hegemony: Cooperation and Discord in the World Political Economy*. Princeton.

Kindleberger, Charles P. (1978). 'Dominance and Leadership in the International Economy: Exploitation, Public Goods, and Free Rides'. In: Centre Nationale de la Recherche Scientifique (ed.), *Hommage à François Perroux*, Vol. I. Grenoble, pp. 283–91.

Kleemann, Josef (1965). *Die internationale Freizügigkeit der Arbeit – Wirtschaftliche und gesellschaftliche Aspekte*. Winterthur.

Klodt, Henning (1990a). 'Industrial Policy and Repressed Structural Change in West Germany', *Jahrbücher für Nationalökonomie und Statistik*, Vol. 207/1, pp. 25–35.

(1990b). 'Technologietransfer und internationale Wettbewerbsfähigkeit', *Aussenwirtschaft*, Vol. 45, No. 1, pp. 57–79.

Klodt, Henning, and Karl-Heinz Paqué (1993). *Am Tiefpunkt der Transformationskrise: Industrie- und lohnpolitische Weichenstellungen in den jungen Bundesländern*. Kiel Discussion Paper No. 213. June.

Kloten, Norbert (1976). 'Erfolg und Mißerfolg der Stabilisierungspolitik (1969–1974)'. In: Deutsche Bundesbank (ed.), *Währung und Wirtschaft in Deutschland 1876–1975*. Frankfurt-on-Main, pp. 643–90.

Knappe, Eckhardt (1983). 'Reform der Krankenversicherung'. In: Herbert Giersch (ed.), *Wie es zu schaffen ist. Agenda für die deutsche Wirtschaftspolitik*. Stuttgart, pp. 287–325.

Kock, Karin (1969). *International Trade Policy and the GATT 1947–1967*. Stockholm.

Koller, Martin (1987). 'Regionale Lohnstrukturen', *Mitteilungen aus der Arbeitsmarkt- und Berufsforschung*, Vol. 20, pp. 30–44.

Kornai, Janos (1980). *Economics of Shortage*. Amsterdam.

Krämer, Hans R. (1968). *EWG und EFTA: Entwicklung, Aufbau und Tätigkeit*. Stuttgart.

Kreinin, Mordechai E. (1979). *Effects of European Integration on Trade Flows in Manufactures*. Institute for International Economic Studies, Seminar Paper No. 125. Stockholm, August.

Krengel, Rolf (1958). *Anlagevermögen, Produktion und Beschäftigung in der Industrie im Gebiet der Bundesrepublik 1924–1956*. Berlin.

Kromphardt, Wilhelm (1947). 'Marktspaltung und Kernplanung in der Volkswirtschaft'. In: Sozialforschungsstelle an der Universität Münster zu Dortmund, *Dortmunder Schriften zur Sozialforschung*, No. 3.

Krugman, Paul R. (1981). 'Intraindustry Specialization and the Gains from Trade', *Journal of Political Economy*, Vol. 90, pp. 959–73.

Kühl, Jürgen (1970). 'Zum Aussagewert der Statistik der offenen Stellen', *Mitteilungen aus der Arbeitsmarkt- und Berufsforschung*, Vol. 3, pp. 250ff.

Kühne, Karl (1957). 'Das Feilschen um den Gemeinsamen Markt', *Gewerkschaftliche Monatshefte*, Vol. 8, pp. 287–95.

Küsters, Hanns Jürgen (1982). *Die Gründung der Europäischen Wirtschaftsgemeinschaft*. Baden-Baden.

Lampert, Heinz (1989). '20 Jahre Arbeitsförderungsgesetz', *Mitteilungen aus der Arbeitsmarkt- und Berufsforschung*, Vol. 22, pp. 173–6.

Langfeldt, Enno (1987). *Wiederaufleben des Korporativismus? Zur Rolle der Verbände in der frühen Nachkriegszeit*. Institut für Weltwirtschaft, Kiel Working Paper No. 283, March.

Langhammer, Rolf J., and André Sapir (1987). *Economic Impact of Generalized Tariff Preferences*. Thames Essay No. 49. London.

Layard, Richard, and Robert Jackman (1985). *European Unemployment is Keynesian and Classical, but not Structural*. Center of European Policy Studies, Working Document 13. Brussels.

Layard, Richard, and Steven Nickell (1985). 'Unemployment, Real Wages and Aggregate Demand in Europe, Japan and the United States', *Carnegie–Rochester Conference Series on Public Policy*, Vol. 23, pp. 143–202.

Lehment, Harmen (1978). *Der Bremer Plan für ein europäisches Währungssystem – zurück nach Bretton Woods?* Institut für Weltwirtschaft, Kiel Discussion Paper No. 59.

Lindbeck, Assar, and Dennis Snower (1986). 'Wage Setting, Unemployment and Insider–Outsider Relations', *American Economic Review*, Vol. 76, pp. 235–9.

Lohse, Rolf (1958). *Zur Finanzpolitik der Deutschen Bundesrepublik*, Vol. II, *Die Zollpolitik vom westalliierten Außenhandelsmonopol zum Gemeinsamen Markt*, Berlin (DDR).

Ludlow, Peter (1982). *The Making of the European Monetary System*. London.

Lundberg, Erik (1985). 'The Rise and Fall of the Swedish Model', *Journal of Economic Literature*, Vol. 23, pp. 1–36.

Lutz, Friedrich A. (1949). 'The German Currency Reform and the Revival of the German Economy', *Economica*, Vol. 16, No. 2, pp. 122–42.

McCracken, Paul, et al. (eds.) (1977). *Towards Full Employment and Price Stability – A Report to the OECD by a Group of Independent Experts*. Paris, June.

Machlup, Fritz, et al. (eds.) (1983). *Reflections on a Troubled World Economy. Essays in Honour of Herbert Giersch*. London.

Maddison, Angus (1987). 'Growth and Slowdown in Advanced Capitalist Economies – Techniques of Quantitative Assessment', *The Journal of Economic Literature*, Vol. 25, pp. 649–98.

Magee, Stephen P. (1984). 'Endogenous Tariff Theory: A Survey'. In: David C. Colander (ed.), *Neoclassical Political Economy*. Cambridge, Mass., pp. 41–51.

(1987). 'The Political Economy of US Protection'. In: Herbert Giersch (ed.), *Free Trade in the World Economy: Towards an Opening of Markets*, Symposium Kiel 1986. Tübingen, pp. 368–402.

Marris, Stephen (1985). *Deficits and the Dollar: The World Economy at Risk*. Institute for International Economics, Washington, D.C.

Meadows, Donella H. et al. (1972). *The Limits to Growth*. New York.

Mendershausen, Horst (1949). 'Prices, Money and the Distribution of Goods in Postwar Germany', *The American Economic Review*, Vol. 39, No. 3, 646–72.

Merx, Volker (1972). *Ausländerbeschäftigung und Flexibilität des Arbeitsmarktes der Bundesrepublik Deutschland*. Cologne.

Messerlin, Patrick A. (1989). 'The EC Antidumping Regulations – A First Economic Appraisal, 1980–85', *Weltwirtschaftliches Archiv*, Vol. 125, No. 3, pp. 563–87.

Meyer, Fritz W. (1953). 'Der Außenhandel der westlichen Besatzungszonen Deutschlands und der Bundesrepublik 1945–1952'. In: A. Hunold (ed.), *Wirtschaft ohne Wunder*. Zurich, pp. 258–85.

Miksch, Leonhard, (1947). *Wettbewerb als Aufgabe – Die Grundsätze einer Wettbewerbsordnung*, 2nd enlarged edition. Godesberg.

Milward, Alan S. (1984). *The Reconstruction of Western Europe 1945–1951*. Berkeley/Los Angeles.

Mises, Ludwig von (1926). *Kritik des Interventionismus: Untersuchungen zur Wirtschaftspolitik und Wirtschaftsideologie der Gegenwart*. Jena.

Mitchell, Brian R. (1980). *European Historical Statistics 1750–1975*, 2nd revised edition. Cambridge.

Möller, Hans (1976). 'Die westdeutsche Währungsreform von 1948'. In: Deutsche Bundesbank (ed.), *Währung und Wirtschaft in Deutschland 1876–1975*. Frankfurt-on-Main, pp. 433–83.

(1981). 'The Reconstruction of the International Economic Order After the Second World War and the Integration of the Federal Republic of Germany into the World Economy', *Zeitschrift für die gesamte Staatswissenschaft*, Vol. 137, pp. 344–66.

Motz, Walter (1954). *Die Regelung des Außenhandels in Deutschland 1945–1949.* Lörrach.

Müller, Georg (1982). *Die Grundlegung der westdeutschen Wirtschaftsordnung im Frankfurter Wirtschaftsrat 1947–1949.* Frankfurt-on-Main.

Müller, Ulrich (1983). *Wohlstandseffekte des internationalen Handels unter den Regeln des Allgemeinen Zoll- und Handelsabkommens (GATT).* Cologne.

Müller-Armack, Alfred (1946). *Wirtschaftslenkung und Marktwirtschaft.* Hamburg.

Mundell, Robert A. (1962). 'The Appropriate Use of Monetary and Fiscal Policy for Internal and External Stability', *IMF Staff Papers,* Vol. 9, pp. 70–9.

Neue Zeitung of 20 February 1950, 'Wortlaut des alliierten Memorandums'.
of 6 March 1950, 'Bundesregierung beantwortet alliiertes Memorandum'.

Niklas, Wilhelm (1949). *Ernährungswirtschaft und Agrarpolitik, Ausführungen des Bundesministers für Ernährung, Landwirtschaft und Forsten Prof. Dr. Niklas über die Ernährungs- und Agrarpolitik in den Sitzungen des Ausschusses für Ernährung, Landwirtschaft und Forsten des Deutschen Bundestages am 19. und 27. Oktober 1949 in Bonn.* Bonn.

Nogues, Julio J., et al. (1985). *The Extent of Nontariff Barriers to Imports of Industrial Countries.* World Bank Staff Working Papers, No. 789, Washington, D.C., February.

Oberhauser, Alois (1976). 'Geld- und Kreditpolitik bei weitgehender Vollbeschäftigung und mäßigem Preisanstieg (1958–1968)'. In: Deutsche Bundesbank (ed.), *Währung und Wirtschaft in Deutschland 1876–1975,* Frankfurt-on-Main, pp. 609–42.

Olson, Mancur (1982). *The Rise and Decline of Nations – Economic Growth, Stagflation and Social Rigidities.* New Haven/London.

Organization for Economic Co-operation and Development (OECD)
(1970). *National Accounts of OECD Countries 1950–1968.* Paris.
(1975–7). *Economic Outlook.* Paris, various issues.
(1979). *Collective Bargaining and Government Policies in Ten OECD Countries.* Paris.
Foreign Trade, Series B. Paris, various issues.
Foreign Trade by Commodities. Paris, various issues.
Monthly Statistics of Foreign Trade. Paris, various issues.

Organization for European Economic Co-operation (OEEC). *Annual Reports 1950–1959* (German edition edited by the Bundesministerium für den Marshallplan from 1950 to 1953, by the Bundesministerium für wirtschaftliche Zusammenarbeit from 1954 to 1957, and by the Bundesministerium für Wirtschaft from 1958 onwards).
Foreign Trade, Series I. Paris, various issues.
Foreign Trade, Series II (Series B). Paris, various issues.

Paqué, Karl-Heinz (1987). *Labour Surplus and Capital Shortage – German Unemployment in the First Decade after the Currency Reform.* Institut für Weltwirtschaft, Kiel Working Paper No. 290, July.
(1988). *The Mixed Blessing of Labour Shortage – German Overemployment in the 1960s.* Institut für Weltwirtschaft, Kiel Working Paper No. 332, July.
(1989a). *Is Structural Unemployment a Negligible Problem? A Critical Note on the Use of Mismatch Indices.* Institut für Weltwirtschaft, Kiel Working Paper No. 357, February.
(1989b). *Wage Gaps, Hysteresis and Structural Unemployment. The West German*

Labour Market in the 1970s and 1980s. Institut für Weltwirtschaft, Kiel Working Paper No. 358, February.

(1989c). *Micro–Macro Links in West Germany's Unemployment*. Institut für Weltwirtschaft, Kiel Working Paper No. 378, August.

(1990). *Unemployment in West Germany – A Survey of Explanations and Policy Options*. Institut für Weltwirtschaft, Kiel Working Paper No. 407, January.

(1993a). 'Germany: Living with Tight Corporatism'. In: Joop Hartog and Jules Theeuwes (eds.), *Labour Market Contracts and Institutions. A Cross-National Comparison*. Amsterdam.

(1993b). *East/West-Wage Rigidity in United Germany: Causes and Consequences*. Institut für Weltwirtschaft, Kiel Working Paper No. 572. May.

Preiser, Erich (1950). 'Geldschöpfung oder Sparen', *Jahrbuch für Nationalökonomie und Statistik*, Vol. 162, pp. 245–59.

Presse- und Informationsamt der Bundesregierung (1951–9). *Deutschland im Wiederaufbau*, Progress Reports of the Federal Government for the years 1950–1958. Bonn.

Putnam, Robert D., and Nicholas Bayne (1987). *Hanging Together: The Seven Power Summits*, revised and enlarged edition. Cambridge, Mass.

Quante, Heinz (1950). 'Die moderne Beschäftigungstheorie und die gegenwärtige Arbeitslosigkeit in Westdeutschland', *Weltwirtschaftliches Archiv*, Vol. 65, pp. 283–303.

Riess, Artur (1955). 'Harmonisierung der europäischen Soziallasten?', *Gewerkschaftliche Monatshefte*, Vol. 6, pp. 105–7.

Ritschl, Albrecht (1985). 'Die Währungsreform von 1948 und der Wiederaufstieg der westdeutschen Industrie', *Vierteljahreshefte für Zeitgeschichte*, Vol. 33, pp. 136–65.

Rittershausen, Heinrich (1955). *Internationale Handels- und Devisenpolitik*, 2nd enlarged edition. Frankfurt-on-Main.

Röper, Hans (1951). 'Die Lohnschraube', *Frankfurter Allgemeine Zeitung* of 28 July.

Röpke, Wilhelm (1942). *Die Gesellschaftskrisis der Gegenwart*. Erlenbach/Zurich.

(1944). *Civitas Humana. Grundfragen der Gesellschafts- und Wirtschaftsreform*. Erlenbach/Zurich.

(1947). 'Offene und zurückgestaute Inflation: Bemerkungen zu Jacques Rueffs L'Ordre Social', *Kyklos*, Vol. 1, pp. 57–71.

(1950). *Ist die deutsche Wirtschaftspolitik richtig?* Stuttgart/Cologne.

(1951). 'Das Deutsche Wirtschaftsexperiment: Beispiel und Lehre'. In: Schweizer Institut für Auslandsforschung (ed.), *Vollbeschäftigung, Inflation und Planwirtschaft*. Zurich, pp. 261–312.

(1953). 'Sozialpolitik der freien Gesellschaft', *Blätter der Freiheit*, Vol. 5, pp. 347–52.

(1958). 'Gemeinsamer Markt und Freihandelszone: 28 Thesen als Richtpunkte', *ORDO*, Vol. 10, pp. 31–62.

Roskamp, Karl W. (1965). *Capital Formation in West Germany*. Detroit.

Rüstow, Alexander (1932). Untitled contribution to a discussion. In: Schriften des Vereins für Socialpolitik, Vol. 187, *Deutschland und die Weltkrise*, pp. 62–9.

Rüstow, Hans-Joachim (1966). 'Gastarbeiter – Gewinn oder Belastung für unsere Volkswirtschaft'. In: *Probleme der ausländischen Arbeitskräfte in der Bundesrepublik* (Beihefte der Konjunkturpolitik, 13). Berlin, pp. 35–48.

Sachverständigenrat zur Begutachtung der gesamtwirtschaftlichen Entwicklung. *Jahresgutachten* (various issues).

Salin, Edgar (ed.) (1948). *Synopsis, Festgabe für Alfred Weber*. Heidelberg.

Sarcinelli, Mario (1986). 'The EMS and the International Monetary System: Towards Greater Stability', *Banca Nazionale del Lavoro, Quarterly Review*, No. 156, March, pp. 57–83.

Schade, Peter (1963). *Die Entwicklung des Zolltarifes der Bundesrepublik Deutschland bis zum EWG-Außentarif*. Tübingen.

Schatz, Klaus-Werner (1974). *Wachstum und Strukturwandel der westdeutschen Wirtschaft im internationalen Verbund*. Institut für Weltwirtschaft, Kieler Studie No. 128. Tübingen.

Scheide, Joachim (1987a). *Der Beitrag der Konjunkturpolitik zum deutschen Wirtschaftswunder nach der Währungsreform*. Institut für Weltwirtschaft, Kiel Working Paper No. 281, March.

(1987b). *Anstieg und Fall des Dollarkurses – Folgen der amerikanischen Geldpolitik?* Institut für Weltwirtschaft, Kiel Discussion Paper No. 131, April.

(1988). 'Lehren aus dem Scheitern des Bretton-Woods-Systems', *Die Weltwirtschaft*, No. 1, pp. 53–71.

Scheide, Joachim, and Stefan Sinn (1989). 'How Strong is the Case for International Coordination?'. In: J. A. Dorn and W. A. Niskanen (eds.), *Dollars, Deficits and Trade*. Dordrecht, pp. 397–422.

Schiller, Karl (1951). 'Vollbeschäftigung und Kreditpolitik'. In: Gerhard Albrecht (ed.), *Die Problematik der Vollbeschäftigung – Verhandlungen auf der Tagung des Vereins für Socialpolitik in Bad Pyrmont, 1950*. Berlin, pp. 111–25.

Schillinger, Reinhold (1985). *Der Entscheidungsprozeß beim Lastenausgleich 1945–1952*. St Katharinen.

Schlesinger, Helmut (1976). 'Geldpolitik in der Phase des Wiederaufbaus 1950–1958'. In: Deutsche Bundesbank (ed.), *Währung und Wirtschaft in Deutschland 1876–1975*. Frankfurt-on-Main, pp. 555–607.

Schmahl, Hans-Jürgen (1971). *Globalsteuerung der Wirtschaft*. Hamburg.

Schmid, Günther (1989). 'Modell Schweden als Vorbild? Licht- und Schattenseiten der schwedischen Arbeitsmarkt- und Beschäftigungspolitik', *Mitteilungen aus der Arbeitsmarkt- und Berufsforschung*, Vol. 22, pp. 75–84.

Schmidt, Klaus-Dieter, et al. (1984). *Im Anpassungsprozeß zurückgeworfen – Die Deutsche Wirtschaft vor neuen Herausforderungen*. Institut für Weltwirtschaft, Kieler Studie No. 185. Tübingen.

Schmieding, Holger (1987). *How to Fill a 'Dollar Gap'? Observations on the Liberalisation of West Germany's External Trade and Payments 1947–1958*. Institut für Weltwirtschaft, Kiel Working Paper No. 291, July.

(1988). *The Dynamics of Trade Diversion – Observations on West Germany's Integration into the 'Little European' Common Market 1958–1972*. Institut für Weltwirtschaft, Kiel Working Paper No. 334, September.

(1989a). 'Strategien zum Abbau von Handelshemmnissen. Ordnungspolitische Lehren des bundesdeutschen Liberalisierungsprozesses 1949–1957 für die Gegenwart', Schriften des Vereins für Socialpolitik, new series, Vol. 190, *Währungsreform und Soziale Marktwirtschaft*, pp. 253–67.

(1989b). 'Zu den Ursachen der Investitionsschwäche in der Bundesrepublik Deutschland 1974–1987', *Die Weltwirtschaft*, No. 1, pp. 58–75.

(1990). 'Eine deutsch-deutsche Währungsunion wird nur als Bestandteil eines radikalen Reformpaketes akzeptabel', *Handelsblatt* of 8 February 1990.

(1991). 'Die ostdeutsche Wirtschaftskrise: Ursachen und Lösungsstrategien. Anmerkungen im Lichte der westdeutschen Erfahrungen von 1948 und des polnischen Beispiels von 1990'. *ORDO*, Vol. 42, pp. 183–211.

Schwarz, Hans-Peter (1981). *Die Ära Adenauer, Gründerjahre der Republik 1949–1957. Geschichte der Bundesrepublik Deutschland*, Vol. II, Stuttgart/ Wiesbaden.

(1983). *Die Ära Adenauer. Epochenwechsel, 1957–1963. Geschichte der Bundesrepublik Deutschland*, Vol. III, Stuttgart/Wiesbaden.

Servan-Schreiber, Jean-Jacques (1967). *Le Défi Américain*. Paris. (English translation: *The American Challenge*. New York, 1979.)

Siebert, Horst (1990). *The Economic Integration of Germany – An Update*. Institut für Weltwirtschaft, Kiel Discussion Paper No. 160a, September.

Sinn, Stefan (1988). 'Zur Wechselkursdebatte in der Bundesrepublik Deutschland in den sechziger Jahren', *Die Weltwirtschaft*, No. 1, pp. 72–86.

Soltwedel, Rüdiger (1980). *Rückwirkungen sozialpolitischer Maßnahmen der Tarifpartner und des Staates zugunsten bestimmter Erwerbstätigengruppen auf dem Arbeitsmarkt – Identifikation und Vorschläge*. Kiel.

(1988). 'Employment Problems in West Germany – The Role of Institutions, Labour Law and Government Intervention', *Carnegie–Rochester Conference Series on Public Policy*, Vol. 28, pp. 153–220.

Soltwedel, Rüdiger, and Peter Trapp (1988). 'Labour Market Barriers to More Employment: Causes for an Increase of the Natural Rate? The Case of West Germany'. In: Herbert Giersch (ed.), *Macro and Micro Policies for More Growth and Employment*. Symposium 1987. Tübingen.

Soltwedel, Rüdiger, et al. (1986). *Deregulierungspotentiale in der Bundesrepublik*. Kieler Studien 202. Tübingen.

Spittäler, Erich (1970). 'The 1961 Revaluations and Exports of Manufactures', *IMF Staff Papers*, Vol. 17, No. 1, pp. 110–26.

Stäglin, Reiner, and Hans Wessels (1969). *Input-Output-Tabellen und Input-Output-Analysen für die Bundesrepublik Deutschland*. Berlin.

Statistisches Bundesamt (1956). *Einkommen- und Körperschaftsteuerstatistik 1950*. Wiesbaden.

(1974). *Lange Reihen 1950–1973*. Wiesbaden.

Fachserie A, Reihe 3 (since 1975: Fachserie 1, Reihe 2.3), *Wanderungen*. Various issues.

Fachserie 7, Reihe 7, *Außenhandel nach Ländern und Warengruppen der Industriestatistik*, various issues.

Statistisches Jahrbuch für die Bundesrepublik Deutschland, various issues.

Volkswirtschaftliche Gesamtrechnungen (tape of the Institut für Weltwirtschaft).

Wirtschaft und Statistik, various issues.

Stehn, Jürgen, and Holger Schmieding (1990). 'Spezialisierungsmuster und Wettbewerbsfähigkeit: Eine Bestandsaufnahme des DDR-Außenhandels', *Die Weltwirtschaft*, No. 1, pp. 60–77.

Stolper, Gustav (1964). *Deutsche Wirtschaft seit 1870*. Tübingen.

Stolper, Wolfgang F., and Karl W. Roskamp (1979). 'Planning a Free Economy, Germany 1945–1960', *Zeitschrift für die gesamte Staatswissenschaft*, 'Currency and Economic Reform in West Germany After World War II – A Symposium', Vol. 135, No. 3, pp. 374–404.

Trapp, Peter (1982). 'Frankreich: Ausbruch aus der Rezession gescheitert', *Die Weltwirtschaft*, No. 1, pp. 48–63.

Treuhandanstalt (1993). *Monatsinformation der THA*, December.

Triffin, Robert (1957). *Europe and the Money Muddle, From Bilateralism to Near-Convertibility, 1947–1956*. New Haven.

Tumlir, Jan, and Laura La Haye (1981). 'The Two Attempts at European Economic Reconstruction after 1945', *Zeitschrift für die gesamte Staatswissenschaft*, Vol. 137, pp. 367–89.

Tüngel, Richard (1949). 'Pariser Hemmungen bei der Bewertung der D-Mark', *Die Zeit* of 9 September 1949.

United States. 1989. *Economic Report of the President*. Washington, D.C.

US Department of State (1947). *Occupation of Germany – Policy and Progress 1945–46*. Publication 2783, European Series 23. Washington, D.C.

US Office of Military Government for Germany OMGUS (1946). *A Year of Potsdam – The German Economy Since the Surrender*, prepared by the Economics Division. N.p.

The United States Strategic Bombing Survey (1945). *The Effects of Strategic Bombing on the German War Economy*. Overall Economic Effects Division, 31 October. Washington, D.C.

Vanberg, Viktor (1988). '"Ordnungstheorie" as Constitutional Economics – The German Conception of a "Social Market Economy"', *ORDO*, Vol. 39, pp. 17–31.

Vaubel, Roland (1979). *Choice in European Monetary Union*. Wincott Memorial Lecture, IEA Occasional Paper 55. London.

(1983). 'Coordination or Competition among National Macroeconomic Policies?'. In: Fritz Machlup et al. (eds.), *Reflections on a Troubled World Economy. Essays in Honour of Herbert Giersch*. London, pp. 3–28.

(1985). 'International Collusion or Competition for Macroeconomic Policy Coordination? A Restatement', *Recherches économiques de Louvain*, Vol. 51, pp. 223–40.

(1989). 'Möglichkeiten für eine erfolgreiche Beschäftigungspolitik'. In: Schriften des Vereins für Socialpolitik, new series, Vol. 178, *Beschäftigungsprobleme hochentwickelter Volkswirtschaften*, pp. 17–35.

Verwaltung für Wirtschaft des Vereinigten Wirtschaftsgebietes (ed.) (1949). 'Außenhandel als Lebensfrage', *Wirtschaftsverwaltung*, No. 10 (May), Frankfurt-on-Main, pp. 265–9.

Vetter, Ernst-Günther (1959). 'Sturmzeichen in der Lohnpolitik', *Frankfurter Allgemeine Zeitung* of 21 December 1959.

Der Volkswirt of 30 January 1954, 'Lärm an der Lohnfront'.

Wagenführ, Rolf (1950). *Der Weg zur Vollbeschäftigung. Eine allgemeinverständliche Einführung*. Cologne.

Wallich, Henry C. (1955). *Mainsprings of German Economic Revival*. New Haven.

(1968). 'The American Council of Economic Advisers and the German Sachverständigenrat. A Study in the Economics of Advice', *Quarterly Journal of Economics*, 82, pp. 349–79.

Wallich, Henry C., and John F. Wilson (1979). 'Thirty Years (Almost) of German Surpluses', *Zeitschrift für die gesamte Staatswissenschaft*, 'Currency and

Economic Reform in West Germany After World War II – A Symposium',
Vol. 135, No. 2, pp. 480–92.

(1981). 'Economic Orientations in Postwar Germany: Critical Choices on the
Road Toward Currency Convertibility', *Zeitschrift für die gesamte Staatswissenschaft*, Vol. 137, pp. 390–406.

Wall Street Journal of 13 October 1949, 'West Germany: Free Economy Trend
in Occupied Land is Hit by Money Devaluation'.

of 16 October 1956, 'German Experience in Labour Management Program is
Described'.

Watrin, Christian (1979). 'The Principles of the Social Market Economy –
its Origins and Early History', *Zeitschrift für die gesamte Staatswissenschaft*,
Vol. 135, pp. 405–25.

Weiss, Frank D., et al. (1988). *Trade Policy in West Germany*. Institut für
Weltwirtschaft, Kieler Studie No. 217, Tübingen.

(1989). *The Rise of the New Protectionism: A Phenomenon of the 1970's?*. Paper
presented at the seminar. 'Die siebziger Jahre – Der Weg in die Stagmation',
Institut für Weltwirtschaft, Kiel, 24–6 January, mimeo.

Werner, Heinz (1987a). 'Ermittlung der Arbeitslosigkeit und Leistungsbezug in
der EG'. *Beiträge zur Arbeitsmarkt- und Berufsforschung 108*. Nuremberg.

(1987b). 'Arbeitsmarktpolitische Maßnahmen in den Ländern der Europäischen
Gemeinschaft und in Schweden – Eine Übersicht', *Mitteilungen aus der
Arbeitsmarkt- und Berufsforschung*, Vol. 20, pp. 441–52.

Willgerodt, Hans (1989). 'Wertvorstellungen und theoretische Grundlagen des
Konzepts der Sozialen Marktwirtschaft'. In: Schriften des Vereins für
Socialpolitik, new series, Vol. 190, *Währungsreform und Soziale Marktwirt-
schaft*, pp. 31–60.

Willgerodt, Hans, and Alan T. Peacock (1989). *German Neo-Liberals and the
Social Market Economy*. Basingstoke.

Winham, Gilbert R. (1986). *International Trade and the Tokyo Round Negotiations*.
Princeton.

Winkler, Heinrich (ed.) (1979). *Politische Weichenstellungen im Nachkriegsdeutschland 1945–1953*. Göttingen.

Wirtschaftswissenschaftliches Institut der Gewerkschaften (1950). *Vollbeschäftigung*. Ergebnisse einer Arbeitstagung des Wirtschaftswissenschaftlichen
Instituts der Gewerkschaften in Oberhausen vom 16.–19. März 1950. Cologne.

Wirtschaftswoche of 9 June 1989, 'Langzeitarbeitslosigkeit – Neuer Anlauf'.

Wissenschaftlicher Beirat beim Bundesministerium für Wirtschaft (1973). *Sammelband der Gutachten von 1948 bis 1972* (edited by the Bundesministerium für
Wirtschaft). Göttingen.

(1987). *Sammelband der Gutachten von 1973 bis 1986* (edited by the Bundesministerium für Wirtschaft). Göttingen.

Wolter, Frank (1980). *The Impact of Manufactured Imports from Developing
Countries in the Federal Republic of Germany*, Institut für Weltwirtschaft,
Kiel Working Paper No. 99, February.

Wünsche, Horst-Friedrich (1979). 'Wirtschaft in Westdeutschland 1945–1948.
Bemerkungen zu dem gleichnamigen Buch von Werner Abelshauser', *Orien-
tierungen zur Wirtschafts- und Gesellschaftspolitik*, No. 2 (December),
37–40.

Yoffie, David B. (1983). *Power and Protectionism*. New York.

Die Zeit of 28 January 1954, 'Ein lohnpolitischer Fanfarenstoß – Die neuangelegte "Gruppentheorie" des Herrn Agartz gibt doch etwas zu denken'.

Zeitschrift für die gesamte Staatswissenschaft, 'Currency and Economic Reform in West Germany After World War II – A Symposium', Vol. 135, No. 2.

Zijlmans, Hendrik (1970). 'Die Finanzierung der Gemeinsamen Agrarpolitik', *Agrarwirtschaft*, Vol. 19, pp. 253–61.

Zis, George (1984). 'The European Monetary System 1979–84: An Assessment', *Journal of Common Market Studies*, Vol. 23, No. 1, pp. 45–72.

Index

Note: All references are to West Germany unless specifically indicated otherwise.

Abelshauser, W., 23n, 40, 99n
Adenauer, Konrad, 66, 74, 81, 86, 103, 122, 125, 167
Advisory Council to Federal Minister of Economics, 41, 65, 102, 119, 121, 177
and demand management (1960–74), 139–41, 155
and economic growth (1950–60), 55–60, 62, 68, 85, 94
Agartz, Viktor, 33, 74, 76, 77n
agriculture
assistance, rates of, 228
comparisons on eve of unification, 261
employment changes (1960–73), 129
employment changes (1973–89), 129, 199
employment in protected sectors, 235
policy in European Community, 173–6, 232
structural change in, 7–9
tariff protection: 1951 and 1958, 111
Allied Bizonal Control Office, 37
Amelung, T., 226n
anti-trust and anti-cartel policies, 84–5
Artis, M. J., 252n
Artus, J. R., 197n
assistance, rates of by industry, 228–9
Austria, 97–8

Baade, F., 52, 118, 119n
Baker, James, 244n
Balabkins, N., 16n, 20n, 22n
balance of payments
(1950–90), 237
and foreign trade (1960–73), 165
and Korean War, 101–5
and oil imports, 239
Baldwin, R. E., 117n
Barnikel, M.-H., 47n
Bayne, N., 242n

Belgium–Luxemburg, 98
and establishment of Common Market, 117
Bell, L. A., 205n
Bellmann, L., 205n
Belongia, M. T., 253n
Berg, Fritz, 121–2
Berlin Wall, 260–2
Bismarck, Otto von, 27, 81
Bizonal Economic Administration, 33–4, 106
Bizonal Joint Export and Import Agency (JEIA), 24, 91–2
Bizonal parliament, 33, 36, 43
Blanchard, O., 199, 200n, 248n
Böckler, Hans, 74, 86
Bofinger, P., 254n
Böhm, F., 34, 52
Bonn Summit (1978), 189, 242–3, 250
Borchardt, K., 43n, 99n
Boss, A., 38n, 60n, 79n, 81n, 83n, 193n, 220n
Bothe, A., 82n
Bracher, K.-D., 157n, 160n, 163n, 170n, 214n
Brandt, Willy, 157
Braunthal, G., 112n
Bretton Woods agreement, 142, 254, 274
erosion of, 176–84, 240, 252
and inflationary pressures, 151–2
and recession of 1974/5, 186
Bruno, M., 131n, 196–7n
Buchheim, C., 20n, 21n, 23n, 38n, 40n, 43n, 99n, 115n
Büchtemann, C. F., 207
budget deficits, forbidden, 37
Burda, M. C., 197n, 198n, 202n
business cycles, 9–10
and currency (1950–60), 66–7
(1960–73), 140–54
and stabilization, 143–5

297